Stepping Out
WITH THE
Sacred

Other books by Val Webb:

In Defense of Doubt: An invitation to adventure
John's Message: Good news for the new millennium
Why We're Equal: Introducing Feminist theology
Florence Nightingale: The making of a radical theologian
Like Catching Water in a Net: Human attempts to describe the Divine

Stepping Out

WITH THE

Sacred

HUMAN ATTEMPTS TO ENGAGE THE DIVINE

VAL WEBB

continuum

Continuum International Publishing Group
The Tower Building, 11 York Road, London SE1 7NX
80 Maiden Lane, Suite 704, New York, NY 10038

www.continuumbooks.com

British Library Cataloguing-in-Publication Data
A catalogue record for this book is available from the British Library

ISBN 13: 978-1-4411-9642-2 (Hardback)

Typeset by Kenneth Burnley, Wirral, Cheshire
Printed and bound in the United States of America

Contents

To my grandchildren

Preface

> Behind all . . . questions is a fundamental one: How can people be in touch
> with what is ultimately real, that unlimited source or sources from which they
> derive life and meaning? . . . We designate this focal point of the religions, as
> the sacred, the ground of ultimate vitality, value and meaning. The modes of
> experiencing the sacred, and the responses to this experience, are many and
> varied; these are the forms and expressions that make up the religious
> traditions of the world.
>
> *Theodore M. Ludwig*[1]

It is February 7, 2009. I am at my computer trying to concentrate as the
television flashes live updates of "Black Saturday", Australia's worst natural
disaster. Multiple bushfires, driven by winds gusting over 80 miles an hour,
have swept through idyllic villages and hamlets in the rolling hills north of
Melbourne with absolutely no warning. People glanced out of windows to
see walls of flames already devouring their fence-lines. Some managed to
jump into cars with nothing in their hands. Many did not have time for that.
Others perished in their vehicles, blocked by fallen trees and burned-out cars
on their only escape route out, or disorientated by smoke clouds that oblit-
erated visibility. Story after story unfolds, told by shell-shocked folk with ash
still on their faces and make-shift bandages hiding burned feet and scarred
hands. Mothers with small children were trapped in homes; elderly parents
struggled to save a wheelchair-bound son; husbands stayed to help neighbors. All are gone. Two hundred and ten people lost their lives; over 2,000
properties were destroyed; 800,000 acres of land were burned and an estimated one million native animals, horses, cows, sheep, family dogs, cats and
chickens were incinerated or so badly burned they had to be destroyed.

What is the point of this preamble? In horrific events, people, religious or non-religious, need to make sense of the events. One reclusive couple wandered into town from the hills, eyes glazed and faces stunned, only to discover they had been listed as deceased. "But I'm here," the man said, his dazed partner staring past the reporter. He shook his head, as if to brush away the image that clung like a fly. "I've never been to church, but perhaps I might go now." A young father, a paraplegic from a roof fall, had just returned from a long re-habilitation. "I don't know what I've done, but I've sure upset somebody," he said with a wry grin. If he had not been in a wheelchair, he would have stayed to fight the fire and perished with his neighbors. Far from the smoke, Members of Parliament in the nation's capital made speeches of condolence. One of them, frustrated at human impotence before nature, said, "If you are someone who prays—PRAY!" We feel in control of our world until something happens that renders us powerless. While we may not believe that prayer helps, or we see such events as nothing but chance or luck, our final recourse in these moments is to plead for help to Something we may have long dismissed.

There are always those who know exactly why things happen. The leader of Catch the Fire Ministries announced in the press that the bushfires were a direct result of laws decriminalizing abortion, leaving Australians an "open target for the devil to destroy". Apparently he dreamed about the fires a few months earlier, waking with

> . . . a flash from the spirit of God: that His conditional protection has been removed from the nation of Australia, in particular Victoria, for approv-ing the slaughter of innocent children in the womb.

One of his Christian political friends objected to his remarks—"It is beyond the bounds of decency to try to make moral or political points out of such a tragedy." But such prophets with a hotline to the Divine are never thwarted by mere humans who oppose them. "I must tell people what they need to hear," he answered to charges of bad taste, "not necessarily what they want to hear."[2]

Ever since humans began to take notice of things around them, they looked beyond what could immediately be seen and understood to ponder the bigger picture. The yearning for an explanation for everything, an encounter with something ticking away beyond our ken, has always driven the human spirit. Something in us wants to make sense of the world and especially our part in it. "Wonder" is a "wonder-*full*" word for this quest, with its double meaning of breathtaking awe before mystery and wondering *about* that mystery. Philosopher Sam Keen calls wonder the source and prin-ciple of all philosophy, science, art, and religion—"The fact that something exists rather than nothing."[3] Keen even maps an itinerary for wonder. We first experience surprise or amazement—we are "wonderstruck". Words fail to capture the moment because the experience "jolts us out of the world of common sense in which our language is at home".[4] Puzzlement follows as our ordinary categories of explanation are shattered and questions come, laced with ambivalence and fear of the unknown, as well as tentative anticipation of the possibilities. Admiration ("admire" originally meant "to regard with wonder or astonishment") sweeps over us, moving us to contemplation and celebration.[5] I'm not suggesting we consciously proceed through all these steps when we see an exceptionally beautiful sunset, but they remind us of the complexity in our reactions to mystery.

Richard Elliott begins his book *Falling in Love with Mystery* with a childhood experience he still remembers in vivid detail:

> It was during my eleventh year on the planet that it happened. I was walking through a pasture on our family farm and came upon a cow lying on the ground. It seemed strange to me that she would be lying so prone on the ground. I wondered if she were sick. However, it soon became apparent to me that she was in the process of giving birth to a calf. Until that time I was quite innocent about such things and was not convinced that calves were born in such a seemingly impossible way, but now all of that doubt vanished away. I was seeing with my own eyes a calf coming into the world. After a time of labor, the calf came gently out onto the green grass. It lay perfectly still for a moment and I wondered if it were dead. Then it took a deep breath and began to move. In a few moments the mother stood and began to lick her newest creation. Soon the calf was standing and nursing. I was absolutely blown away! I was overwhelmed by awe. The mystery of life was as real and powerful in that moment as it has ever been for me. That is to say, I had a real life encounter with God. Then I returned to my normal religious training.[6]

Elliott's final sentence jolts us back to the gulf that exists between experiences of awe and wonder and how they have been domesticated into religious forms that curb the imagination and define how we can think and feel, that artificial gulf between the Sacred and the secular.

In this book, I roam across religious traditions, listening for examples and explanations of how people have engaged the Sacred. I also leave open the question of whether or not there *is* Something to engage and, if so, whether this is possible, hence the title "human *attempts*". We live in a global community where we share education, political ideas, medical breakthroughs, trade, disasters, wars and, hopefully for longer periods, peace and harmony. We also share "faith" in believing that we are not alone—whether this means being part of the universe, a community, a family, or a Presence some call GOD. This is expressed in many different ways, some of which are religious, but all of which reflect what it means to be human and, as such, are valuable to share with others. We have not been good at this in the past, because we have met each other carrying our boxes (religions) and have insisted that others put down their boxes to take up ours. Many of us have more sense now, realizing that different religions are humanly constructed descriptions of the universal human search for Something More, according to particular contexts and experiences.

My mind works rather like ink on blotting paper, soaking up the breadth of a question until saturated with the idea, rather than like wax paper where a thought simply stays where it lands. It will be obvious to the reader that this book has been written in many different places around the world and from many different churches, temples and even kitchen tables, as I went in search of how ordinary people have engaged the Divine, or have experienced the Divine reaching out to them. Rather than coming up with a "This is the way it is folks" conclusion, I have gathered these stories together, describing them as best I can to invite your consideration and decision. This is not a textbook on the religions of the world—that would take volumes. To be too generic is not helpful; to be too specific is not mind-expanding. Since the majority of readers will have roots in the Christian tradition, even if not adherents, I will focus on that tradition but draw examples from across religions to show the breadth of the human search and to offer ways of stepping beyond our personal "boxes". It is not a *comparative* religion book where different religious approaches are evaluated against each other as if they can be graded. How could anyone absorb all religions sufficiently to make such value comparisons, unless they simply decide that one is superior to all? I have tried not to use phrases like "It is said" or "It is claimed to be" when referring to religious claims which I may not personally espouse (although I am sure I am guilty of this somewhere in the book). Such comments are a subtle grading in themselves. Instead, I present ideas as they are believed and taught within their religions and leave it to your own judgement. For each topic, I feature only a few examples because of space, making choices that introduce ones of which you may not be aware. I do not single out the religiously strange or obtuse, because this is a distortion of any tradition. To focus on such, "lifting it out of context and waving it before the public drool", religion scholar Huston Smith said, "is, where not straight sacrilege, the crudest kind of vulgarization".[7] Instead:

To take [religions other than our own] seriously, only two things are required. We need to see their adherents as men and women who face problems much like our own. And second, we must rid our minds of pre-conceptions that could dull our sensitivity to fresh insights.[8]

Writers have only words at their disposal with which to paint pictures and tug at hearts. Nikos Kazantzakis, author of *Zorba the Greek* (1883–1957), of whom you will hear much through this book, described (in unfortunately militaristic images) his writing process: "I was setting words as traps, setting them with all the cunning I possessed, so that I could capture the uncapturable Cry which kept advancing in front of me."[9] Despite this:

We suffocate inside every word. Seeing a blossoming tree, a hero, a woman, the morning star, we cry, Ah! Nothing else is able to accommodate our joy. When, analysing this Ah! we wish to turn it into thought and art in order to impart it to mankind and rescue it from our own dissolution, how it cheapens into brazen, mascara-ed words full of air and fancy! But alas, there is no other way for us to impart this Ah!— the only bit of immortality in us—to mankind! Words! Words! For me, alas, there is no other salvation. Under my authority I have nothing but twenty-six lead soldiers, the twenty-six letters of the alphabet. I will proclaim full mobilization.[10]

For those who want a quick perusal of the book, Chapter 1 summarizes my previous book *Like Catching Water in a Net: Human attempts to describe the Divine*,[11] since we cannot speak of engaging the Divine unless we have something in mind when we say the word GOD. We also need an image of where we think the Divine is located, the theme of Chapter 2. Chapter 3 examines what humans *want* in trying to engage the Divine, and Chapter 4 asks whether the Sacred engages us or we engage the Sacred. Moving into ways of engaging, Chapter 5 talks of experiencing the Sacred in nature, Chapter 6 looks at sacred places, and Chapter 7 explores sacred things. In Chapter 8, I consider how people, whether saints, founders, shamans or Divine incarnations, act as intermediaries, and, in Chapter 9, how communities and priests carry that function. Chapter 10 examines sacred texts as ways to GOD, and Chapter 11 describes how rituals and action facilitate such contact. In Chapter 12, the five senses—smell, touch, taste, hearing and sight—are explored as participators in this process. In Chapter 13, I move from external mediators to human experience, those who engage the Sacred and receive a response within themselves. As an extension of this, Chapters 14 and 15 look at prayer, meditation and contemplation. Chapter 16 considers how people have engaged the Sacred in the world here and now (and also has a bit to say about "heaven"). Since religions evolved from one another, Chapter 17 looks at borrowing and adapting between religious action, and Chapter 18 raises the question of inter-religious dialogue and what we learn from that. As a conclusion, Chapter 19 gathers up and invites us forward in the search for, and engagement with, whatever we name as Sacred—or not.

As in my previous book,[12] I capitalize the word GOD (except in quotations from other people) to remind us that I am using the term simply as a three-letter symbol across religions, free of any particular baggage or theology. The New Revised Standard Version is used throughout in quotations from the Bible, and I have included dates for people when I first mention them (unless they are still alive). I have reluctantly left gender-exclusive terms, such as "man", "he" or "she", in other people's quotes. While aware of their inadequacy, editing them out with brackets and "*sic*'s" becomes more disruptive to the flow of the quote than the exclusive language itself— I hope readers feel for themselves the inappropriateness of gendered language as they read.

Many people, past and present, have contributed indirectly to this book through their life stories, experiences and ideas. My family has participated by always encouraging the process and being patient when I slipped away to write—from my mother Joan Skerman to my children and their spouses, Helen and Steve, Paul and Alexis and Karen and Sean, and the wonderful grandchildren Daniel, Rhys, Kyle, Calvin, Lola and Max. I would like to thank Burke Gerstenschlager who began as my editor at Continuum, and Thomas Kraft who saw the book to completion and into print, along with the host of Continuum people who worked with the book through its gestation and birth. As always, there is one person without whom my books would never see the light of day. My husband Maurice is my inspiration in life and in writing, my partner of 45 years, my "editorial consultant" from the very first draft (reading each chapter to see, he says, if a "simple surgeon" can understand the theology) and the one who takes over the hassles of life so the writing can be done. Thank you, Maurice. I forever count my blessings.

Pinning Down the Sacred

Some call on the Lord, "Rama", some cry, "Khuda",
Some bow to Him as Gosain, some as Allah;
He is called the Ground of Grounds and also the Bountiful,
The Compassionate One and Gracious . . .
Says Nanak, Whoever realizes the will of the Lord,
He will find out the Lord's Secrets!

—*Adi Granth*[1]

O   O   O

sac'red, a. [pp. of old *sacre*, to set apart, consecrate; Fr. *sacré*, from L. sacer, sacred, from root seen also in *sanus*, sane, and in Gr. *Saos*, safe].

di-vine, a. [ME. *divine*; OFr. *divin*; L. *divines*, divine, inspired, pertaining to a deity, from *divus*, a deity].

ho'ly, a. *comp*. holier; *superl*. holiest. [ME. *holy, holi, halig*; AS. *halig*, holy, sacred.] n. something holy; a sanctuary. **ho'ly-day,** n. a religious festival; hence a *holiday*: also *holy day*.[2]

Words describing Something More—holy, sacred, divine, spirit, transcendence, mystery, presence, GOD—pile up like soiled clothes on a teenager's floor. While this may not concern you, it makes me nervous, since my training in an earlier life was in science. The basic principle of scientific writing is to state clearly one's hypothesis at the beginning and carefully describe throughout the paper the terms used so that their borders are clearly drawn without gaping holes, to avoid misinterpretation. When I checked the dictionary for the above definitions, something became apparent. Each word began life as an adjective descriptive of the One known—Sacred Name, Divine Lord, Holy Spirit—but

1

significantly they have now become nouns—"the Holy", "the Sacred" and "the Divine"—suggesting we are more comfortable today describing *qualities* we attribute to the Unknown than claiming to know what the Unknown is in Itself.

While this book stands alone, it is also a sequel to my book *Like Catching Water in a Net: Human attempts to describe the Divine*[3] where I examine how people across the globe and centuries have described intimations of Something More and asked if there *is* such a thing as GOD. If we are to spend this book discussing how human beings have attempted to engage the Divine or celebrate Its engaging of them, we need to know what we mean by GOD as this will have bearing on how the Divine is engaged. If GOD is described as an external Being, we will engage It differently from a Spirit in the depth of our being. I will therefore summarize my previous book in this chapter to lead into the discussion of engaging the Sacred. Those who have read that book have my blessing to move to Chapter 2—unless, of course, a refresher course would not go astray.

How we describe the Divine *matters* because it determines how we relate to the Sacred and whether we can believe in Something More at all. Many people think their sacred texts, whether the Qur'an, the Bible or the Hindu Vedas, tell us all about GOD, yet none of these texts gives a single description. The Bible, for example, is a collection of stories from various tribes in different places over different eras who also exchanged ideas with neighboring tribes holding other beliefs. The Bible talks about an all-loving GOD, then describes a Divine Warrior slaughtering local residents to give their land to a chosen few. The Sacred is called Father, yet many biblical passages describe GOD as a mother comforting her child or an eagle gathering chicks under her wings. According to the mystic Julian of Norwich (c. 1342—1416) who lived most of her life as a hermit (anchoress) in a cell in the churchyard of the Church of St Julian at Norwich:

> As truly as God is our Father, so truly is God our Mother . . . I am he, the power and greatness of fatherhood; I am he, the wisdom and lovingness of motherhood; I am her, the light and the grace which is all blessed love; I am her, the Trinity; I am her, the unity; I am he, the great supreme goodness of every kind of thing; I am he who makes you to love; I am he who makes you to long; I am he, the endless fulfilling of all true desires.[4]

The Sacred has been portrayed in art and language as a supernatural Being with human characteristics of power, goodness and love, yet we first meet a Divine Wind brooding over the waters at creation, Breath breathed into humanity, cloud, pillar of fire, whirlwind, thunder, fortress or shield—not a human shape among them. The Hebrews were told in no uncertain terms not to create GOD in any image, making an idol (Deut. 4:15–19), yet by the Renaissance, the paintings and frescos that covered European church walls showed *exactly* what GOD was like—a man with a grey beard ruling from the heavens.

Despite hundreds of biblical descriptions of the Divine, we have fished from a fairly shallow pond of ruling males—King, Father, Lord. Because of this selectivity, ordinary people *assume* these are the most common biblical images and thus the correct way to think about GOD. Yet this is not so. Father is not a dominant Divine image in the Hebrew Bible and is used disproportionately in John's Gospel compared with other Gospels.[5] Its dominance in Christianity was established centuries later when the metaphor of a Trinity was assigned to the Godhead consisting of Father, Son and Spirit. To further cement the imagery, GOD the Father's earthly representatives were called Pope (*Papa*) and fathers. Similarly, King was not ascribed to Yahweh until the wandering Hebrew tribes established a settled kingdom around 1,000 BCE. According to contemporary scholars, the translation "kingdom of GOD" in the New Testament is better translated, given Jesus' location within the Roman Empire, "empire of GOD", a phrase cryptically suggesting a non-violent, justice-led alternative to the Roman Empire. Even the term "Lord" translating the Greek title of dignity or honour, *Kyrios*, is rarely used in ordinary conversation today (except for formal titles such as Lord Mayor)—it belongs to an earlier time and social structure. We have, over time, basically limited formless Mystery to these few, powerful images. We have created GOD in our image. Even though the New Testament defines GOD as "love", a powerful image that does not control or dominate, we continue to opt for images which claim that the Divine can do anything, even though we get ourselves into knots when GOD either cannot do everything or chooses not to, given the horrific tragedies that happen to both little children and devout adults.

What is wrong with this focus on a few images? Plenty. I called this chapter "Pinning Down the Sacred" because that is what we continually try to do. Christian art has depicted a butterfly superimposed on the cross, suggesting that the Spirit in Jesus was not captured by death but emerged like a butterfly from a chrysalis. However, as one who has seen her fair share of butterflies pinned out in butterfly collections, *this* thought also comes to my mind, depicting what we have done to the Spirit—capturing it securely so we can focus our magnifying glasses on It to create our own descriptions. We need images to help us think about the Sacred, but these *matter* since they determine how we try to engage the Sacred and live out our lives as a result.

If we see GOD intervening in natural laws to bring about natural disasters as punishment and reward, we will live as passive victims of our environment. Theresa Maggio describes a Sicilian family whose hazelnut orchard was covered by lava from Mount Etna. They now milk ewes and make ricotta on the same slopes of this active volcano, living "as God wills"— "There are dangers anywhere you go . . . We aren't afraid of staying here, not at all," the woman said.[6]

If GOD is all-powerful, ordaining everything that happens, we spend our lives accepting horrendous events as the Divine Will. After 9/11, a woman, whose brother had been the pilot of one of the doomed planes, was interviewed. When asked where she found her comfort, she said, "I usually find it in my church, but I can't go back to church as yet because our religion says I must forgive and I'm not at that point yet." If, on the other hand, we imagine GOD as universal Spirit or Energy within us and the universe, this becomes the wind in our sails that spurs us on and enables us to do great things. Our ideas of the Sacred are therefore as much about anthropology as theology—we live differently, depending on how we image the Ultimate.

Anything we say about the Sacred is a metaphor, a construction of language and images and not a description of the real thing, as we have never seen GOD and cannot know in totality what the Divine might be. Metaphors are word pictures borrowed from within particular cultures, traditions and worldviews to describe something otherwise difficult to describe. Metaphors make the best sense *within* a shared cultural experience. When touring the ruins of Pompeii, our guide said that an early Italian historian had described the eruption of Mount Vesuvius as like a pine tree. When we looked puzzled, she explained that pine trees in that area are not pointed like Christmas trees, but have tall, leafless trunks with a mushroom-like outgrowth at the top, a perfect metaphor for the smoke cloud from a volcano but lost on those whose pine trees are different. While Divine protection imagined as sword and shield gave comfort to ancient desert tribes at war with neighbors, a present-day soldier would shrink in fear if these were the weapons issued for his protection. In the same way, computer-savvy city children are asked to visualize GOD as a Good Shepherd when they have no practical experience of a wandering, odoriferous herdsman protecting stray sheep against wild beasts on rugged Palestinian hills. The metaphors don't work in a different time and place, yet many people continue to use such images for the Divine as if the *metaphor* is sacred, rather than what it tries to describe.

From earliest times, people asked the same questions—Who are we? Where did we begin? Does Something pull our puppet strings? Our ancestors, powerless against the natural elements that gave life and destroyed, used these elements as metaphors for the Unknown—mighty Wind, consuming Fire, thirst-quenching Water. They also borrowed metaphors from the natural world. Since mountains stretched through the clouds into the heavens, they were seen as Divine, the abode of the Gods or at least the closest point to them. The desert eagle suggested Divine power. Not only did it perch on the point nearest the heavens, it also swooped down on its enemies and its huge wings covered its eaglets—"God will cover you with his pinions [wings], and under his wings you will find refuge" (Ps. 91:4). Similarly, GOD was called a rock, fortress, high tower, hiding place, all metaphors describing not what the Unknown *was*, but how ancient desert people experienced Divine protection.

As humans became more in control of their world, human metaphors moved into vogue. GOD was imaged as a warrior, shepherd, potter, mother hen—images of power, creativity and protection from everyday life. In time, as already mentioned, images of human power and authority—king and lord—became the dominant metaphors. For primal human beings, "belief in the continuity of all life resulted in a feeling of intimate belonging—of being at home in the world, even as it remained mysterious, sacred, and unpredictable", philosopher Sam Keen says, but by the nineteenth century, "Western man had come to stake his claim to dignity not on being part of a natural order, a cosmos . . . but on being above the natural order . . . being related to nature not as a brother but as a lord—not in the spirit of co-operation and thankfulness but in the spirit of domination."[7] Metaphorical language is all we have to talk about the Divine. The problem arises when certain metaphors from sacred texts, formulated within the power struggles and culture of a particular era, become literal descriptions of the Divine on which infallible doctrines are built and which some people go to endless lengths to defend as reality. Many descriptions of the Sacred, whether from ancient deserts or medieval monasteries, are simply not applicable today and desperately need to be retired. Some are downright offensive, such as GOD accepting the slaughter of Jephthah's only daughter in payment for Jephthah's military victory (Judges 11) and GOD demanding the death of all the occupants of conquered land—"do not spare them, but kill both man and woman, child and infant, ox and sheep, camel and donkey" (1 Sam. 15:3).

The reality is, however, that Mystery is exactly that—Mystery. It has made a career of obscurity and silence. Israel's GOD was always disguised in clouds, thunder or burning bushes. Even in the Genesis Garden, it is the *Sound* of the Creator walking in the Garden and the Divine Voice they hear

(Genesis 3). Moses was told, "You cannot see my face; for no one shall see me and live" (Exod. 33:20). The Hindu Brahman "comes to the thought of those who know him beyond thought, not to those who imagine he can be attained by thought".[8] Islam refuses to depict Allah in any form other than designs combining calligraphy of the Divine names and elements from nature, Allah's creation. Talmud scholar, Maimonides (1135–1204), rather than trying to describe Mystery, said "It is better by far to be silent and to be, simply, before God with the intention of your mind, as the Psalm again says: 'Ponder upon your beds, and be silent.'"[9] This is the mystical tradition, with its intuitive unknowing that Something *is,* rather than a cerebral knowing of *what* It might be. Mystics either say nothing about the Divine or say what It is not—GOD is not powerless; GOD is not ignorant—to avoid the trap of claiming to know what Mystery *is.* Others talk of Divine Darkness or Absence, meaning we can never capture GOD in our dogmas or claims of absolute truth. "Blessed absence of God," the German Beguine mystic Mechtild of Magdeburg (c. 1210–85/91) sang, "how lovingly I am bound to you."[10]

Divine Absence is not something desired by all, however, because there is a thin line between celebrating Divine Hiddenness and deciding that hiddenness is a veil for no-GOD-at-all. I picked up a little book in a hospital chapel explaining GOD to children and was reading excerpts to a chaplain friend who struggles, as I do, with descriptions of the Divine in human shape. The book called GOD a child's best friend who loves to play with you in the Divine playground, the world. You play hide-and-seek with GOD, it says, by looking for GOD hiding in nature.[11] "That's religious life," my chaplain friend said ruefully, "God hides and you seek and sometimes God doesn't appear at the end of the game when we call "Come out, come out, wherever you are.'" We make excuses for such Absence, blaming ourselves for lack of insight, rather than, as the famous atheist Bertrand Russell (1872–1970) said when asked what he would say to God if his atheistic convictions turned out to be wrong, "God, you gave us insufficient evidence!"[12]

If we *do* want to say something descriptive about the Sacred rather than nothing, "formlessness" finds consensus across religions. Yahweh was formless, always appearing in secondary forms—pillar of cloud, voice, wind. "Where can I go from your spirit?" the Psalmist said, "or where can I flee from your presence? If I ascend to heaven, you are there. If I make my bed in Sheol, you are there. If I take the wings of the morning and settle at the farthest limits of the sea, even there your hand shall lead me, and your right hand shall hold me fast" (Ps. 139:7–10). This is a far cry from a male Being sitting on a cloud throne, directing the world from outside its messiness and pain. Formless Spirit in, with and around everything, is also a New Testament image, blowing where It chooses (John 3:8), within us all (John 14:17) and sweeping into a room "like the rush of a violent wind filling the entire house" (Acts 2:2). The Hindu *Upanishads* say, "Where the fire of the Spirit burns, where the wind of the Spirit blows, where the Soma-wine of the Spirit overflows, there a new soul is born."[13]

We are dealing with Mystery, yet this word has had a rocky career in religion. It can mean something not yet clearly known that will be revealed with more knowledge, thus innocent ignorance is mystery. As twenty-first-century people, we are aware that the more we know about our amazing universe, the more there is to know. When scientists talk about 10,000 grains in a handful of sand and more stars in the universe than grains of sand on earth, we cannot begin to imagine it. On the other hand, mystery has been used to silence those who question religious authorities—"Don't ask such questions. It's a Mystery—just believe." There is something of this in the thoughts of the monk Thomas à Kempis (1380–1471) who spent most of his life with the Brothers of the Common Life in Holland. In his best-selling book *Imitation of Christ*, he says:

> A pious and humble inquiry after the truth is allowable, provided we be always ready to be taught and study to walk in the sound doctrine of the Church . . . Many have lost devotion whilst they sought to search into high things. Faith is required of thee, and a sincere life; not height of understanding nor deep delving into the mysteries of God . . . If the works of God were such that they might be easily comprehended by human reason, they could not be justly called wonderful and unspeakable.[14]

Mystery can also describe something well known and loved through experience, a feeling of awe that something *is*, rather than something we can describe. Jewish philosopher and theologian Martin Buber (1878–1965) called this the "I–Thou" relationship, where Something reaches out to engage us, and the more we experience It, the more mysterious It becomes. His contemporary, German theologian Rudolf Otto (1869–1937), called this "Numinous" (the Holy) the "aspect of deity which transcends or eludes comprehension in rational or ethical terms—the *feeling* which remains when the concept fails".[15] According to Otto, this feeling is not simply some emotion "engendered or stimulated in the mind" but also an awareness of "something in the objective situation awaiting discovery and acknowledgment". Otto was not replacing objective or rational religious thought with something subjective or irrational, but ensuring that both elements, rational *and* non-rational, be regarded "as the warp and the woof of the complete fabric, neither of which can dispense with the other".[16] He wrote:

> If one subjects everything to reason our religion will lose its mystery and its supernatural character. If one offends the principles of reason our religion will be absurd and ridiculous . . . There are two equally dangerous extremes, to shut reason out and to let nothing else in.[17]

Evolutionary biologist Richard Dawkins and some other scientists who write for the general public today think that the more sweepingly ultimate and religiously down-grading their arguments against a GOD are, the faster religion will disappear, even though science itself, at its best, talks in open-ended degrees of certainty or probability. It is strange that such dismissals of religious enquiry come in a postmodern age that celebrates the relativity of all thinking and the absence of universal truths—this should keep *all* conversations about the unknown open. Good scientists are the first to acknowledge they cannot prove or disprove what people have called the Divine; and whether one includes a GOD-shape in their worldview or not is a faith statement beyond the bounds of scientific investigation. In an article "Does the Universe have a Purpose?" American physicist Lawrence Krauss, who sees purpose in the universe unlikely, acknowledges that

> While nothing in biology, chemistry, physics, geology, astronomy, or cosmology has ever provided direct evidence of purpose in nature, science can never unambiguously prove that there is no such purpose. As Carl Sagan said in another context, absence of evidence is not evidence of absence.[18]

Perhaps science and religion can talk today about "wonder" and "mystery", each interpreting this human experience in their own methods and metaphors. Sam Keen said:

> To wonder is to perceive with reverence and love . . . and in wondering we come close to the feeling that the earth is holy. Historically, the notion of wonder has been closely bound up with a religious mode of being in the world . . . In my experience, the substance of wonder is more frequently found in the prose of the secular than in the often quaint poetry of religion . . . Whether we continue to talk about God is not so important as whether we retain the sense of wonder which keeps us aware that ours is a holy place.[19]

How and if we imagine Something More is not just an academic exercise. It determines the way we relate to, engage, or live with that Mystery and whether we can believe in a Something at all. Having just lived through the lead-up to Christmas and the excitement of receiving his gifts, my nephew's four-year-old asked his daddy, "Are we God's *toys*?" His was, no doubt, a happy image of GOD sitting cross-legged, as he did, enjoying cars, trucks and dolls spread around the Divine knees and making up stories in which the toys played their part, but for others, the image of being GOD's toy has a fearful ring if it brings to mind a fickle Child playing, destroying or abandoning at whim. We need all the metaphors and descriptions we can get from people's experiences across religions in order to speak of the Unknowable. Different people have come up with different images, throwing back over their shoulders hints and visions from another place and time that need careful unpacking if they are to help us today.

I will use *many* metaphors in this book—Sacred, Holy, Numinous, Divine, Mystery, Presence, GOD/GODDESS—in order to diffuse the idea that there is only one form, image or metaphor, or that one descriptive image takes precedence over all others. This is how Hindu devotees see their plethora of incarnations of the One, many of them fanciful and outrageous, to remind them that nothing they can imagine will capture the Divine. When I asked a Jewish friend, in the process of being bat-mitzvahed as a middle-aged adult, how she imagined the Divine, she said that Jews don't talk much about that. In fact, when she asked questions about GOD in her bat-mitzvah class, the rabbi replied, "Do you want to talk GOD-talk? I don't really feel comfortable with that." This was not because he didn't know what to say but because, in Judaism, there is never just one answer and the whole point is to allow people to discuss and think for themselves. My friend has broad life experience as a social worker, in contact with people of many religions and in many difficult life situations. She sees the Divine in everyone— *everyone* is chosen—and so, to answer my question about how she imagines GOD, she laughed and said, "A black Jewish female who has studied Buddhism." In all our searches for the Divine, traditional or non-traditional, with certainty or with skepticism, we can take comfort in the words of theologian and author Frederick Buechner:

Theology is the study of God and God's ways. For all we know, dung beetles may study humans and their ways and call it humanology. If so, we would probably be more touched and amused than irritated. One hopes that God feels likewise.[20]

Location,
Location, Location...

God is formless, colorless, markless,
He is casteless, classless, creedless,
His form, hue, shape and garb
Cannot be described by anyone.
He is the Spirit of Eternity,
Self-radiant, He shineth in His splendour.
—Guru Gobind Singh[1]

○   ○   ○

"You know [the Spirit of truth],
Because He abides with you,
And He will be in you."
—John 14:17

Thomas, one of Jesus' disciples, was prone to question and, as a result, was labelled for eternity as "doubting Thomas". Other stories about him, however (recorded only in John's Gospel), suggest he was, in fact, one of the brightest in the bunch. When Jesus said he was going away and would prepare a place for them all to join him, Thomas asked a rather crucial logistical question—"Lord, we do not know where you are going. How can we know the way?" (John 14:5). Jesus' answer has been blown up from a simple response to a small band of followers asking a local question, to a statement of religious exclusivity with global dimensions over the centuries, yet the basic question of "Where are you?" is crucially important.

To step out with the Sacred or engage the Divine, we need some idea of where the Sacred *is*. Is the Divine within us, within nature, within everything, or is everything within the Sacred? Or, is GOD somewhere else, separate from us, perhaps in the heavens? Are we journeying towards the Sacred up ahead of us, or is the Sacred waiting for us after death in a realm beyond human experience? Are *we* sacred ourselves, living on holy ground, and is the whole linguistic division between sacred and secular something of our own creating? For those who grew up with a church school education, it was rather confusing if we stopped long enough to think about it. We sang about a friend for little children above the bright, blue sky, yet prayed that GOD would come into our hearts. We read about GOD declaring creation very good, while the whole purpose of salvation was about escaping this world of sin, where we were "strangers", to gain another world of heaven.

The technical terms for describing how the Divine is related to the world are transcendence or immanence. Like any language terms, the definitions have evolved through history.[2] In general, transcendence is anything that is altogether beyond the bounds of human understanding or thought, that cannot be the object of experience or enter consciousness through our sense experiences, that is beyond and independent of history, affecting it but not affected by it, totally other than humanity. Although the Hebrews experienced Divine encounters through burning bushes and Voices, Divine transcendence was assumed, not as a definable location but rather the inability to confine Mystery to our limitations. Divine transcendence does not necessarily mean distance but complete freedom from time and space such that transcendence enables immanence, allowing GOD to be interior to things, closer to us.

> For my thoughts are not your thoughts, nor are your ways my ways, says the Lord. For as the heavens are higher than the earth, so are my ways higher than your ways and my thoughts than your thoughts. (Isa. 55:8–9)

This reflects an ancient cosmology where the heavens, the Divine throne, were above the firmament or sky and the earth was GOD's footstool (Matt. 5:34–35). Thus Moses went up Mount Sinai to receive his Divine instructions, the closest place to GOD, and the mountain was shrouded in smoke when GOD came down to meet Moses there (Ex. 19).

Immanence has more than one meaning. It can mean "near", in terms of something around us or close by—the Divine Spirit present throughout the universe—or it can mean "operating within" or "an integral part of"—the Divine Spirit as part of nature or Nature itself. In terms of immanence as "with" or "near", Yahweh was not confined to shrines like local deities, but the wandering Hebrew people pitched a small tent outside the camp to symbolize Yahweh's presence with them. When Moses entered the tent, "the pillar of cloud would descend and stand at the entrance of the tent, and the Lord would speak to Moses . . . as one speaks to a friend" (Ex. 33:9–11). Later, when the wanderers settled for longer periods in one place, a more elaborate structure, the Ark of the Covenant (Ark of Yahweh), became the actual manifestation of Yahweh with them. It was basically a portable shrine like those used in Egypt, Mesopotamia and Canaan—prior to the prophet Muhammad (570–632 CE), Arabs also had a portable tent-shrine which was taken into battle, the *qubba* containing two sacred stones.[3] Hebrew people would camp around the tabernacle containing the Ark in their tribes, signifying that Yahweh was the center of everyday life. There was no concept of life *outside* of the Divine presence.

When a kingdom was formed about 1,000 years before Jesus, King Solomon built the first temple in Jerusalem to replace tent and tabernacle as the symbol and place of the Divine presence. The Ark was placed in the Holy of Holies in Solomon's new temple as the throne of the invisible Deity present with them.[4] This temple was destroyed and rebuilt twice in Jewish history, the last being the temple that Jesus frequented. When *this* temple was destroyed by the Romans some 40 years after Jesus, synagogues became the place where the Law was read and taught, the *new* location of the Divine Spirit present among the people. Our Gospels were written after the destruction of this temple, so it is not surprising that John's Gospel, written perhaps as late as early second century, calls Jesus the *new* temple, the new location where the Divine Spirit is encountered. Since the community from which John's Gospel emerged had recently been excluded from the synagogue, this assured them that GOD was *still* in their midst, still pitching a tent with them, as it were, as the comforter Spirit that had also been in Jesus.

The other meaning of immanence defines the Sacred not as "near" but "in"—part of nature or Nature itself. For indigenous people whose stories stretch back far beyond recorded history, the Sacred was encountered every-where in nature, and demonstrated, not through dramatic or extraordinary occurrences but in the everyday. Romanian-born comparative religion scholar Mircea Eliade (1907–86) wrote, "One of the major differences sep-arating the people of early cultures from people today is precisely the utter incapacity of the latter to live their organic life (particularly as regards sex and nutrition) as a sacrament."[5]

There are two variations on immanence in nature. "Pantheism" sees the Sacred and the world as identical, whereas "panentheism" sees the world and GOD as interacting and interdependent, but the world does not encompass all there is of GOD—there is still Divine transcendence we cannot know. In panentheism, it is not necessary to seek this transcendence since we interact with Divine action in the *world*. Bishop John Shelby Spong quotes the words on a tenth-century gravestone in Lonköping, Sweden:

Envoi
God within me, God without,
How shall I ever be in doubt?
There is not place where I may go
And not there see God's face, not know
I am God's vision and God's ears
So through the harvest of my years
I am the Sower and the Sown
God's self unfolding and God's own.[6]

In Sikh doctrine, the Unknowable One is transcendent, but there is sufficient revelation communicated by the grace of the Gurus, the Divine Voice mystically uttered within a person. Although the Divine Presence is without form, It is visible to enlightened believers because GOD is immanent in all creation.

Where GOD is raises the question of revelation. Some say the Divine can be known through human ability to see evidence of this Mystery in nature. For the Greeks, the holy could be encountered anywhere, revealed not through extraordinary events but through ordinary experiences of life—when philosophers looked at the cosmos, they saw Divine reason present in the order of the universe. In Judaism, however, while Yahweh was experienced speaking *through* natural elements, Divine revelations were recorded events in history—GOD was never homogenized with or within the cosmos. This battle between natural theology, the knowledge of GOD within the universe, attainable by "natural reason", and specific revelatory events, such as a burning bush or the man Jesus, waxed and waned through church history. Following the thoughts of the great medieval theologian Thomas Aquinas (c. 1227–74), the First Vatican Council (1869–70) declared that "If anyone shall have said that the one true God, our Creator and our Lord, cannot be known with certitude by those things which have been made, by the natural light of human reason: let him be anathema."[7]

Protestant reformers, on the other hand, were concerned about human depravity after the fall and were suspicious of the idea that humans were capable of knowing GOD apart from faith in Jesus Christ or through the work of the Holy Spirit. While the Enlightenment gave credence to human reason, any emerging theological suggestion that GOD could be known through reason and nature was bulldozed under by Protestant theologian Karl Barth's (1886–1968) booming voice through two World Wars declaring bankrupt any notion of knowing GOD apart from the revelation in Jesus Christ. This great divorce between knowledge of the Divine through the natural world and Divine revelations only through the special experience and history celebrated in synagogue and church led, according to Sam Keen, to

> a desacralization of nature, a destruction of the presence of the holy at the heart of the everyday . . . The story of the eclipse of wonder (which is the same story as the death of God, the loss of the holy, the secularization of Western culture, and the loss of cosmic reason) is the outcome of the unsolved dichotomy between the sacred and the profane which was bequeathed to Western man by the Judeo-Christian tradition.[8]

The Divine's location became more and more defined in the Middle Ages and the Renaissance, not only by Christian theology but also in church art. A quick searchlight around European museum and church walls finds the male humanlike Being firmly planted in the heavens, reaching down to earth or else holding the cross bearing the crucified Christ as the symbolic bridge between heaven and earth. The Vatican's Sistine Chapel ceiling, painted by famous Italian Renaissance artist Michelangelo (1475–1564), depicts "The Creation of Man" as an elderly greybeard GOD reaching out from atop a heavenly cloud to almost touch the finger of earth-bound Adam (a scene madly reproduced today to advertise just about everything). With that heavenly vantage point, it was not rocket science for illiterate sinners to realize that the Divine eye saw everything—both good and bad news. While It could watch over us, It also saw when we did evil or dishonest things and thus we could join the list for punishment. While the Bible mentions that GOD sees each sparrow fall (Matt. 10:29)—no doubt intended meta-phorically to indicate Divine attention—this later became literalized to depict an overworked Being micro-managing every detail of the universe. Symbolically, this was depicted in art as an eye within the Trinitarian triangle. In the Neamt Orthodox Monastery I visited in northern Romania, a huge GOD's-eye stares down from a high tower into the enclosed courtyard where the monks live and walk, symbolizing the two aspects of the Seeing-eye GOD—protection and punishment. Similarly, in a magnificent old hunting lodge near Kosice in Slovakia, I noticed as we swept past the kitchen on tour that the master of the house had hung a triangulated GOD's-eye over the kitchen door to remind the servants that GOD was watching when they arrived and left. No doubt there was little separation in the servants' imagination between GOD and their master—both had the power to arbitrarily punish or reward.

The risen Christ in Christian art was also firmly ensconced in heaven, seated beside the Father GOD and depicted as a younger, beardless clone to indicate a biological likeness (shared genes, we would say today) between Father and Son. The Holy Spirit, shown as a white dove, is the one of the Three on the move, whispering various messages from the two elevated males into the ears of saints, or impregnating Mary with the Divine seed. Such art was not the random wielding of a paintbrush by an inspired artist. Church art taught the doctrines of the time—they were theological instruction manuals for the illiterate and, as such, deliberately executed. In *The Coronation of the Blessed Virgin* hanging in the Musée de Villeneuve-les-Avignon, Father and Son have identical faces and ages, unlike many paintings where GOD is an older, bearded man and Jesus the younger, beardless lookalike. The specifications and contract for this altarpiece, commissioned by Lord Jean de Montagnac of the artist Master Engueran Quarton as the altarpiece of the Holy Trinity in the Carthusian Church of Villeneuve-les-Avignon, was signed on April 24, 1453 and are kept in the Museum. Twenty-six articles describe how the painting is to be executed, the first being:

> Heaven must be represented and in this Eden the Holy Trinity has to be seen without showing any difference between Father and Son; the Holy Spirit must be represented as a dove with our Lady in front, displayed to Master Engueran's liking. The Holy Trinity will be putting the crown on Our Lady's head.[9]

The rest of the instructions for the painting cover the type of clothing for the figures, which angels and saints to include and what symbols they should hold, the world "where a part of the city of Rome can be seen", followed by instructions as to which of Rome's buildings be included and the "river Tibre [Tiber] rejoining the sea on which will be some galleons and ships". Jerusalem must be depicted on the other side of the sea and extensive instructions follow as to who and what should be featured there. Hell and Purgatory must be shown and include "all the world states to Master Engueran['s] liking". As a final instruction, "Master Engueran will demonstrate all his skills in designing the Holy Trinity and the Virgin Mary, and will do his best with the rest." This contract was signed "in the spice shop of Jean de Bria . . . spice trader, citizen of Avignon, in the presence of John and Lord

Guillaume Gui, priest, canon of St Agricol Church of Avignon, witness, etc. and me, Jean Morel (the notary)".

This City of GOD in the sky containing the Holy Trinity, the goal of faithful pilgrims, was reiterated in the sacred literature read to and by pilgrims, many of them poor and enduring suffering in their medieval world and thus were attracted to such blessed relief. "O most happy mansion of the city which is above!" Thomas à Kempis wrote, "O most clear day of eternity . . . Oh, that that day would shine upon us, and that all these temporal things were at an end! . . . O merciful JESUS, when shall I stand to behold thee?[10] For now, however, according to à Kempis, the Divine is not engaged in the "world" but enthroned in the heart—"Thy Beloved is of such a nature that He will admit no rival but will have thy heart alone and sit on His own throne as King. If thou wouldst empty thyself perfectly of all created things, Jesus would willingly dwell with thee."[11]

The GODS' location also depended on who was doing the describing. Two people standing on a beach staring at the horizon could be a twenty-first-century couple ending their day on a remote island resort, or a primal couple wondering what happens where the water meets the sky. The latter is what sent humans to sea in boats. Imagine the anxiety as that first boat became smaller and smaller and disappeared on the horizon. Will we see them again? Will they drop off the edge of the earth? Not surprisingly, the "other side" of the ocean came to represent the after-world or the realm of the GODS. Ancient Egyptians believed a boat transported the sun across the sky each day and sailed through the after-world to return at dawn. Perhaps this boat also took the souls? Early Indonesian tribes thought the dead travelled to the next world in boats and built boat-shaped coffins to help their departure; and we all know that the River Styx in Greek mythology formed the boundary between earth and the underworld. The nave of a church comes from *navis* meaning "ship", with the tower the mast and buttresses the oars—the ship that takes the faithful to heaven.

My boat meander leads into the story of Pitcairn Island. After mutiny on board the British ship *Bounty* in 1789, Fletcher Christian and a handful of mutineers, together with some Tahitian men and women, landed on Pitcairn Island in the Pacific. Christian chose Pitcairn to avoid being found and hung because, although recorded on naval maps, it was drawn in the wrong position. It's a long and fascinating story but, in time, only one mutineer, Alexander Smith, plus some Tahitian women and their children, remained. Smith had found religion by reading the *Bounty*'s Bible and Prayer Book and converted his little clan into devout Christians. When a British ship arrived in 1808, the crew were amazed to find an Anglican community under Smith's pastoral care (he later changed his name to John Adams). Rather than being deported and hung, Smith was praised for his pious flock and commended to English mission societies and the Queen, who began sending financial support to this Christian outpost. The Pitcairners were eventually re-settled on Norfolk Island, but some returned later and continued their religious life under the blessings of the Crown. Today, Pitcairn Island Christianity reflects this history of isolation, hardship, rejection, closeness to death and hope of glory. When I was on Norfolk Island where many Pitcairn descendants still live, I purchased a DVD of their favourite hymns in the Anglican mission church. Several written by Pitcairners are biblical texts set to music (reflecting a people formed by a King James Bible and a Church of England Prayer Book)—verses pleading for Divine protection on a dangerous life journey and a hope of heaven. The bulk, however, are about the sea and heaven as a place across the ocean—"There is a Land of Pure Delight" whose lights will "light us from the shore" and "In the sweet by and by we shall meet on that beautiful shore." Another talks of heaven's "peaceful shore", something not experienced by these island people whose only landing place on Pitcairn involved riding the waves heading for shoreline rocks until the very last minute. "Let the lower lights be burning" was also included:

> Brightly beams our Father's mercy
> From his lighthouse on the shore,
> Unto us he gives the keeping
> Of the lights along the shore.
> Let the lower lights be burning
> Send a beam across the wave,
> Some poor fainting struggling Christian
> You may rescue, you may save.[12]

"The Ship of Fame" is the most memorable hymn with rollicking tune and chorus—I can hear Pitcairners singing this as their boat shoots the waves towards the rocky shore:

> What ship is this you're sailing in,
> This wondrous ship of fame?
> The ship is called the "Church of God"
> And Christ's the Captain's name.
> Do you not fear the stormy seas
> Your bark may overwhelm?
> You need not fear—the Lord is near,

And Christ is at the helm!
Then hoist the sails and catch the breeze,
And soon the journey's o'er.
The ship will land you safe at last
On Canaan's happy shore.[13]

For these island people whose only "road to anywhere" involved boats and the sea, and whose safety while at sea depended on lights on the shore, it made perfect sense to imagine heaven as a long boat-ride away.

Mystics located the Divine, not up in heaven or across the ocean, but *within* them. Julian of Norwich described Jesus enthroned in the midst of her heart:

> Our Lord opened my spiritual eyes, and showed me my soul in the midst of my heart. I saw my soul as wide as if it were a kingdom, and from the state in which I saw it, it seemed to me as if it were a fine city. In the midst of this sits our Lord Jesus, true God and true man, a handsome person and tall, honourable, the greatest Lord. And I saw him splendidly clad in honours. He sits erect there in the soul, in peace and rest, and he rules and he guards heaven and earth and everything that is . . . The place which Jesus takes in our soul he will nevermore vacate, for in us is his home of homes, and it is the greatest delight for him to dwell there.[14]

While the term "soul" has suffered pretty intense analysis over the centuries by theologians from all brands of religion, it is a word ordinary people use for inner feelings and experiences that can't be talked about in any other way. Our "soul" belongs exclusively to us where we can live in private, even in the midst of a crowd. If you come too close to a nesting killdeer, she will pretend to have a broken wing and stagger around on the ground to distract you from getting to her eggs. We humans also have the habit of pretending all sorts of things to stop people getting too close to our souls, not in order to take something from us but to expose our innermost being for what we really are. Just as some people don't ask friends home because their private space may reveal too much about them—their wealth, reading choices, private living arrangements, habits—many don't ask friends into the "home" that is our soul. Thus it is the perfect place for the mystical experience, that "fundamental unitive experience of love and communion with God" (a theistic definition) or the "intuitive, contemplative approach to ultimate reality (a non-theistic definition)".[15] There is still some theological imagery confusion within Christianity however, although not in the Eastern religions, as to whether the Divine Spirit resides naturally within the human heart or whether some search and invitation is necessary to begin this indwelling process.

Religion scholar Raimon Panikkar, son of a Catalan Catholic mother and Indian Hindu father, was an early participant in contemporary inter-religious dialogue. When asked why Eastern religions became attractive to Westerners, Panikkar suggested that Christianity has given insufficient attention to general contemplation, silence and the well-being of the body. Christian traditions, for the most part, have sought a GOD of difference and otherness, even though its picturesque creation story tells of Divine Breath being breathed *into* clay in order to create human beings. Hinduism and its religious offspring, on the other hand, locate Divine Mystery *in* human beings and the world, something so profound and real that one cannot be separated from it. The Indian greeting "Namasti" with hands together and a slight bow means "The Divine in me greets the Divine in you"—"To see another person is to see the face of God" is how it is worded in the song from *Les Miserables*. A monk on Mount Athos in Greece told Nikos Kazantzakis of his long, unsuccessful struggle to "experience" the Divine through renunciation and obedience:

> [L]et me be able to feel His invisible presence so that I too may rejoice if only for a split second and know that I am a Christian and that my years in the monastery were not spent for nothing. I cried out, wept, fasted—in vain![16]

At one point, the monk was sent to the country where he lived among children, families, fields and harvests. He was seduced by a local woman and, in that experience, finally felt GOD come near him. While his fellow monks would be horrified at this form of epiphany, for him it was this embodiment of love that revealed Divine Love:

> For the first time in my inhuman, cheerless life I understood to what degree God is all-good, to what degree he loves man, and how very much he must have pitied him in order to have created woman and favored her such grace that she leads us to paradise along the surest and shortest of roads . . . A woman had given me this certainty—a woman, I repeat, and not prayer or fasting . . . brought the Lord into my room . . . I did not and will not repent! If I had the chance to do it again, I would.[17]

The Ultimate has long been described as an external Being tinkering with the laws of the universe to work miracles and change physical circumstances for some and not others, like sending floods as punishment and finding car-parks for the faithful. We now have *other* explanations for how the universe works. We can no longer bury our heads in the sand and hold on to pre-scientific descriptions of a Divine train-driver steering the universe from somewhere outside it, not even on automatic but using a manual gear-stick. We need language and imagery today that makes sense in the presence of our scientific knowledge, not over against it or separate from it. This is not to say that scientific inquiry can or must explain everything, as even that language is always tentative, but rather that we can no longer describe Divine activity in the world in ways that contradict with what can be scientifically demonstrated as the working of natural laws. Prior to the Enlightenment, philosophy, science and theology were all the property of the Church, as Galileo discovered the hard way, but after the Enlightenment, philosophy excluded a Divine Being from its discussions just as science would soon stop including the Creator in its explanations—rightly so because the scientific method strictly limits itself to what can be investigated by physical experiment. We now need to find ways, if at all possible, to talk about locating and engaging the Divine that allow philosophy, science and theology to be in the same conversation. Ursula King, citing the opinions of two American scholars involved in science and religion discussion, John Haught and Ian Barbour, says:

> [I]t would be of great benefit to the human community if the new scientific worldview, especially the understanding of natural history and the stunning evolution of life, could be integrated with the enduring wisdom and spiritual quest that form an essential part of humanity's religious and cultural traditions.[18]

Scientists have gone to the moon and travelled in space, showing us that medieval images of heaven "up there" separated by a membrane beyond the clouds and hell under the ground no longer make sense for our universe.

Contemporary science concerns itself with the energy and interrelatedness within an organic universe rather than the Newtonian ideas of a mechanistic universe. While science labels the elements of unpredictability and chance within the universe with its particular metaphors, these can, as a faith statement, also be described metaphorically in terms with religious overtones, such as Energy working within us and the universe, urging towards richness and wholeness. Just as scientists express awe and wonder at the mysteries of the universe, we can do the same from our own spiritual quests. Such imagery moves us from an External Being pulling our puppet strings and overriding our free will to Energy within the world mending and re-creating the planet or, alternatively, our fragile universe as the Divine Body nurturing all life within it, as Paul described to the Athenian philosophers—GOD "in whom we live and move and have our being" (Acts 17:28). This imagery as to the location of the Sacred is also important in indigenous traditions and contemporary GODDESS traditions which see the Sacred as Mother Earth or Nature itself:

> The drama of birth, death and rebirth does not take place outside the Goddess but within Her; the universe is seen and experienced as the divine body itself. As "parts" of the whole body, the many facets and factors of nature do not exist apart from each other, but as interconnected strands of the whole: all depends on all . . .[19]

Such imagery calls for a very different engagement with the Sacred. Rather than hands lifted up to the GOD in heaven, we are part of the Divine, working with Mother Earth or the Divine Spirit within the universe to preserve this planet and show reverence for it.

> What alienates us from the divine is hubris: we imagine not only that we are not part of the divine, but the divine is apart from us. This separation from divine nature may give the appearance of divine order, but does not reflect intuited reality.[20]

Moreover, if this Life-Force is within *all* people and living things, not just those who believe the "correct" religious creeds like us, we are jolted into repentance over how we have treated our siblings of different races and religions. A student in a class of mine on World Religions had spent some years as a missionary in Bangladesh, during which time she realized that Muslims were not all "pagans" in need of conversion as she had been taught in her church and mission society in Australia. They could also tell of their experiences of the Divine in ways from which she learned much. From this revelatory perspective, she was horrified when her mother came to visit and would say in a loud voice when they were in taxis or restaurants, "It's terrible to think that all these nice people aren't converted."

Just as our metaphorical descriptions of the Divine determine how we act towards that Divine, where we imagine the Divine to be—location, location, location—is crucial if we are to engage the Divine or if we are to recognize the Divine engaging us. We may think we know exactly where GOD is because that is where we have looked for the Sacred and told GOD to remain, but surprises await us along the journey as the Divine refuses to be where we have proclaimed or we find more authentic places in which to search—or the other possibility that there is nothing to find. The other day I received an email from my daughter with the heading "So this didn't go quite to plan." As the first one to read and critique my draft manuscript for *Like Catching Water in a Net: Human attempts to describe the Divine*, she was dutifully trying to instil a broader view of GOD into her three-year-old son, Calvin. The conversation apparently went like this:

> Me: "Some people think God is a person up in the sky, like an angel, that looks after everything. And some people think God is the good things inside of us. And some people think there is no God at all."
> Calvin: "Do you have God inside you?"
> Me: "Yes."
> Calvin: "And does Daddy?"
> Me: "Yes."
> (Shocked expression, then shrieks of laughter from Calvin)
> Calvin: "Daddy has a little *man* in his tummy?"

3

What Do
Humans Want?

Religion is not primarily a matter of facts in the historical sense; it is a
matter of meanings. An account may speak endlessly of gods and rites
and beliefs, but unless it leads us to see how these things help men to
meet such problems as isolation, tragedy, and death, it may be impec-
cably accurate, but religion has not been touched at all.

—*Huston Smith*[1]

In a *Peanuts* cartoon, Lucy and Charlie Brown are engaged in a "heavy, deep,
and real" conversation about the meaning of life. Lucy says, "Life is like a
deckchair. Some people place it so they can see where they are going. Some
people place it so they can see where they have been. And some people place
it so they can see where they are now." Charlie thinks deeply about Lucy's
soliloquy and then replies, "I can't even get mine unfolded."

What do humans *want* from engaging the Sacred? What is this search for
meaning all about? In halls of theological education, certain words such as
eschatology, neo-orthodoxy, epistemology and determinism are codes for
lengthy theological debates that a hearer in that setting will know without
having to spell out the details each time. It's like new parents talking about
potty training—you know what the other person means by the word without
having to list each time the changing theories of when, where and how.
Learning these terms is a large part of theological education and, by the time
you have them all in place, you return to the real world and unlearn them
so those around you know what you're talking about. There are also *ethnic*
terms in different religious groups, usually arising from the founder. Lutherans have a host of these—"between the times", "two kingdoms", "works
religion", "theology of the cross", to name a few. I did my PhD in an American Lutheran Seminary where I satisfied four "minority" groupings in one—

non-American, non-Lutheran, non-male and non-ordained. Although I had a religious studies degree when I arrived, I thought I had stumbled on a whole new religion, although the main protagonist—GOD—was still recognizable. At first I felt intimidated, wondering how I missed so many pages in my theology textbooks, but one frustrating day I interrupted my small doctoral class and said, "Excuse me, can someone *please* tell me what that phrase means?" From the silence, you would have thought I had stripped bare. Another student, more Lutheran than Luther, snorted and said, "We shouldn't have to deal with such questions in a *doctoral* class!" To my professor's credit, he said, "No, Val has a right to ask" and, turning to the one who objected, said, "Perhaps *you* could explain the history of the term to her?" I hope I didn't look too jubilant when he made a hash of his explanation—he had used the short-hand so long its actual origins had departed him!

The "human condition" is one such code phrase. While this may not keep you awake at night, it lies at the heart of religion and has been answered differently across the globe. It is the awareness that something is wrong with us and asks what is it, where do we want to go from here, and how can we get there? As writer George O'Brien says, religion is about singing, praying, talking and gesturing "about the humanly unfixable"; and prayer is the evolution of primal swear-words "Oh Fudge!" when things went wrong or were beyond our control.[2]

If we were to ask a group of people about their particular concerns (human condition) and what they wanted from a Divinity, you'd get different answers. Some want an afterlife insurance policy, some want Divine protection now, some want supernatural experiences to wow their mundane existence, some want to feel a part of something bigger than themselves, some want to feel closer to nature, some want a line either to pull them to a more secure shore or to save them from hell. Our answer to the "human condition" will influence how we engage the Divine because, in most religions, the Divine is part or all of the solution. "For practical life, at any rate, the chance of salvation is enough", William James (1842–1910) wrote. "The existence of the chance makes the difference . . . between a life of which the keynote is resignation and a life of which the keynote is hope."[3]

In their book *Faith, Religion and Theology,*[4] the authors examine the human condition and its solution in different religions, finding a mix of responses. For Middle Eastern religions from Abraham (Judaism, Christianity and Islam), the human problem is described as sin or disobedience, argued from Adam and Eve's disobedience in the Garden of Eden. While this story has been variously interpreted and is currently being reprieved from its dastardly disgrace, the outcome in traditional understandings is alienation from

GOD. The where-do-we-want-to-go solution is reunion with the Divine and we get there through faith in the One who did not abandon humankind and demands love and obedience, according to specifications in the Torah, Bible or Qur'an. In South Asian religions, such as Hinduism and Buddhism, the human condition is not sin or disobedience, but ignorance of our true nature. Since we don't know who we really are, we grasp at external things that cause us suffering and the solution is to discover our true nature. In Hinduism, this comes through realizing that what we think is real is actually unreal and that our individual self, *atman*, is actually the universal Self, *Brahman*. In Buddhism, the solution is to shed layers of things that cause us suffering and discover for ourselves, through meditation, yoga and compassion, our "non-self" and our Buddha-nature—work out your own salvation with diligence, the Buddha said. In Confucianism and Taoism, the religious traditions of China, the human condition is disharmony. The natural, dynamic balance in society, relationships with people, among nations, in nature and in the universe is disrupted. The goal is to regain that harmony in all things and it is achieved in Confucianism by education and the structuring of society, and in Taoism by union with the *Tao*, the mysterious way of nature.[5]

It is difficult evaluating another religion. We can discuss it from the outside, describe how it started, what its practices are and how they function in people's lives, or we can try to look from the inside by listening to what people say about the meaning and purpose of their religious practices. Either way, it is not easy. None of us can belong to every religion and know them all "from the inside", nor can we be completely objective in our descriptions "from the outside" because these are always colored by our personal scale of what is good and bad, logical and illogical, civilized and primitive. We are limited to being on the outside trying to look into the personal experiences of others and thus we miss the individual drive and meaning that a religion has for a devotee. Since most people are grossly ignorant of other religions, there has been a tendency in Christianity to simply file the universal human condition under the label "sin" and its solution under "salvation", applying *Christian* meanings of these terms across the board. As I have said, however, not every religion identifies the same problem, nor do people solve it in the same way. American naturalist Henry David Thoreau (1817–62), who wrote about living alone for two years in the woods in Massachusetts, was asked on his deathbed if he had made his peace with God. "I didn't know we had quarrelled," he replied.[6] "Salvation" comes from the Latin root for "health" or "deliverance" and the original Hebrew term meant "safety, deliverance or liberation", but it became limited in Christianity to a specific, defined event around the person and purpose of Jesus, and the Christian discussion of other religions became absorbed with whether there is truth and/or salvation anywhere else. Some have denied any truth or salvation outside of Christianity because "Jesus is the way, the truth and the life" (John 14:6). Others concede some truth, but not salvation, in other religions and thus interfaith dialogue is to bring the other to full truth. Thankfully, there are more and more people today who see religions as different paths to the Sacred and thus dialogue is not about Christian salvation but about enhancing *both* with fresh insights into the Divine.

Not only does what we want (our human condition) vary across religions, it also varies according to our particular time, place and experience; as someone jokingly said about teaching children to deal with life, "The only truly educational toy we might give to our children is a jigsaw puzzle, no two pieces of which fit together."[7] Valerie Saiving, a rare species of *female* theological student in the 1950s at the University of Chicago, sat through endless discussions with male colleagues about the "human condition" which, at that time in theological education, went under the code word "existentialism"—anxiety and loneliness brought on by the human need to stand apart from the world and survey it, manipulating and organizing it for one's purposes. Sin was seen as the temptation to overcome this anxiety by magnifying one's *own* power and making oneself like GOD:

> Man knows that he is merely part of the whole, but he tries to convince himself and others that he *is* the whole. He tries in fact to become the whole. Sin is the unjustified concern of the self for its own power and prestige; it is the imperialistic drive to close the gap between the individual, separate self and others by reducing those others to the status of mere objects which can then be treated as appendages of the self and manipulated accordingly.[8]

The remedy for this sinful pride and urge to dominate, the students decided, was the opposite—total self-giving love that ignored one's own interests and sought only the good of others. Apart from *our* discomfort as readers with this exclusively male language, Saiving felt very uncomfortable with this conversation because it did not line up with her experiences as a *woman*. While anxiety about maintaining power and control might be problematic for a 1950s *male*, it was certainly not something 1950s women experienced. Besides, their solution—total self-giving love and seeking the good of others— was what women did all the time in families. Saiving's doubts took thirteen years to compost into an article for the *Journal of Religion* that began:

I am a student of theology; I am also a woman. Perhaps it strikes you as curious that I put these two assertions beside each other, as if to imply that one's sexual identity has some bearing on his theological views. I myself would have rejected such an idea when I first began my theological studies. But now, thirteen years later, I am no longer certain as I once was that, when theologians speak of "man", they are using the word in its generic sense. It is, after all, a well-known fact that theology has been written almost exclusively by men. This alone should put us on guard, especially since contemporary theologians constantly remind us that one of man's strongest temptations is to identify his own limited perspective with universal truth.[9]

Saiving's male colleagues had described the "human condition" according to *their* experiences. Women, on the other hand, had no access to dominating power, either at home (the male was still listed as head of the household) or in the world. The male solution, to love sacrificially and surrender to others' needs, was a woman's everyday role. The "human condition" for women was constant *surrendering* of power and self-identity to others as wives and mothers. Their "sin" (or "fall" from their GOD-given image) was *lack* of pride in its best sense, diffuseness, lack of focus and negation of themselves as people. Women's solution was not more of the same, but claiming their own personhood and power. The gender, experience and context of those describing the human condition *matter*. As liberation theologian Dorothee Sölle (1929–2003) said:

> There is something liberating about knowing that particular thought forms, convictions and customs do not hold from eternity to eternity but are historical forms of expression which must necessarily be subject to examination and understood in terms of their origin.[10]

In his classic book *The Varieties of Religious Experiences: A study in human nature,* psychologist William James (1842–1910) showed that the needs of human beings are different and different types of people need different types of religious experiences. There is not some universal "religious emotion" in itself, but "a common storehouse of emotions upon which religious objects may draw".[11] In probably the first book on the psychology of religion, James outlined different personality types and the religious experiences that would be more attractive or satisfying to each, rather than the "one size fits all" approach with which, for the most part, religions have been packaged. According to James' categories, there are healthy-minded "once-born" people who see life optimistically and focus on the good. Rather than wallowing in guilt, they get up and act on what needs improving, believing the old slogan that "God's in his heaven, all's right with the world!" On the other hand, there are morbid people who live in failure and depression, focusing on the evil in things. They despair of the condition of the world, their own inner state and also maintain a general fear of the universe. The famous German writer Goethe (1749–1832) said, despite all his successes:

> At bottom, [life] has been nothing but pain and burden, and I can affirm that during the whole of my seventy-five years, I have not had four weeks of genuine well-being. It is but the perpetual rolling of a rock that must be raised up again for ever.[12]

To such people, healthy-minded, positive people seem shallow. I am a "cup half-full rather than half-empty" person and I always worried a devout friend who regularly commented on my usual analysis of an event—"It was fun", together with my farewell greeting—"Have fun!" He was not comfortable with someone so geared to "fun" when there were so many lost souls and evil things about which to fret. James quotes American evangelist Henry Alline (1748–84) who obviously had the same affliction—"I had now so great a sense of the vanity and emptiness of all things here below that I knew the whole world could not possibly make me happy, no, nor the whole system of creation."[13] James called these solemn people "twice-born" because they needed a religious conversion in order to deal with the world, to find an evil and battle against it.

Although Florence Nightingale (1820–1910) is most famous for her time spent at the Crimean War (1854–56) and her contributions to nursing, this was only a fraction of her life-work. What is little known is her scholarship and interest in religion such that she wrote an 800-page manuscript offering a new religion for the poor, something that was never published in her lifetime and has only recently had any wide circulation.[14] In my book *Florence Nightingale: The making of a radical theologian,* I examine Nightingale's religious ideas and vocation and show her to be a progressive theologian in dialogue, at the time, with those who were challenging many of the doctrines of the Church of England.[15] One of her chief concerns was the theology that said GOD ordained some to be rich and some poor, a doctrine that held people in poverty and worked against reform as the rich were only required to give charity, not change the social situation. Nightingale's "new" religion was that the Divine Spirit within everyone enabled all to *challenge* their particular lot in life:

Instead of talking about man being "desperately wicked", we should say, as we sometimes do say of great heroes, we did not know of what man was capable. Instead of that hideous, hopeless repetition every day for years of "there is no health in us", we should be living with a purpose, a purpose of moral improvement, which would be constantly realized till we were "perfect, even as God is perfect". What a difference there is between those thus living with a purpose and those who live with no purpose at all.[16]

Different people will have different views on the human condition and will need different solutions for resolving it. James said:

[T]he Divine can mean no single quality, it must mean a group of qualities . . . it takes the whole of us to spell the meaning (of human nature) out completely. So a "god of battles" must be allowed to be the god for one kind of person, a god of peace and heaven and home, the god for another . . . If we are sick souls, we require a religion of deliverance; but why think so much of deliverance, if we are healthy-minded? . . . for each man to stay in his own experience, whate'er it be, and for others to tolerate him there, is surely best.[17]

Today, the Myers-Briggs Type Indicator (MBTI) tests used to assess personality types can also help explain why different religious practices attract different people (and also why many people feel uncomfortable in the religious styles into which they were born). Introverts are energized by the inner world of ideas and prefer meditation and private prayer as ways to engage the Divine, while extroverts will seek the Sacred in the world of people, public worship, group discussion and social action. Some will be attracted to a focused study of scriptures and books while others find that rituals and experiences capture their emotions. Some will espouse religious ideas through logic and reason while others "know" GOD in the heart. Some will want spontaneity in worship while others prefer the orderliness of liturgy. Some will see religious practices as a means to an end while others will value them for themselves. Some will want instruction as to what to do, while others venture out on their own spiritual quest. Some will seek the Sacred in nature and others in ceremonies and cathedrals.

What we want from the Divine also depends on the stories on which we were raised about how GOD acts. According to psychologist of religion E. D. Starbuck (1866–1947):

A child who is early taught that he is God's child, that he may live and move and have his being in God, and that he has, therefore, infinite strength at hand for the conquering of any difficulty, will take life more easily and will probably make more of it, than one who is told that he is born the child of wrath and wholly incapable of good.[18]

In my own childhood, sermons and altar calls that raged against the total depravity of human beings, and thus the constant need to confess *all* sins to avoid the fate of hell, were the fashion. As a well-protected child whose opportunities for "big" sins were few and far between and whose overall disposition was one of enthusiasm rather than despair, I struggled to find personal sins sufficiently large enough for the necessity of Christ's horrific death for *me*. Pinching my sister or miscalculating the number of cookies I'd eaten hardly seemed in the same league. On the other hand, I was a GOD-intoxicated child who intuitively longed to *experience* a loving Presence, a feeling of belonging to and being loved by GOD, such that my basic psychology leaned towards loving rather than being afraid of GOD. The French Carmelite nun, Saint Thérèse of Lisieux (1873–97), who was also in love with GOD from childhood (no, I'm not comparing myself to a saint), was raised in a family where both parents had hoped to follow a religious vocation. When her mother died when Thérèse was four and a half, Thérèse was already longing for heaven rather than earthly life so susceptible to the Devil. Her father felt greatly honored when, one by one, his daughters became nuns—Jesus chose many brides from *his* house. All Thérèse wanted growing up was to become another bride for Jesus:

If people who are as weak and imperfect as I am only felt what I feel, not one of them would despair of scaling the summit of the mountain of love. Jesus does not demand great deeds. All He wants is self-surrender and gratitude.[19]

Yet this was not enough to satisfy her religious, psychological and sexual needs—she also wanted to *suffer* for GOD to appease, in some way, for what she saw as her sinful childhood:

I don't want to suffer just one torment. I should have to suffer them all to be satisfied . . . My heart leaps when I think of the unheard tortures Christians will suffer in the reign of anti-Christ. I want to endure them all. My Jesus, fling open that book of life in which are set down the deeds of every saint. I want to perform them all for You![20]

As well as the personal stories we imbibed as children, the communal religious stories in which we were raised, in church, temple or mosque, shape our desire (or not) to engage the Divine. We can talk all we like about doctrines, theories and definitions of religions, but there is also a lived experience that formed our particular religious tradition and a context that made it attractive to our clan. Huston Smith says:

> Ideas are important in life, but they seldom, of themselves, provide starting points. They grow out of facts and experiences, and torn from this soil lose their lives as quickly as uprooted trees. We shall find ourselves quite incapable of understanding Christian theology unless we manage to see clearly the experience it tried to account for.[21]

Few people convert between religions. Most of us are born into a particular religion and remain under that umbrella all our lives, even though we may adapt it, grow away from it, ignore it or denounce it. When people become entranced by the Dalai Lama's Buddhism, or more likely the personality of the Dalai Lama himself, he always urges them to stay within their own religious tradition because it *culturally* suits them best and, within it, they will feel most at home.

This is not surprising because religions are not pure entities dropped from heaven but significantly reflect the culture and location in which they were formed—they are as much about these as about theology. Religious ideas are also not eternal, but emerged out of a particular "landscape" which included the problems people faced within that situation (the human condition) and the solutions they embraced. Although theology is often portrayed as specialist language and action within academic halls, it is always an attempt by human beings to talk about GOD in their particular place and time in order to decide how to act in the world—it is functional, not an end in itself. Prior to the Holocaust, Judaism saw itself as GOD's chosen people but, after the Holocaust, such claims were problematic. Judaism had to rethink its theology in terms of burning children, gas chambers and an absent GOD. "Nothing justifies Auschwitz", survivor Elie Wiesel says.

> Were the Lord Himself to offer me a justification, I think I would reject it . . . The barbed-wire kingdom will forever remain an immense question mark on the scale of both humanity and its Creator. Faced with unprecedented suffering and agony, [God] should have intervened, or at least expressed Himself. Which side was He on? . . . This is the dilemma confronted by the believer . . . by allowing this to happen, God was telling humanity something and we don't know what it was.[22]

In the same way, *German* Christians could no longer do their theologizing without incorporating their shame over the Holocaust. What had happened to this nation that was so confident it had reached the pinnacle of civilization and had produced some of the finest theologians and biblical scholars whose works were studied across the globe? How could this Lutheran and Catholic country have perpetrated such a heinous crime against so many, justifying its actions with religion? The reformer Martin Luther (1483–1546) had written in 1543:

> These Jews should be treated with a sharp mercy, their synagogues set on fire with sulphur and pitch thrown in, their houses be destroyed. They are to be herded together in stables like gypsies in order to realize that they are not masters in the land but prisoners in exile.[23]

This was acted upon by Nazi mobs celebrating Luther's birthday in 1938 and praised by a Lutheran bishop at the time as "a right and glorious way of honoring the reformer's legacy".[24] In light of our chapter's topic, what had gone wrong with their estimation of themselves as a grand civilization and a Christian nation, and also their estimation of GOD? Albert Schweitzer (1875–1965), the Alsatian-German theologian, organist, philosopher and missionary doctor, also asked these questions from his mission hospital at Lambaréné, French Congo, prior to the outbreak of the First World War (1914–18):

> It seemed to be assumed everywhere not only that we had made progress in inventions and knowledge, but also that in the intellectual and ethical spheres we lived and moved at a height which we had never before reached, and from which we should never decline . . . and now war was raging as a result of the downfall of civilization.[25]

Schweitzer had long wanted to write a book about the philosophy of civilization and, ironically, war made it possible when he became a prisoner of war in his home in the French colony, initially forbidden to work at the hospital or make contact with those around him. This was no detached exercise. For a Germany that had convinced itself "it no longer needed any ethical ideals but could advance to its goal by means of knowledge and achievement alone, terrible proof was being given by its present position of the error into which it had sunk . . . Many a night did I sit at [the manuscript]," Schweitzer says, "thinking and writing with deepest emotion as I thought of those who were lying in the trenches."[26]

Any theology would now have to be forged in earshot of gunfire and the screams of the wounded. Schweitzer was in his African hospital while the Second World War (1939–45) raged and, again, there was dissonance between what was preached and what was experienced by the people. Schweitzer wrote to a friend:

> We are all of us conscious that many of the natives are puzzling over the questions raised by the war. How can it be possible that the whites, who brought them the Gospel of Love, are now murdering each other, and throwing to the wind the commands of the Lord Jesus? When they put the question to us, we are helpless.[27]

How we evaluate the human condition and what we want from our engagement with the Sacred will always be shaped by that through which we have personally lived. New Zealand's famous theologian, Sir Lloyd Geering, who recently celebrated 40 years since his landmark heresy trial for saying things that are said by many theologians today, wrote in his latest book:

> Humans show themselves to be religious whenever and wherever they take the questions of human existence seriously, and then create a common response to whatever they find to be of ultimate value to them. The only truly non-religious person is one who treats human existence as trivial or meaningless, for ultimately the religious phenomenon arises out of human experience as we reflect on the fundamental nature of human existence. With but rare exceptions, people everywhere and at all times have made some kind of response to the demands of human existence. They have tried to make something of life. They have looked for meaning and purpose. They have hoped for some kind of fulfillment. For such reasons humankind has in the past been universally religious, and there is no good reason to suspect that in the future people will cease to be religious. And this is true even though an increasing number have grown dissatisfied with the religious forms of the past, having found them to be irrelevant in the new cultural age we have entered.[28]

4

Does the Sacred Engage Us or Do We Engage the Sacred?

A lover seeks his beloved, but he also wants his beloved to seek him.
God seeks every human being, but he also wants human beings to seek him.
A lover feels flashes of lightning in the heart—flashes of joy—
and wants to know that his beloved feels the same.
God takes joy in humanity, and wants to know that humanity takes joy in him.
Have you ever heard one hand clapping? God is one hand; humanity is the other.

—*Rumi*[1]

○   ○   ○

Primal religious behavior is language addressed at the mute or the mysterious.
Language is our self-conscious communication, and normally we know how
and when it works. We address our friends and relations and even believe that
the dog understands our tone of voice. Then we find ourselves talking on when
we are not sure that there is anyone to address yet when we also refuse silence
. . . we can only guess at the life of the One who slumbers not nor sleeps. We
are by no means sure how to name the Holy Mystery which we project
as the audience for these strange linguistic turns.

—*George Dennis O'Brien*[2]

These two quotations highlight the continuum of the religious struggle—the
assurance of Divine love and attention that the Sufi mystic Rumi (1207–73)
described, and O'Brien's refusing to accept Divine silence. Few of us have
the luxury (or misfortune) of approaching religion with a blank slate. Most
of us have been raised in a society steeped in religious ideas and a culture
that confirmed those "truths". Even if our family was not religious, these

values and morals shaped the mindset in our slice of the world, such that we absorbed their influence with our mother's milk. We enter this environment with our first breath and spend the rest of our lives responding to these inherited traditions positively, casually or negatively. Russian writer Leo Tolstoy (1828–1910) described his struggle with his inherited Russian Orthodox faith:

> Had I simply understood that life has no meaning I might have accepted it peacefully, knowing that it was my lot. But I could not be calmed by this. If I had been like a man in a wood from which he knows there is no way out, I might have been able to live; but I was like a man in a wood who is lost, and terrified by this rushes around hoping to find his way out, knowing that with each step he is getting more lost, and yet unable to stop rushing about.[3]

All the famous atheists have also spoken, not as observers from another planet but from within particular cultural experiences shaped by religious beliefs, which is why philosopher Karl Marx (1818–83) named the struggle against religion as "indirectly the struggle against that world whose spiritual aroma is religion".[4]

Because of this inevitable ingestion of religious ideas, the chicken–egg question is difficult—which came first, the Sacred engaging humans or humans striving to engage a Divine, or alternatively, did GOD create religion or religion create GOD? Sigmund Freud (1865–1939), the father of psychoanalysis, called religion a learned mechanism to control basic energy and release tension and frustration and thus a product of people's helplessness, but could he *prove* there was not a reciprocal reaching out or encouragement from the other side of the veil? Marx declared religion to be "the sigh of the oppressed creature, the heart of a heartless world, and the soul of soulless conditions . . . the opium of the people",[5] yet could Marx *demonstrate* that such happiness was always illusory and that there was, in fact, no Object of that happiness that some claimed to encounter? History of religion scholar E. O. James (1888–1972) believed that religion gave people something to hold on to in face of life's uncertainties, especially death, because eternal rewards were painted as better than those of life. People could fulfil unfulfilled desires by locating them in the transcendent realm of a future life and explain life's present struggles as having an ultimate purpose we can't see, yet could James *show* there is nothing beyond death and nothing supporting us in time of need? "While [the human being] has dispelled many of the demonic ghosts of ignorance," Sam Keen says, "he has at the same time fallen prey to the pretention of omniscience, to the foolish pride of believing that he can eliminate the mystery of being."[6]

How we resolve this debate as to whether the Divine engages *us* or we can engage the Sacred is always and inevitably a faith statement. First, we cannot prove there is a Something More, nor can we prove there is nothing. Second, what do we mean by GOD—a universal Force, a Presence, a personal Genie, an external Being manipulating universal laws, or none of these? Third, how can we demonstrate conclusively to anyone else something that we personally experience, or don't experience? The spectrum of answers over the centuries to the question of whether the Sacred engages with humanity ranges from the Deists' belief in a Creator that had no further interest in creation, to Nature itself as Sacred, to a Divine life-force or Persuasive Urge within the universe, to GOD directing every event in our world from outside, changing its laws in answer to prayers. How we answer basically comes down to how we *interpret* what we experience in the world. Theresa Maggio, writing about life in the farming village of Santa Margherita, Sicily, described the people sowing wheat by hand in December and going to Mass twice a day to beg for rain. "We had no technology, so we used religion," one farmer said. "We prayed, 'Dear Lord, let it rain, let it rain. The grain is dying of thirst. Give us a good one, with no lightning and no thunder.'" The Holy Crucifix was carried through town three times a year, first to beg for rain, then in April to ask for warm sun and then on May 3 to celebrate the Crucifix's feast day. In June the people harvested. When it was time to winnow, they prayed to Saint Mark, patron saint of wind, for a breeze to blow off the chaff, leaving a pile of grain. Then they prayed that the ants wouldn't eat it.[7]

The Religious Experience Research Centre, founded in Oxford in 1969 by British zoologist Sir Alister Hardy (1896–1985), has carried out research on people's religious experiences around the question, "Have you ever been aware of or been influenced by a presence or a power, whether you call it God or not, which is different from your everyday self?" In its survey in Nottingham, David Hay reported that 62% of people said they had had such an experience at least once or twice in their life.[8]

In a similar 1973 survey in America by sociologist priest Andrew Greeley, 35 percent of American adults claimed to have had a religious experience,[9] while in a 2005 survey in America's *Newsweek* magazine, 80 percent of Americans called themselves "spiritual".[10] Despite the flurry of books in today's marketplace denying the existence of any Deity and labeling claims of religious experience "delusional", British philosopher and theologian John Hick, hardly known for toeing a traditional line, argues for an inbuilt human capacity for awareness of the Sacred, given the millions of people across centuries who have claimed experiences of such a Presence, albeit described in culturally conditioned ways. How many seriously mystical people do we need, he asks, in order to take notice, both inside and outside, of religions?

> The Real, or the Transcendent—whose nature is transcategorical, beyond the scope of our human concepts—is that which there must be if human religious experience globally is not delusion. We cannot know it as it is in itself, but we know it as it affects us.[11]

Whether we believe that the Divine engages us, or we have created GOD as the object of our religion, boils down to our own experience (or not) of the Sacred, or the experiences of others we accept as truth, for example religious authorities.

In Christian history, however, individualistic faith or personal experience has not been the central thrust. Yahweh's covenant was with the Hebrew *people*, mediated through leaders and prophets—"I will take you as my people, and I will be your God" (Ex. 6:7). One such prophet was Jesus, whom some Jews accepted as a *Messiah* or "anointed one" (the term was applied to any person "anointed" and sent by GOD) and others did not. After Jesus' death, the Divine Comforter promised by Jesus engaged the fledgling *community*, guiding them "into all the truth" (John 16:13). The New Testament letters of Paul do not focus on his personal spiritual journey, but his call to be GOD's emissary to all the world, Jews *and* non-Jews. The Bible is not an anthology of personal religious journeys of individual saints. It is a story of Divine engagement as experienced by *chosen people* of the biblical world—the word of the people of GOD rather than the word of GOD.

Once Christianity became established as part of the Roman Empire in the fourth century, the *Church* was the focus of Divine engagement, with the Pope as Christ's earthly representative and the Holy Spirit domesticated and operational only *within* the Church—there was no salvation outside it. The Church created the rules by which GOD could access humanity and also the rules by which the people could engage GOD—through priests, prayers and sacraments. When mystics challenged this monopoly of the Divine, claiming personal, unmediated GOD-experiences, they were marginalized and regarded with suspicion, especially women mystics (given their supposedly irrational and unreliable nature) who were placed under a male confessor's control if claiming Divine visions or revelations. Julian of Norwich was safely secluded in her anchorite cell under the authority of her English bishop when she received Divine visions:

[O]ur Lord showed himself to me, and he appeared to me more glorified than I had seen him before, in which I was taught that our soul will never have rest till it comes into him . . . Again and again, our Lord said, I am he, I am he.[12]

Joan of Arc's (1412–31) private Divine Voices, experienced as a young peasant girl, left her more vulnerable. When she appeared before the French Dauphin offering her visionary services against the invading English, she was stringently examined by learned bishops and theologians before being allowed to lead the army. Riding into battle in men's clothes in front of 6,000 soldiers, she chased the English out of Orléans. When the Dauphin, now King, dragged his feet about expelling the English completely from France, Joan led a few sorties without his support and was captured by troops secretly aligned with the French *and* the English. The King abandoned her, no longer needing her visions, and the Church did not fancy a female "loose cannon" with messages from GOD. She was sold to the English and tried in a church court for "crimes" including abandoning female attire (against nature) and claiming she was sent from GOD and had received Divine secrets. Refusing to tell what her Voices said, Joan was declared a witch, in league with the Devil. Recanting at the scaffold, she was found wearing male clothes again, declared a relapsed heretic and burned at the stake. Saint or Devil is a fine line. In 1456, her trial was reopened and she was found innocent and declared a martyr. Canonized in 1920, she is now a patron saint of France.

The Reformation also challenged the Church's control of GOD and moved the place of engagement to scripture—people could read for themselves, guided by GOD's Spirit. Martin Luther translated the Latin Vulgate Bible into everyday German, and his English contemporary William Tyndale (1494–1536) fled to Germany to publish his English translation of the New Testament. When these arrived in England, they were collected and burned by church officials—perish the thought of lay people reading in their own language! Tyndale himself was burned at the stake in 1536. While such translations were revolutionary, in practice the authority to interpret GOD simply shifted from Catholic Church to Protestant preacher since so many could not read. More radical reform groups, however, preached that the Divine engaged the individual soul *directly*, not through those ordained for church office. Quakers, who had no clergy, believed that *everyone* had direct, unmediated access to the Divine by turning to their inward Light.

The Enlightenment loosened further the Church's stranglehold on knowledge, celebrating individual human reason, experience, observation and experiment. Methodism's founder John Wesley (1703–91) added another leg to the Church of England's three-legged stool of scripture, tradition and reason as ways to "know" the Divine. He had felt his heart "strangely warmed" and had been greatly influenced by Moravian personal piety and so he added personal "experience" to the mix. Reason and experience added to scripture and tradition gave a blessing to those who sought the Divine themselves, or claimed a personal experience of the Sacred. Wesley's ideas crossed the Atlantic, inspiring revival and "holiness" movements that continue in modern-day evangelical traditions. A devoutly evangelical student of mine sat through three-quarters of my university course on "Christian Traditions" with a disapproving and often disgusted look on her face. When we finally reached the Wesleyan revival movements in America, she wrote in her reflection paper, "This is the first thing in class that sounds anything like *real* Christianity."

The Enlightenment also ushered in critical historical study of the Bible, revealing a human book with contradictions and cultural infiltrations, rather than an inerrant, inspired dictation from GOD. As biblical scholar Antony Campbell says, "The Bible is evidence *of* faith in God's being; it is not direct evidence *for* God's being."[13] This research opened up new ways to both challenge and interpret the Bible and also began the ongoing search to discover the historical Jesus under layers of theological accretions. Naturally, this was very threatening to those who wanted to keep control with their infallible claims for Bible or Church. Albert Schweitzer, who wrote a definitive book in this discussion, *The Quest of the Historical Jesus*, experienced this tension:

> The satisfaction which I could not help feeling at having solved so many historical riddles about the existence of Jesus, was accompanied by the painful consciousness that this new knowledge in the realm of history would mean unrest and difficulty for Christian piety. I comforted myself, however, with the words of St Paul's which had been familiar to me from childhood: "We can do nothing against the truth, but for the truth" (2 Cor. 13:8).[14]

Karl Barth drew in the reins of this open-ended pursuit of truth during the two World Wars, declaring that we cannot know GOD by human reason and speculation, only by what the Divine chose to reveal through Jesus Christ, as recorded in the Bible. Having tasted the liberty of thinking outside the box, however, theologians Rudolf Bultmann (1884–1976), Dietrich Bonhoeffer (1906–45) and Paul Tillich (1886–1965) led an explosion of challenges that would become the "Death of God" movement in the 1960s, with its flagship book *Honest to God* by Bishop John A. T. Robinson (1919–83). These scholars showed that our GOD-descriptions were outdated and needed to die so that new ways of thinking about the Sacred could emerge for a contemporary world.

Human beings must decide for themselves who, or if, GOD is to be for them. Faith is always a first-hand experience, whereas beliefs are second-hand, someone else's experiences of the Divine cemented into doctrines by which we are supposed to live. "All Christians must have a *working theology*, one that can actually function in their personal, professional, and public lives", theologian Sallie McFague says. "We need a theology that begins in experience and ends with a conversion to a new way of being in the world."[15] Experience is the key to deciding whether Something More engages us or whether we are we simply listening to our echo returning to us. We need to decide what has been initiated by Something in our lives, or by us. We have to judge whether our experiences of wonder and awe in nature are encounters with Mystery or simply natural human reactions to beauty. Bede Griffith (1906–93), a British Benedictine monk who formed a Hindu-style ashram in India, came to *his* decision through reading 1 John 4:10—"In this is love, not that we loved God but that he loved us."

> I suddenly saw that all the time it was not I who had been seeking God, but God who had been seeking me. I had made myself the centre of my own existence and had my back turned to God. All the beauty and truth which I had discovered had come to me as a reflection of his beauty.[16]

My father kept a journal from the age of seventeen throughout his life, still making entries a month or so before he died at 86. I followed his example, recording in detail my various religious thoughts and experiences along the way. We all have regrets over things we wished we had not done—mine is burning, just before my wedding, any of my diaries that also recorded my various infatuations (so tame compared with today's romantic literature) over different males that crossed my adolescent path. The regret is not about losing those romantic sagas, but about losing my equally emotive record of longing for the love of a present/absent GOD. I do have my journals *since* marriage, tracking that ongoing and evolving search. Sometimes I read things written at a place where I no longer stand theologically, or in GOD-images with which I am no longer comfortable, but they still speak of a place on the religious experience continuum where others stand and thus may be helpful to them. I wrote this poem some twenty years ago:

I was the creator of my life,
yearning to do my own thing—find myself!
So I resolved to search for God.
I followed a new trail to the left
but it was marked with fresh footprints.
God had been there already
searching for me.
I cut an uncleared track to the right,
a lingering aura of light clung to the leaves.
God walked ahead, calling my name.
I retraced my steps backwards a distance.
The grass was newly trampled, the dew scattered.
God had been there before me,
reaching out to hold my hand.

Confused and defeated, I stood still.
I abandoned the search,
and cried over my failure.
I waited helpless in the silence of my mind.
All at once I heard a voice calling.
I watched a hand stretch out to me.
Strange I had not seen these before.
Now a trail stretches ahead, fresh and unmarked.
Footprints appear in the sand
asking only that I follow.
A hand clasps mine firmly,
making it difficult to stumble or fall.
A voice of love within me speaks,
urging, luring, encouraging.[17]

Human experiences of the Sacred spawned "religions" around their revelations. We cannot talk about engaging the Sacred without also talking about religions. There are many definitions in scholarly books of what "religion" is and what it does—binding the sacred to the profane or unconditioned reality to conditioned reality, belief in spiritual beings, consciousness of the infinite, finding what is highest and deepest in our experience, an uneasiness about the human condition and its solution, a house of meaning built on the edge of despair, a shelter from meaninglessness, a set of symbolic forms and acts that relate us to the ultimate conditions of our existence, stories to live by, a unified system of beliefs and practices related to sacred things which unite into a moral community all who adhere to them. Paul Tillich called religion "the state of being grasped by an ultimate concern, a concern which qualifies all other concerns as preliminary and which itself contains the answer to the question of the meaning of life".[18] This Ultimate concern can be transcendent or immanent, a Being or a mysterious No-thing (Nothing). It can be personal or beyond personality, all-powerful or all-gentle. "Religion" is therefore a very slippery object, even before we consider its varieties and particularities.

Religions, formed around a belief that it is possible to engage the Sacred, have elements in common. Huston Smith's list includes *authorities* who specialize to help others and *rituals* to help people act together in celebration or concern. While a religion may start spontaneously, *speculation* about its source and goal follows, shaping *traditions* that bind the faithful. There is usually a concept of *Divinity* and a consciousness of *mystery* beyond mundane human existence.[19] These elements are also a religion's problems. Each can be abused, dragging it from its initial inspiration into static forms and rigid, humanly constructed rules shaped both by those in power and the prevailing culture. Designated authority can shrink to personal or corporate power, with secrets held from laity. Rituals can reduce to empty shells of offerings and chants. Speculation about the cosmos and the human condition can become obscure, irrelevant and outdated. The Divine can be trapped in unhelpful human constructs, and mystery can descend into magic and divination.[20]

While the initial flush of excitement around a prophet or teacher holds the followers in a state of fluidity, things need to be written down and authority passed on to others when a founder dies. Without the founder's charisma, rules and forms take his or her place and these give shape to what becomes the "religion". Inevitably, some of the original ideas of the founder and fledgling community will be adapted to changing contexts, evolving worldviews, emerging questions and reflective scholarship, regardless of the original "truth" claims. A Greek Orthodox friend recently gave me Matthew Gallatin's autobiography of growing up Seventh Day Adventist, becoming a fundamentalist pastor, joining the charismatic movement, exploring Roman Catholicism and finally converting to Orthodoxy.[21] This winding journey was driven by Gallatin's search for, and discovery (for him) of *original* Christianity—"[T]he Faith of the Apostles preserved in the Holy Orthodoxy is an historical reality, not just a theological school of thought", he says. "Until the eleventh century, to be Christian meant to be Orthodox."[22]

Yet it is impossible to recover the original form of any ancient religion in order to see it through its founder's eyes. The fourth-century Christian creeds were not there from the beginning and say nothing of Jesus' life and teachings apart from noting his birth and death. They are already a dramatic progression of ideas from the original events, forged under Emperor Constantine (285–337 CE) through battles, even to death, between bishops, political intrigue, imperial interference and deep-seated theological splits—pretty much like any church council today! Finding the original Jesus is equally difficult since the Gospels were written up to 80 years after Jesus' death by different communities who shaped their versions of his legacy. There is also serious scholarly debate today as to which sayings of Jesus actually came from his lips. Beliefs that later became central to Christianity, such as the virgin birth, are not even mentioned in the earliest New Testament writings (the letters of Paul and the earliest Gospel, the Gospel of Mark). As for original manuscripts, the earliest fragment we have of a New Testament Gospel is part of a chapter from a second-century copy of John's Gospel—we have no original texts. While Christianity claims the Holy Spirit as its guide against error, the host of denominations claiming the Bible as their source of truth demonstrates a certain difficulty with this argument. Thus, while a founder's visions (GOD engaging humanity) may have been the initial impetus for people to gather together, the way the group then structured itself and created its doctrines, rules and rituals to continue engaging this Divine is a human creation through which the Divine is said to respond.

The Buddha is an interesting case study in this discussion. Born Siddhartha Gautama (Siddhattha Gotama) into a noble family in the foothills of modern Nepal in the sixth century BCE, he became aware as an adult that suffering was the "human condition" to be addressed. He tried the religious solutions of his day, studying under gurus and starving himself in renunciation. When neither worked, he vowed to sit under a tree until he found enlightenment—and he did. When then asked if he was a GOD or an angel, he said, "No, I am awake." Buddha means "one who is awake". The Buddha's solution was not religious speculation, but *living* a life that avoided the religious excesses of the religion into which he was born (later called Hinduism). To follow Smith's religious elements, authority had become personal power for the Brahmin upper caste and the Guilds. Rituals were performed by priests for payment. Speculation about cosmology had become rife, producing answers divorced from the needs of the people; and mystery had become the magical cajoling of a genie-in-the-lamp. Buddha's Middle Way had no external authorities. He ridiculed rites and prayers to helpless GODS, calling them fetters that bind. He refused speculation as to whether the world was eternal and what the soul might be, developing instead a way of living so people did not get diverted from life. He addressed the human condition—suffering—and proposed a solution not locked into traditions so that people could pursue their own way. He advocated self-effort, working out your own salvation, rather than dependence on GODS, offerings to priests and endless rebirths—his path of personal action could lead to enlightenment for everyone in *this* life. He did not deny a Deity but, since we cannot know, refused to waste time speculating about it, describing instead a way not dependent on GODS or miracles.[23] The metaphysical question of whether the Divine engages humanity or we engage the Divine did not interest the Buddha. The solution for the human condition (suffering) is in our hands by following the Four Noble Truths—One: Life is naturally *dukkha* (suffering), dislocation through birth, circumstances, illness, dying. Two: The cause of dislocation is desire (*tanha*), our selfishness and ego clinging to what does not last. Three: Selfish desire must be overcome. Four: The cure is following the eightfold path with the help of the *sangha* (community)—right knowledge, right aspiration, right speech, right behavior, right livelihood, right effort, right mindfulness and right absorption, e.g. yoga practices. It is all about how we live.

It is not surprising that Buddhism has appealed to many people beyond those born into it. Its teaching became popular in the turbulent 1960s as disenchantment with Western Christianity met the spirituality of the East. In the following decades, more and more people have walked away from churches, temples and GOD, not abandoning the search for meaning but finding it in fresh, more authentic forms. Biologist and author Rupert Sheldrake lists their options:

> For those for whom traditional religious practices seem empty and meaningless, there are three possibilities: first, to recognize no living power greater than humanity and hence to recognize neither a need for gratitude nor a means of expressing it; second, to feel such gratitude privately but with no means of public expression; third, to find new ways of expressing gratitude collectively and new conceptions of the life-giving powers to whom thanks are due.[24]

Throughout this book, the question of whether there *is* Anything to engage necessarily remains open. Some have declared with certainty that religion has simply created GOD, while others live with a comfortable agnosticism, opting, with the Buddha, for a way of life rather than a basketful of speculation. Religion scholar Karen Armstrong, who spent her young adult life as a nun in a convent and now writes about the religions of the world, says:

The experience of an indefinable transcendence, holiness and sacredness has been a fact of human life . . . I don't think it matters what you believe in—and most of the great sages of religion would agree with me. If conventional beliefs make you compassionate, kind and respectful of the sacred rights of others, this is good religion. If your beliefs make you intolerant, unkind and belligerent, this is bad religion, no matter how orthodox it is.[25]

Earth as a
Sacred Site

To wonder is to perceive with reverence and love . . . and in wondering we come close to the feeling that the earth is holy. Historically, the notion of wonder has been closely bound up with a religious mode of being in the world . . . In my experience, the substance of wonder is more frequently found in the prose of the secular than in the often quaint poetry of religion . . . Whether we continue to talk about God is not so important as whether we retain the sense of wonder which keeps us aware that ours is a holy place.

—*Sam Keen*[1]

American cartoonist Billy Ireland (1880–1935) rarely attended church. "I'd rather see the sun shining on trees and streams", he confessed, "than elbowing its way through stained glass."[2] Ask any group of people, religious or not, where they most feel in touch with the Sacred and the vast majority will point to nature—a sunset, the Grand Canyon, hiking in the mountains, staring out at the ocean, in the forest or the bush. As I gaze out of the window above my desk, trying to formulate the next sentence, I see red and pink sweet-pea flowers and purple-pink daisies in the garden below; nectarine and plum trees awash with white and pink blossoms in the orchard; protea buds like pointed pink ice-cream cones about to open on their stubby branches; a sea of yellow bush wattle outside the cultivated garden area and encroaching on a sweeping paddock of green where horses graze; neat rows of grapevines in the vineyards nestling under the feet of rolling hills covered in the grey-green of eucalyptus trees and denser green of Botobolar pines, until their various summits touch a blue, cumulus-cloud-filled Australian sky. Nature is too big to define because it is *everything*, including the one doing the defining. We can never stand outside of nature and speak of it as something beyond ourselves, an "it" rather than "me". Yet humans continue to claim (erroneously, I think) a special uniqueness from the rest of living things at being able to move beyond their creatureliness and reflect on nature as if from the outside—and then they argue all sorts of superiorities from it. Yet this cannot describe nature, only how it appears from one particular viewpoint. There would be significant difference from the perspective of a bee or an elephant, something we can imagine but not know.

Eco-theologian Sallie McFague describes two different ways of looking at nature—landscape or maze.[3] We can stand on a hill looking at the panorama in front of us, capturing the view within our gaze as painters capture a two-dimensional scene on canvas or photographers through a lens. What we see is a framed object at a distance with us the invisible spectator. A maze, on the other hand, puts us in the midst of nature. We are no longer controlling the experience or view, but are a part of a multi-dimensional experience and controlled by it. Rather than surveying and analyzing something other than us, we are one of its many details, scurrying around to find our way or, in the case of a maze, a way out. Neither are we the center of this maze. Each tree is the center of its own universe, its roots drawing nutrient from the earth and its leaves absorbing carbon dioxide from the atmosphere regardless of my presence. The bushes around me hide a myriad of insects and small animals I cannot see, but I know they are there, organizing events in their own world and sharing common oxygen. How different are these pictures of nature—a sole, external observer or a small living part of an organic whole.

These contrasting perspectives represent the struggle that human beings have had with nature—being part of it, yet wishing to be above it or superior within it. Indigenous people, for the most part, saw themselves in the maze, part of the changing, pulsing world around them, interdependent and interconnected, the Sacred sharing space with them. They developed their cosmology from their particular knowledge of possibilities in their time. Sacred significance was attributed to rivers, mountains, animals and heavenly bodies. Many saw the sun and moon as GODS whose movements represented wonderful journeys of Divine beings across the sky. Ancient Egyptians watched the antics of the little scarab beetle, laying its eggs in dung and pushing them around until they formed a ball, and wondered if the sun was being pushed across the sky by a giant beetle. In a Chinese story, ten suns crossed the sky each day as beautiful, shining birds. The archer Yi shot down nine of them with his arrows until only one remained.[4] In Japanese Shinto tradition, *Kami* are the mysterious forces or life-powers associated with natural features—mountains, springs, forests—and also with special people, anything seen as awe-inspiring or impressive. Festivals, offerings, visits to shrines and prayers are performed to make peace with, and appeal for protection to, these powers that maintain cosmic and relational harmony.

Holy places were located in nature and myths described their importance. Rituals helped create the necessary balance and harmony both within this world and with the Sacred realm. While Western culture delighted in describing such rituals as primal fear of, or bribery to, the deities, gratitude and thanksgiving also drove the actions of the first human beings. "He was governed by a *spirit of cooperation*", anthropologist Bronislaw Malinowski (1884–1942) wrote. "His life was defined with nature rather than against her. So long as he observed the practical and ceremonial rules governing planting, fishing and hunting, he had every confidence that nature would care for him."[5] While Malinowski's gendered pronouns grate on the ears, as if women were not yet invented, they also demonstrate the contrast between primal ideas of co-operation with earth described as female (Mother Nature) and the dualistic thinking of earth as something to be dominated and controlled, interpreted from Genesis ". . . fill the earth and subdue it; and have dominion over the fish of sea and over the birds of the air and over every living thing that moves on the earth" (1:28). The gendered image in the phrase "*His* life was defined with nature rather than against *her*" (my italics)—man over nature—reflects a patriarchal culture of male control over females, just as ships "commanded" by (usually) male captains are called "she"; and the "virgin" Australian bush referred to as "she", had to be "tamed" and "conquered" by the male English settlers.

Ancient cosmologies were accompanied by cosmogonies, stories of *how* things came to be. These descriptions were human experiences projected onto supernatural events and beings, usually male *and* female as in real life. The Maori creation myth from Aotearoa New Zealand features two Creator Beings, Rangi the male sky and Papa (Papi) the female earth, pushed apart from their passionate embrace by children crammed between them in the dark, thus forming complementary parts of the cosmos. The indigenous religion of southern Peru has two great deities, Roal the Creator Spirit, at the top of the hierarchy, and Pachamama the earth. In other creation stories, life came from death—Saharan Africa's world was made out of parts of the sacrificed cosmic serpent Minia, the first creation; and in the Babylonian myth, the younger GOD Marduk kills Tiamat, GODDESS of the watery, unformed chaos, dividing her corpse into heaven and earth.[6] Other myths have a cycle of cosmic creation, destruction and rebirth. The Hindu preserver Deity Vishnu rests on the cobra couch in a sea of milk between the destruction of one world by the GOD Shiva and the emergence of Creator Brahma (from

Vishnu's navel) to create the next world. The Hebrew creation story varies from its Mesopotamian heritage by imagining a single, uncreated Voice and Spirit speaking the world into existence from the void and calling this creation "very good". Australian Aboriginal people also saw the land as a void, flat landscape in the "Dreaming", from which giant Spirit Beings emerged, their trails crossing the country to form rivers and exploding the land into mountains and rocks (like Uluru) where they still rest.

The early Greeks believed the *universe* created the GODS. Chaos (unformed darkness) separated itself, according to playwright Aristophanes (446–386 BCE), into Night and Tartarus, the dwelling of the dead. "Black-winged night" laid an egg in Tartarus which separated into Gaia (Mother Earth) and Uranus (Father Sky), from whom the GODS sprang.[7] In time, however, the stories of the Greek GODS became, according to Sam Keen, "so vulgar and so transparently anthropomorphic that neither the morally earnest nor the religiously sensitive found them credible".[8] The philosophers finally stepped in and introduced ideas of reason, ideals and archetypes to explain order in the universe. This Greek idea of Mind would merge in Christianity with the Hebrew Creator God, revealed to humanity in the man Jesus. While the Hebrew Creator proclaimed creation good, Jesus would eventually be described as a Divine rescuer of humanity from its fall into sin, an idea which raised questions as to whether fallen human beings were capable of "knowing" GOD from nature *at all*.

The creation story's little phrase "Let us make humankind in our image" (Gen. 1:26) was captured by humans to name themselves the pinnacle of creation, the bearers of a special GOD-like quality and thus assigned dominion over the rest of nature which was created to serve humans and be the backdrop for the drama of human salvation. Such imagery ploughs a large furrow between humans and the rest of nature, severing any ideas of the interconnectedness of it all. Lutheran theologian Johann Gerhard (1582–1637) wrote:

Man was created . . . after all other creatures. For man is the epitome of all other creatures . . . [M]an partakes of both spiritual and physical nature. In the words of Augustine [354–430 CE], "In man is found almost every creature; man is the center of creation and nature" (*De Civitae Dei* 10:12). All things were created on behalf of man. For, as man was made for God in order that he might serve him, so the world was made for man in order that it might serve man. Man, therefore, was set in the middle in order that he might be served and, in turn, that he himself might serve . . . For God intended that he should be served by man in such a way that not God, but rather man, might be benefited. Everything, then, was intended for the good of man; both that which was made on his behalf, and the purpose for which he himself was made . . . Let [man] make use of the creatures, and yet not abuse them. Let him make use of the creatures not as the ultimate end of his desire, but as means to render homage and service to the Creator.[9]

While this might have been something the medieval worldview could have swallowed as truth, our knowledge of a universe some thirteen to fourteen billion years old in which human life forms did not emerge through evolution until somewhere between two million and 100,000 years ago (depending on what you call "life"), makes it difficult to argue that the world was created just for humans.[10] Bertrand Russell picked up this difficulty in his day:

At what moment in evolution did our ancestors acquire free will? At what stage in the long journey from the amoeba did they begin to have immortal souls? When did they first become capable of the kinds of wickedness that would justify a benevolent Creator in sending them into eternal torment? Most people felt that such punishment would be hard on monkeys, in spite of their propensity for throwing coconuts at the heads of Europeans. But how about *Pithecanthropus Erectus*? Was it really he who ate the apple? Or was it *Homo Pekiniensis*?[11]

Does the Sacred engage us through nature and can we "know" the Divine by experiencing nature? This question raised its head early in Christianity. Originally, the church fathers seemed to have no difficulty with seeing Divinity in nature, as it was a Divine creation, but there was a problem—what then was the point of a special revelation through Jesus? Thomas Aquinas declared that knowledge of GOD was possible through natural reason and observation of creation, but that knowledge of the divine "mysteries" was only possible through faith. His Muslim contemporary Rumi, living in what is now Afghanistan, said:

Those who deny God often say: "If the spirit of God were present in Nature, we would be able to see it." But if a child cannot see the intellect within an adult, does that mean that the intellect does not exist? If a rational person is insensitive to the movements of love, does that mean that love is an illusion?[12]

Vatican I (1869–70) affirmed Aquinas' position—"If anyone shall have said that the one true God, our Creator and Lord, cannot be known with certitude by those things which have been made, by the natural light of human reason: let him be anathema."[13]

Protestant reformers were nervous about all this. With their emphasis on human depravity after the fall, they questioned whether humans *could* interpret nature properly as a Divine revelation, apart from GOD's revelation in Christ. French reformer John Calvin (1509–64) believed that "God himself has implanted in all men a certain understanding of his divine majesty" and "daily discloses himself in the whole workmanship of the universe" such that "men cannot open their eyes without being compelled to see him". However, human beings "by extinguishing the light of nature, deliberately befuddle themselves" and "furiously repel all remembrance of God, although this is freely suggested to them inwardly from the feeling of nature".[14] GOD is therefore comprehended in Christ alone—"He that does not have the Son does not have the Father" (1 John 2:23).

> For even if many men once boasted that they worshipped the Supreme Majesty, the Maker of heaven and earth, yet because they had no Mediator it was not possible for them truly to taste God's mercy, and thus be persuaded that he was their Father. Accordingly, because they did not hold Christ as their head, they possessed only a fleeting knowledge of God. From this it also came about that they at last lapsed into crass and foul superstitions and betrayed their ignorance. So today the Turks, although they proclaim at the top of their lungs that the Creator of heaven and earth is God, still, while repudiating Christ, substitute an idol in place of the true God.[15]

The Enlightenment and the emerging scientific endeavor changed the focus from what we can know about GOD to what we can observe and interpret by reason. English theologian Matthew Tindal (1657–1733) wrote in *Christianity as Old as Creation*:

> There's a religion of nature and reason written in the hearts of every one of us from the first creation, by which all mankind must judge of the truth of any institutional religion whatever.[16]

His contemporary, Enlightenment philosopher John Toland (1670–1722), thought it offensive to believe that GOD was not capable of expressing the Divine Self in a clear, reasonable way through nature, but others were less willing to make the speculative leap from observations of nature to proof of the Divine and looked instead for evidence of GOD in human consciousness and morality, pointing to a universal Moral Principle. English poet William Wordsworth (1770–1850), along with many poets and writers experiencing the religious uncertainty of the nineteenth century, sought spiritual comfort in everyday experiences and a pantheistic view of nature rather than church dogmas:

> And I have felt
> A presence that disturbs me with the joy
> Of elevated thoughts; a sense sublime
> Of something far more deeply interfused . . .[17]

Karl Barth, whose theology reigned supreme in Protestant Europe during the World Wars, was totally opposed to *any* natural theology (knowledge of GOD through nature). For him, human reason was utterly corrupted by the fall, and an entirely transcendent and free GOD cannot be known except through Divine self-revelation in Christ. Any speculation from nature or Divine revelation in another religion were merely human attempts to create GOD. While Barth was influential in his day and continues to be in some theological circles, his attack on natural theology has been criticized by many in the Christian tradition and, it seems, by verses in Romans proclaiming GOD's universal revelation in creation (1:20) and also written on the human heart (2:15). There is thankfully an emerging consensus among ecumenical theologians that "God's universal presence in creation and in the moral and religious consciousness of humanity . . . finds expression outside the Hebrew-Christian traditions."[18] Sallie McFague, whose early career followed Barth's ideas, describes how hiking in nature moved her from his negativity towards experiencing the Divine in nature, to seeing GOD "incarnate" in everything:

> I found a sense of belonging, of being the "proper size" in the forest . . . I felt in nature; it surrounded me; I was part of it . . . What had been an experience of overwhelming and distant transcendence became one of equally awesome but now immanent and intimate transcendence. God's magnificence, God's pre-eminence, God's "Godness" was manifest in and through and with the earth and all its creatures.[19]

Like everything else to do with theology, our defining minds have assigned various categories to capture the relationship between the Sacred and nature. *Theism* describes an external Being that created the world and has an active role in its history, but is entirely independent of, and separate from, the world. *Deism* was coined in late seventeenth-century Europe to describe a Divine Creator that had no further involvement, through revelations, miracles or incarnations, after creation—such intervention was seen as degrading Divine omnipotence and unchangeableness. *Pantheism* sees GOD and the world as identical, a single reality—GOD is nature and nature *is* GOD. *Panentheism* sees GOD and the world dynamically interacting and interdependent, with GOD immanent in the world but also transcending the world—the cosmos is part of GOD. *Atheism* initially argued that a Divine was not provable by empirical methods and, when the term *agnosticism* emerged to cover this inability to know something that cannot be proven, atheism was applied to those who dismissed *any* belief in a GOD.

Today is a whole new day for talking about nature and the Sacred, firstly because of the Ecological Movement's concern for nature; and secondly because of the explosion of scientific knowledge about the universe, raising all sorts of questions about the relationship between religion and science. While Ecology is the biological science that studies the relationship between living things and their environment, the Ecological Movement, energized in the 1960s by Rachel Carson's book *Silent Spring,* represents the growing concern for our planet with its threats from agricultural chemicals, nuclear weapons, ozone depletion, deforestation, overpopulation, species extinction and climate change. A small pond near where we once lived, and which I watched out of my study window as I wrote, sported fish, turtles and other life for some twenty years. In one heavy rainfall, this pond lost twenty years of its future when a toxic, mud-clogged runoff from a building site flowed into it, blocking the natural springs seeping through its gravel floor with a layer of cement-like mud. We are using up the world's non-renewable resources and straining renewable cycles that have worked for centuries. Can GOD, or the planet, afford to keep humans alive? Will GOD, or the planet, once again regret creating humans, as the story of Noah recounts, and who, like Noah, will get a reprieve from destruction, I ask in my poem:

> Like the consummate mother,
> the divine Heart of the universe
> picks up, mends and medicates
> the planet in our wake.
> But how long until tough love prevails
> and our desecration is reigned in
> to protect other subjects of creation,
> even creation itself?
> How long, O God, will you

suffer the pride and destruction
of this willful generation?
The ancients feared your wrath
in lightning, quakes and plagues.
We, fearless new creators,
have invented our own destruction
and are determined to carry it through.[20]

We need to treat the world as our home, not a temporary motel where we use everything and leave our rubbish behind for someone else to clean up. Some people are starting to realize that the over-consumptive lifestyles of the planet's richest nations and the over-population of its poorest nations are causing a great threat to planetary survival—"The protection of Earth's vitality, diversity and beauty is a sacred trust", the Earth Charter states.[21] This *is* a theological issue if we believe the planet is GOD's "good" creation. Zoroastrians have known this for centuries. They claim to be the first ecologists because, since the world is the good, perfect creation of Ahura Mazda, they are instructed to care for it and not reject it through asceticism or indulgent materialism. Regulation #5 for inmates at the infamous island prison of Alcatraz in San Francisco Harbor reads, "You are entitled to food, clothing, shelter and medical attention. Anything else you get is a privilege." This should be the regulation issued to us as inmates of planet earth.

"The renewal of religion in the future will depend on our appreciation of the natural world as the locus for the meeting of the divine and the human", eco-theologian Thomas Berry (1914–2009) said. "The universe itself is the primary divine revelation. The splendor and the beauty of the natural world in all its variety must be preserved if any worthy idea of the divine is to survive in the human community."[22] The desecration of nature and the planet is especially confronting for contemporary theologies that see the Divine, not as an external Being manipulating the world from outside, but as the Life-blood, Breath, Spirit or Energy *within* everything in the universe, or the world as GOD's body (panentheism). Anything destructive done to our world necessarily affects the Divine *within* the organic network of the universe. While imagery of the Sacred-within-the-world is contemporary theology, it is as ancient as the earth for indigenous peoples. When missionaries first went to Bolivia, they introduced the sacraments to the new converts but were distressed when the locals poured a little of the consecrated wine onto the ground for *Pachamama,* the Earth Mother and nurturer of all earth beings. For Australian aboriginal artist Wandjuk Marika, "This land is not empty, the land is full of knowledge, full of story, full of goodness, full of energy, full of power. The earth is our mother, the land is not empty."[23] At the Parliament of the World's Religions in Melbourne, Australia (2009), an Indian scholar suggested that, to address the ongoing problem of climate change, we must not differentiate between the Sacred and the secular—all has Divinity in it. We would only need one religion, he said, the religion of the environment where we unite to co-operate and act for the preservation of Mother Earth. Such a religion would have to be dynamic, able to improvize according to what we now know. In his country of India, this means using modern technology for disposing of bodies rather than polluting with open cremation fires along the Ganges.[24]

Ancient ideas of the living earth as Sacred Mother have been revived through women's movements, GODDESS spirituality and Celtic traditions today. The thermal Cross Bath Spring in Bath, England was originally sacred to the Celtic GODDESS Sulis who, as well as the water, possessed healing powers. Under the Romans, the baths were dedicated to Sulis Minerva, a hybrid Celtic–Roman GODDESS, and accessing the waters provided direct contact with the Sacred. When the Romans left Britain, a church was built over the site to claim this "pagan" place for Christianity. Coming under civil control in the sixteenth century as a place of healing and fertility, it received its present name from a cross erected in thanks for the pregnancy of James II's queen and became a fashionable place with little religious connection, closing when amoebae in the water stopped bathing. In 1991, Cross Bath was restored by Margaret Stewart as a place where the GODDESS Earth Mother had once been contacted, because "There are those who believe that the springs of Bath are bringing about a change in people's attitude to, and relationship with, the sacred."[25]

In the same way in Australia, groups under the umbrella of "Paganism" began forming around the Creative Force (usually a GODDESS) manifested through nature, the seasonal cycles and the spirits of place—an overlapping of the spiritual and natural realms such that the Divine is in every part of nature. Since their ancient rituals came from the northern hemisphere, Pagan adherents had to adapt their "Wheel of the Year" for the reverse seasons— winter solstice is around June 21 instead of December 21 and Samhain (end of summer or Harvest Festival) is April 30, not October 31 (or November 1). Not only are the dates different, but Australia offers better weather for outdoor ceremonies than its European ancestors experienced, allowing oppor- tunity for creative new ways of engaging the Sacred *in* nature. There is also growing interest by non-Aboriginal people in Australian indigenous ideas around land, nature and spirituality, although this has to be pursued in a way that is not seen as yet another way to steal or appropriate indigenous culture.

It is now standard policy at the beginning of conferences, official meetings and public gatherings in Australia to pay tribute to the original Aboriginal owners of the land on which the event is being held. Aboriginal Christians are also trying to recover their ancient spirituality and introduce it into the Christianity that once took it away, a spirituality of the land as sacred for *all* Australians. Religion scholar Lynne Hume says:

> It is a curious irony that two hundred years after Europeans arrived, Aboriginal Christians are trying to find correspondences between an imposed belief system and their own ancient past, while Pagans and other nature carers are looking to the land that Aborigines have always said is sacred to articulate their own spirituality.[26]

Within Christianity, as in other religious traditions today, hard challenges are being made to the way we have treated nature. The creation story's language of human dominion over earth's creatures has been exposed as a human mandate for nature's desecration. "Dominion" was originally replaced with "stewardship" of the earth, but this still keeps humans in control. In *An Inconvenient Text: Is a green reading of the Bible possible?*, Professor Norman Habel argues that the Bible is an inconvenient text that includes "green" texts *and* "grey" texts. To be green is "to have empathy with Earth because we know ourselves as . . . Earth beings in solidarity with Earth, not as God-like beings who happen to be sojourners on Earth".[27] "Made in the image of God" is a grey text because it suggests humans are superior to the rest of the earth and justifies their domination of it. The flood story is grey because it also destroyed innocent earth creatures *and* the natural features of earth. The Exodus story is grey because those mighty acts of deliverance were also mighty acts of destruction of the earth—plagues that poisoned rivers and destroyed crops and animals. As for a promised land, this grey idea sanctioned a divine right to conquer, kill and destroy. All this is a shock for those who claim that the Bible is the literal word of GOD and an infallible guide for living, but as ecologically concerned Earth beings, Habel says, we must stand with earth so grey texts are not used against it. Russian novelist Fyodor Dostoevsky (1821–1881) wrote:

> Love all God's creation, the whole and every grain of sand in it. Love every leaf, every ray of God's light. Love the animals, love the plants, love everything. If you love everything, you will perceive the divine mystery in things. Once you perceive it, you will begin to comprehend it better every day. And you will come to love the whole world with an all-embracing love.[28]

We are currently working on a creation story for our time, the one scientists call the Big Bang. Human creation stories, whether about the explosion of the Chinese cosmic egg containing the Divine ancestor Pan Gu, or the Big Bang, share the human desire to understand the universe and our place in it. Our new creation story does not deal with *why* things happened, but tries to determine from scientific investigation *what* happened and how. Scientists don't claim to have answered all the questions about nature or found the theory of everything. In fact, they wonder whether *anyone* will ever know what happened immediately before the Big Bang and, in a few hundred years, we will probably look back at what scientists are saying today as limited and even naïve cosmology. Science works within a certain methodological parameter—that natural effects have *natural* causes and we can try to find *natural* explanations for such observed phenomena by constantly testing our hypotheses by controlled experiment to demonstrate whether they can withstand such examination. Religious descriptions of the Sacred in nature are beyond science's mandate and are always faith statements because GOD cannot be tested by experiment. There is nothing wrong with faith statements—we make them every day about a host of topics from refrigerator brands to correct doctrine—but we have to recognize the type of claim they are.

Since GOD-descriptions are metaphorical, we must, in our scientific world, use metaphorical language that is viable within our scientific understanding, not over against it or opposed to it. As already mentioned, a Divine Being breaking natural laws and readjusting the natural world in response to human requests may have fitted the biblical and medieval cosmology, but it does not work today. This does not mean everything has to bow to science, but that we respect what science does within its parameters. Many scientists are the first to acknowledge that there are crucial questions about which science has little or nothing to say; and many theologians conversant with scientific advances see these as exciting new avenues of knowledge, not threats. Oxford immunologist and Nobel Prize winner, Sir Peter Medawar (1915–87), said:

> That there is indeed a limit upon science is made very likely by the existence of questions that science cannot answer, and that no conceivable advance of science would empower it to answer . . . I have in mind such questions as: . . . What are we all here for? What is the point of living?[29]

To ascribe everything—creativity, arts, altruism, love—simply to genes, molecular activity and what science can explain, is an inadequate, truncated and sterile description of human existence.

Science and religion can meet for coffee today, not only over the tired old discussions about evolution, but over another word—"wonder"—which describes their joint passion. Together, they can respond to the metaphorical imagery of "earth is a magic moment in the cosmos, a sacred site".[30] As long as scientists remain within their defined limits and theologians acknowledge their different interest in meaning, they can meet on an open playing field and hopefully find moments of shared mystery. Australian physicist Paul Davis shares with many of his colleagues a feeling that there is "something going on in nature, that the world seems amazingly ingenious, in some way contrived":

> It's so beautiful, it's put together with such delicacy and there are so many felicitous qualities about it when you look at it at a fundamental level . . . I don't know what's going on and I don't quite know where we fit into it, but I do not believe that our existence, as human beings, is trivial. I'm not saying we're literally made in God's image but I do think that the emergence of life and consciousness, somewhere and somewhen in the universe, is a fact of the deepest significance . . . I think the universe has something like a purpose or a meaning and that we human beings have a part to play in that . . . It's not a central place, by any means, but it's not an insignificant place either.[31]

Davis is not advocating any Intelligent Design theory or "childish" notion of GOD that "would meddle and tinker and move matter around, violating the laws of physics". Instead, he suggests what many theologians describe—something "grander and, in some ways, a bit more inspiring . . . a timeless underpinning, a timeless purposefulness behind existence".[32] Rather than begin with questions of who or what created the earth, we should look for "a truly plausible God" in nature itself, in the laws of physics which are "omnipotent, universal, absolute, unchanging, utterly dependable and perhaps even transcendent in that they exist beyond the visible, physical universe with which we're familiar . . . they are both the grandest and the most fundamental things we know".[33] The laws of physics order, maintain and direct the universe—functions and qualities previously reserved for GOD. How we interpret this in religious metaphors is open to each of us, since that is as far as scientific exploration can go. Davis says:

> For the pure rationalists among us, here ends the search for God. It ends with an ingeniously designed universe, teeming with coincidences and

alluding to the existence of a consciousness behind it all but falling short of raising the curtain and exposing that consciousness to its creation.[34]

From the theologian's team in the open playing field of wonder, Australian biblical scholar Antony Campbell says that, since the ever more complex world we are discovering is beyond even *science's* imagining, theologians are more able to talk about mystery:

> Given that our world is vastly more complex than we can ever hope to imagine, is it the least bit suprizing that God should escape the limits of our understanding? For centuries, theologians have called it mystery. It still is mystery but today it is just that little bit more okay for it to be mystery. After all, so much else is.[35]

The challenge, Campbell says, is to describe Something "*big* enough to be thought of in matching terms with the vastness of our universe".[36] Over 100 years ago, William James wrote, "The God whom science recognizes must be a God of universal laws exclusively, a God who does a wholesale, not a retail business. He cannot accommodate his processes to the convenience of individuals."[37] The Milky Way with its 100–400 billion stars is only *one* of billions of galaxies in the observable universe. Surely such a universe *mocks* those who promote a micro-managing GOD counting hairs on our heads and finding parking spots for the faithful. We have to do better than this. The words of poet, historian and English language professor William McNeile Dixon (1866–1946) seem to express appropriate sentiments with which to end this chapter:

> If there be a skeptical star I was born under it,
> Yet I have lived all my days in complete astonishment.[38]

6

Sacred Places

The Pilgrims sailed west to found a holy colony which would be a beacon
unto the world. When Massachusetts would not do, Roger Williams moved on
to holiness in Rhode Island. The Mormons trekked to the great Salt Lake.
Hippies and their heirs . . . thumb their way to the Golden Gate. Somewhere
there is a holy land, a perfect pad . . . We remain like the Pilgrims at sea
searching for the landfall of the holy land.

—*George Dennis O'Brien*[1]

O   O   O

[T]he holy, the sacred, the wakan (as the Sioux call it) need not be exclusively
attached, or consciously attached at all, to a distinguishable Supreme Being.
Something may even be lost by so attaching it, that loss being the removal of
holiness from the world that remains when God is factored out.

—*Huston Smith*[2]

Heaven joins earth at sacred places and the Divine brushes against the
human in sacred shrines. This conviction has not been limited to any one
faith. In tidy Austrian villages where Roman Catholicism reigns, the crucified
Christ is never far from mind, not only because of crosses that crown the tips
of buildings and soaring church spires, but also at roadside shrines dotted
even into the mountains. These glass-covered pill-boxes with plastic flowers
draping a tortured, impaled Christ are sacred places where village folk pray
for good fortune, health and rain and passing motorists en route to somewhere (or nowhere) are reminded, "Have you said a prayer today?" In shop-
windows, doorway entrances, courtyard corners, or even nestled between
rice bags and white china teapots in Asian markets, elaborate red and gilded
shrines glow with small candles and receive the offerings of fruit, milk and
rice in praise of good fortune, or protection against bad fortune. On a

Singapore building site, I saw an old paint tin filled with sand serving as the workers' shrine, with a handful of incense sticks burning long and strong, hedging bets against a cruel, unreliable world.

In the main square of any Australian town, a war memorial crowned with a soldier's statue reminds Australians of events, as sacred to many as Jesus on the cross, when not just one, but hundreds of mothers' sons and true mates were crucified for something they did not do, for a cause they did not create. They died as heroes, not trouble-makers. They died for others, slaughtered in cruel ways for children they never knew and relatives they would never see again. Their deaths launched a religion as staunch as any, with sacred sites in Gallipoli, the Somme, Tobruk, New Guinea, Korea and Vietnam. ANZAC[3] Day memorial rituals cause the most hardened, macho Australian man to weep as the *Ode to Remembrance* is said, recalling those "who shall not grow old as we that are left grow old", and promising that we shall always remember them.[4]

While the whole universe may be a sacred site, our small minds function better with specific and tangible places in which to engage the Divine. But what makes a sacred place? Anthropologists and religion scholars have played with this for centuries. Emile Durkheim (1858–1917) divided the world into two domains, sacred and profane:

Sacred things are those which are protected and isolated by prohibitions; profane things are those to which the prohibitions apply, and they must keep their distance from sacred things.[5]

The problem with Durkheim's divisions, while neat and seemingly watertight, is that they are *not* mutually exclusive and things can be more or less sacred in varying degrees. Human rituals can take on so many different forms that it is difficult to box them as one or the other, or even describe them in the first place. Religion scholar Mircea Eliade (1907–86) continued these categories in his book *The Sacred and the Profane* but, rather than being language distinctions that humans impose on experiences in their physical environment, Eliade said that the Sacred *acts* on humanity such that things possess sacred or profane properties of themselves:

Man becomes aware of the sacred because it manifests itself, shows itself, as something wholly different from the profane. To designate the act of manifestation of the sacred, we have proposed the term *hierophany* . . . i.e. that something sacred shows itself to us.[6]

A much-loved violin teacher was laid to rest in our church. During the memorial service, the sun suddenly came out from behind a cloud, and a ray of light beamed down through the stained-glass window onto a small violinist, one of her pupils, playing *Ave Maria*. Such rays probably happen many times a day in many different places, but because it happened at this moment and focused on the violinist, people whispered for days about the "miracle", the tangible evidence of the Sacred. Was it a natural occurrence that, given its perfect sense of timing, was named sacred, or was Something sacred being manifest to the mourning crowd, a hierophany?

Today we are moving away from dualisms that once organized our world into hierarchical opposites—good/evil, male/female, black/white, mind/matter. We're finding that the world doesn't work that way, even though we tried to name it thus. We can experience a profoundly sacred moment sitting in a quite ordinary place in the woods, yet feel nothing while receiving the Eucharist, as if the Divine has lost the page of instructions as to where and when such moments of epiphany are allowed. We designate sacred places, only to find that no one comes there for supper, when some great party is in full swing down the road in the most dubious of dwellings. What we designate as profane has the uncomfortable habit of revealing the Sacred. Rather than GOD residing only in great temples operated by richly garbed priests, "Each human being, each animal and each plant is beautiful, if that creature is living as God ordained," Rumi reminds us, "thus we can worship God by loving all that is beautiful."[7]

Sacred space or time, as opposed to profane (*pro* and *fanum*—"outside the temple", routine and unconsecrated), is a common idea in religion, designated in different ways by different cultures. This is not surprising when cultures differ in their rules about *ordinary* space and time. The more affluent Westerners become, the more space they put between themselves and their neighbors, even establishing rules as to how close one can build to another house. There are also unwritten rules about how much space we should leave between people. We get decidedly uncomfortable if someone stands too close to us, invading our personal space—for me, it is also that they become out of focus! In a crowded room, we try not to touch each other accidentally, while other cultures have absolutely no problem with hugging everyone, holding hands with the same sex and kissing twice with no sexual or invasive intentions—it would be unfriendly not to do so and even worse if the recipient backed away to maintain distance. Some cultures are pedantic about being on time, while others see such promptness as quite rude and operate almost without time impositions. In some cultures, people might agree to go fishing and simply do not show up because it would be more impolite to say "No" in the first place.

Sacred time reflects a culture's idea of time. Primal people described their life by seasons coming and going—solstice, harvest, new moon—rather than an historical dateline. Hindus think of time as circular, just as we represent time on a watch as circular, not linear. Rather than a lifetime moving towards a single finale, people are born, die and reborn in ongoing cycles. There are sacred cycles of the universe—times when Brahma is creating a world, Shiva destroying it and Vishnu either preserving the world or sleeping on his serpent couch between worlds. Christianity is linear, an idea of time inherited from the Hebrews that began in a creation, progressed with GOD working in history and looks forward to a time when the Messiah will come. Christian sacred time is also a progression towards an end (*eschaton*), a fulfillment, a new heaven and earth, not something we can predict but GOD's time when one day is "like a thousand years, and a thousand years as one day" (2 Peter 3:8).

For ancient societies that saw the natural world as the abode of the Sacred, significant features of the environment such as mountains, springs, unusual landscape shapes and caves, were singled out as sacred places where the Divine seemed more acutely present. The River Ganges (Ganga) is sacred in Hinduism. Flowing from the Himalayas, it is said to come from Lord Vishnu's toe and spreads through the world through the long matted locks of Lord Shiva's hair. Sips of Ganges water are given to the dying, and bathing in its waters brings *Svarga*, the paradise of the Divine Indra, to worshippers, as does leaving something of themselves, like a hair or a bone, on the left bank.[8] In September 2005, the *Times of India* reported that a company was collecting Ganges water from Gangotri and packaging it to sell further down the river where the water was more polluted, giving people pure water for their *puja* (worship). While many agreed that the water would be safer, others were perturbed, preferring to risk using polluted water—"How can I know it is Ganges water?" they said. Others thought the packaged water might lose its pristine quality through packaging, while others simply wanted the virtue of collecting the water themselves.

Indigenous Australians feel deeply responsible for the flourishing of the land, which is not owned but entrusted to them by the Creator Spirit. Different Aboriginal groups are responsible for different portions of "country", and their elders have sacred laws by which to tend it. Each has a sacred song about their land and a sacred place within that land where ceremonies are performed, songs sung and dances performed.

These ceremonies are part of our responsibility as custodians of the land: they ensure that we preserve our connections with the Creator Spirit, that we maintain the resources and life-forces of the land, and that we keep alive the law and culture given us by our ancestors.[9]

After the renewal "burn-time" ceremony where portions of the land are burned by elders to enable better production of food, dew on the grass the next morning means the Creator Spirit has blessed the land and their efforts.[10] Each person has a specific "country" to which they belong, linked with their particular story and a creature or part of creation as their living symbol. Sacred places are where spiritual forces are concentrated, places linked with beginning ancestors and the Creator Spirit, often represented as the Rainbow Serpent. When Australia was overtaken by British settlers in 1788, Aboriginal people were chased from their "country" and many children taken from parents such that they lost their personal symbol and story place, their roots and connection with the Creator Spirit. They have no answer to the Aboriginal form of greeting "What is your story?", "Where is your country?" Sacred places were also desecrated as highways pushed through them, mines dug into them, cities built over them and fences separated them off from the original caretakers. The elders say:

> The Creator Spirit is crying because the land is dispossessed. The land is crying because the people assigned by the Creator Spirit to be its custodians have been torn from the land by force. The people of the land are crying because they are unable to fulfill their responsibilities as custodians of the land.[11]

The most famous Aboriginal sacred site for tourists is Uluru, the giant red rock standing, as if dropped from on high, in the center of Australia. It has now been handed back to Aboriginal owners after thousands of tourist feet tramping over it. Just as Western Christians would be horrified if tourists sat on their churches' altars, visitors to Uluru are being encouraged to treat it with equal respect as a sacred site.

Places where important events in religious history took place also become sacred pilgrimage places. In Bodhgaya in Bihar, India, where the Buddha is said to have gained enlightenment, a seventh-century CE temple stands beside a papal tree (*ficus religiosa*), a direct descendant of the original bodhi tree under which the Buddha sat. Traditionally, anyone making a pilgrimage with sincere faith to this site will be reborn in favorable circumstances.[12] Mecca, the birthplace of Muhammad, is the holy site for Muslims towards which Muslims around the world turn to pray. A pilgrimage (*hajj*) to the Ka'ba, the cube-shaped holy shrine of Islam in the great mosque Masjid al-

Haram, is one of the Five Pillars of Islam, with everyone dressed in white robes to demonstrate the equality of all. The Ka'ba is recorded as built by Adam and rebuilt by Abraham and Ishmael (Qur'an 2:125, 22:126). When Muhammad conquered Mecca in 630 CE, he cleaned the Ka'ba of some 300 statues to various GODS, dedicating it as the "House of Allah", the one GOD and the earthly place designated by Allah as the focal point for communication with the Divine. In the east corner of the Ka'ba sits a Black Stone, thought to be of meteorite origin, which Hajj pilgrims try to kiss and touch as they walk seven times around the Ka'ba.

By contrast, the rock that stands as a monument to the landing of the *Mayflower* Pilgrims in 1620 in Plymouth, USA, had sacredness thrust upon it. Neither William Bradford (1590–1657) nor Edward Winslow (1595–1655), the earliest chroniclers of the landing, record any particular rock on which the first English foot stepped, neither do several explorers who came ashore there. The rock first became important in 1741 when plans were made to build a wharf at that site. Thomas Faunce, a 93-year-old man who had been the town record keeper, asked to be carried down to the site and pointed out the exact rock his father had told him was the one that welcomed the first Pilgrim foot (although it is now thought that rock was about 650 feet from the actual landing). In 1774, Colonel Theophilus Cotton and the townspeople decided to move the rock and it split in half—a sign, in retrospect, of the American Revolution the following year. It was decided to leave the bottom half where it was and relocate the top half to the town meeting house. Thus began a series of rock journeys around Plymouth town as its sacred aura increased and different locations were deemed suitable. During its travels, pieces were removed as souvenirs, with a piece now in the Pilgrim Hall Museum and another in the Smithsonian. Its final resting place is near the rebuilt shoreline such that it lies at water level once again, where thousands of tourists gaze on it with holy awe. Alexis de Tocqueville (1805–59), the French historian who wrote *Democracy in America* (1835) wrote:

This Rock has become an object of veneration in the United States. I have seen bits of it carefully preserved in several towns in the Union. Does this sufficiently show that all human power and greatness is in the soul of man? Here is a stone which the feet of a few outcasts pressed for an instant; and the stone becomes famous; it is treasured by a great nation; its very dust is shared as a relic. [13]

As with Mecca, whole cities are designated as sacred places. Jerusalem immediately springs to mind, a holy city for Jews, Christians and Muslims.

According to biblical accounts, Jerusalem was captured from the Jebusites by King David and became his royal capital (2 Sam. 5) and the site of King Solomon's temple. When captured by the Babylonians in 587 CE, this temple was destroyed and many inhabitants taken to Babylon. At the end of this exile, the rebuilt temple became the center of Jerusalem's life. In the second-century BCE, the Jews were under Antiochus, King of Syria, who decreed that sacrifices be offered to the great Deities, and built a "pagan" altar on the temple altar in Jerusalem. Devastated at this desecration, the Jews under the Macabees family staged a courageous revolt, recapturing Jerusalem and restoring the defiled temple. The rededication of the temple in 164 BCE is celebrated with the Feast of Dedication—Hanukkah. Just as the temple candelabras were re-lit at that time, Jewish people light the Hanukkah candelabra, adding a light each night of the festival. However, history's punctuation marks are wars and uprisings. The temple in Jerusalem was destroyed by the Romans in 70 CE, leaving only the western (wailing) wall. After the Bar Kokhba revolt (135 CE), Emperor Hadrian renamed the city Aelia Capitolina, built a sanctuary to the GOD Jupiter Capitolinus and forbade Jews from entering the city.

Christian history was also enacted within this framework, as Jerusalem was the place of Jesus' death and resurrection and also became the metaphor for heaven, the Christian hope—"Jerusalem the golden, with milk and honey blessed".[14] The Jerusalem church faded by the end of the first century and did not revitalize until Emperor Constantine (fourth century) introduced pilgrimages to holy places—Constantine's mother Helena (c. 250–330 CE) is said to have traveled to Jerusalem and returned to Constantinople with part of the real cross. The Church of the Resurrection (Church of the Holy Sepulcher) has become the Christian center of Jerusalem, although disputes between rival Christians erupt from time to time. In July, 2002, eleven monks were treated in hospital after a fight between monks of the Ethiopian Orthodox and the Coptic Church of Egypt for control of the church's roof, an ongoing battle for centuries. When an Egyptian monk moved his chair into the sun, the Ethiopians saw this as "violating the 'status quo', set out in a 1757 document which defines ownership of each chapel, lamp and flagstone".[15] The Egyptian monk sits there to demonstrate the Coptic claim to the rooftop, which is mostly used as an Ethiopian monastery with African-type huts since they have been evicted from the main church. The church is actually a bed of rivalry between *six* Christian denominations, with the more powerful ones taking advantage of weakness in their rivals.

For Muslims, Mecca, Medina and Jerusalem, in that order, are all sacred cities. Jerusalem is where Muhammad traveled by night through the sky with the angel Gabriel and, after prayer and worship, ascended to the seven heavens. He found paradise in the seventh and conversed with Allah before returning to Mecca. Muslim prayers were originally said towards Jerusalem, but later changed to Mecca when the Ka'ba became the focus for Muslims. *Qubbat as-Sakharah*, the Dome of the Rock, was built in 691 CE on the rock from which Muhammad ascended—the rock is said to have split when it tried to follow Muhammad, and his footprint can still be seen. We know only too well what has happened in Jerusalem since the establishment of the State of Israel in 1948 and the capture of the Arab quarter in 1967 by Israeli forces, declaring it the capital of the State of Israel. Is it inevitable that a place considered sacred by three religions will become the epitome of all that is destructive in religion, with wars between opposing doctrines, sects and claims?

Places associated with saints and religious founders acquire sacred status and become designated places at which to engage the Divine. Recently, we were near San Giovanni Rotondo in Italy and thought we might visit this town, famous for Father Pio (1887–1968), a Capuchin priest canonized by Pope John Paul II in 2002. Father Pio decided at age five to become a priest and began experiencing visions and ecstatic episodes. Ordained in 1910, he spent from 1916 until his death (except for military service) in Our Lady of Grace Capuchin Friary where he received permanent stigmata (wounds corresponding to Jesus' crucifixion wounds). Accusations were made against him, however, by high-ranking archbishops, bishops, theologians and physicians, with charges of insanity, immorality, misuse of funds and deception about his stigmata. The tide would turn in his favor and, in 1939, Pius XII encouraged devotees to visit his friary. John XXIII did not share this enthusiasm, but his successor Pope Paul VI dismissed all accusations against him. Father Pio died in 1968 and was canonized by Pope John Paul II in 2002. This monastery town, the second most visited Catholic shrine in the world with eight million pilgrims a year, has developed a veritable industry around this man. For sale in our hotel were hologram cards that changed at the twist of the fingers from Father Pio to Jesus, lace-edged, heart-shaped satin pillows with an embedded metal statue of Father Pio, cigarette lighters with Father Pio's face, bracelets with a different Pope on each bead, books, rings, rosaries and statues. His body has been exhumed and is on display as some 15,000 people a day file past the crystal coffin in his old cell within a modern sanctuary and complex that includes the large hospital Father Pio built. We felt that we met most of these 15,000 people *and* their cars as we wound up a beautiful hill past olive trees to this hill-side shrine and encountered traffic police, souvenir stalls, a carnival atmosphere and long entrance lines. In the end, we didn't go into the sanctuary but stopped instead outside the town to readjust our spiritual bearings—there is a difference between a religious site and a religious sight.

The great mosque Al-Masjid an-Nabawi in Medina is built over the prophet Muhammad's tomb, just as St Peter's Basilica in Rome is built over Saint Peter's tomb. King Ashoka, a third-century BCE Indian ruler who converted to Buddhism, was responsible for building some 84,000 *stupas* (dome-shaped monuments to contain the Buddha's relics) as sacred places of pilgrimages. Assisi in Italy attracts millions of pilgrims each year to the crypt of Saint Francis (1181–1226), a wealthy cloth merchant's son who espoused a life of poverty and formed the order of Friars Minor that became the Franciscans. When I visited this crypt, I thought of my Franciscan friends at their motherhouse, Assisi Heights, in Minnesota. Despite being a Protestant not very familiar with candles and rituals in Roman Catholic shrines, I purchased a candle in honor of them from a non-English-speaking monk at a table near the tomb. When my postcard telling of my actions reached their motherhouse, it was circulated around with affectionate chuckles—"Crazy Protestants—she could have burned the place down!"

In the beginning, the Hebrews experienced Divine encounters wherever God chose such revelation. When Yahweh called Moses, the medium of choice was a burning bush and, when Moses approached it, Yahweh said, "Come no closer! Remove the sandals from your feet, for the place on which you are standing is holy ground" (Ex. 3:4–5). As wandering nomads, they erected a "tent" for Yahweh whenever they camped, but when they settled in Jerusalem, King Solomon built the first temple. There was some reluctance, however. While Solomon believed GOD had given him a pause in warfare in order to build (1 Kings 5:3–4), he was conscious that the Divine could not be limited to any place—"But will God indeed dwell on the earth? Even heaven and the highest heaven cannot contain you, much less this house that I have built!" (1 Kings 8:27). For Hindus, a *mandira* (dwelling place or temple) is where the Divine lives, embodied in a *murti* (meaning "embodiment" of a GOD). This *murti* can be a sacred stone under a tree with the *mandira* a small, sacred space around it, or the *murti* can reside like royalty in a "womb house" deep inside a massive temple where it is symbolically woken with prayers and music, washed, dressed, fed, entertained and tucked back into bed at night by the priests.

After a day of touring some of Europe's magnificent cathedrals, my friend was sitting quietly in the taxi with his chin held high. When I asked if anything was wrong, he said, "My head is holding so much culture that I'm keeping my chin up in case it all leaks out." The creation of Christian sacred places has produced much of the art and architecture of the Western world. In centuries when most of the faithful were illiterate, churches were their "Bibles", telling the stories, with art and architecture reflecting the theology of the day. The followers of Jesus first met in private homes—there were some 25 house churches in Rome when Emperor Constantine began building churches in the fourth century.[16] The original churches were rectangular basilicas with interiors representing the "House of GOD"—you entered GOD's dwelling place and the mosaics and wall-paintings told the salvation story. After the lull of what was called the "Dark Ages" for Christianity, church building began again in the ninth century, combining features of Roman and Byzantine buildings with thick walls, round arches and sturdy buttresses. This Romanesque style incorporated the triumphant, transcendent GOD in its dome, with heaven full of angels and saints. After the Second Council of Tours (567 CE), the chancel area was elevated above the nave and lay people were banned from standing with the clergy, a move from the assembly (*ekklesia*) of the people of GOD to the hierarchy of priest closest to the heavenly entourage in the dome. The crucifix in the chancel was raised above the level of the priest as the symbolic bridge to GOD. Although tourists usually sweep their eyes around Europe's ancient cathedrals for a superficial smorgasbord, the positioning of each visual symbol once spelled out a message for the illiterate as clearly as letters of the alphabet ordered into words and doctrines do for us.

The medieval walled city was all sacred space, separated off from the world outside with a Gothic church at its center, its soaring church tower and tall, arched windows drawing everything upward towards the heavenly Jerusalem where the Divine Father and Judge was seated on the heavenly throne. In turn, stained-glass windows brought the transcendent Light down into this earthly space where the nave continued the city road towards heaven, and stories of the saints covering the walls assured people that they were part of the eternal city, experienced here in part but fully in the life to come. The Renaissance, on the other hand, would emphasize humanity and this human realm. Its churches were built as classical Greco-Roman temples re-creating the ancient classical world, considered the high point of human thought. The Christian stories were now depicted in classical humanist forms with the supernatural Christ, once enthroned in heaven, returned to earth as a super-human classical male enduring super-human suffering, with GOD as Light shining on him.

When the Reformation focused on hearing GOD through the scriptures and preaching, rather than doing the Mass and praying to the saints, church icons were removed, wall paintings white-washed out, priestly garb replaced with black robes, and pulpits moved to the center of the chancel to replace the altar—Word over Mass. In response to this "turning down of the lights", the Roman Church over-responded with triumphant and lavish baroque art and architecture, taking its flourish from the Opera with the "performance" at the high altar decked with candles and flowers (although the scholarly Jesuits brought their pulpits closer to the people so they could hear as well as see). Rococo design followed, still with flourishes but a softer, gentler effect in pastels and pastoral scenes. The church was not just a building—it was a theological teaching aid and its changes of style reflected the different messages it wanted people to hear.

As theology continues to change, GOD's house is also changing. Vatican II allowed the priest to face the people across the altar, indicating that *all* are gathered around the table rather than the priest doing the Mass on his own at the altar. Protestants have warmed to ritual, introducing candles, crucifixes and incense that would have appalled their predecessors who died over such distinctions. The beautiful icons of the Eastern Church have found their way into the West as mirrors of the Divine. With declining attendance, churches have been "deconsecrated" and "desacralized" to become art galleries, restaurants and bed-and-breakfasts—I once slept in a luxurious king-size bed where the altar of a convent chapel once stood, a strange experience I must say. As George O'Brien, comparing GOD to the New Haven railway, wrote, "Where Church and Temple were once grandiose constructions suggesting all sorts of adventurous journeys to the beyond, they seem today reduced to humanity's arrivals and departures."[17]

In an advertisement for an Australian animal and bird repellent, a letter of recommendation came from a Catholic nun who wrote about bird infestation in their church. "Our church had been declared unsafe some seven years ago," she said, "so was not used" (which could be said of a lot of churches today and nothing to do with birds). Once they used the bird repellent, however, the birds exited "as if they had an electric shock" and did not return to the building (a problem many churches have with people). Some people have returned to house churches for community worship, seeing church buildings as bastions of inflexibility, immobility and lack of connection with those in the pews. Others have fled church buildings altogether for the great outdoors as the theater of GOD. An American pastor going to Zimbabwe took a print of a religious picture that hung in his church to present to the congregation, only to find that the Zimbabwe church was outdoors with no walls on which to hang his imitation print—they had a 360-degree picture of creation instead.

Asian temples as sacred spaces are more like central stations or a busy market. GOD seems more in residence than in the dark, usually closed structures of Christendom and also seems to have many more guests at all hours of the day. While Hindu temples are usually dedicated to one particular incarnation of the Divine, they contain a host of little worship centers inside and outside the temple. Surrounded by crowded shops and traffic, the Sri Veeramakaliamman Temple in Serangoon Road, Singapore is, according to its sign, "dedicated to the Goddess Kali, ferocious incarnation of Lord Siva's wife Meenachi", and it claims to be the first Singapore temple to venerate her. It was built in 1855 by Tamil lime workers as the "Temple of the Village of Lime". On the day I visited, like any day, flocks of people bustled throughout the open-sided building and into the courtyard, lighting clay oil lamps and buying strings of fresh flowers from the flower-sellers to give as offerings to the Deity's *murti*. A giant pot of milk was constantly filled beside one shrine and trays of bananas were being prepared in an outside shed, all as gift offerings. Many devotees prayed earnestly at various shrines or circled a shrine carrying oil lamps—none seemed distracted by the bustle or the crowds. Others stood in line with their purchases before a shrine, peering around each other to catch a glimpse of the Deity in the half-dark of the "womb house". When they reached the head of the line, a priest took their offering into the shrine and placed it near the Deity or around its neck. In a temple in Goa, India, I wandered around the courtyard to the back of the temple and found a large shed where a handful of women sat on the floor in brightly colored saris, sorting large piles of raw rice that had been offered to the temple Deity and was now being prepared for distribution to the poor and needy.

The same activity is true for Asian Buddhist temples. In Hanoi in Vietnam, many of the temples I encountered were a mix of Buddhism, ancestor worship, nature worship and indigenous traditions—places where everyone can go to engage the Sacred of various names and descriptions with prayers and offerings. Some of the many side shrines in the temples feature photos of dead ancestors, with spiral incense sticks burned for them to represent the eternal spiral of life. Some housed Buddha statues, usually the three representing the past, present and future Buddhas. An appropriately named yellow fruit that looked like gnarled fingers, "Buddha-hand", was placed in front of the Buddhas as an offering. In the Dien Huu Pagoda (One Pillar Pagoda), bowls of fake $100 American notes were being offered, no doubt considered very generous but also ironically capitalist in this temple bordering Communist leader Ho Chi Minh's (1890–1969) mausoleum. Pepsi-Cola bottles containing oil to fill the candles had been placed as offerings before many shrines, said to bring enlightenment but also a reminder that more than religion has spread around the world. In another shrine in the Dien Huu Pagoda, a row of statues of female midwives could help in one's reincarnation, but they also helped infertile women in *this* life—women could always multi-task. In the courtyards, burning towers gave opportunity to burn money for good fortune, but always in odd numbers and they must completely burn to be effective.

This chapter could go on for ever—and you may be wondering if it will, since the topic could fill whole books and then some. Even as I end, I realize I have hardly started. Sacred places and space are more than just the buildings. They are places where the Divine is engaged, or the Sacred, whether nature, Spirit, Presence or simply our more aware selves, is experienced. An authentic sacred place is primarily *functional* and, as such, can be anywhere and anything.

Sacred Things
and Symbols

For the ancient Greeks the gods were real.
A Greek who saw a thunderbolt was reminded of Zeus, and so reminded of
another, simultaneous system of reality.
In contrast, when we see a thunderbolt, we see a weather pattern and are
probably reminded to watch the six o'clock news for the weather report!
—*Robert A. Johnson*[1]

When the taxi-driver picked me up at my hotel in Goa, India, to spend a day
looking at Portuguese Catholic churches and Hindu temples, I noticed he had
two statues attached to the dashboard below his rear-vision mirror—Ganesh,
the elephant-headed son of the Hindu Lord Shiva, and the Virgin Mary.
When I asked him why he had both, he laughed and said, "Two is better—
I need all the protection I can get." I observed that he was right when we
entered the busiest parts of the city, weaving between cows, strolling people,
roadside stalls, motorcycles with whole families on board and cars using
horns for brakes. The Ganesh and Mary statues are *things*, mass-produced
objects sold in the local market for only a few cents, yet they are more than
that. They are "signs" that "signify" that he believes they will protect him
from harm. This message is successfully transmitted to me if I understand
what these particular figures, placed in this position in his taxi, mean. Had
he had a key swinging from his rear-vision mirror to signify protection from
Saint Peter who holds the keys to heaven, this sign would not have worked
if I had thought it was his house-key, safely in view so he did not lose it.

Semiotics is the study of signs and symbols and how they work in communication. We are so used to responding to signs every day and in every
place that we hardly pause to consider this whole process of communication,

73

whether it be a road sign warning us of deer crossing, dark, grumpy clouds as a sign of rain, a signature on a letter, or a propitious natural event as a sign of good luck. I am currently sitting in my American daughter-in-law's home, surrounded by every imaginable representation of an orange pumpkin—soft, felt ones with gaping smiles of missing teeth, pumpkin-shaped salt-and-pepper shakers, night-lights glowing orange through pumpkin casings and even orange leaf-bags shaped like giant pumpkins for the falling leaves outside. In sync with these leaves, plastic Fall-colored leaves are glued to the window-glass, indicating that somehow these changing leaves are important at this time. All these signs, incomprehensible to someone unfamiliar with American holidays, celebrate Fall (Autumn) and Halloween. The signs are very specific—a green pumpkin like we grow in Australia would just not do for Halloween.

There are three types of signs—an icon, an index or a symbol. An *icon* is a sign that actually looks like what it signifies. When my toddler grandson looks at my photograph on my driving license, he points to the photograph and then to me—the photo is a sign of me that actually looks like me. An *index* is a sign that does not look like what it signifies, but there are recognizable connections. When that same toddler finds my shoes at the door, he picks them up and says "Grandma". The shoes don't look like me, but he associates them with me. A *symbol* is a sign that looks nothing like what it signifies, yet there is common agreement that this symbol stands for a particular thing. Numbers and letters are symbols. When my grandson can read, he will look at the letter symbols G-R-A-N-D-M-A on his birthday card and know immediately that it came from me. Symbols can be anything—passwords, badges, flags, applause, music notes, wedding rings, and a cross—so long as they communicate by transmitting a message. The word "symbol" (meaning "to throw together") originally described two halves of a tablet the Greeks would split between themselves as a sign of hospitality or covenant. It was later applied to engraved shells with which people in certain secret societies identified themselves, like a secret handshake.[2] In the early Church, Christians under Roman surveillance would draw in the dirt with their stick as they spoke with strangers, making a half circle so that, if the others were also Christian, they would casually add a reverse half circle to complete the Christian symbol of a fish.

Religions depend heavily on signs and symbols to represent Divine Mystery. "For the religious person," Hans Biedermann says in his *Dictionary of Symbolism*, "the symbol is a concrete phenomenon in which the idea of the divine and the absolute becomes immanent, in such a way as to be more clearly expressed than in words."[3] There is something very comforting about a "thing" that can be seen, felt or experienced to represent Something non-tangible. Statues of Mary weep tears, sacred rivers heal illnesses and kissing an icon makes us feel we are encountering the one portrayed in it. For ancient Egyptians, creatures such as cats, crocodiles and ibises were sacred things and repositories of divine power. Fire is sacred for Zoroastrians as a visible symbol of the all-pervasive Divine, Ahura Mazda—the flame rising upwards challenges all kinds of darkness. The fire in a Zoroastrian temple is fed five times a day by the priest and, in the home, an oil lamp (*divo*) burns 24 hours a day. Fire was also the vehicle for Divine communication to Moses—"the angel of the Lord appeared to him in a flame of fire out of a bush" (Ex. 3:2). In his classic book on symbols, Count Eugene Goblet d'Alviella (1846–1925) wrote:

Without doubt the symbols that have attracted in the highest degree the veneration of the multitude have been the representative signs of gods, often uncouth and indecent; but what have the gods themselves ever been, except the more or less imperfect symbols of the Being transcending all definition Whom the human conscience has more and more clearly divined through and above all these gods?[4]

Goblet d'Alviella's comment that religious signs can be "uncouth and indecent" shows how symbols mean different things to different people, according to their cultural maps. Because of Christianity's pathological negativity to sex throughout its history, it has poured out harsh judgements on religions that celebrate sexual intercourse, especially between Deities. Hindu temples positively vibrate with the multi-positioned sexual activity of their Divine incarnations (Avatars) and indigenous religions of the world always sought help for themselves and their crops from fertility-inclined GODS and GODDESSES. No wonder the Christian story of a GOD who "birthed" a universe without a female partner and impregnated a woman, later declared virginal before and after childbirth, spawned a cult of celibacy and suspicion of sex. Bertrand Russell, in his typically iconoclastic style, noted one such idiosyncrasy in his time:

. . . for instance, the nuns who never take a bath without wearing a bathrobe all the time. When asked why, since no man can see them, they reply: "Oh, but you forget the good God." Apparently they conceive of the Deity as a Peeping Tom, whose omnipotence enables Him to see through bathroom walls, but who is foiled by bathrobes.[5]

In a complete misreading of religious symbols, John Stoddard, an American traveler at the beginning of the twentieth century, described India's religious art as "too disgusting to be illustrated, and some of the carvings on the temples of Benares are too vile to be described".[6] Yet the general Sanskrit word *linga* for "symbol" is also the specific term for the penis symbolizing generative energy. Not surprisingly, in a culture with a healthy regard for sex, the penis became a symbol for *Divine* generative energy such that Lord Shiva is often imaged in Hindu temples simply as a penis. Goblet d'Alviella recorded a story in *The Times* in 1891 of a boy in British-run India being flogged by order of the Madras Police Magistrate for "exhibiting an indecent figure in public view". According to custom, he had placed a *linga* in front of a house being built inviting blessing from the Divine

> . . . in whose strength alone can any work of man be surely established, and as a devout and public acknowledgement that, in the words of the Hebrew Psalmist:—"Except the Lord build the house, they labor in vain that build it."[7]

The *linga* does not stand alone as a sacred symbol but is mounted on a pedestal symbolizing the *yoni*, the female sex organ. Thus Divine creative energy is the *union* of the two rather than the individual players. Whenever the One *Brahman* (a neuter noun) is incarnated, whether as Shiva, Vishnu, Kali, Durga or Krishna, sexual union with their consort is an essential part of their activities. Tourists who stare in amazement (and pleasure or disgust) at graphic Hindu carvings of Divine Beings in various sexual positions are simply reflecting their own religious and cultural sensitivities, missing entirely this beautiful symbolism of Divine creative *Energy* at work in the universe. Hindu devotees choose only one Divine Avatar to worship, since all are depictions of the One (not polytheism), and male and female Avatars are equally sought. Durga, the female consort of Shiva, killed the buffalo demon Mahisa whom neither human nor beast could destroy and is depicted with ten arms carrying an arsenal of weaponry and accompanied by a lion or tiger—not just a pretty face. Avatars are always portrayed with not strictly anthropomorphic embellishments—they possess multiple hands, eyes and heads, take animal form and adopt strange postures, emphasizing that the formless One is not just a human being writ large. Their appearance is geared to reach our emotions, bring delight to our eyes and engender confidence in their multi-tasking abilities with all their tools of trade in many hands.

Sacred symbols and objects do not have a singular religious meaning. For indigenous Australians, the Rainbow Serpent (snake) is the Creator Spirit that emerged from the land, traveled the void of the earth creating all that is and leaving its trails as rivers and hills, before returning to the earth through caves, water holes and sacred sites. Many Christian missionaries forbade snake imagery for the Creator because, in their tradition, the snake is associated with sin, Satan and also "pagan" fertility rites.[8] In Asian religions, snakes are the guardians of temples and sacred spaces, perhaps because the cobra rises up to defend its territory. In Greek mythology, the Golden Fleece was guarded by a massive serpent that never slept and snakes were also protectors and companions of GODDESSES. Since snakes shed their skins, they were also symbols of death and rejuvenation—the Minoan snake GODDESS held a serpent in each hand to signify both of these, yet because of their poison they also symbolized the threat of death *without* rejuvenation.

Snakes are cousins to dragons, sea serpents (Leviathan), lake serpents (Loch Ness Monster) and cosmic serpents that regularly appear in myths and legends. The serpent with its tail in its mouth appears in Greek mythology, Central American and West African stories, symbolizing the cycle of the eternal return or eternal life. In Hindu mythology, Lord Vishnu rests during world cycles on a many-headed serpent couch called Ananta, floating in a cosmic sea of milk. When a storm threatened to interrupt Buddha's meditation under the bodhi ("enlightenment") tree, the many-headed serpent Mucalinda came up from under the earth to envelop him in its coils and protect him. There is also something about serpents and trees. In Greek mythology, Ladon coiled around a tree in the Garden of the Hesperides to *protect* its golden apples, while the snake in the Hebrew Garden story, portrayed in medieval paintings as coiled around the Tree of the Knowledge of Good and Evil (and often with a female face), was giving the fruit *away*. The staff with a coiled serpent symbol, an extension of the tree imagery, is found in Sumerian, Greek and Hebrew stories—the rod of Asclepius with its coiled snake symbolized medical healing and Moses' brass serpent on a pole brought healing for those bitten in a snake plague (Num. 21).

With such diversity of meaning across cultures extracted from a single symbol, it is crucial that the symbol is correctly interpreted. To continue the snake example, John Stoddard, our nineteenth-century travel writer, commented on the large number of snakes in Ceylon (now Sri Lanka) and that 19,000 people died in India in 1892 from snakebite, mostly field-workers whose bare feet were exposed. Because of this "danger", Stoddard said, "a common sight, therefore, is that of natives worshipping deities in the form of snakes, in order to propitiate their wrath".[9] For evidence, photographs of Ceylonese people squatting in front of headstone-like tablets accompany the statement with captions reading "worshipping snakes". The images on the tablets, however, are not random snake carvings before which animist villagers propitiate the creatures' wrath, but rather the ancient Hindu sacred symbol of the many-headed serpent Ananta that forms Lord Vishnu's couch.

The meaning of symbols can also change over the centuries as they are borrowed, adapted or used in entirely different ways. The staff of authority carried by Orthodox Christian bishops is topped with a cross and two snakes. Hold your hats as we track this imagery down the centuries. Moses erected a bronze serpent on a pole when the Hebrew people were attacked by poisonous snakes sent as Divine punishment for their complaining—"[T]here is no food and no water, and we detest this miserable food" (Num. 21:5). Those bitten could look up at the pole and live. This story might have faded into obscurity in Christianity except that John's Gospel (and *only* this Gospel) mentions it in a conversation between Nicodemus and Jesus about the reign of GOD as eternal life here and now—"[J]ust as Moses lifted up the serpent in the wilderness, so must the Son of Man be lifted up, that whoever believes in him may have eternal life" (3:14–15). There is no mention of Jesus' *death* in their discussion—Moses' snake was not crucified but "lifted up" so people could see it and be healed, just as teaching about the reign of GOD as eternal life *now* should be "lifted up" before people to give them abundant "life" in the present. Biblical scholar John Dominic Crossan says:

> The Kingdom of God . . . was what this world would look like if and when God sat on Caesar's throne, or if and when God lived in Antipas's palace . . . It is about the transformation of this world into holiness, not the evacuation of this world into heaven.[10]

"God gave his only Son" (v. 16) calls Jesus a gift to the world, although by the time John's Gospel was written at the end of the first century (or later), the image of Jesus on the cross would also come to mind.

In time, this symbolism would take a further theological step when John 3:16, beginning with "For God so loved the world . . .", became seen as the gospel-in-a-nutshell, interpreted now as Jesus being "lifted up" on the cross as a *sacrifice* in order to remove human sin and offer eternal life in the hereafter, just as Moses' serpent lifted up (cross) saved people from death by a snake (a Christian symbol for sin). Evangelically inclined Christians still lift up banners reading "John 3:16" behind television news reporters at anything from a national disaster to football games, believing that sinners will be saved by looking up at this—the symbol has a life of its own. Return with me now to the Orthodox Bishop's staff with two snakes facing each other across the cross. Some say it represents this Moses–Jesus–sin trajectory, while some see in it the snake-entwined staff of Asclepius, the Greek GOD of medicine, suggesting the bishop is the healer of *spiritual* illnesses. Yet the bishop's staff has two snakes, not one, and is almost identical to the caduceus, the staff of Hermes, the Greek GODS' messenger, which has two snakes facing each other under a pair of wings symbolizing Hermes' speed. The caduceus became the badge for heralds and ambassadors in ancient Greece and Rome, so why not GOD'S ambassador in the Greek Church? Others have suggested that the snakes symbolize holy wisdom, as in Jesus' commission to the apostles, "Behold, I send you out as sheep in the midst of wolves; so be wise as serpents and innocent as doves" (Matthew 10:16), while others see two agitated serpents facing off against each other, with the cross in between, as symbolizing the bishop's need for diligence in guarding the flock.

Mention of "the flock" brings us to the bishop's staff in the *Roman* Church. The image of Jesus as the good shepherd spoke volumes to the early Church as a metaphor for Divine care such that bishops, in time, carried a shepherd's crook (crosier) with its hooked end to symbolize "pastoral" care (pastoral meaning "of or relating to shepherds or herders")—interestingly, the hook on some crosiers ends in a snake's head. The purpose of the hook on a shepherd's crook was to catch wayward sheep that got themselves into awkward places. Since sheep varied in size, small-legged sheep needed a small hook while bigger sheep needed a larger one. In the twenty-first century, where the image of shepherd is almost obsolete, what would a hooked crosier symbolize—church authorities hooking free thinkers into line? Popes since Pope Paul VI's reign (1963–78) have not used the crosier, but carry instead the Papal Cross, a staff topped with a crucifix which is also a custom that goes back to before the thirteenth century.

The cross became a Christian symbol during Emperor Constantine's reign when Christianity became a tolerated religion favored by Constantine. Before this, the cross meant a criminal's death, and so other symbols, such as the fish and the anchor, were used. When I was a child, the cross symbol emitted loud denominational signals. Roman Catholics used crosses with the figure of Jesus (crucifix) in their churches, on rosaries and hung around their necks. In my Presbyterian tradition, however, crosses were few and far between in case they were seen as idols and worshipped. Never would they have the figure of Jesus on them because an empty cross symbolized the resurrection, the completed Easter event. Rarely did Protestants wear crosses around their necks, yet today most Protestant pastors have a stylized cross as part of their clothing and the cross has become a fashion statement in itself, worn by people with absolutely no interest in the meaning of the symbol and accompanying mini-skirts, high-heeled boots, multiple body piercings and hairy chests.

The swastika, an ancient form of a cross, was found in most cultures across the world including Egypt, Persia, Tibet, India, Africa's Gold Coast, Cyprus, Mycenae, England, Scotland and Israel. It symbolized the GOD of Light associated with the sun, is the sacred symbol second only to Om in Hinduism, is depicted in the footprint of the Buddha, represents the Greek GODs and is associated with the GOD Thor in Nordic traditions. In the 1920s it became the peace symbol for the United Nations and appeared in the 1930s on the national flags of Estonia, Finland and Latvia as the cross of Freedom. Author Rudyard Kipling (1865–1936) combined the swastika with his signature as a personal logo on many early editions of his books. As a symbol of good fortune and well-being, Swastika Clubs flourished in the United States and the nationally circulated Girls' Club magazine was called the *Swastika*. All would change when Adolf Hitler (1889–1945) adopted this symbol as the insignia and flag of the German Nazi Party in 1920. No symbol has been so completely transformed, from good fortune and well-being to the epitome of evil. In a film on Dietrich Bonhoeffer depicting the closing of the underground seminary of the German Confessing Church that opposed Hitler, the Gestapo ransacked the lecture room, symbolically changing the crucifix behind the podium into a swastika by extending each point at right-angles with paint. Today, few would dare to re-establish the swastika as a positive symbol, given the revulsion it carries across the world. One of my students wrote a paper on the swastika as a symbol in the world's religions and was quite nervous as she photocopied examples of its ancient usage in the university copying room, fearing that someone would ask questions—she even took home the discarded photocopies rather than drop them in the bin beside the public machine.

While a religious symbol represents something else, there is often a fine line between objects as symbols pointing to the Divine and objects that actually "become" sacred or facilitate in themselves some tangible contact between humans and the Divine. The centuries-long debate in Christianity as to whether the elements of bread and wine in the Eucharist are mere symbols of the body and blood of Christ or whether they change *into* Christ's body such that the recipient actually "eats" Christ is a classic example. Many things are said to be imbued with supernatural power. In Polynesia, anything possessing this *mana* is taboo—the tombs of chiefs, sacred shrines or sacred stones.

Taboos govern things connected with their fishing, building and carving indus-tries, since these important industries require Divine protection. The Chief and his family were also carefully protected so the *mana* they possessed did not weaken through contact with mundane things. In the twelfth-century chronicle of Henry of Huntington, *Historia Anglorum,* girdles containing supernatural power were placed around women in difficult labor and noblewomen had their girdles embroidered with mythical figures to ensure the birth of heroes. The Church forbade this "pagan" activity, said to originate with the Druids, and midwives were forbidden to use any "sorcerie, invocations, or praiers, other than suche as be allowable and may stand with the laws and ordinances of the Catholic Churche".[11] Perhaps the friars did not like competition, because unscrupulous ones were doing a nice trade in pieces of cloth said to have come from the Virgin's own cloak to lighten the pain of childbirth.

Possessions and relics of the saints are seen as physical transmitters of Divine power, or things through which Divine power is miraculously made visible. Thérèse of Lisieux (1873–97) described the sisters in her Carmelite convent rushing to seize a relic of the Mother Superior when she died. As for Thérèse:

> During her last agony, I noticed a tear shining on an eyelash like a lovely diamond. It stayed there, the last of all she had shed on earth, and I saw it glittering when her body was placed in the choir. In the evening I took a scrap of linen and went to her without anyone seeing me. And now I possess a saint's last tear.[12]

In Kandy, Sri Lanka, the seventeenth-century Temple of the Tooth (Sri Dalada Maligawa) holds the left eyetooth of the Buddha, taken from his funeral pyre. This sacred tooth used to be taken out of the temple once a year during *Esala Perahera*, a ten-day festival attracting over one million people— due to political tensions, only the casket has been paraded since 1990. In late July or early August, a royal male elephant bearing the casket heads the procession, flanked by two smaller elephants and followed by up to 100 magnificently decorated elephants that parade into town with fire dancers and torches to chase off evil. Acrobats, musicians, dancers and pilgrims follow the elephants, the parade ending on the last night in the temple to circle the shrine.

While claiming great respect for the Buddha and his teachings, John Stod-dard's 1912 travel journal describes that final evening ceremony as the blowing of discordant horns and beating of drums by a "horrible orchestra" with devotees "blear-eyed and half-naked":

[B]etween Buddha and the ordinary Buddhism of today there is a heaven-wide difference. Of this the Buddhistic Holy of Holies in Kandy is a proof; and, since this has for its conspicuous features the gross imposture of the "Sacred Tooth", a half-barbaric style of worship, and an environment of dirt and beggars, we realize how polluted has become the stream from so pure a spring.[13]

It is amazing that Stoddard could be so critical of this Buddhist ceremony when, apart from cultural differences of dress, language and ceremony, relics of the saints are honored in similar, often strange ways in Christianity. Wandering through Naples a few years ago, I stumbled on the festival of the miracle of San Gennaro (Januarius) at the Duomo. The cathedral was crowded with expectant people watching and waiting, especially at the altar rail. At 4 pm, an elaborately garbed priest entered the chancel and reached up to a gold case above the candles and red anthuriums to retrieve a round glass container with the congealed blood of San Gennaro. After turning it around in his hands for a while, he held it up to the crowd. A hissing sound began, changing to a chant that grew louder and louder as the crowd encouraged the blood to liquefy, no doubt feeling some small power in co-operating with GOD and the saint. Although I couldn't see from a distance, the blood liquefied and the priest walked back and forth at the altar rail as people kissed the container, some asking for it to be placed on their heads. The aisle was filled with people waiting in line to get to the altar rail and, every few moments, the priest rotated the container again to show it had liquefied. The street outside the cathedral had turned into a carnival, but without the elephants. Temporary stalls of candy, gifts and balloons lined the sidewalks, and men handed out cards of the saint for a donation. Two little girls had set up their small table with a few statues of saints. At 5 pm, when I hired a taxi to return to my hotel, the line waiting to kiss the blood was still long and there was an extra euro on my five-euro taxi fare, "supplemental" for St Gennaro's Day. Michael Kelly, an Irish singer, actor, composer and friend of Mozart's, witnessed this ceremony in 1770:

> It happened by some accident, that the Archbishop could not make the miracle work. The Lazzaroni and old women loudly called on the Virgin for assistance. "Dear Virgin Mary! Blessed Madonna! Pray use your influence with St Gennaro! Pray induce him to work the miracle! Do we not love him? Do we not worship him?" But when they found the saint inexorable, they changed their note, and seemed resolved to abuse him into compliance. They all at once cried out, "Porco di St Gennaro!"—"You pig

of a Saint!"—"Barone maladetto!"—"You cursed rascal!"—"Cane faccia gialutta!"—"You yellow-faced dog!" In the midst of this, the blood (thanks to the heat of the Archbishop's hand) dissolved. They again threw themselves on their knees, and tearing their hair (the old ladies particularly) with streaming eyes, cried, "Oh! Most Holy Saint, forgive us this once, and never more will we doubt your goodness!"[14]

Statues of Sacred Beings are also believed to contain the Divine, or at least facilitate Divine action, somehow bringing the Divine into our presence in a tangible way. Thus they are seen as sacred in themselves. One of my students doing a class presentation on Hinduism visited several Hindu services and festivals in our Midwest USA town and arrived for her presentation in a beautiful Indian sari borrowed from a new Indian friend, complete with a *bindi* (red dot) on her forehead. From a basket covered with a Red Riding Hood-style red and white checkered cloth, she produced statues of Shiva, Ganesh and Krishna, her new friend's family collection of Deities, lent on condition she returned them before night was over. A Catholic student in the class was very perturbed that she was handling them as a non-Hindu and asked what she had to *do* to them before returning them. Would they have to be "re-sacralized" after being handled this way? No, it seemed these Deities could happily be traveling GODS, even where other religions were being celebrated or hands other than Hindu ones handled them, so long as they returned home. People long indoctrinated in *their* traditions about the sacredness of statues and how to treat them are often nervous with someone else's symbols—a theophobia in the presence of "other" GODS. What if something "foreign" or "pagan" rubbed off on them?

Vietnamese Buddhist monk Thich Nhat Hanh, who has worked with many Christians in his peace efforts around the world and has shared the Eucharist with some of them, has images of both Buddha and Jesus on the altar at his hermitage in France:

[E]very time I light incense, I touch both of them as my spiritual ancestors. I can do this because of contact with these real Christians. When you touch someone who authentically represents a tradition, you not only touch his or her tradition, you also touch your own . . . For dialogue [between traditions] to be fruitful, we need to live deeply our own tradition and, at the same time, listen deeply to others. Through the practice of deep looking and deep listening, we become free, able to see the beauty and value in our own *and* others' traditions.[15]

8

Gurus and
Go-betweens

Prophets and religious teachers are like signs on the road, to guide spiritual travelers.
But those who have encountered God directly no longer need signs.
Their inner eye, combined with the divine lamp, is sufficient to keep them on the
right path.
Such people then become signs for others.

—Rumi[1]

Nikos Kazantzakis loved the Greek Orthodox saints of his childhood. As
soon as he could read, he bought a book of saints and spent each afternoon
reading the stories to the women and children of his Cretan village, embel-
lishing their ordeals until his mother would cry. Kazantzakis imagined the
saints' adventures as his own and even promoted his intrepid grandfather to
the rank of saint. He once tried to run away to become a saint but a fisher-
man at the wharf sent him home. His special hero was Saint Minas, patron
saint of his town. Since Crete was occupied by the Turks, the locals saw
St Minas as more than a saint—he was also their military captain against the
occupiers and they secretly brought their weapons to him to be blessed. The
icon of St Minas, which held pride of place in the local Orthodox church,
stirred Kazantzakis' young imagination:

Astride a gray horse, holding a red lance pointed at the sky, [Saint Minas]
remained motionless all day in his diminutive church, upon his icon—
fierce-eyed, sunburned, with a short curly beard. All day long, weighed
down by the silver ex-votos—hands, feet, eyes, heart—which the Kastri-
ans had attached to him so that his grace might heal them, he remained
immobile, pretending to be only a picture: paint on a piece of wood. But

as soon as night fell and the Christians gathered in their homes and the lights began going out one by one, he pushed aside paints and silver offerings with a sweep of his hand, spurred his horse, and went out for a ride through the Greek quarters, went out on patrol. He closed whatever doors the Christians had forgetfully left open, he whistled to night owls to return to their homes, he stood outside the doorway and listened absorbedly, with satisfaction, when he heard singing . . . Afterwards he made a tour of the ramparts which gird Megalo Kastro, and at cockcrow, before daybreak, spurred his horse, entered the church with a bound, and climbed onto his icon. Once more he put on a show of indifference. But his mount had perspired, its mouth and flanks were covered with froth, and when Mr. Haralámbis, the verger, came first thing in the morning to dust and polish the candlesticks, he saw Saint Minas' horse drenched in sweat. This did not surprise him, however, for he knew (everyone knew) that the saint patrolled the streets the entire night.[2]

Communities have always selected out a few people with seemingly magical or supernatural powers, or have trained selected individuals to become mediators of the Sacred, taking their petitions to the Divine and receiving Divine messages back. When such people die, they remain effective, able to work for you in the Divine realm, such as those canonized as saints. The role of these go-betweens depended on how their communities saw themselves in relation to the Sacred—whether they felt worthy to engage the Divine, whether the Divine was fickle or in need of bribes in order to act, or whether the Divine longed to make human contact and seek the human good. Richard Rodriguez received mixed messages about Divine interest in him as he grew up Mexican-American and attended an American Catholic school. The nuns at school introduced him, a sinner, to the Divine Judge. By third grade, he could distinguish between venial and mortal sins, perfect and imperfect contrition, sins of commission and sins of omission. He knew why some souls went to limbo, others to purgatory and others to heaven or hell for ever and ever. Confession was his only escape, with Christ the mediator between him and GOD. At home, however, the members of his family were suppliants, not sinners. The Divine wasn't the stern judge that could change their lives at a whim. They approached GOD not out of fear and guilt, but in confidence and out of need:

We prayed for favors and at desperate times. I prayed for help in finding a quarter I lost on the way home. I prayed with my family at times of illness and when my father was temporarily out of a job . . . Whether by man or women however, God the Father was rarely addressed directly. There were intermediaries to carry one's petition to Him. My mother had her group of Mexican and South American saints and near-saints (persons moving towards canonization). She favored a black Brazilian priest who, she claimed, was especially efficacious. Above all mediators there was Mary . . . the Mexican Virgin, *Nuestra Senora de Guadalupe*, the focus of devotion and pride for Mexican Catholics. The Mexican Mary "honored our people", my mother would say. "She could have appeared to anyone in the whole world, but she appeared to a Mexican." Someone like us. And she appeared, I could see from her picture, as a young Indian maiden—dark just like me.[3]

Some community intermediaries were chosen from birth or during their lifetime, while others chose themselves with claims of Divine messages or a "calling" to be a go-between. The latter path has, down the centuries and across religions, become the ultimate power trip for some, used by both the cunningly sane and the severely disturbed. Many proclaimed prophets had feet of clay which their holy calling somehow did not transform into solid rock. "Praise the Lord" (PTL)'s founder Jim Bakker ended up in prison after sexual misdemeanors and fraud charges, followed fast on his heels by television prophet Jimmy Swaggart, frequenter of sleazy motels and call-girls. Dotted through history, prophets have proclaimed a date for the end of the world and lived to see successful dates pass by without catastrophe. Smaller-sized prophets regularly proclaim "God told me . . .", guilting the faithful into paying special attention—and often money—for their privileged information. Others simply find the prophetic role handy in emergencies. A nineteenth-century cardinal, who took great delight in organizing and performing in elaborate ceremonial events, was once thwarted by a Master of Ceremonies who claimed that GOD had told him to stop the procession. Not at a loss, the cardinal replied, "Let the procession go on. I have just obtained permission, by special revelation, to proceed with it."[4]

Many indigenous go-betweens have been clumped under the term "shaman". In general, they were said to possess many powers, whether controlling and communicating with spirits, entering trances and ecstatic states, levitating, journeying outside the body or receiving visions and revelations. Some shamans could absorb spirits into themselves in order to protect the community from their powers, or invoke the presence of supernatural beings into selected sacred spaces. Shamans were essential in cultures that believed in a universe filled with good, evil and neutral spirits, in order to control these spirits. In Native American traditions, the shaman was also what became known as the "medicine man", the one with access to supernatural healing power and knowledge. As shamans aged, younger men groomed from an early age, like a prince to be king, took over the role. For hunting and fishing people of the central Arctic, the shaman (*angakok*) is the one who has made contact with the *Sila*, the fundamental all-pervasiveness of the universe. An *angakok* is prepared for this role and authorized by his society through ordeals and fasting and has ecstatic experiences that bestow special gifts on him.[5] In Shinto tradition, young female shamans (*miko*) are chosen early from selected families and face a rigorous life of celibacy, assisting the priests and performing sacred dances.

Bishop Jack Spong met Domingo, a practicing shaman, in the Amazon rain forest. Domingo saw himself as "spirit-filled" in the sense of one through whom the spirit flows and had served his people for 40 years banishing evil spirits and contacting the dead to check on their happiness. Selection for this role involved entering the forest as a youth and experiencing an ecstatic or visionary moment. To test these new powers, hallucinogenic leaves were used, allowing them to see things others could not, including causes of illness and the actions of evil spirits. Thus chosen by the "spirit of the forest", he or she was confirmed, if the tribe approved, as the next shaman and apprenticed to an ageing one. As Spong points out, all humans have a common search to ease life's anxieties and fear of death, and they design rituals and empower individuals to help with this task, whether it be Domingo the shaman or Jack Spong the bishop.

Are our modern explanations better than those of a people who inhabit the Amazon Rainforest? We do see through a wider lens. We have lived through changes in the perception of reality that have been given to us by the intellectual giants of our cultural past. We know things about the universe, about the laws of cause and effect, about our evolutionary history and about germs and viruses as the causes of sickness that they do not know . . . Every explanation is always an expression of cultural knowledge, but no explanation can ever be substituted for the human experience, which is common, universal and real . . . [Domingo] works within his animistic world view to make sense out of life. I work within my Western mechanistic world to make sense out of life. The goal of us both is to create human wholeness, to introduce us to transcendent dimensions of reality that our experience tells us must either be real or be delusional. Both Domingo and I are convinced that we are in touch with reality.[6]

Shamans see a world filled with spirits sharing space with humans. As anyone who has shared space with dogs, cats, boa constrictors or even other humans knows, co-operation and appeasement is the name of the game in the competition for space and power. Spirits have taken different shapes— angels, jinns, kachinas, mimi spirits—basically anything invisible with intermediary connections to the Deities. North American Hopi Indians see co-operation between lower and upper realms as central for harmony, good health, community peace and a reliable food supply. Kachinas serve as the symbolic intermediaries to help this happen, and kachina dolls are created as visible representations of these, not much different from the statues of saints in Christianity. Sometimes the most effective spirit intermediaries are departed relatives. In many African traditions, a deceased relative remains alive within the family as a spirit until there is no one left who can remember them in the flesh. Until then, they are consulted in decision-making and beseeched to help out with their spirit-power. When no longer personally remembered, these spirits can become fickle, unpredictable and thus unreliable. In the Lovedu religion of Transvaal, the most important ancestral spirit is a woman's mother—which certainly dampens all the mother-in-law jokes.

Angels and archangels are the Divine messengers and assistants in the Bible. An angel guarded the gates of the Divine Garden after Adam and Eve left; three angelic messengers visited Sarah and Abraham's tent with baby news, while another angel comforted Abraham's expelled mistress Hagar in the wilderness. A Jewish teenager, Mary, also received news of her impending pregnancy from an angel. In religious art, angels painted in clouds depicted the Divine realm. Italian artist Giotto di Bondone's (1267–1337) skies simply overflow with angels, and neutered, winged cherubs hold up the pedestals of saints and draw back marble curtains for glimpses of heavenly scenes in many a European cathedral. Angels diminished somewhat after the Enlightenment, when the supernatural was downplayed, but have reappeared with vengeance today far beyond the bounds of religious tradition. In my "Art and Religion" course, I had to remove "angel" from the list of religious symbols about which my students could write because their internet searches pulled up such a huge mishmash of "angel" literature which my students treated as absolute truth—personal angels, angelic miracles, angel dolls and pins, even *The Angel Bible: The definitive guide to angel wisdom* which, according to a reviewer, gives guidance on invoking angels, setting up an angel altar and invite angel messages, a far cry from the avenging angel that struck down the eldest child in each Egyptian family (Ex. 12:29). In Islam, angels *(mala'ika)*, such as Gabriel and Michael, are thought to be made of light. The tempter or Devil Iblis is a rebel angel made of smokeless fire, like a jinn. These angels are superior to humans but inferior to the prophets as Divine messengers.

Speaking of prophets, Jewish, Christian and Islamic prophets, according to the sacred texts, were chosen by GOD to communicate a special Divine message for a particular time, not people predicting the future as the word is often used today. Despite different circumstances into which the Hebrew prophets were sent, they had basically one message—repent of whatever the people were doing or suffer Divine consequences. In fact, much of the Hebrew Bible is a roller-coaster ride of the Hebrews disobeying Divine rules, snubbing their noses at their covenant with Yahweh, receiving warnings from the prophets, persistence in disobedience bringing on Divine punishment, then repentance and reunion, until the next act of disobedience. The prophetic role was not necessarily a safe or pleasant one. We can only imagine Daniel's terror as he had watched three friends thrown into the furnace for displeasing King Nebuchadnezzar! Although personally in the king's good books for interpreting a previous dream, this time Daniel had to tell the king that GOD would cut him down to size for his pride and drive him from society to live like an animal until he repented (Daniel 4).

Biblical prophets couldn't simply claim that role—they had to be tested to avoid false prophesy. GOD tells Ezekiel to testify against some other prophets who were misleading the people by prophesying "out of their own imagination" (Ezek. 13:17). John the Baptist was a prophet, preaching the need for repentance, as was Jesus, the one who followed him. Muslims acknowledge Abraham, Moses, Amos, Micah, Isaiah and Jesus (plus others) as prophets, with Muhammad the final prophet—all conduits through whom GOD spoke, but not GOD. As theologian Hans Küng says, "Muhammad never thought he had brought anything fundamentally new; he had merely brought something new *to his people*—and that was only because the first proclamation had fallen into oblivion."[7] "Final" is a hard act to maintain. In the early nineteenth century, a Shi'ite Muslim sect emerged in Iran under a leader who claimed to be the *Bāb*, "gateway" to the hidden Imam, and later the Imam himself who was long predicted to return and bring peace and justice to the earth. *Bāb* was executed in Persia, but under a new prophet Bahā'u'llah, a follower of *Bāb*, the Baha'i faith emerged. While the *Bāb*'s group had been both authoritarian and sectarian, Baha'i became a universal religion with no formal rituals, priesthood or dogmas and stressed unity of all faiths. Baha'is do not claim that Bahā'u'llah will be the *final* prophet, but rather the one sent from GOD for this time.

Sometime prophets, like Bahā'u'llah, become leaders of new religious movements as their followers recognized them as mediators of the Divine or aids to enlightenment. Jesus began as a prophet like Elijah and John the Baptist, but became (not in his lifetime) the leader of a new religion. The Buddha was a prophet, teaching how to live in his day, but his followers transformed his teachings into a new religion that would flourish across Asia. "The blind can only find the path if they are guided by people with eyes," Rumi said. "In the same way the spiritually blind can only find their path to God if they are guided by people with religious vision."[8] Rumi also began as a prophet in thirteenth-century Afghanistan. He came from a family of religious leaders and taught at the royal court at Rum (Konya). At 37, after an intense spiritual experience, Rumi abandoned his "arid" doctrines to join an eccentric wandering Sufi named Shams. Rumi eventually gathered his own brotherhood of ecstatic mystics, the Mevlevis, around him, resisting intellectual knowledge for the Divine Light within:

> Knowledge acquired through learning, and knowledge as a gift from God, are as different and as far apart as earth from heaven. Knowledge from God is like the light of the sun; knowledge through learning is merely the dull reflection of that light. Knowledge from God is like a raging fire; knowledge through learning is like a spark from that fire.[9]

His followers whirled and sang for joy, hence their name Whirling Dervishes, and Rumi's writings were gathered into the *Masnavi*, known to many as "the Qur'an of the Persian tongue".

While Rumi formed a group within Islam, other prophets started new religions altogether. Zoroaster (Zarathustra, *c.* 628–551 BCE) from eastern Iran taught that there were two Divine Forces, the bounteous Ahura Mazda and the destructive Angra Mainyu, a cosmic divide between good and evil. Humans had to choose between these two. After death, those who have done good deeds and harbored good thoughts will cross the Chinvat Bridge (the Bridge of Judgement) into paradise, but the wicked fall from the bridge to be "guests in the house of the Lie", [with] poor food, foul smells, torment and woe.[10] Initially, Zoroaster was not heeded, but when he miraculously cured the king's horse, things changed. His teachings are contained in seventeen hymns (*Gāthās*), making up their holy scripture, the *Avesta*. For the Parsis (Zoroastrians) of India, Zoroaster was more than human, the Divine presence on earth, but in Iran he is a human prophet.[11] This ancient religion first gave the Hebrew people, exiled in Babylon, ideas of an afterlife and a cosmic battle between good and evil. King Cyrus, the Persian (Zoroastrian) king who captured Babylon in 539 BCE, allowed the Jewish exiles to return to Jerusalem, making Cyrus the only non-Israelite designated in the Hebrew Bible as GOD's anointed, a *Messiah* (Isaiah 45:1).

Prophets come in all shapes and sizes—some relatively harmless, some weird and some lethal. Religion is one of the few places people can gain absolute control over others simply by claiming a "call" or "anointing" from GOD. Since fear of death or Divine judgement is never far beneath the human surface, claims to alleviate these uncertainties attract the fearful like moths to a flame, especially if benefits are painted in glowing terms, either in this life or the next. American Jim Jones (1931–78) left the Methodist Church and formed his own church, Wings of Deliverance, in 1954 (later the People's Temple). By the 1960s, the Christian Church (Disciples of Christ) had ordained Jones without any formal theological training and he began to see himself as a prophet and manifestation of the Christ principle with power to heal. He moved his temple to Ukiah, California and established a second temple in San Francisco but, on losing tax-exempt status in 1977, he moved his followers to a remote area of Guyana where members lived in a tightly controlled community, with public confession and punishment for transgressions. Concerned relatives initiated a Congressional investigation, led by Congressman Leo Ryan (1925–78), who flew to Jonestown and was murdered, with others, by a commune member. That night in 1978, a "revolutionary suicide" with cordial mixed with poison ended the cult—their premeditated finale if their idealistic goals failed.

A similar mass suicide occurred in San Francisco in 1997 in order that members of the "Heaven's Gate" cult could board their arriving spaceship, Haley's Comet, for a place where Ti and Do reigned. A more earthly conflagration occurred with the Branch Davidians, a Texas offshoot of Seventh Day Adventism led by prophet David Koresh (Vernon Howell, 1959–93). Howell began work as a handyman in a group founded by Benjamin Roden (1902–78). When Roden died, his wife Lois (1905–86) claimed leadership, and David, her prodigy and lover, became leader after her death. Claiming Divine sanction, Howell began taking "spiritual wives", first the unmarried women and then wives of members, saying that, as Messiah, he was the perfect mate to spawn a lineage of God's children who would rule the world. Howell adopted the name David Koresh—Koresh is Hebrew for the Persian King Cyrus already mentioned and David cemented a link to the biblical King David. Koresh taught that Christ died for those *prior* to his death, while Koresh was to bring salvation for subsequent generations. In contrast to the "sinless" Christ model, Koresh was a "sinful" Messiah, showing that sin did not prevent humans attaining salvation. By 1992, Koresh had predicted that the final apocalypse (Armageddon) would happen in the United States with an attack on them, so they began stockpiling food and weapons. He basically invited fulfillment by resisting a Bureau of Alcohol, Tobacco and Firearms raid in 1993 which ended in an inferno, killing over 80 members.

Koresh is one of many who have claimed to be the Jewish Messiah or the second coming of Christ. In Manchester, England, Ann Lee (1736–84) received notice from GOD that she was the female element of the Godhead and the new bringer of salvation. Moving to the United States, she founded the Shakers, a celibate community living a simple, communal celibate life. "Shaker" came from an involuntary Spirit possession that developed into a formalized type of dancing as part of worship. Initially, community numbers increased by taking in orphans, but when this source dried up, their celibacy caught up with them such that, in December 2009, there were only three members left. In 2002, the Raëlians made world news when Dr Brigitte Boisselier, a Raëlian bishop and head of its organization "Clonaid", announced they had successfully cloned the first human baby. The founder Claude Vorilhon, born in 1946 in Vichy, France, is a motor-racing journalist and singer known as Raël who claimed to see a flying saucer and talk with a space alien in 1973. For Raël, the Bible is the story of human interaction with the *Elohim* (plural Hebrew term for GODS), extraterrestrial beings who created the world and humankind.[12] One group, the Nephilim, had sex with humans (Gen. 6:1–2) and produced a race with superior intelligence, the Jews. Jesus resulted from sex between the human Mary and an Elohim, and Raël also claims a human–extraterrestrial conception. As the new Messiah (their calendar dates from Raël's birth), Raël is preparing humans for the Elohim's peaceful arrival on earth and their adoption as our leaders. Their government will admit to office only those with an intelligence 50 percent higher than average, and scientific development, material prosperity and increased leisure time will be promoted, with robots doing menial tasks. After death, the Grand Council of the Eternals determines whether a human should be re-created by cloning from cell banks held inside an embassy to be built in Jerusalem, or experience oblivion, unless re-created for other purposes such as returning suicide bombers to earth to stand trial.

Divine incarnations are naturally the most direct messengers to humanity. Hinduism has many incarnations (Avatars) of the One Brahman that have appeared at different times according to need. Brahman's three major incarnations are Brahma the Creator, Vishnu the Preserver and Shiva the Destroyer. Vishnu, as preserver of each world era, has ten incarnations—fish (Matsya), turtle (Kurma), boar (Varaha), man-lion (Nrusimha), dwarf (Vamana), Rama with ax (Parasurama), Sree Rama the Ideal (Ramayana), Krishna, Buddha and Kalki, the one still to come, leaving incarnational activity possible in the future. It is not hard to see why Hindu gurus simply incorporated Jesus and his message into their own tradition—a new messenger (Avatar) of the One. Buddha was named in Hinduism as the eighth incarnation of Vishnu, and in later evolutions of Buddhism the bodhisattva emerged as someone on the final path to Buddhahood who, with compassion for all, postpones enlightenment to help others—"Though I attain Buddhahood, I shall never be complete until everyone in my land is certain of entering Buddhahood and gaining Enlightenment."[13] In Mahayana Buddhism, bodhisattvas are always present and helping in the world, using their own powers, through meditation and merit, to help others.

The bodhisattva that incarnates the supreme qualities of compassion is Avalokiteshvara, appearing in whatever form is necessary to help living beings. Although originally male in India, in Chinese and Japanese Buddhism he is portrayed as the female Quan (Kuan or Shih) Yin, the GODDESS of Mercy and protector of women, children and sailors. She is a universal image in that her qualities of mercy, love and compassion are those also imaged in the Virgin Mary in the West. In fact, when I visited a marble factory in Vietnam, I was intrigued to notice that the statues of the Virgin Mary were on one shelf and those of the bodhisattva Quan Yin next to them, almost identical in appearance and pose. In Tibet, the succession of fourteen Dalai Lamas (the first one born in 1351 CE), are reincarnations of each other and of Avalokiteshvara (Chenrezig, the bodhisattva of compassion).

Kings, chiefs and emperors were once seen as incarnations of the GODS. Emperor worship in ancient Rome began with Augustus (31 BCE) and took priority over any other worship, something early Christians found difficult. The Emperor was called the "Son of God" and "Saviour" of the people, language that biblical scholars today think was metaphorically applied to Jesus as a subversive claim that Jesus was an alternative, non-violent "Son of God" and "Saviour" to Caesar. John Dominic Crossan says:

[I]magine this question. There was a human being in the first century who was called "Divine", "Son of God", "God", and "God from God", whose titles were "Lord", "Redeemer", "Liberator", and "Savior of the World". Who was that person? Most people who know the Western tradition would probably answer, unless alerted by the question's too-obviousness, Jesus of Nazareth. And most Christians probably think that those titles were originally created and uniquely applied to Christ. But before Jesus ever existed, all those terms belonged to Caesar Augustus.[14]

And so we come to Jesus. Volumes of books have been written on who Jesus was, hardly something to cover in one paragraph in one chapter, but for many serious biblical scholars today (and many in the past), Jesus began his adult life as a Jewish prophet proclaiming the reign of GOD, a non-violent alternative to the dominant Roman Empire under which the Jews suffered, and was murdered for speaking out against the authorities. As Dorothee Sölle said, "The basis of faith is not that it was Christ who spoke with divine authority; the basis of faith is the praxis of the poor man from Nazareth who shared his bread with the hungry, made the blind see, and lived and died for justice."[15] His followers believed that the Spirit in him was still with them after his death and that he was, in fact, the promised Messiah (anointed one). After the Jewish War of 70 CE when the Temple was destroyed, Jesus' followers were evicted from the Jewish synagogues and the emerging sect became dominated by Greek-speaking converts across Asia Minor. The Jewish man with a message from GOD would become, with the help of the Caesar terminology just described, the Greco-Roman Divine–human "Son of GOD", second Person of the Divine Trinity. This metamorphosis was obviously gradual, since the fourth-century Councils, called to decide on orthodoxy, were still arguing whether Jesus was actually GOD or simply "like" God and, if so, how could the human and Divine be mixed in one body?

There is a big difference between the biblical statements, "God was in Christ reconciling the world to Himself" (2 Cor. 5:19) and "Jesus *is* GOD." Jesus as a messenger of GOD was so attuned to the Divine message that he could say, "Whoever has seen me has seen the Father" (John 14:9), without this meaning he was GOD. To the disciples he did not claim to be GOD in these words, "I do not speak on my own; but the Father who dwells in me does his works. Believe me that I am in the Father and the Father is in me; but if you do not, then believe me because of the works themselves" (John 14:10–11). A student once raised his hand in a World Religions class when I began to talk about Hinduism and its many Divine incarnations. "But they're wrong," he said. "The Bible says that *Jesus* is the Way, the truth and the life." "How do you think your comment would sound to a Hindu?" I asked, "or to a Muslim who feels that Christianity distorted the story of GOD by making Jesus more than a prophet and equal to God? How would you prove that your 'truth' statement is more 'true' than theirs?" Theologian Sallie McFague writes:

God is incarnate *in the world*. Jesus is the clue to this, the place where Christians look to see what it means, but divine incarnation is not limited

to Jesus . . . This in no way lessens the importance of Jesus Christ to Christians, for he is, to us, the revelation of God, the one who allows us to see
what divine incarnation means and how we, too, can live within God's
reality.[16]

American author Thomas Cahill suggests that such a reassessment of
what Christians mean by GOD incarnate in Jesus would allow for a
Jewish–Christian reconciliation where Jews could

> acknowledge Jesus as one of their own, not as the Messiah, but as a
> brother who called God "abba". For Christians, it may be time to
> acknowledge that we have misunderstood Jesus in virtually every way that
> matters. As Raymond Brown [biblical scholar and priest, 1928–1998]
> was fond of remarking, if Jesus were to return to earth, the first thing we
> would do is crucify him again.[17]

As the role and person of Jesus evolved, so did his mother's, from poor
Jewish teenager to *Theotokos*, Mother of God and Queen of Heaven. The
church San Luigi el Francese in Rome has three sixteenth century Caravaggio
paintings of the life of Saint Matthew but, according to a guidebook, these
paintings could not be viewed publicly for many years because the artist had
painted the saints and the Virgin Mary realistically—with dirty feet. Exalted
in Roman Catholicism and almost ignored in Protestantism, Mary finds an
appreciative home in the Qur'an, receiving more attention there than any
other woman. Of 114 chapters (surahs) in the Quran, only eight people have
a chapter named after them, yet the nineteenth chapter is named after Mariam
(Maryam, Mary). In Christianity, as Mary's status rose as both virgin and
mother, the status of Eve and all non-virginal mothers (temptresses, sinners
and polluted bodies) fell. Crowned in heaven (but not quite Divine), she
became the blessed one who could best mediate between sinners and her
Divine Husband and Son. Miracles too numerous to mention have been attributed to her, this accessible one. In Heviz, Hungary, a site of natural mineral
springs, I found a new shopping center named after the Roman Emperor
Flavius who ruled this area and the eastern Roman Empire between 279 and
295 CE. On the wall of the center, I read the story of a Christian nurse who
begged the Virgin to cure a little crippled boy, and a mineral spring gushed
out, healing the child. He grew up to be Flavius Theodosius and, remembering
his miraculous cure, made Christianity the state religion of his region.

Close to, but lower than Mary, stand the saints, those who have led exem-
plary lives on earth and, in their place of reward, convey help and blessings

on others. In everyday speech, we call people saints—"You are such a saint to do this!"—meaning that someone is living in a way that causes others to respect and honor their behavior. In Islam, a saint or holy man is a *wali* meaning "a friend or person near God". People make pilgrimages to their tombs after their deaths and their anniversaries are celebrated. Catholic saints are officially created after their death, depending on certain criteria about their lives. According to the Apostolic Constitution *Divinus Perfectionis Magister* promulgated by Pope John Paul II in 1983, five years must pass after the death of the candidate to ensure objectivity. The bishop of the person's region must begin the process, a diocesan tribunal is formed and witnesses called as to the person's virtues. A postulator resident in Rome prepares the case, under the direction of the Congregation for the Causes of Saints, which is examined first by nine theologians, then the cardinals and bishops, and then the Pope. A miracle performed by the proposed saint must be produced and investigated and then the Pope decides about beatification which gives them the title "Blessed". Another miracle attributed to the intercession of the beatified and occurring after beatification is needed for canonization. Again, the Pope decides for or against canonization and the title of "saint".[18]

Saint Thérèse of Lisieux was canonized just 28 years after her death in 1897, aged 24. Few people knew her except for the little book she wrote, *The Story of a Soul* (1898), which sold millions around the globe. The book's simple message was of GOD's unshakeable love and instant forgiveness, thus no one need fear GOD, and every act done for GOD takes on great value because of the motive behind it. Thérèse and her four sisters all entered a convent where they could "wait for heaven" together.[19]

> How happy simple nuns are! The will of their superiors is their only compass and so they are always certain of traveling in the right direction. They can never feel mistaken, even if they are certain their superiors are wrong.[20]

Why was Thérèse canonized when she lived such a short time and spent almost half that time in an enclosed monastery? Because her book became a "missionary" in itself, endearing her to millions as the saint who could mediate for them. I once heard a retirement lecture by a professional man ending a great career. He talked of three people who had most influenced his life, all men from different centuries. Chatting with him afterwards, I commented that women did not have such mentors from long ago because their writings were not kept. The next day he confessed to me that, if he had been really honest, three *women* had most influenced him, one of them being Saint Thérèse because his fiancée had given him her book as he went off to the Second World War and he had read it and carried it with him all through that time.

As links between us and the Divine, saints specialize, usually in association with their own history. The third-century martyr Saint Appolonia, who was burned alive after having her teeth smashed out by an Alexandrian mob, is the patron saint of toothache and dentists. Fourth-century martyr Saint Lucia, patron saint of her home town of Siracusa (Sicily), was stabbed in the throat and her eyes put out before being killed. Depicted in religious art with her eyes on a plate, she is the patron saint of eye problems and blindness. Third-century Saint Agatha, patron saint of Catania (Sicily), refused to marry a Roman proconsul because she was promised to GOD. He had her breasts cut off with pincers before being roasted in a kiln and she died two days later. Her relics—a breast, parts of her arms, a foot and her veil—lie in Catania's Cathedral, and since Catania is close to the active volcano Mount Etna, many averted lava flows are attributed to Saint Agatha, or her veil held high before the flow. During the week of her death (February 5), a massive pro-cession takes place in Catania as her remains are taken from her vault in the Cathedral and paraded through the streets in a silver carriage, complete with her statue encrusted with precious jewels, all donations from wealthy petitioners in exchange for favors. Practically everything in Catania is geared to Saint Agatha, from her many statues, pincers in one hand and breasts on a plate in the other, to special St Agatha cupcakes in the coffee shops with white icing and a red cherry for the nipple.

Saints are kept very busy around the world. When I visited St Peter's Church in Vienna, I described the scene in my journal:

It was eternally busy, something like Central Station or a video on fast forward, a cacophony of gold, marble, tapestry, ceramics, plastic flowers, plaster saints, martyrs, angels and cardinals earnestly pursuing their own path to God, bumping into each other in petrified motion. While God and Jesus looked down from the heavens, accompanied by their entourage of angels, church fathers and prosperous laymen, monks were being slain on the walls in grim detail, women were being raped and Jesus was being crucified—so many miracles, murders and marvels in process at once. No wonder the poor peasants were wowed with the lives of saints when their own seemed so tame and bare. Although they suffered, ordinary folk never expected *their* humble lives would deserve miraculous intervention and so they worshipped those to whom the miracles happened. It was patently obvious, as they clutched their many children around them, that only those who had chosen the path of celibacy, preferably with martyr-dom, received the blessings of stigmata, visions and healing powers.

Writer Luigi Barzini (1908–84) called Italy one of the last Western coun-tries "where the great Pan is not dead, where life is still gloriously pagan, where Christianity has not deeply disturbed the happy traditions and customs of ancient Greece and Rome, and where the Renaissance has not spent itself".[21] According to him, Roman Catholicism is a thin veneer over older customs, and the many saints venerated as protectors in villages are the old local GODS disguised. Even their names are thinly disguised. Santa Venerina, whom the people around Mount Etna believe makes barren women fertile, is like Venus or *Venere* (Italian) of old. The relics of Saint Gennaro (Januarius), the patron saint of Naples (whose dried-up blood liquefied), stopped Mount Vesuvius' lava flow at the very gates of the city. Was he Janus, the Roman protector of all portals and doors?[22] Saint George, patron saint of England, was martyred at Lydda around 303 CE, and statues of him slaying the dragon are found in practically all Christian churches around Europe such that my husband began photographing, for entertain-ment, the various artistic interpretations of him while trailing after me through churches (his other project is recording which of Jesus' feet is crossed over the other in crucifixes). The slaying of the dragon was probably bor-rowed from the Greek myth of Perseus rescuing Andromeda from the sea monster, but it also appears in many legends of Saint George rescuing damsels in distress. Saint George rose to fame when Richard the Lionheart's (1157–99) crusade to the Holy Land (1189–92) conquered Lydda, and Richard made George the patron saint of his army and of soldiers. Medieval knights wore George's ensign on their shields and military attire (a red cross on a white background) and shouted his name as a battle cry. After the Battle of Agincourt in 1415, a national religious feast day was declared in England in his honor.

Popes continue to canonize saints. Mother Teresa (1910–97) was beauti-fied in 2003 by Pope John Paul II, the shortest time after a saint's death in modern history—she is now being examined for canonization and sainthood. On December 21, 2009, the Pope approved a second miracle for Mary MacKillop (1842–1909) and named her Australia's first saint in February 2010. But are there other ways to be a saint? Trappist monk Thomas Merton (1915–68) said that a saint preaches sermons by the way he talks and the way she walks and the way he stands and the way she sits down and the way he picks things up and holds them in his hand:[23]

For me to be a saint means to be myself. Therefore the problem of sanctity and salvation is in fact the problem of finding out who I am and of discovering my true self. Trees and animals have no problem. God makes them what they are without consulting them, and they are perfectly satisfied. With us it is different. God leaves us free to be whatever we like. We can be ourselves or not, as we please.. But the problem is this: since God alone possesses the secret of my identity, He alone can make me who I am or rather, He alone can make me who I will be when I at last fully begin to be.[24]

9

Community, Clergy and Caretakers

In springtime in the lands of the sun the church is the Lord's sitting room; his friends, men and women alike, go there, seat themselves in the rows of chairs, and engage in small talk, at one moment with God, at the next with their neighbors. God's servant comes and goes, habited in white lace and a black or red dress. He rings the little bell and in a sweet voice chants the praises of Saint Francis, the master of the house. Then the guests rise, say goodbye, and head for the door. They have paid their visit to the Saint; now the visit is over. Heaven laughs with satisfaction, and below on earth the taverns open their doors.

—Nikos Kazantzakis[1]

A three-storied Georgian revival building stands in Market Square, Newport, Rhode Island. This Seamen's Church Institute was founded in 1919 by local residents to assist sailors docked in their harbor. The building houses a café, library, internet service, chaplaincy and a memorial garden. The walls of its Chapel of the Sea are covered in murals featuring saints linked with the sea and stories about the sea. Eleven beds provide transitional housing and donated clothing, and food is distributed to those working on the waterfront. Volunteers also take soup to workers on the lobster and fishing piers. Of the many people helped in this haven away from home, one man had been released from prison and was offered his old job back in a Newport marine business. Because his family lived out of town without transport, he would lose this fresh start unless he could find affordable housing. The Institute took him in. The guest book records oceans of emotion—"Would that every harbor has a warm, dry, friendly haven like this! Many thanks" . . . "The chapel was a peaceful haven for me today" . . . "Very moving and peaceful, a home off the boat."

What comes to mind when you hear the word "home"? Do you think of a country, a town, the house in which you grew up, the home you have now? Do you think of your nationality or certain people in your life, or do you think of all this as temporary with heaven your home? When our children were little, we lived in England and would spend each weekend driving around the country, staying in bed-and-breakfasts. Although easier to find last-minute than now, we would start looking at around 4 pm. If I came out of too many places saying "They're full," our three-year-old would start asking, "when will we find a home?" Once installed in someone's upper room, she would jump up and down singing "We're home! We're home!" No doubt the Hebrew exiles in Babylon felt the same way when told by GOD that they would return to their homeland and "settle on their own soil that I gave to my servant Jacob. They shall live in safety in it, and shall build houses and plant vineyards . . . And they shall know that I am the Lord their God" (Ezek. 28:25–26).[2]

While "home" for most of us is the place where we live, what also helps define home is recalling when we have said "I feel really at home here" when it was not our home, or when we did *not* feel at home. Home is more than a place or people—it has to do with a shared ethos, whether religious, ethnic, or genetic. Many years ago as a theology student, I read up about the Puritans in order to write an essay on them. Prior to that, I knew only the stereotypes, but when I began to read, I wrote this journal entry:

There is such wealth in discovering your roots—not where you were born but where your thought patterns originated. I never knew what the Puritans really thought—they were always just a term for restrictive religious practices—but when I read about where they came from and what they thought, it is the story of who *I* am, raised Presbyterian with definite Puritan leanings. While much is said about who we are according to where we were born, the important test is where we learned our moral and ethical compass. Life is about making choices, and these are not made according to whether you are Australian or African, but how you were trained to choose—my training had a Puritan bent. Many people never know how subtly influential their religious history has been if they have shucked it off long before. Their moral principles may now be a protest, the opposite of their religious origins. Half of our life is spent revising and adapting our upbringing. The best definition of home has to do with relationships.

Australian cartoonist Michael Leunig, noted for his weird, wacky but thoughtful humor, was scribbling one day, lost for something to draw, when he drew a man with a large curl on his head returning home and called it "Mr Curly Comes Home". At the time, he simply saw it as interesting. He drew Mr Curly's wife and children running to meet him, all with a curl on their head. The dog, the pet duck, the roof of the house, the garden plants and trees all had the curl. As he pondered what he had drawn, it struck him it was about "reunion". The very thing that made Mr Curly odd in the world was the thing that defined him at home where everything was curly! We all need a place where what defines us as odd, alien or estranged in the world is "normal", where we belong and are "at home".

To feel at home, we first need a relationship with *ourselves*, the only human relationship guaranteed to last until death. A man was seen parading through downtown Chicago with a sandwich board saying, "Bad news! Bad news! The world isn't coming to an end. You're going to have to cope."[3] Along with relating to ourselves, we need intimate relationships with a partner, close friends or a family, biological or chosen. Even though it is legendary that many people hate family reunions, the party goes on because there is something about being family that makes us endure the worst people for a few hours so the ritual of gathering can happen. American poet Robert Frost (1874–1963) said, "Home is the place where, when you have to go there, they have to take you in."[4] We also have relationships in communities where we feel at home—church, temple, mosque, Rotary club or neighborhood. Richard Rodriguez writes of his childhood Mexican village—"The steps of the church defined the eternal square where children played and adults talked after dinner. [My father] remembers the way the church building was the center of town life. [My mother] remembers the way one could hear the bell throughout the day, telling time. And the way the town completely closed down for certain feast days."[5] Those who have traveled and made friends across the globe have a world "home" as well—there are so many places where we have been invited into a stranger's home in another country and felt "at home", even when we do not share a language. Finally, with the largest circumference of all, we can feel a relationship with, and be at home in, the universe with the Sacred. "It is entirely reasonable, rational, sane", philosopher John Hick says, "for those who participate in what is apparently an awareness of the Transcendent to believe, and to base their lives on the belief, that in living as physical beings within the natural world we are at the same time living in relation to a transcendent-and-immanent reality whose presence changes the meaning for us of everything that we do and happens to us."[6]

We tend in the West to think of ourselves first as individuals who *then* decide to join groups or, if born into a group, decide whether or not to stay. This is why many people today identify themselves as "spiritual" rather than "religious", a fear of being labeled part of a group that has gone out of fashion, lost its standing in the world or clings to ideas past their use-by date. Young adults who will no longer go to church or temple will identify with self-help groups or follow gurus outside traditional religious boxes. People *want* to belong to something, even though we are a generation that celebrates individuality. Television evangelists know this. You can belong to their "church" without venturing outside your door. You are invited into their pad of opulent drapes, Raphaelite cherubs and glittering jewelry—and seemingly into their confidence. You may meet grandson Chad, tour their sumptuous home and gaze into their bedroom. They pour out tears of compassion for you and tears of contrition *to* you for their latest scandal. You are *important* to them—and need to give money because, if you don't, people might spend eternity in hell if the program closes. Your special lapel pin tells you that you belong and you can be part of a prayer "family" without having to meet the rest of your tribe. You can even buy a miracle, or have your name on a prayer tower, like buying indulgences in Luther's time. Television has created your "reality", tidying up any disconnect with a hot, dusty Jesus trudging between Jerusalem and Galilee. In the same way, Facebook, Twitter, Skype, internet dating and i-Phones are filling the human need for community—young people today probably spend more time with disembodied friends than with flesh-and-blood ones. While preachers, prophets and popes have claimed to be GOD's face and voice, GOD may now have to sign on to a Facebook page.

Despite this turn to individual spirituality, religion and community have always gone together, like the song "You can't have one without the other". Religions are practical and social, and shared ideas about the Sacred have to be *lived*, not just believed. "It is no use magisterially weighing up the teachings of religion to judge their truth or falsehood before embarking on a religious way of life," Karen Armstrong says, "you will discover the truth—or lack of it—only if you translate these doctrines into ritual or ethical action. Like any skill, religion requires perseverance, hard work and discipline. Some people will be better at it than others . . . but those who do not apply themselves will get nowhere at all."[7] Significantly, when the Buddha put together a way to live, the three essentials in which one could take refuge were the Buddha, the dharma (teachings) and the sangha, the community. At the Parliament of the World's Religions (2009), having said that all religions have a similar message of compassion, love, harmony, contentment and peace, the Dalai Lama challenged the assembly to take a more active role in promoting world peace, bringing compassion to the planet and listening to indigenous people about caring for the environment. Such action would allow the next Parliament to talk about what we have actually *done*.

In religious communities, we act together in rituals, prayers, social concerns and celebration. A community provides a structure in which to seek the Sacred and offers an opportunity for "sacred time" within the world and the everyday. By marking the stages of our lives together, we become part of a long history of those who also celebrated their stages of birth, puberty, marriage and death before us. Such regulating of life drives away the fear of meaninglessness and chaos. Even those who walk away from religious rituals keep other rituals that renew and re-create their otherwise humdrum lives. We even call them "recreation"—national holidays, sporting events, days at the beach or hiking in the mountains. Whatever motivates us has to be constantly renewed as it tends to run down and become impotent. Religious communities know the need to move regularly into sacred time "in which the realities of the sacred story are experienced as new and present once again. Ordinary time is transcended, and the people of now become contemporary with the gods and the founders and heroes of the Beginning Time. The rituals and festivals provide a rhythm of periodic renewal."[8]

At a time when many young people are abandoning traditional churches, American mega-churches are booming with some five million weekly attendees. According to Professor Scott Thumma, author of a recent survey on mega-church attendees, "Participants interact with the mega-church on their own terms, to meet their individualized needs rather than following some prescribed or idealized plan created by the church's leadership."[9] These people are mostly under 45, more educated and affluent than the average church attendee, and one-third are single. While most are not new to Christianity, one-quarter of them have not been recently associated with another church. Forty-five percent of mega-church attendees never volunteer at church and 40 percent don't attend small groups. In an age of individualism and self-absorption, these people have not lost the need for community in their search to engage the Divine, but they want it on their own terms, in their own timetable and with a say in what involvement they will accept.

Communities exist around shared stories. In such company, a story need not be told in its entirety to make sense—just a few words are necessary. "Remember Uncle Joe's fishing trip" is enough to send ripples of laughter through a family as they recall something they have heard many times, but the memory still brings joy. Take a minute to think of phrases in your family that do the same. Such family stories become apocryphal with embellishments that may or may not represent original events, especially if the protagonist is dead and families remember him or her as larger than life. Religious communities have *their* shared stories, with ritual and liturgy serving as codes to remember the stories over and over. There is both the mega-story of GOD and a local way of telling it, as different denominations demonstrate. "Nothing changes more constantly than the past," writer Gerald White Johnson (1890–1980) said, "for the past that influences our lives does not consist of what actually happened, but of what men believe happened."[10] In the past, people were imprisoned or killed for telling the mega-story of GOD the "wrong" way. From calculations done as a canon at Fromback's Cathedral (Poland), Nicolaus Copernicus (1473–1543) decided that the earth revolved around the sun. Only on his deathbed did he allow his work to be published, because he knew the scorn—or worse—he would receive from the Church for describing the universe in a different way. Ecclesial opposition came not from the Church's own research, but because they believed that the philosopher Aristotle (384–322 BCE) could not be wrong. "They wish never to raise their eyes from those pages," Galileo (1564–1642) said of the church fathers, "as if this great book of the universe had been written to be read by nobody but Aristotle, and his eyes had been destined to see for all posterity."[11]

Religious communities tell their mega-story according to their context. It must be transformative or "good news" for *their* particular situation, and their trials and troubles will be reflected in their worship, symbols, prayers and liturgy. South American poor found "good news" in the Christian story when they realized that Jesus was actually on the side of the poor, rather than their rich and powerful oppressors. Grace Cathedral in San Francisco tells its mega-story from living with HIV/AIDS and losing thousands of members to this disease. The Cathedral's interfaith HIV/AIDS memorial chapel exudes beauty and peace to counteract the shame, devastation and rejection usually forced on such sufferers. In beautiful calligraphy, a handmade book lists those who have died, complete with their birth and death dates to ensure they are not forgotten—Grace Cathedral cannot tell its GOD story apart from this. Sometimes, one community's story becomes a source of inspiration for others. On the first Saturday after 9/11, many people made their way to the devastated area in New York to help or simply mourn with those who lost loved ones. A group of black gospel singers held hands and sang the old songs forged by their grandmothers and grandfathers during the horrors of slavery. As they sang "Amazing Grace" and "Hold Somebody's Hand" and "Needing Someone to Lean On", the circle of joined hands grew and grew and many tears flowed. From slavery's vocabulary of hopelessness and sorrow, others, now speechless in their helplessness and pain, found solace.

Religious communities form around a new way of thinking offered by a teacher in response to local circumstances, usually some significant crisis otherwise people tend to stay in familiar territory, even if the new ideas are appealing and Divine claims are made for them. The Chinese scholar Confucius (551–479 BCE) was born into tribal fighting after the Chou Dynasty's control collapsed. Opinions differed as to how people could live peacefully together. The Realists said that reason did not work against a mob, only force. The Mohists, followers of Mo Tzu (Mo Ti), saw the solution as love, not force—"When all the people in the world love one another, then the strong will not overpower the weak, the many will not oppress the few, and the wealthy will not mock the poor."[12] Mohists saw the universe ruled by Shang Ti (the Sovereign on High), a personal GOD who "loves people dearly. He rewards the virtuous and punishes the wicked, and has prepared everything for the good of humankind."[13] Heaven and earth were a continuum, with the ancestors occupying heaven but still dominating earthly life, demanding spirit money, incense and food offerings, and speaking through omens and signs. Confucius thought that brutal force was wrong, but the force of love utopian. Tradition was the answer, not randomly repeating the past but teaching people how to behave. Everything—temples, music and art—should be part of this education such that goodness became second nature. Confucius shifted the focus from heavenly ancestors to living in *this* world, emphasizing the earthly family and filial piety to bring community order while not ignoring the ancestors and cosmic order. When he put his ideas into practice in a community, he changed China.

The Prophet Muhammad also found himself in a land torn with tribal warfare. Convinced that Allah was the *only* GOD among the many worshipped, he began receiving Divine revelations and set out to preach a message of peace when life is surrendered to GOD. This was not a new religion but the culmination of GOD's story told through Abraham, Moses, the Hebrew prophets, Jesus and now Muhammad, the seal of the prophets. At first Muhammad had little success and he left Mecca, but later returned victorious with an almost mass conversion of the city. Once again, Muhammad taught a way of life in community, emphasizing deeds not creeds. Theologian Hans Küng says:

> In the Western world, religion (from *religio*, bond) has become a more or less personal bond of commitment. In the Islamic world the corresponding Arabic word, *din*, still means an all-encompassing way of life, which is upheld by external controls.[14]

The five pillars of Islam hold Muslims together—(1) reciting "There is no God but Allah and Muhammad is his prophet", (2) praying five times daily, (3) giving charity, (4) fasting at Ramadan, (5) pilgrimage to Mecca. This is not about orthodoxy but about orthopraxy. The community is key, and all Muslims are urged towards unity with their brothers and sisters. Wealth has to be distributed equally with provision for the poor, and racial discrimination is forbidden such that, at the *hajj* (pilgrimage to Mecca), all wear the same robes, rich or poor. The lot of women was also greatly improved in Muhammad's time, with inheritance to daughters and better rights within marriage, although recent treatment of women in some Muslim countries raises questions around the globe from Muslims and non-Muslims alike.

Where there is a belief in an afterlife or a realm beyond the physical world, communities who engage the Divine together do not end at death. In many African religions, ancestors receive prayers from the living asking for good fortune, and they punish the living if neglected—they are still elders but with additional powers. In traditions with a GOD-image, ancestors are emissaries between the living and the Divine—Zulus use *ukukhonza* for worshipping GOD and *ukuthetha* for worshipping ancestors, both meaning "speaking with".[15] In Polynesian religions, the spiritual power *mana* flows from the GODs through ancestors to living chiefs who are responsible for controlling these powerful forces. The Hebrews did not originally have an afterlife—Sheol was merely a shadowy place of dead spirits. Immediately prior to Jesus, however, ideas of an afterlife borrowed from the Zoroastrians came into vogue. The debate was alive and well in Jesus' day, with the Pharisees promoting an afterlife against the Sadducees who did not. Jesus was drawn into this debate and supported the afterlifers. In Christianity, Abraham, Moses, Jacob and many others became the "heavenly" cloud of witnesses, and the saints continued this tradition in the heavenly city, to whom one could pray for help.

Communities vary as to *who* can engage the Divine and receive messages on behalf of all. In Native American traditions, while some have special people, the prayer, songs and dances that prepare the tribe for special events (hunting, seasons, war) are performed by everyone without need of priests to act for others. Since all life is infused with the Sacred, every action by every person within the tribe is a religious action.[16] With the *Nuer* people of Southern Sudan, since tribal life and wealth revolve around cattle, their central ritual to creator GOD Kwoth is the sacrifice of an ox which anyone can do any time in any place. The Baha'i faith, which emerged under the prophet Baha'ullah into a universal faith, has no formal public rituals or priesthood—local congregations meet, have a devotional time together and discuss contemporary concerns. The Religious Society of Friends (Quakers) believe that everyone can have a direct experience of the Divine within, so there is no need for any external mediation by clergy or sacraments—one "hears" GOD in the heart. The original Quakers sat in silence, allowing the Spirit to work within each heart and cause members to respond aloud if so led. During a meeting of biblical scholars in a Quaker college, a Quaker lay-woman accidentally stumbled upon an intense discussion on biblical criticism, something from which she felt excluded. She stood up suddenly, Bible in hand, and interrupted the shocked group. "I assert my prerogative as a Friend to speak, moved by the Spirit. In John 21:15, Jesus says, 'Feed my lambs.' He did not say, 'Feed my giraffes.' Well, brothers, when are you ever going to put the food where the lambs can get it?"[17]

On the other hand, religions that had sacrifices and a temple at their center appointed priests to do their rituals and care for the temple Deities. In Ancient Egypt, temples (mansions for the GODS) were decorated with scenes of kings performing rituals while priests cleansed, dressed and fed the Deities, carrying them in procession to the neighboring temples of their consorts. Magi in ancient Iran were a hereditary order of Zoroastrian priests with religious training to perform the rites and ensure ethical and ritual purity, an important task because dirt was associated with evil and decay— they wore masks so their contaminated breath did not defile the Sacred temple fire.[18] The priestly task in Roman times was to recognize *prodigia*— signs that the harmonious order between GODS and humans had been disturbed, by events such as natural disasters and abnormal births. The priest had to identify offended GODS and find ways to restore this balance.[19] The Hebrew priesthood was limited to the family of Jacob's son Levi. Originally, the head of a clan performed any sacrifices but, once in the promised land, although families could still sacrifice in holy places, only Levitical priests could sacrifice in temples. Under Josiah (639–609 BCE), other temples were demolished and priests served *only* in the Jerusalem temple, performing purification rites and doing the sacrifices. When the second temple was built (sixth century BCE), the ark of the covenant was no longer there and many earlier practices were abandoned. With the destruction of this temple (70 CE), sacrifices ended and the priestly role disintegrated further.[20] Priesthood has a fuzzy history in Christianity. Jesus was seen as the great High Priest who mediated between GOD and humanity rather than priests and sacrifices. The Church was the "priesthood of all believers", sharing in Christ's priesthood. In the first century, presbyter, deacon and bishop were terms used for various church leadership roles, without clear definition of function and degrees of separation, and church referred to people gathering and sharing a meal in someone's home to remember Jesus. As Melanie Johnson-DeBaufre points out, it took a community to propel Jesus into history:

> In order to be a unique and powerful individual, people have to recognize you as such. And even when people acclaim someone as "the One", it may be as much because that person voices the concerns and hopes of many people than that a distinctive new thing has come upon them.[21]

The Jesus communities shared things in common and cared for the poor among them. The homes in which they met were often presided over by wealthy women who orchestrated the gathering and took the leadership role. Women also traveled with Paul as apostles of the good news. Only in the second century were leadership roles given exclusively to male bishops and presbyters, but even then confusion reigned as to what these roles meant and what authority was conveyed. The language of "sacrifice" and "priest" was not used in first-century Christianity, as it could be confused with Jewish animal sacrifices and Greco-Roman sacrifices to the GODS. In time, however, the Eucharist moved from a ritual in memory of Jesus to a sacrifice, a re-enactment of Christ's death on the cross. The priesthood of all believers regressed to only priests and bishops allowed to offer this sacrifice to GOD, by virtue of their status. The once-for-all sacrifice of Jesus was no longer suf-ficient, needing its constant repetition in the Mass:

> The financial stipends received for the celebration of masses, originally meant to support the day-to-day living of the priests, became the monetary base for the considerable power of monasteries, cathedrals and dioceses. This complex social unity of power, wealth, and religious piety was part of the scandal against which Luther and other church reformers of the sixteenth century preached.[22]

Debates about the role of priests and ordination rites continue, stalling many ecumenical debates.[23] On what basis is someone considered able to engage the Divine on our behalf? The answer rests on the authority claims developed within various traditions. The first split between the Eastern and Western churches involved questions of leadership and authority. The Western church claimed the Pope as the continuing representative of Christ on earth, with authority to decide between truth and error. Bishops continued a line of unbroken succession from the apostles, and priests were ordained by these bishops to convey grace to the laity. The Eastern church, on the other hand, has no Pope—the Patriarch is the first among equals. Church teaching is determined through consensus in church councils which only make judgements on things *in* the Bible, interpreting it rather than initiating doctrines such as purgatory, Mary's assumption and indulgences. Laity elects their priests—the bishop cannot appoint without this. Priests do the sacraments, but laity can read the Bible and preach. The church in England also broke with Rome over Papal authority under Henry VIII, but it still claims apostolic succession for its bishops who, in turn, ordain the priests who officiate at the sacraments.

Although the scriptures became authoritative in the Reformation, they were still interpreted by the ordained clergy. An essay on the pastoral office in Methodism in 1835 said:

Christ has made his ministers accountable for the purity and good discipline of the church, and unless it can be shown from scripture that He has made others equally accountable with his ministers, the latter cannot share their responsibility with others.[24]

Presbyterian and Reformed communities (from John Calvin) located their governance in a body of clergy and laity that performed the bishop's role. Since preaching the word was central, clergy were ordained on the basis of proper theological training rather than an office or apostolic succession. They earned respect by being able to think and teach, not through an Episcopal sash. I once attended an ecumenical meeting where someone from the Presbyterian tradition stepped to the floor microphone and asked if he could speak. The bishop on the raised dais said back to him, "You have no power." There was a shocked look on the face of the Presbyterian until he realized that the bishop was telling him the electricity to the microphone had gone off.

Charismatic authority is a third model of authority in a community, allowing for the free movement of the Spirit. A charismatic leader must demonstrate a spiritual relationship with the Divine (often through claims of "God spoke to me") to earn his or her place. Governing structures in these denominations—Pentecostal, Baptist and Holiness groups—are shared and spiritual leadership is granted primarily through a "call" and spiritual evidence rather than an institutional office or theological skills, although these are also in place. Yet this type of authority can also get out of hand since it rests on personal claims of spiritual power and special contact with GOD, especially in independent churches with no external audits. In the 1970s, the Universal Brotherhood emerged in Western Australia with a vision of a simple life of peace, love, harmony and saving the planet. Many young people left successful careers to join and pool their resources. It grew into a wholesome, self-sufficient community with an alternative spirituality and old-fashioned Christian values. In time, a few people rose to leadership by claiming visions to be believed and obeyed. Power became concentrated in a central "core" and, like George Orwell's (1903–50) *Animal Farm*, you could only express uneasiness to this more "spiritual" core and probably be disciplined for weakness, threatened with expulsion and forbidden to speak to the others. After a number of years, a single event opened the can of worms and people started talking out loud. Everything fell apart within a week as 40 people left. One of the core who "sold" his brand of religion now sells single roses in coffee shops and restaurants. In another contemporary group of independent churches in Australia called "Christian Fellowships", a small male elite have nominated themselves as elders and claimed Divine authority to examine the moral and spiritual lives of everyone in their tight communities, especially the wives who must be totally obedient to both husbands and elders. Women make regular confessions to the elders and are re-examined if they are not satisfied. Mothers may not attend their children's weddings if shown, by examination, to be rebellious or not good enough mothers, and they can also be forced out of marriages and the community, losing access to their children, if they do not satisfy the elders' standards.[25]

Some communities demand a greater commitment. The sangha is the community of Buddhist monks who follow a Buddhist monastic code. Saffron-robed monks and begging-bowls are a common sight in Asian villages. Since they don't eat after lunch, the monks go out begging for food each morning and lay people are expected to support them. They are not priests, although they can give blessings or preach at marriages and funerals. Many parents in Thailand send their young children to become monks so they can be educated in the monasteries—they must be at least eight when they shave their heads, don the orange robe and surrender all their possessions except their begging-bowl. It is not a lifetime vow—most adult Thai males have spent some time as a monk during their student years, learning a discipline and training they take into their careers. Christian monasticism (Greek *monachos,* solitary), on the other hand, was first recorded in Egypt in the fourth century. Men and women fled city life and a "worldly" church to seek a life of repentance, prayer, poverty, asceticism and hard labor in order to engage the Divine. These desert fathers and mothers first lived as hermits in individual, scattered cells until some built cells around a teacher, forming a religious community under an abbot or abbess with strict rules of obedience. The Coptic monk Pachomius (292–348 CE) turned this model into a monastery, establishing the first monastic community. As asceticism was already known in Greece, India and Egypt, monasticism took it on board as an ordered, disciplined life under an abbot as spiritual father.[26] The Reformation challenged monastic life as a "work" to gain merit, opening up the monasteries, but this spawned even more austere forms in Catholicism as a reaction, such as Capuchins and Trappists, where fasting, hair shirts and long prayer vigils strengthened the soul.

In a Jewish community, rabbis are the teachers of the Torah. Initially they were responsible for interpreting the scriptures and oral law but, by the Middle Ages, they had become leaders of Jewish communities. This was not a priestly or sacramental role, but ordination as an educator and spiritual guide. Today, a rabbi has a similar function to a Christian minister—preaching, leading worship, counseling and teaching. An Islamic community gathers in the mosque to worship under their worship leader, the imam. Again, this is not a priestly function and, in smaller mosques, imams are not paid. There is no ordination, although the imam may be theologically trained, and he is only an imam as long as he acts in that capacity. Imams have a higher status in Shi'ite tradition where ayatullahs ("miraculous sign from God") are charismatic leaders recognized by the community at large. The Ayatullah Khumaini (1902–89), who became famous as the Shah of Iran's opponent, was thought by some to be the "hidden Imam" predicted to return before the end of the world and battle against evil forces. In the Hindu tradition, Brahmans (Brahmins), the highest level of the social classes, are responsible for teaching the sacred Vedic texts and performing priestly sacrificial rituals in a way acceptable to GOD. In the temple, they receive offerings for the Deities and are permitted into the womb chamber to dress and care for the *murti* (Deity statue). In the past, Brahmans, as the educated and ritually pure ones, became rich through royal patronage but now they choose professional careers in law, business and medicine—those in rural areas who pursue the occupation of priest barely making a living.

Does gender have a bearing on who can help a community engage the Divine? It would need volumes to spell out the arguments made through the centuries and across religions as to why only *men* can serve as intermediaries to the Divine—not surprising since most religions developed in patriarchal societies where males wrote the rules. As a rare exception, Maori women of Aotearoa New Zealand have always been responsible for the traditional call that starts any ceremony at the *marae*, the sacred gathering place. Nothing can happen until the woman makes the call, and it can be whenever she wants to, whatever chant she chooses and for however long she wishes to do it. While this has continued in Maori culture, Maori women have lost out in their adopted Catholicism because women cannot participate as ritual leaders in this imported male-orientated religion. In some branches of contemporary Judaism, women can be rabbis, but the imam in Muslim society is male. Recently, Egypt appointed its first woman *mazoun*, a judicial official like a notary who presides over wedding ceremonies. According to a Cairo report, many men were unhappy. One interviewed said, "There must be religious texts forbidding this. . . [and] there are also obstacles on a social level. She would always take the woman's side." According to Sheik Fawzi Zefzaf, deputy director of the religious institute Al Azhar, this was not a violation of Muslim law, but he added, "When a woman is menstruating she must not enter a mosque or read Koranic [Quranic] verses and that will affect her job, so for this reason we say it is not advisable to have a woman."[27]

Women in Christianity have had a rough time ever since Eve, a history I trace in my book *Why We're Equal: Introducing feminist theology.*[28] Although Jesus had significant women followers and Paul worked with women apostles, by the fourth century the Church had declared itself a male-run institution by soliciting a few Bible verses and Aristotle's Greek household codes. Paul's words in Galatians 3:28 that "there is no longer Jew nor Greek, slave or free, male and female" were ignored in favor of non-Pauline letters that returned the household codes of master over slave and male over female, demanding that a woman be subject to her husband and "learn in silence with full submission. I permit no woman to teach or have authority over a man; she is to keep silent. For Adam was formed first, then Eve; and Adam was not deceived, but the woman was deceived and became a transgressor" (1 Tim. 2:11–15). Although the Genesis 1 creation story describes men and women created together out of dust, the different creation story in Genesis 2 was adopted by the Church where Eve was made from Adam and thus, theologians said, derivative and subordinate. Yet these same people argued the superiority of the male human over animals because of the creation sequence from simple to the crown of creation—which, on this reasoning, should be *Eve* as the last creation. Eve was blamed for tempting the male, thus initiating sin and the fall (although neither word is *in* the fruit-eating story), and also "cursed" under an eternal natural order of submission to the male (although Adam was not eternally condemned to toil in the fields). Add the Greek influence of celibacy for scholarly philosophers and the fear of women as temptresses like their mother Eve, and we have church father Tertullian (c. 155–245 CE) describing women, not only with loathing but as Christ's murderers:

And do you not know that you are each an Eve? The sentence of God on this sex of yours lives in this age; the guilt must of necessity live too. You are the devil's gateway . . . the first deserter of the divine law; you are she who persuaded him whom the devil was not valiant enough to attack. You destroyed so easily God's image, man. On account of your desert—that is, death, even the son of God had to die.[29]

As Mary evolved into a virgin mother whose hymen was not broken before or after Jesus' birth (an impossible role model for women), Eve and her daughters sank lower in their bodiliness, weakness, irrationality and evil. By the Middle Ages, witch-hunts and executions became ecclesiastical sport, with a textbook by two Dominicans, *Malleus Mallificarum* (Hammer of Witches), for spotting women who supposedly cohabited with the Devil. As I surveyed items in the Museum of Torture in Posnan's (Poland) Town Hall, most of the instruments were from witch-hunts—a pyramid on which women sat to pierce their vaginas, chairs with spikes in them and pincers that tore off their breasts (there was an unwritten agreement against torture of the penis except for severe crimes). This museum estimated that nine million women were killed as witches in Europe. It is not surprising then, that a church that described women thus would not allow them into the ecclesiastical club or near the sacred altar. If we think such attitudes to women are in the past, it was not until 1918 that Texas altered a law that said everyone had the right to vote except "idiots, imbeciles, aliens, the insane, and women".[30]

While many churches allow women to be ordained today as a result of feminist scholarship, Roman Catholic, conservative Anglican and some independent churches still hold out, citing tired old Bible verses and the fact that a woman cannot substitute for Jesus' *maleness* at the altar—and anyway, didn't Jesus call all male disciples? This history, despite recent inclusions for women, still reverberates through church halls and theology, denying or downgrading women's ability to engage the Sacred for themselves or others. As long as ancient sacred texts of any religion continue to be interpreted, for the benefit of some, as Divine words such that the cultural patriarchy of the time is re-enforced and not challenged, we *all* suffer. As David James Duncan said of such uncritical approaches to ancient holy books and doctrines:

I could end up worshipping—or worse, obeying—nothing more than my misunderstanding of another man's misunderstanding.[31]

Sacred Texts and Holy Books

He [Allah] sent down upon you the Book in truth, confirming what went before it, and he sent down the Torah and the Gospel before this as a guide to all people.

—*Qur'an, Surah 3:2*

O   O   O

There is no book so holy that it cannot be misunderstood and abused.

—*David James Duncan*[1]

The Torah (Judaism), Bible (Christianity), Qur'an (Islam), Tao Te Ching (Taoism), Book of Mormon (Latter-Day Saints), The Most Holy Book (Baha'i Faith), TriPitaka, Lotus Sutra and Dhammapada (Buddhism), Avesta & Gathas (Zoroastrianism), Vedas, Bhagavad Gita and Ramayana (Hinduism), Adi Granth (Sikhism), Lun Yu and I-Ching (Confucianism)—and that's only a portion of religion's holy books. Most of us are familiar with one, perhaps two, and know another few by name, but beyond that, what is sacred to someone else on our planet has not even registered on our horizon. The most likely reason for this is that we have, for so long, been taught that *our* sacred texts, whichever they are, contain the truth while others don't, or that ours is the fulfilment of previous sacred texts. Christians see the New Testament as the fulfilment of the Hebrew scriptures, and the Qur'an is seen by Muslims as the final revelation in GOD's story since the beginning of the world. People have not explored other sacred texts because, having not grown up within another's stories, they seem strange and alien to us. Many students in my World Religion courses express incredulity that someone would believe the feats of the Greek GODs, the many Hindu incarnations of Brahman or the miraculous birth stories around the Buddha, yet don't blink an eye at the parting of the Red Sea, Mary's perpetual virginity, turning water into wine, a corpse coming alive after three days, and a host of saints performing impossible miraculous feats.

Sacred texts come out of specific communities. The founder of a religion gathers followers around him or her and, in time, often after the founder has died, the community gathers together its stories in order to preserve the founder's teachings as to how they should understand GOD, the universe and their place in it. Their solutions, preserved in holy books, will differ, even though they all seek to engage the Mystery. At a recent theology conference, the speaker was describing the Divine *within* everything, rather than an interventionist GOD breaking into earth events from outside the world. I enthused afterwards to the professor next to me that this imagery meant that GOD is active in all religions, but he disagreed, claiming an exclusive Divine incarnation only in Jesus. I asked how he knew this was so—had he studied other religions? "No," he said with irritation, "I don't need to. I can see it from how they act." For once I was speechless, as visions of the Christian Crusades, Inquisitions, witch-hunts, burning of heretics, apartheid and slavery reeled through my mind. How blind religious people can be about their own tradition and their valuation of others. It is reminiscent of the colonial attitudes of previous centuries where missionaries were sent out, not just to convert but to "civilize".

According to religion scholar Karen Armstrong, pre-modern cultures had two ways of knowing and speaking—*mythos* and *logos*. Both were essential and complementary without any hierarchy or conflict. *Logos* (reason) described how humans operated in the world—making weapons, building houses, educating people and governing a city—but *logos* "could not assuage human grief or find ultimate meaning in life's struggles".[2] *Mythos* (myth) accounted for that. Today's scientific world (*logos*) demands that we must prove whatever we say and has basically down-graded *mythos,* or reserved it for once-upon-a-time stories that aren't literally "true". Yet when most sacred texts were written down, *mythos* was an equally valued way of explaining our world and larger than real life because it created a vision of what could be without being locked into boxes of truth or fantasy. When a hero went underground to wrestle with evil forces, these were not to be read as factual stories, nor critiqued as "not true", but rather "they were designed to help people negotiate the obscure regions of the psyche, which are difficult to access but which profoundly influence our thought and behavior".[3] As retired Bishop Richard Holloway says:

Not only have we separated ourselves from nature, we have cut ourselves off from the power our myths possess to alert us to the danger of our own excesses . . . [we] have lost the feeling for myth, the dark poetry of our unremembered past, and replaced it with the fraudulent veracity of religious claims to "historical reality". This accounts for the peculiar ugliness of both religious and anti-religious protagonists today, neither of whom has any feel for the creative power of metaphor. By literalizing it, either in the name of dogmatic orthodoxies of religion or the dismissive orthodoxies of science, we have cut ourselves off from the ability of myth to hold a mirror in front of ourselves.[4]

Somewhere I collected a lovely "story" to illustrate the difference between our modern categories of "truth" and "story".[5] The fact that I am using a "story" to explain something I have already said in words is an example in itself of the power of "story".

Truth and Story were twins who had lived together in the same house in the same village for fifty years. They were much loved in their community and went together every night to visit all their neighbors. Story dressed elaborately for the visit almost always in costumes. She wore elegant robes, strings of seashells, pearls or glass beads, garlands of flowers, fanciful wigs and crowns or hats. Every night Story looked a bit different but always intriguing. Truth never wore clothes at all. When they made their rounds each night, everyone they visited embraced Story warmly and greeted Truth more distantly with great respect. One night Story was too ill to make the traditional visit, so Truth went without her. The visits lacked the joy and warmth they had when Story went along. After several nights of visiting alone and feeling bereft without Story, Truth decided to comfort herself by making the visit dressed in some of Story's finery. That night wherever Truth went she was greeted warmly with great hospitality and embraced, for you see, Truth dressed as Story is easier to embrace.

Myths in pre-modern times were not something you simply believed in— they were challenges to make the myth experience true in your own experience. Creation myths and stories of why human beings are different from the GODS appear in every religion, as do hero myths, encouraging us to imitate this model of dealing with suffering, enduring hardship, staying loyal to ideals, protecting others and saving the world from whatever threatens. Whether or not the stories actually happened in real time or exactly as told is not the point—they have a self-authenticating feel to inspire us to do likewise. Beethoven's "Ode to Joy" is not good just because Ludwig van Beethoven (1770–1827) wrote it, nor do people follow Jesus' teachings just because they are in the Bible—they make sense in their own right. India's famous son, Mahatma Gandhi (1869–1948), studied Jesus' teachings and found them inspiring, but did not abandon his Hindu traditions in order to follow them. Gandhi said:

> I must say that I have never been interested in an historical Jesus. I should not care if it was proved by someone that the man called Jesus never lived, and that what was narrated in the Gospels was a figment of the writer's imagination. For the Sermon on the Mount would still be true for me.[6]

This is true today, although we've shied away from the term "myth" as an explanation, as this has come to mean something not actually true. We watch television programs and read books about people who overcome all sorts of impossible odds, sacrifice their own interests and comforts in order to help others, or risk their lives to pull people from danger, and we call them "heroes". Do these stories grab us because we actually know the people, or are assured the story is literally true? No. We respond to them because they show how noble human beings can be and inspire us to be the same, to make their courage and compassion our story as well. Rama, Krishna, the Buddha, Jesus and Muhammad all model the ideal hero, which is why their followers imitated them. Thomas à Kempis entitled his bestselling book *The Imitation of Christ* and wrote, "O Lord Jesus, forasmuch as thy life was narrow and despised by the world, grant me to imitate thee, though the world despise."[7] Actually, à Kempis' monastic life imitated more closely a revered *church* lifestyle rather than the Jesus who engaged with the world, ate with sinners, practiced compassion in the marketplace and publicly confronted injustice and oppression which led to his murder. It is hard to see Jesus' lifestyle "imitated" in what à Kempis described:

> . . . there is no other way to life and true inward peace but the way of the holy cross and of daily mortification . . . the more the flesh is wasted by affliction, so much more is the spirit strengthened by inward grace. And sometimes [the afflicted] is so comforted with the desire of tribulation and adversity for the love of conformity to the cross of Christ, that he would not wish to be without grief and tribulation, because he believeth that he shall be unto God so much the more acceptable the more grievous things he is permitted to suffer for Him.[8]

A sacred text contains the myths and stories of the religion from which it arose, yet many people want to argue that these stories are *logos*—ancient realities that occurred at one time and can and will occur in the same way in our totally different world. If demons caused disease and could be expelled by exorcism in Jesus' day, this is still a valid cure today. If prayer and faith could move mountains—although no such event was actually recorded in the New Testament—GOD can do the same today without recourse to heavy-duty construction equipment. In a recent church magazine, an older woman missionary, sick and alone in her Asian village, said she found comfort in her daily reading from Joshua as a literal promise to her—". . . the Lord said unto [Joshua], 'You are old and advanced in years, and very much of the land still remains to be possessed'" (13:1). She read this "land to possess" as souls for Jesus, yet the promise was about conquering other people's land and slaughtering its inhabitants.

Our religious instruction to children about sacred texts has not always made clear distinctions between *logos* and *mythos*. Thus, when a child reaches a certain age, Santa Claus who served her well in earlier years turns out to be a fictional creation of parents, like fairies and wizards, but stories about GOD, that often bear a decided likeness to Santa Claus with rewards and punishment for good and bad children, have to be retained as true. Sacred history was Nikos Kazantzakis' favorite subject growing up, but, for some reason, he developed a fear of Abraham and imagined Abraham's footsteps following him and heard a panting whenever he repeated Abraham's name. When he learned that Abraham went through the motions to slaughter his son, he hid behind his desk so Abraham couldn't find him, and when he heard that the good go to Abraham's bosom, he decided to break all the rules. When he *did* ask a question for clarification, however, his teacher raised his switch and shouted, "Stop this impertinence! . . . These are God's doings . . . We're not supposed to understand. It's a sin!"[9] A Catholic sister once told me a similar story of her early childhood ideas. Upset by blood running down Jesus' face from the crown of thorns, she asked a nun why this was happening and why Jesus hung on the cross. "Because of your sins", was the answer. A few years later, she was taught, in that vague style of sex education, that the *worst* sins had to do with sex. Although not understanding what sex meant, she resolved never to get involved with "it" because of what it did to Jesus. She entered a convent in her late teens, both to avoid sex and to apologize to Jesus. In her mid-fifties, she still reflected back on this troubling blurring of physical acts and theological *mythos*.

Sacred texts tell stories of how humans engaged the Divine in ancient pasts and experienced the Divine engaging them and thus they offer different answers to the universal human questions—where did we come from, what is the meaning of life, how should we live, does Something greater exist and how does It relate to us and us to It? In what way are they "true"? Are they GOD's actual words, words of inspired humans encountering GOD, or words of wise sages who reflected deeply on their life experiences? Are some more true than others and on what basis can we decide this? The Arabic words in the Qur'an are said to be Allah's actual words, revealed by the angel Gabriel to Muhammad over some twenty years. As each revelation was emblazoned on Muhammad's mind, he called scribes to write it down, with Allah preserving literal accuracy. Faithful followers also learned it by heart. These revelations were collected and compiled into the Qur'an within fifteen to twenty years of Muhammad's death, with 114 chapters (surahs) arranged from longest to shortest (except for the first). It is the great miracle of Islam.

> Ask you a greater miracle than this, O unbelieving people! Than to have your vulgar tongue chosen as the language of that incomparable Book, one piece of which puts to shame all your golden posey and suspended songs?[10]

Other Muslim sacred texts include the Hadith, sayings of the prophet, and the Sunnah which includes the Prophet's actions and practices.

The Guru Granth Sahib (Adi Granth) is the Sikh sacred text, containing the writings of ten gurus from 1469 to 1708. The earliest hymns were oral compositions by the first guru, Guru Nanak (1469–1539), later written down with additional hymns by successive gurus. Since Sikhism endeavored to bridge the divide between Hinduism and Islam in its day, it contains the teachings of some fifteen holy men from the Islamic and Hindu traditions. The tenth guru, Gobind Singh (1666–1708), aware that he was dying, addressed the Khalsa (the assembly of initiated Sikhs) and bowed before his successor, not another guru but the sacred scriptures, Guru Granth Sahib, as the community's eternal guru:

> O beloved Khalsa, let him who desireth to behold me, behold the Guru Granth. Obey the Guru Granth. It is the visible body of the Gurus. And let him who desireth to meet me, diligently search its hymns.[11]

The story of the Book of Mormon begins some 600 years before Jesus with prophets from an ancient people that GOD led from Jerusalem to America. The last prophet, Moroni, buried the record of this group, engraved on gold plates. Joseph Smith (1805–44) was visited by Moroni in a vision, who revealed this buried treasure in a hill near Smith's Manchester home in upstate New York. Smith was ordained to translate them from their "reformed Egyptian" script, which he began in 1828, aided by an interpreting instrument called Urim and Thummim—two crystals or "seer stones" set in a bow like spectacles. When put in a tall hat with the light blocked out, they allowed him to "see" the translation which he then dictated to scribes. Smith's further revelations also became the scriptures of his church, the Church of Jesus Christ of Latter-day Saints, formed in 1830.

While some sacred writings are considered holy because they are the actual words of a Deity, others *become* holy when accepted by a religious community as stories by which it will live. Both claims have been made for the Christian Bible. Some say it is the "Word of God", meaning it contains GOD's actual words or, alternatively, GOD ensures that the words will not lead us astray. The former is a difficult argument, given its recorded editing and altering through history and also the evolution of thought *within* the Bible. The latter argument is also difficult, given the many denominations that have emerged from reading the same text and claim guidance for their "truth" from the Holy Spirit. Others see the Bible simply as a collection of writings from the Jewish tradition, together with the stories of the Jewish Jesus, that became the "canon" authorized by the Church (*kanōn* is Greek for a carpenter's ruler and is used as a metaphor for accuracy, definiteness and truth)—around 100 Gospels and letters were freely circulating in early Jesus communities before the canon was set towards the end of the fourth century. Of the New Testament writings, Paul's letters are the earliest, with the four Gospels written between 70 CE and the end of first century. Only late into the second century were these Gospels assigned titles, representing the apostles thought to be the founders of the communities from which these Gospels came.

There were many and varied opinions about these writings circulating in the first few centuries of Christianity. The theologian Origen (185–232 CE) doubted whether 2 Peter was genuinely from an apostle and questioned whether 1, 2 and 3 John had the same author.[12] Many strains of Christian teaching existed such that the second-century philosopher and anti-Christian writer Celsius claimed that Christians did not know what they believed. Eusebius, Bishop of Caesarea (260–341 CE) wrote an *Ecclesiastical History*, offering a suggested list of 27 best writings judged on their links to early apostles and their popularity with the church fathers. He noted the public dispute about the letters of Jude, 2 and 3 John and 2 Peter and thought Revelation "spurious"—only an allegorical reading of it was considered acceptable.[13] While Eusebius did not claim that his list was exhaustive or closed, Emperor Constantine made his list official, and non-canonical writings were banned under threat of exile. Constantine basically changed Christianity into imperial Christianity:

> Once the bishops and priests began to receive salaries from the state, once church councils could be called and their business personally directed by the emperor, once huge buildings were built at the emperor's personal expense and given to the Catholic Christians for Sunday worship, once the emperor had personally ordained Sunday as the universal day of rest, it was just a matter of time before the canon law became inextricably intertwined in the process of deciding which writings of the Lord's disciples should be read at Sunday worship (the Holy Scripture) and what was the proper interpretations of the doctrines contained in them (the Creed.)[14]

Christian sacred writings also included selected works by church theologians. "[T]his truth and rule are contained in written books and in unwritten traditions which were received by the apostles from the mouth of Christ himself," a sixteenth-century ecclesiastical decree states, "or else have come down to us, handed on as it were from the apostles themselves at the inspiration of the Holy Spirit."[15] The Reformers, however, made the Bible their final authority rather than the Church, but did not abandon other writings or talk of an infallible Bible. Martin Luther was heavily influenced by Saint Augustine and also judged some New Testament books unhelpful—he put James, Hebrews and Revelation in a non-canonical group at the end of his German New Testament, instructing that doctrines not be based on them. The Enlightenment's challenge to the religious control of all knowledge led to a reinforcement of biblical authority in some circles but, in the mid-1800s, a group of progressive Anglican scholars published *Essays and Reviews*, arguing for a more enlightened understanding of the Bible in the face of emerging scientific knowledge (*The Origin of Species* by Charles Darwin (1809–82) had been published the year before). Benjamin Jowett (1817–93), Master of Balliol College, Oxford, included an essay "On the Interpretation of Scripture", summarizing his argument:

> Of what has been said, this is the sum: That Scripture, like other books, has one meaning, which is to be gathered from itself without reference to the adaptations of Fathers or Divines; and without regard to *a priori* notions about its nature and origin. It is to be interpreted like other books, with attention to the character of its authors, and the prevailing state of civilization and knowledge, with allowance for peculiarities in style and

language, and modes of thought and figures of speech. Yet not without a sense that as we read there grows upon us the witness of God in the world, anticipating in a rude and primitive age the truth that was to be, shining more and more unto the perfect day in the life of Christ, which again is reflected from different points of view in the teaching of His Apostles.[16]

For those who claim the Bible as GOD's actual words, nowhere does it say that GOD over-rode the humanity of the Bible's writers. The author of John's Gospel made choices as to what stories to include and which to leave out (John 20:30–31) and Paul offered opinions he did not claim to be "GOD-given" (1 Corinthians 7:12). Besides, we don't have original manuscripts, only copies—the earliest full Gospel being a copy of Mark's Gospel made 140 years after its original creation. Biblical scholar Bart Ehrman asks:

[H]ow does it help us to say that the Bible is the inerrant word of God if in fact we don't have the words that God inerrantly inspired, but only the words copied by scribes—sometimes correctly but sometimes (many times!) incorrectly? What good is it to say that the autographs (i.e. the originals) were inspired? We don't have the originals! We have only error-ridden copies, and the vast majority of these are centuries removed from the originals and different from them, evidently, in thousands of ways.[17]

At the beginning of his New Testament classes in the Bible Belt of the American south, Ehrman asks his students, "Who thinks the Bible is the inspired Word of GOD?" Almost all hands shoot up. He then asks, "Who has read the *Da Vinci Code*?" Again, almost all hands go up. Then he asks, "Who has read the Bible right through?" A few hands go up. He then says, "If GOD had actually written a book, wouldn't you want to read it?"[18] People who make claims of an inerrant, Divinely inspired Bible are themselves selective about which parts are eternally inspired and which are adaptable. 1 Timothy 2:11–14 has been used to deny women's ordination and ban women from teaching men in some churches, yet two verses before, instructions that women not braid their hair or wear gold and pearls, have been dismissed as culturally outdated. Why is one instruction all-binding and another flexible in an inerrant book? On what or whose authority are some verses disposable as culturally outdated or metaphorical, yet verses reflecting the ancient subordination of women eternally binding? Who stands to benefit from such selective reading?

While sacred texts are believed to contain messages to us from GOD, different claims are made as to how a text delivers Divine messages to us.

Some say the words have no power in themselves but, like a spoon, they become effective when used, when the Spirit works on someone's mind and heart through the words. In Parramatta Road, an ultra-busy commercial street in Sydney, Australia, a huge sign covers a billboard saying "The Son of Man is come to seek and to save that which is lost". The Bible reference is in small print underneath. But who is the audience—some wayward soul who knew the scriptures as a child such that these words will jolt a memory? It wouldn't mean anything to someone not schooled in biblical language— "Who is this 'son of man'?" would be the first question from Australia's young unchurched and, on a busy road, who is there to ask? Those who post such signs believe that somehow GOD will dramatically interpret this strange sentence in someone's heart and zap them into belief because GOD can do anything. I once ate lunch at the elegant restaurant, Branka House, on Norfolk Island, once a prison for incorrigible convicts shipped from Australia. Its living-room floor was once the roof of twelve underground prison cells 4½ by 7 feet, their only ventilation and human contact being through a roof-grate into the living-room floor. If that was not punishment enough, when they slid their roof open for light and air, they had to listen to the Bible being continually read in the room above by another convict, in order to save their souls but not their bodies.

Others say that the words and stories of sacred texts are effective in themselves, as if GOD speaks to us directly—a person in the deepest jungle who had never heard of GOD would believe if they picked up a Bible and read. Others argue that GOD regulates the text so we only understand what GOD wants to reveal—no human can exhaust Divine Mystery. The ancient Druids would not commit their sacred knowledge to writing, even though they knew how to write, in case their years of study to reach the highest learning got into the wrong hands.[19] The *Avesta*, the Zoroasterian scriptures, were said to be revealed in entirety to Zoroaster as oral texts and memorized by the priests since writing was considered unsuitable for a sacred text. Much later, a special alphabet was devised to commit these oral stories to writing, and copies were kept by the scholar priests in the temples. Only a fraction of the original writings remains after so many invasions, mainly liturgical parts memorized by priests.

Many religious communities believe that only religious authorities can properly interpret the text, uncover hidden meanings and expose new ideas under Divine guidance. Richard Rodriguez was taught in Catholic school never to read the Bible alone, but trust the Church through whom GOD was best known. In fifth grade, when he told the nuns he planned to read the New Testament over the summer, they were not thrilled, saying he should wait "to read it in class" where he would be guided by the "continuous interpretation of the Word passing through generations of Catholics".[20] Yet this continuous interpretation has varied with time and with different ways to interpret—literal, historical, allegorical, moral, metaphysical, transcendental or eschatological meanings. For many early church fathers, the literal meaning was least important—Origen urged readers to aim above this mundane level in their search for meaning. Whether Abraham and Sarah existed is trivial compared with their allegorical meaning. Saint Augustine proposed a four-fold scheme for examining scripture—a literal reading, the purpose for the writing, analogy and a hidden meaning. In this scheme, "Jerusalem" could mean a literal place, the symbol of GOD's realm, the human soul, or the heavenly city and New Jerusalem.[21] Yet even Augustine realized his limits:

> I have not the strength to comprehend this mystery, and by my own power I never shall. But in your strength I shall understand it, when you grant me the grace to see, Sweet Light of the eye of my soul.[22]

All this made it difficult to say what the "Word of God" was, such that Thomas Aquinas in medieval times preferred one single meaning, the literal. When he could not understand scripture this way, he assumed it was because it could not *yet* be understood. While some say reason must always submit to faith in a stalemate, others say that only what is "reasonable" in a sacred text should be followed. Frederick Buechner's illustration is helpful for modern-day readers: "The Bible is like a window—looking through it you see the world. If you look at the window you see fly-specks, dust, and the crack where Junior's Frisbee hit it. If you look through it, you see the world beyond."[23] Jewish rabbis were happy to use all four methods for their sacred texts with an openness that did not demand a single interpretation. They recognized that their story emerged from a much wider tradition of written sacred texts in the ancient Near East—the *Epic of Gilgamesh* came from the Old Babylonian period and the Hittite literature included scientific works, together with creation and resurrection epics such as *Slaying the Dragon Illuyankas* and *The Missing God*.[24] From all these ancient stories, we discover "truths" about the human encounter with the Sacred and everything can have multiple meanings, with new meanings expanding traditional interpretations. Ask "Why was this written?" and you invite a new set of meanings to be discovered. These "explanations" of the Torah (the first five books of law in the Hebrew Bible—TaNaKh) are called *midrash*, making the text useful for life and renegotiating it in new contexts to allow it to be a living, evolving communication from GOD. The ability to do *midrash* helped

Judaism survive the loss of the temple in 70 CE—they could reinterpret their status of "chosen" people. Much later, it would allow them to cope with the Holocaust. The Hebrew Bible was initially an oral tradition, written down after the Exile (sixth century BCE). It was translated into the Greek Septuagint before the time of Jesus. Other Judaic texts include the Dead Sea scrolls, the Apocrypha (in the Catholic but not Protestant Bible), the Mishnah, the Jewish oral law, the Gnostic writings from Nag Hammadi, the Talmud, a commentary on the Mishnah (a fourth-century CE Palestinian (Jerusalem) Talmud and the fifth-century CE Babylonian Talmud) and the Zohar, the twelfth-century Kabbalist *midrash* interpreting the Torah.[25] To visualize the importance of the Torah, some adult Jewish males wear *tefilin* (black leather boxes) containing passages from Exodus and Deuteronomy on their left arm and head during weekday morning services, from the Divine instruction to bind the word of God as a sign on their hand and between their eyes (Deut. 6:8).

The Buddha wrote nothing down, even though he taught for 45 years— it was 150 years after his death before any texts of his sayings appeared. There are two types of Buddhist writings, the words of the Buddha and commentaries on these words, but there is no single volume like a "Buddhist Bible" (we can use this term because "bible" means a collection of books or a little library). Many schools evolved from the Buddha's teachings (*dharma*), perhaps as many as 34, some playing down his break with Hinduism (after all, Buddha became the eighth incarnation of Vishnu) while others widened the break. Buddhism is not about rigid doctrines but about how to live, learned not just from the Buddha's words but also from a teacher's example of living in the world. The *dharma* is like medicine to the heart, according to the *Anguttara Nikaya*:

> Just as if there were a beautiful pond with a pleasant shore, its water being clear, agreeable, cool and transparent, and a man came by, scorched and exhausted by the heat, fatigued, parched and thirsty, and he would step into the pond, bathe and drink, and thus all his plight, fatigue and feverishness are allayed; so also . . . whenever one hears the Buddha's Dharma . . . all one's plight, fatigue and the feverish burning of the heart are allayed.[26]

While Theravada Buddhism, the oldest surviving form, pays more attention to doctrine and sacred texts, Zen Buddhism (part of Mahayana Buddhism) rejects study and scholarship for "sudden enlightenment". *Zazen* (seated meditation) combined with *koans* (non-rational poems to challenge the mind) and *sanzen* (working with a Zen master) lead to *satori* (sudden enlightenment). The *dharma* (teaching) is not something sacred in itself, but the vehicle by which you cross the river from ignorance to enlightenment. Different teachings are different vehicles but, once on the other side, all boats are abandoned. No one, the Buddha said, would carry a boat on their shoulders after crossing a river simply because it helped with the crossing.

Crossing the river is not as straightforward as it might sound, however. Ordinary village folk don't even think of gaining enlightenment any time soon, but seek to add up cumulative merit by doing *punna*, such as giving food to monks and making temple offerings of flowers and candles. In a Pagoda in Hui, Vietnam (where I broke my foot staring up at the decoration rather than watching the uneven floor), our woman guide told me that she goes to the temple on Saturday to pray, bringing food, flowers and money which is used to care for orphaned young monks living in the grounds. She takes these gifts to the temple to get a blessing and, when she asks for things, she says she feels better. She had not learnt any of Buddha's teachings or read anything about Buddhism—they have some talks at the temple, she said, but not much. Ordinary people simply offer basic prayers to the Buddha or a bodhisattva in the hope of reward—not much different from religious traditions anywhere. My guide said she could eat pork, chicken and beef, but not dog or cat. When I pursued the reason for these religious exclusions, she laughed, "Because they look after people and greet them when they come home—woof, woof, woof", she said in her limited English.

Because sacred texts carry messages from the Divine, the texts themselves are treated with great honor and ritual as representing the Divine presence in the community. Elaborate ceremonies facilitate their public reading. In Judaism, the Torah scrolls are kept in a special chest representing the Ark of the Covenant (*aron ha-berith*) in a niche on the wall facing Jerusalem, the holiest part of the synagogue. People stand when the ark's doors are open, or when the scrolls are removed or replaced, and a mat is placed under a scroll when it is laid on a desk for reading. This honoring of the written word continued in the Christian tradition, with the Gospels as the symbol of Christ present in the gathered community. The early church fathers extended the Eucharistic metaphor to the eating and drinking of the Word through the reading of scripture and "feasting" on it. By the Middle Ages, the reading of the Gospel had become complex, with processions carrying the Bible to the altar, much kissing of it by assorted church hierarchy and other elaborate rituals before reading. About the same time, similar rituals for the Torah developed in Judaism, honoring not just the words but the Torah itself as an icon. Since the scriptures became the focal point for the Reformation, the

Bible continued to be carried in and prominently displayed on a lectern, either as a symbol of Christ present for Lutherans or a reminder of the centrality of the word for other reform traditions. For Muslims, the Qur'an is the uncreated Word of GOD pre-existent to the world and, as such, must never be held lower than the waist for fear of dishonoring it, hence special wooden holders that support the Qur'an for readers sitting on the floor. People must also be ritually pure before touching it, which highlights the magnitude of the offense when American soldiers deliberately denigrated copies of the Qur'an in front of Iraqi prisoners.

Sacred texts paraded and read in churches, synagogues and mosques remind people that GOD has communicated with humanity. The Torah, Qur'an and the Vedic scriptures are memorized and recited in synagogues, mosques and temples so that people "hear" the Divine word. We read our own scriptures in the privacy of our room and meditate on them in our hearts as a way to engage the Divine behind the words. We seek the One within the limits of our own imagination, language and history. Recognizing these limitations, a Hindu temple invocation says:

O Lord, forgive three sins that are due to my human limitations:
Thou are everywhere, but I worship you here;
Thou are without form, but I worship you in these forms;
Thou needest no praise, yet I offer you these prayers and salutations.
Lord, forgive three sins that are due to my human limitations.[27]

Rituals as
Religious Action

Without ritual, myth makes no sense and would remain as opaque as a
musical score, which is impenetrable to most of us until interpreted
instrumentally. Religion, therefore, was not primarily something that
people thought but something they did. Its truth was acquired by
practical action.

—Karen Armstrong[1]

○   ○   ○

In his religious experience, the humbling awareness comes to man that it
is not he who establishes a relationship or communion but rather that he
is established by and through performance of the religious act.

—Joachim Wach[2]

On Easter Thursday in 2009, my husband and I landed at Palermo airport
in Sicily. The travel guidebooks tell you that, if you are in Italy over Easter,
Trapani in Sicily is the place to be for the *I Misteri* (the Mysteries) procession on Good Friday which attracts thousands of visitors each year. This
procession began in 1602, during Spain's domination of Sicily, with the
establishment of the Spanish brotherhood *Confraternita del Preziosissimo
Sangue di Cristo* in Trapani. Local artists were commissioned to create
twenty life-size tableaux of wooden figures representing the events leading
up to Jesus' crucifixion. Later, the *Maestranze* (guilds of grocers, fishermen,
bakers, butchers, etc.) became involved, each guild responsible for a
tableau. Pride, competition and secrecy surround the decoration of these
tableaux until Good Friday when, stunningly engulfed with fresh flowers,
they are taken from their home in Chiesa del Purgatorio (Church of Purgatory) and paraded for twenty hours through Trapani's streets on the

shoulders of *i portatori* (volunteer guild members), returning to the church by one o'clock on Easter Saturday.

I hardly know how to start describing this visual, auditory and emotional feast—the most hardened soul would be touched. Life-size figures, clothed in exquisitely carved robes of color and gold and frozen in wood and time, rise out of a sea of flowers to depict Jesus' final hours. So life-like are their expressions of horror, pain and grief as they move slowly past, their feet at eye-level, onlookers weep in devotion as if "I was THERE when they crucified my Lord." Each heavy tableau is mounted on two poles that dozens of muscular guild men, body crushed against body and arms entwined, carry on their shoulders with a slow rocking step to the beat of marching bands between each tableau—a stirring dirge-like but urgent rhythm that remains with you hours later. Between the tableaux, variously costumed locals walk—children carrying nails and crowns of thorns on cushions or loaves of bread in Easter shapes, groups of mature women in black chanting, shy little angels, handsome youths whose past and future are forever entwined in this event, church dignitaries and city officials. While the parading faces are solemn and absorbed, camaraderie engulfs the bystanders lining the narrow streets, jostling for a view and participating in the story simply by being there. People lean forward to touch the floats and hold up their toddlers to kiss them. Awestruck children watch the pageantry and splendor, if not quite grasping the entire story behind it. I felt for an embarrassed young mother whose small son's Shrek-face balloon kept escaping to float irreverently high on its string alongside the tragic tableaux faces—he did not realize it was not yet time to party. We stood in one spot for three hours as the entire parade passed, then caught it again in the evening in another part of town, now glittering with candles and lights swaying to the powerful music, while on a parallel street the party was in full swing as the line between sadness and celebration blurred. In Modica in Sicily, the resurrection is celebrated on Easter Sunday with a statue of the risen Christ paraded into the streets from the Santa Maria Church, with the Virgin's statue emerging half an hour later in a separate procession. The statues "search" for each other, finally meeting at noon in the church square where Mary's black mantle slips from her shoulders to show her signature blue cloak. As the virgin kisses her son, Easter has come!

In another part of the world, an ancient ritual is being questioned. The months of the lunar Islamic calendar begin with the sighting of the first crescent of a new moon. For the important month of Ramadan, when Muslims all over the world fast from sun-up to sun-down, the sighting of the new crescent moon begins this ritual. Since the lunar calendar is shorter

than the solar, Ramadan falls at different times through the year, and the start
varies slightly over 24 hours in different countries because of the moon's
cycle. Most Muslims go by a local physical sighting of the moon or else the
Saudi Arabian declaration determining the start of Ramadan. Some are ques-
tioning the "primitive" sighting method employed by Saudi Arabia's
Supreme Judiciary Council, however, in an age of science and huge telescopes. Two witnesses are sent into the desert to see the crescent with the
naked eye, even though the more accurate use of telescopes has been
approved by the Council of Senior Islamic Scholars. According to religious
scholar Sheikh Abdul Muhsen Al-Obaikan (in 2005), "It is pure backward-
ness", since the *Hadith of the Prophet* was written long before satellites and
telescopes and did not specify that it should be determined *only* with the
naked eye.[3] To back his argument, he reminded Muslims that, unlike Christianity where the medieval Church rejected scientific discoveries, Islam has
always embraced science as Allah's gift to them.

The term "ritual" comes from the Latin *ritus* meaning "structure" or
"ceremony" and describes any actions that are repeated in standard, pre-
dictable ways conveying meaning, whether religious or not. Almost everything we do involves ritual, whether the way we clean our teeth, the way we
greet our neighbors or the way we say our prayers. Friends develop rituals
that seem strange to outsiders but which remind them of their commitment
to an ongoing relationship. My son's friends from college now live in different parts of the country, but still get together whenever possible. What
started as a joke has become a ritual of reunion. A now petrified bagel, once
hidden in someone's backpack for some reason, is passed on secretly,
mysteriously appearing in someone else's belongings at weddings, college
reunions or birthday celebrations. There is no explanation for this ritual—
it just *is*, a sign of enduring friendship despite distance and change. Families
develop rituals around holidays, meals, sibling roles and putting children to
bed. My small grandson has to have "magic dust" blown over him before
he goes to sleep, something his mother did once when he was feeling alone
in the dark. When taking care of him one night, I performed what I thought
was the correct ritual action, blowing imaginary dust off the palm of my
hand towards his head on the pillow. Then, as always, I stroked his head and
said "Goodnight", causing him great distress as that wiped off the magic
dust. While these things seem nonsense from a rational or useful point of
view, they are full of meaning for those who share them and play a part that
nothing else can fill.

Religious ritual includes ceremony, liturgy, rites of passage, seasonal rites,
social drama, theater and dance. Not surprisingly, theater and dance have

their origins in religion, and it seems they are still alive and well in many different forms, according to this announcement in our local newspaper:

> The Adams Family Ministries will be appearing Sunday through Wednesday at the Assembly of God Church . . . The high-energy gospel program includes unicycling, juggling, clowns, stage illusions and a live band. Two bicycles will be given away on Wednesday night.

While the term "liturgy" is mostly used today for public worship, the Greek word *leitourgia* (Latin, *liturgia*) meant "public work or duty" (*leitos*, public; *ergon*, work) and was, in ancient Athens, "a form of personal service which the wealthier citizens were obliged to discharge to the state at their own expense, when called upon. Such services sometimes consisted of the defrayal of the expenses of festivals, dramatic performances, equipment of ships in case of war, etc.".[4]

In religious rituals, beliefs are "embodied and acted out, not just read about, thought about, or believed".[5] Momentarily, we are removed from our present situation and transported into a sacred space and time that is constructed with ritual objects, language and movement, so re-creation, transformation or rebirth can take place. While this sounds awfully wordy and esoteric for simple, repeated actions like praying together or lighting a candle, it describes the importance of ritual as making something *happen* to us and helps us to see ritual as more than boring routine or empty habit, a negative implication often associated with the word. A new initiate into a Buddhist monastery seemed shocked that the monastery's important daily rituals started at 4.30 am. Concerned he would over-sleep, the initiate asked the master if it was all right if he couldn't always wake in time. The master said it was fine. When the initiate then lined up to be assigned his special monastery chore, he found he had been given a very important task—hitting the plank at 3.45 am each morning to wake the monastery.

Protestants and Catholics of my generation usually feel differently about formal religious ritual, although this is changing. Catholicism focused on the Mass as the *action* engendering salvation, while the "protest" of Protestantism was that sinners did not need to *do* anything to earn salvation—it is a free gift, saved by grace through faith. At the time of the Reformation, the Eucharist had become an elaborate performance by priests, and laity were to partake only if feeling worthy and after confession. The belief that the Eucharistic bread and wine actually turned into the body and blood of Christ through the priest's actions at the altar reinforced this priestly hierarchy. While power-plays, personalities and politics also helped the split in

Christendom, the Reformers increasingly rejected the elaborate rites, rituals, robes and riches of the papacy and church, in order to focus on the word— preaching and scripture—and on a Lord's Supper as a memory of Jesus, without miraculous changes in the bread and wine.[6] The priesthood of *all* believers became the Protestant cry and the crucifix was removed from behind the altar where it signified the Mass as a re-enactment of Christ's sacrifice by the priest and the faithful "eating" the physical body and blood.

Many rituals were labeled "popish", a term flung around whenever the "bells and smells" of Catholicism encroached on the pure sands of Protestant beachheads. The Puritans wanted to abolish set prayers, vestments, eating restrictions, candles, incense, bishops, ecclesial hierarchies and the sovereign as head of the Church, substituting instead a plain, simple fellowship centered on good preaching—which is why they left for America. When the Ecumenical Movement in the middle of last century introduced candles, ornate vestments, procession of the Bible and other such rituals into Protestant territory for the sake of unity with Orthodox and Catholic siblings in Christ, many Protestants were uncomfortable with these innovations over which their ancestors fought and died. And Catholics feel at sea in Protestantism where familiar, structured worship has often been replaced with a "best friends for ever" familiarity with the Divine. Camilla Trinchieri, an Italian Catholic, describes being taken to a Southern Baptist church service:

This is an American religion. Democratic. Everyone joins in the singing. We drink grape juice together and shake our neighbor's hand at the end of the service. This sharing makes me uncomfortable. I miss the statues of the saints, the protectors, the intercessors to whom you can make requests. I miss the pomp and the ritual that keeps the worshipper at an adoring distance. A few years later, back in Italy, I will declare my intention to become a nun, attracted more to the absolutes of Catholicism and the idea of belonging to a tight-knit community than by any communion with God.[7]

The rituals we do to engage the Divine are always cultural and contextual –they have much to do with what is considered culturally right and proper at the time. Since most religions have begun in patriarchal cultures, their attitudes to women, established by men, have been claimed as *GOD's* will. The veiling of women, covering women's heads in worship, excluding women from sacred spaces during menstruation, "purifying" women after childbirth and denying women priestly activities, all originated in cultures where women were named as subordinate to men and functioned mainly in private spaces. What can and cannot be worn in church or mosque, for both men and women, although argued from comments in the Bible or Qur'an, reflect ideas of modesty and social etiquette at that time. In 1923, the Dean of Westminster prohibited a radio broadcast of the late Queen mother's wedding because "the service would be received by a considerable number of persons in an irreverent manner, and might even be heard by persons in public houses with their hats on". While laughing at such outdated thinking, we create new ones according to *our* cultural and social norms. At a religion scholars' meeting, a stimulating dialogue between Christian and Buddhist scholars had just taken place such that "you could have heard a pin drop". A business meeting followed the session. The organizer, because of her perceived contemporary "rules" on meeting-space design, insisted on rearranging the whole room into a circle of chairs with no hierarchical head table. While the theory was good, the moment was not. After much fussing, she discovered that the seats were in sets of six and couldn't form a circle in the limited space, at which point she allowed the room to return to its original position while everyone from the Buddhist–Christian discussion stood and waited. Any gains from having a non-hierarchical circle were lost in the disruption to the mood of the previous discussion where participants would have been happy sitting on backless hay bales.

Rather than entering the theoretical jungle of anthropologists and comparative religionists as to how rituals work to engage the Sacred, let's stroll around various religions and watch what they do and what they say about what they do. Matthew Gallatin joined the Orthodox Church because he felt they were more about experiencing and doing than about believing something. Knowledge of the Divine came through spiritual exercises, not the other way around. Gallatin describes the sacraments as a live encounter— "Every time an Orthodox Christian opens the door of his heart by practicing a sacrament, in faith and with a pure heart . . . he enters heaven! He embraces the living Christ!"[8] The supernatural world enters and fills the ordinary space within an Orthodox church so that we experience the Divine presence and share the Divine life of the Trinity—a process called deification. Protestants have trouble with rituals, Gallatin says, because they deal in concepts and ideas, where rituals are living encounters with the Divine. It's like the person who was intent on ensuring that his friend had the right belief package. "Do you believe in infant baptism?" he asked. "Believe in it!" his friend replied with enthusiasm, "I've seen it done!"

The ritual of sacrifice has a long religious history. The word means "to make sacred" and early rituals involved the slaying of an animal and transferring all or part of it to the Divine as a gift offering, an attempt at communication, an exercise in reciprocity, an expiation to remove an offence, a substitution for the wrong act of someone else, or a re-enactment of primordial events.[9] Jesus' death, when interpreted as a sacrifice, has been explained at different times in all these ways—an offering to the Divine, GOD communicating with humanity, a deal between GOD and humanity, a sacrifice to an offended Deity, a substitution for sinful humanity and a re-enactment of primordial events with Jesus as the Second Adam. Christian theologians, struggling to explain why their Messiah was killed as a criminal (an offense for Jews), borrowed the Jewish idea of "sacrifice" to make sense of it. In South American religions, the GOD Huitzilopochtli was honored with human sacrifices at the festival of Raising the Banners, thought to secure both Aztec power and also the power of their GOD—they regenerated the cosmic order and the blood and hearts of the sacrificed fed the GODS. The best sacrificial offerings were captured warriors, but women, children and slaves were also sacrificed on altars by extracting the heart with a knife. This gruesome "deal with the Deity" accompanied the inauguration of buildings and the coronation of kings, with thousands killed to "seal" the event for the kingdom and cosmos.[10]

When we cringe in horror at these "primitive" beliefs, we need to remember that Abraham was told to offer his son as "a burnt offering" to the Divine (Gen. 22:2). We have sanitized the story by focusing on Abraham's obedience and Yahweh's last-minute rescue, yet we shove under the rug the parallel story of Yahweh accepting the mighty warrior Jephthah's bribe—"If you will give the Ammonites into my hand, then whoever comes out of the doors of my house to meet me, when I return victorious from the Ammonites, shall be the Lord's to be offered up by me as a burnt offering" (Judges 11:30–31). This time, Yahweh stages no last-minute rescue when Jephthah's only child, a daughter, rushes to meet him and he "did with her according to the vow he had made" (v. 39). Spelled out in detail, this meant tying her up on an altar, slaughtering her and burning her as a thanks offering to GOD. What do the literalists do with this Bible story?

A sacrificial offering could also be an animal, bird, fruit or vegetable. In Hebrew tradition, cattle, sheep, goats, doves and pigeons were acceptable animals, as well as wheat, barley, olive oil, wine and frankincense. According to Luke's Gospel, when the newborn Jesus was brought to the temple, his parents offered a "sacrifice according to what is stated in the law of the Lord, 'a pair of turtle-doves or two young pigeons'" (Luke 2:24). The normal offering would be a lamb in its first year and a pigeon or turtledove, but the book of Leviticus allowed two turtledoves or pigeons for those who could not afford a sheep (Lev. 12:6–8). As an adult, Jesus would challenge the ethics of temple sacrifice. Since these animals and birds had to be purchased at the temple for purity reasons and with special temple coinage, large rates of exchange were charged. In Holy Week (according to three Gospels—John's Gospel puts the story at the beginning of Jesus' ministry), an angry Jesus evicted these temple "robbers", giving cause for the religious leaders to kill him (Luke 19:45–47). Today, with our awareness of animal rights, we are more likely to drive out those who *slaughtered* the animals and allow the "money-changers" to continue functioning.

In ancient Rome, animal sacrifice made contact with the GODS and ritual correctness was important in order for this to "work". The entrails of the slaughtered animal had to be inspected by *haruspices*, men trained to divine whether the GODS would accept the sacrifice. If not, the ritual started all over again. It's always been a bit of a quandary to know whether or not GOD accepts our offerings and actions and what the Divine actually thinks about them, especially when prayers sometimes don't result in the right answers, even for the most righteous. During the recent economic crisis, the Anglican diocese of Sydney, Australia, renowned for both its literal interpretation of the Bible and its financial wealth, pondered why GOD had allowed them to lose $160 million in their share portfolio. What was the Lord saying to them? Their leader, Archbishop Jensen, pondered this aloud before the synod, suggesting it may be that GOD was "chastening us for our sins. If so, it is only a further evidence of His fatherly love and care." But, the Archbishop added, the Lord may be teaching us something else—"It may not be our sins at all. Perhaps He is challenging our faith to rely on Him more boldly for our finances." We always look for interpretations of GOD's mind that support our theology and cause but, as an irreverent reporter said, it could also be that people "locked in this kind of medieval superstition shouldn't be allowed to . . . be in charge of $200 million"[11] or, I might add, perhaps the Divine is saying something about this diocese's refusal to allow women to preach, or gay unions to be blessed—it all depends on which of our issues we think GOD is supporting.

We do, however, have one unambiguous response to sacrifices from the Divine—"What to me is the multitude of your sacrifices? says the Lord; I have had enough of burnt offerings of rams and the fat of fed beasts; I do not delight in the blood of bulls, or of lambs, or of goats . . . bringing offerings is futile; incense is an abomination to me" (Isaiah 1:11–13). Why? Because GOD wanted no such rituals unless they came with genuine moral behavior—". . . cease to do evil, learn to do good; seek justice, rescue the oppressed, defend the orphan, plead for the widow" (1:16–17). Sacrifices came to an end in Judaism with the destruction of the temple (70 CE), without which formal sacrifices done by priests were no longer possible. A different Judaism emerged, centered in homes and synagogues with rabbis as teachers, not priests. Christianity proclaimed Jesus the final and ultimate sacrifice, although the idea was kept alive metaphorically in the re-enactment of Christ's sacrifice by the priest in the Eucharist. Since a sacrifice required the offering of something of value or purity, we still talk of someone "sacrificing" their time, physical comforts or money for someone else and call the death of a soldier in war, a mother in childbirth, or someone dying to save a friend, the "ultimate sacrifice".

Judaism never focused on creeds or doctrines to be accepted, but on observances—what you *do*. All of life is holy and everything reflects GOD's glory, so if we eat without blessing the meal, we are robbing the Divine of gratitude deserved. Jews see themselves in a covenantal relationship with the One who chose them and cared enough to intervene in their history and give them rules by which to live—613 in fact. Being chosen was both good and bad news—it gave them security, but also made enemies for them as history has shown. The Jewish ritual year is crowded with *chagim* (festivals)—*Rosh Ha-Shanah* (literally "head of the year"), a time of judgement and repentance when the *shophar* (ram's horn) is blown to rouse Jews back to GOD; *Yom Kippur*, the 24-hour Day of Atonement; *Sukkot* (the Festival of Tabernacles) remembering the wilderness wanderings; *Chanukah* (*Hannukah*), the Festival of Lights celebrating the successful second-century BCE revolt against Antiochus IV and the restoration of the Jerusalem temple; *Purim*, the deliverance of Jews, as in the book of Esther; *Pesach* (Passover) with its *Seder* meal recalling the Exodus; and *Shavuot* (Pentecost), God's revelation at Mount Sinai.

Rituals also mark special times, seasons and cosmological occurrences as a way to link human beings with the grand Divine order of things in the universe. In the Ball Court (*Tlachtli*) in ancient Mesoamerican religions, ritual ball games re-enacted the sun's journey through the underworld and its struggle between day and night. The game was won when the small rubber ball was hit through a stone donut protruding from a wall, and the losing captain was often beheaded on a sacred stone to re-enact the death of the sun and its rebirth. By playing the game, participants believed they were actually *involved* in maintaining cosmic order and the regeneration of life. In Chinese tradition, bringing in the New Year (*Hsin Nien*) requires getting rid of the dark yin forces of the old year. Zao Jun (Zao Shen), the GOD of the stove (Kitchen GOD), the ultimate observer of a Chinese family, is sent off to the heavenly court of the Jade Emperor to report on how the family has behaved during the year. Pictures of Zao Jun and his wife (who acts as his scribe) are burned and offerings made of sweet rice and wine, in order to "sweeten" his reports and invite him to give the family good fortune. When he returns on New Year's Eve, a new picture of the couple has been hung and fireworks are set off, along with ceremonies offering food, incense and spirit money to honor the ancestors.

The Baisākhī festival celebrated on New Year's Day of the solar calendar in southern India is the spring harvest festival in North India—Sikhs celebrate it close to the 13th April, the day in 1699 when the khalsa (assembly of initiated Sikhs) was first initiated.[12] The Green Corn Festival of North American Seneca Indians (August) was a three-day thanksgiving harvest festival when the corn was ripe ("green" meant ripe to eat). Native Americans traditionally depended on corn, beans and squash, the "three sisters" which, mixed together, made a vegetable dish called "succotash", which is still a great favorite in the American south. Borrowing the harvest festival from the traditional occupants of the land, the Pilgrim Fathers in Plymouth, Massachusetts, celebrated their first harvest in the autumn of 1621, in thanks for surviving their first year. While this became a national holiday "to thank our beneficent Father", according to President Lincoln, thanks were due in large part to survival assistance given by the local indigenous people whom their descendants would later decimate. Thanksgiving Day is infused with rituals, not least the traditional meal that recreates in general what was available to the early settlers. On our first Thanksgiving Day in America, friends invited us to share the meal with them and so I brightly suggested I would bring a pavlova, Australia's traditional dessert. I soon discovered that Thanksgiving food was ritually prescribed and only pumpkin and pecan pie could follow the turkey, stuffing, cranberry sauce, mashed potatoes, candied yams, green beans and creamed onions.

In medieval days in England, harvest festivals were called Horkey Supper, an excuse to get riotously drunk. Consequently, in the morality driven Victorian era, two West Country rectors came up with a "religious" alternative, a harvest festival service in the church, followed by a tea. In no time, church altars around the country were covered with agricultural produce, breads, vegetables and pickles, with prayers and hymns offered in thanks. At the tea that followed, the farm laborers were both "civilized" and "churched". An added concern for the Victorian clergy may well have been the highly prized last sheath harvested from the field, which was said to contain the loitering harvest spirit. This sheath was plaited and formed into a corn doll to represent the spirit or made into the harvest loaf—perhaps to "kill" the spirit with a bit of heat.[13] Pentecost was also a harvest festival, the Feast of Weeks (*Shavu'ot*) celebrated by Jews 50 days after the first day of Passover, hence the word Pentecost. It originally signified the end of the barley and the start of the wheat harvest when the "first fruits" of the harvest were given to the on-duty temple priest (Deut. 26:1–11). This festival also celebrated the giving of the Torah to Moses on Mount Sinai. The Ten Commandments, the gift of "spiritual bread from heaven", were read, as well as the book of Ruth, the harvest story where Ruth met husband Boaz, and Pentecost was also the traditional birth date of King David, Ruth and Boaz's famous descendant. Some Jews stayed awake all the night before Pentecost reading the Torah to show their willingness to accept the Torah once again.[14] While Pentecost became significant for Christians as the day the Holy Spirit was given to Jesus' followers, few Christians would know what Pentecost meant to the Jews, having simply appropriated the event as their own. For Jesus' Jewish followers, however, the symbolism was very significant—the Holy Spirit was their new "spiritual bread from heaven".

Rituals abound around birth and death, those mysterious times when humans encounter that which is beyond their ken. Extraordinary births are ascribed to leaders and founders across religions. The Hebrew Bible has a pattern of leaders coming from barren women as a special Divine promise. Isaac was born when Sarah was too old. Samuel was GOD's gift in answer to barren Hannah's prayer for a son. John the Baptist's mother Elizabeth was beyond her prime and Jesus' mother Mary was pregnant without "knowing a man". In similar fashion, although the Buddha made no claim to super-natural status, his mother, Queen Maya, barren for twenty years, dreamed that a white elephant entered her womb and made her pregnant. The Buddha was born able to walk, taking his first steps on seven lotus pads that appeared under his feet. Since childbirth was shrouded in the possibility of death, ritual precautions were taken. In an eleventh-century description of the birth of a Japanese prince, everything was draped in white. Female "sub-stitutes" lay on couches beside the queen, faking labor in order to attract the evil spirits to them rather than the queen. A part of the queen's head was shaved so, if close to death, she could be quickly ordained a priestess and welcomed as such into the next world. When the child was safely delivered, the writer says "it was fearful to hear the jealously swearing voices of the evil spirits".[15] In rural Thai villages in the past, most babies died soon after birth. People thought ghosts and spirits took them and so rituals were shaped to keep spirits at bay for the first month. On the first or third day, to confuse or negotiate with the spirits, a midwife placed the child in a winnowing basket and threw it up gently three times before passing it to the godmother to give to the mother, who was lying near a fire to cleanse her impurity and encircled with a magic string to scare off ghosts. Japanese Shinto practices for chasing out evil spirits associated with childbirth and death involved running water and sprinkling salt around while, in purification rituals in temples, priests cleaned the entrance, washed their hands and mouth and waved a *gohei* around (a wand with strips of white paper or cloth), which also indicated that a Deity (*kami*) was present.

The Chinese *P'u Tu* ("saving all souls") festival is celebrated in the seventh month of the Chinese year when ancestral ghosts without descendants or not properly buried are out looking for food. Before we raise our eyebrows at such "superstitious" practices, the popular American celebration of Halloween is linked back to the Celtic Festival of *Samhain* (summer's end), the beginning of the darker half of the year when the division between this world and the "other" world became thin, permitting good and bad spirits to pass through. Something had to be done to welcome friendly spirits but repel harmful ones, thus the various costumes and masks. The term Halloween (All-Hallows-Even) appeared in the sixteenth century when the festival became All Saints' Day and the evil spirits still had to be chased away the night before. The Egyptian pharaohs drove away demons and cleansed sacred places with burning aromatic incense and the Babylonians used it during prayer offerings—Moses was instructed to make an altar on which to offer incense (Ex. 30:1). While used in the temple in Jesus' day, burning incense is not mentioned in Christianity until after the fourth century CE. Today, the swinging of the censer containing burning incense has been reinterpreted, as culture and credibility changes, to the ascending smoke rising, like prayer, as a pleasing offering to GOD.

While rituals such as baptism are practiced in various religions for new babies, children grow up and need to join the group and make their own contact with the Divine. In Melanesian society, a strenuous and painful initiation rite for boys is aimed at "rescuing" them from the weakening effects of being around women growing up. They are ceremoniously washed, separated from the women and children, made to fast and fed a special diet, then beaten and taunted by elders, all to get the approval of the ancestral spirits living in the men's sacred meeting house.[16] I could comment about parallel "rituals" in today's education of boys, but I'll not get diverted, just leave it to your reflection. In Parsi, *naujote* means "new birth", the Zoroastrian ritual of initiation for boys *and* girls that happens as an individual choice at age nine or eleven (even numbers are inauspicious). As an initiation into the army of Ahura Mazda, the child has a ritual bath and dons the sacred cotton shirt (*sudre*) and plaited lamb's wool cord (*kusti*), "the armor of faith" for the war against evil, and first recites the prayers they will now offer five times daily.

Although circumcision has no warrant in the Qur'an, it was later adopted as part of *Sunna* (customary practice). Male circumcision is usually performed after age eight and before puberty, while female circumcision, in countries where it is performed, happens around puberty. Not surprisingly, given the horrendous process, female circumcision has been challenged around the world as psychologically damaging, non-Islamic, physically cruel and based on male control of female sexual activity but, as Muslim women scholars point out, this did not come from Islam but was adopted from prior local customs wherever it is still practiced. In Judaism, circumcision is performed on male children usually eight days after birth and boys are *bar mitzvahed* (initiation into the community) around age twelve or thirteen, when they are called to read the Torah in the synagogue, followed by a celebration (*kiddush*). *Bat mitzvah* is now available for girls in some Jewish traditions. Confirmation is the comparable ritual in Christianity where children renew their baptismal vows and receive the Eucharist (Communion). In Baptist traditions, this rite accompanies baptism at an age of responsible choice, while in the Eastern Orthodox tradition, anointing with oil immediately after baptism (chrismation) signifies the receiving of the Holy Spirit. In each case, these rituals are visible ways a community can mark the religious life of a person within its ranks and formally make contact through this with the Divine.

Worship is the central ritual of religions—offering devotion, praise and thanks to That which is considered worthy, whatever the object of our worship. While not identifying a GOD, Theravada Buddhists worship the Buddha, not as a supernatural being but out of gratitude to him, and also honor the places (*stupas*) where his relics rest—just as Catholics honor saints and their relics. For the most part, however, worship is usually offered to a GOD from whom all things come and who is above, beyond or within all things. Worship is not simply awe, although this is part of it. It is action and ritual, doing something to show our devotion, and doing it regularly and intentionally. Rituals of worship bring a heightened awareness to whatever we are doing, and ritual objects, movements and sounds help to imaginatively create the presence of the Divine in our midst. "One is encouraged to treat whatever object is being employed in ritual as representing ultimate reality", Paramananda says about the rituals of Tibetan Buddhism:

Flowers, for example, are regarded as being imbued with significance, their beauty and fragility reflect the true nature of all reality, which is impermanent and subject to decay, just like our own bodies. Thus we imagine that the flowers we are offering are imbued with a meaning that goes beyond words.[17]

Worship (*puja*) in Hinduism can be done in the home or temple. At home, an area of ritual purity is set aside with images of the family's Deity. I was invited into a friend's home in Mumbai, India, to see where they pray—a simple, quiet room exclusively set aside in a crowded apartment that housed both parents and the son's family. Food is offered here to the Divine and prayers are said, individually or together, as a daily ritual. Rich families often have a priest come and conduct their worship. Devotees also go to the temple to catch a glimpse of their GOD and offer food, milk and flowers in exchange for *prasad* (meaning "a gracious gift"), food offered back to worshippers from the Divine. In Goa, where Portuguese Catholicism reigned from the sixteenth century and left its presence in huge churches and a continuing Catholic presence, I visited the massive Church of the Immaculate Conception in Panjim, which attracts tourists from across India and beyond. A strong note of concern exuded from a roughly painted sign on an aisle column near the altar rail, all in upper-case letters for emphasis:

NOTICE

1. HOLY COMMUNION IS NOT A PRASAD.

2. NON-CHRISTIANS ARE NOT ALLOWED TO RECEIVE HOLY COMMUNION.

3. WHEN A PRIEST OR AN AUTHORIZED MINISTER DISTRIBUTES HOLY COMMUNION, NON-CHRISTIANS SHOULD NOT APPROACH HIM TO RECEIVE HOLY COMMUNION. THANKS.

Whereas *prasad*, the "free action of favor or grace coming to the assistance of individuals" is offered to all worshippers in the temple, the Catholic Eucharist, also signifying Divine grace, is firmly restricted only to those in the "correct" faith.

Similarly, in Islam, worship (*salat*) can be done anywhere as Muslims say their prayers five times a day on a prayer mat facing Mecca. Worship in the mosque on Fridays for noon prayers is important however, because it signifies solidarity with other Muslims. Worshippers ritually wash in a place provided prior to entering the mosque and leave their shoes before entering. Prayers are offered facing the *mihrab*, a niche in the *qibla* wall indicating the direction of Mecca. For the prayer ritual, Muslims stand erect with hands on either side of the face, thumbs touching ear-lobes, and say "Allahu Akbar" (God is most great). They recite the opening surah of the Qur'an (*Al-Fâtiha*) plus other selections, then bow from their hips, hands on knees, while saying "I extol the perfection of my Lord the Great." Upright again, they repeat "Allahu Akbar." They then glide onto their knees and place hands and face to the ground, doing all this several times with prayers and recitations, all in praise or supplication.[18] The Qur'an is displayed on a stand (*kursi*) in the mosque and, since GOD is only known through the Qur'an, reading and chanting it in Arabic is an act of worship in itself, even if one does not understand what is being said. Although there is nothing in the Qur'an to prohibit women entering the mosque, sexuality and religion compete once again. Mixed worship became unpopular as Islam spread, for fear of lustful "temptation", the trap of *Iblis* (Satan). Since the middle of the last century, women are more welcome in mosques, but they worship separately from men, either on the opposite side of the isle, behind the men, in an upstairs balcony or even in a separate room accessible only to women, where acts of prostration with raised buttocks will not cause distraction.

Candles were originally banned in Protestant churches since they suggested Catholic devotion to saints and thus idolatry, but the 1890 "Lincoln Judgement" in the Church of England allowed two candles on the holy table.[19] Since then, the wax has further melted and candles are now regulars in Protestant liturgy, symbolizing the presence of Christ, the Light of the world. Although I have watched many candles burn down to their feet in worship, I recently took part in a retirement service of a minister, his last with his beloved congregation. The main candle signifying the Divine Presence was lit through the service and then snuffed out, as always, at the end. I watched the smoke from the extinguished wick rise slowly for some time afterwards, eventually dispersing into invisibility but still present in the air. In the emotion of the moment, as that smoke and candle-smell was breathed in by all present, it became a wonderful symbol. While the physical gatherings with this minister had ended, the Spirit, made present through the candle symbol, remained within them all and had become part of them, even though dispersed, through its smoke. Such is the power of imagery and ritual, not to spell out meaning in huge explanatory signs but to allow it to percolate up in the heart.

This chapter cannot end without talk about magic and superstition. European colonization of indigenous peoples conquered land, people, cultures *and* beliefs. The religions of the conquered were described and evaluated against colonizing Christianity, so we have comments like "The Tantras [Tantric Hinduism] are generally mere manuals of mysticism, magic and superstition of the worst and most silly kind."[20] Using the words "magic" and "superstition" to describe another's religious rituals is a way of demoting their beliefs and practices in favor of more sophisticated or "true" beliefs. Because the words of tantric mantras were unintelligible, in terms of their rules of language, anthropologists called such chanting "magic", a delusionary belief in the power of irrational words, and yet Catholics have believed for centuries that the priest's words said over the bread and wine actually change it into the body and blood. When the liturgical books of the Russian Orthodox Church were changed in 1666 to equate them with the Greek Orthodox liturgy, some protested because the sign of the cross made in Greek style with three fingers to represent the Trinity had replaced the old two-finger sign representing Christ's dual nature. The protestors became a separate church and were persecuted and killed over the effectiveness of one finger.[21]

Only recently, the Pope ruled that only the actual words "in the name of the Father, Son and Holy Ghost" made a baptism effective—"Creator, Sustainer and Redeemer" simply won't do the trick. St Mary's Catholic Church in Brisbane, Australia, was overflowing with people from all walks of life, gathering from across the city because of the openness to contemporary issues of its priest for twenty years, Father Peter Kennedy, who built the church from almost non-existence. The church also operated a large social outreach ministry for the many disadvantaged in its area. However, because of vigilantes who photographed with phone cameras some of Kennedy's innovations in worship and sent the pictures to Rome, Father Kennedy has been sacked and banned from operating as a priest anywhere in Australia. Kennedy's supporters in the congregation have left in protest with him, as has the social welfare program. About 70 people now worship at the church, while 750 worship down the road with Kennedy at the Trades Hall, calling themselves St Mary's in Exile. What were Kennedy's major "sins?"—allowing priest *and people* to speak the words of consecration at Mass, allowing women to preach, not using vestments at Mass, allowing the blessing of same-sex unions in church *and* using the gender-inclusive terms "In the name of the Creator, the Redeemer and the Sanctifier" for baptism (rather than Father, Son and Holy Spirit), thus invalidating any baptisms done that way.[22]

In a museum in the Seychelles, I found a display cabinet labeled "Witchcraft in the Seychelles". Proof of this witchcraft was a tattered old book with names and crosses randomly written in pencil over its pages—apparently witchcraft notations. Ironically, the book was called *Adventure in Service* and was open at pages 100–1 of the chapter headed "Rotary's Onward March". These pages listed Rotary International's activities from 1930 to 1936 and also a description of the origins of Rotary's "Four Way Test"—Is it the truth? Is it fair to all concerned? Will it build goodwill and better friendships? Will it be beneficial to all concerned? Beside it in the case was a copy of John Bunyan's Christian classic *Pilgrim's Progress,* open at the fearful illustration of the "Flight of Apollyon", the devil against whom Christian fought. Magic or truth? According to Mark Twain (1835–1910):

There are many humorous things in the world, among them the white man's notion that he is less savage than the other savages.[23]

Sensing the Sacred

If our five senses—sight, sound, taste, touch and smell—help us engage our world as human beings, should they not also help us engage the Sacred? Although we say "No" for the umpteenth time when a toddler puts her latest discovery into her mouth, touch was one of her earliest experiences, along with smell when she unerringly found that nipple and discovered taste as a reward. Twitching at a loud noise, we knew that her hearing was intact, and when she followed our hand as it moved, sight was added to her list of accomplishments. Metaphysics, philosophy and religious doctrines were of little use to this fascinating creature, newly emerged from the darkness of the watery womb and confronting the most traumatic moment of her existence thus far.

The previous chapter talked about engaging the Divine through ritual *action*, but rituals also recruit the senses. When religion scholar Sam Gill tried to describe his first experience of a Native American Hopi kachina dance with its stunningly colorful costumes and dances that incorporated highly melodic songs with accompanying rhythms from turtle-shell rattles and sleigh bells, he ended thus:

> Verbal descriptions are dull reflections of such events. Not even photo-graphs and sound recordings (neither are allowed) would do justice to the dances. They engage all of the senses, and at least for the Hopi, the dances resonate with the whole of Hopi culture and history. Over the years I have attended a number of kachina dances at Hopi, and I have always been fascinated and moved.[3]

How do *we* experience the Divine through our senses, or have we discredited them in favor of knowledge and reason, assigning such feelings to children, mystics and the unbalanced? Do we, in reverse, seek to attract the *Divine* senses by hoping that what brings joy to us will also delight GOD?

The sense of taste

In Beach Street, Singapore, where immigrants, traders and adventurers once stepped ashore and erected their places of worship (land reclamation has now sent Beach Street inland), I stepped into a hole-in-the-wall mosque whose only give-away was the crescent moon and star on its roof. The elderly imam and his assistant made me welcome and showed me around. When I asked for a photograph of them both, the younger one whipped upstairs and returned in a few moments in his best robe. "You will send me a copy to this address", he insisted as he scribbled on a scrap of paper. They then invited me to sit with them on the steps of the mosque to eat biryani (biriani) rice wrapped in brown paper packages, donated for mosque visitors by the Pakistani restaurant down the road. Sharing with others in need, including food, is one of the five pillars of Islam, something reciprocated in the days after 9/11 when a New York business adjoining the Center for Islamic Culture began delivering packed lunches to their Islamic neighbors, knowing it would be difficult for them, especially women in hijab (head cov-ering), to go on the streets, given the level of anger against the terrorists.

The sharing of food is also central to the Sikhs. Temples (*Gurdwaras*, "Guru's home") have a kitchen (*langar*), initiated by the original Guru Nanak, where anyone can eat so long as they sit in the same row and eat the same food, free of distinctions of rich or poor, high or low caste, Hindu or Muslim. Guru Amar Das (1479–1574), the third Guru, would not give an audience to anyone, not even Akbar the Great (1542–1605), the Mogul

Emperor of India, if he had not first eaten with others at the *langar*. This was exceptional in a time of both caste distinctions and prejudices against "untouchables". Funded by donations and contributions of food, today's *langar* volunteers cook and do the dishes—it is considered an honor to work in the kitchen or dining-room. Although some Sikhs eat meat, only vegetarian food is served to respect those for whom eating meat is offensive, reminiscent of Paul's plea for restraint before Corinthian church members who were still hesitant about eating food offered to idols. If it offends others, Paul said, don't do it (1 Cor. 8:13). Such hospitality is also the theme of the care of the Deity in a Hindu temple. As religion scholar Diana Eck explains, the Deity does not need the food, water and ornaments offered—it is the other way around:

> Human beings need to refine the arts of service and caring and, according to the Hindu tradition, the Divine graciously condescends to be present in every temple, on every home altar, precisely that they may do so.[4]

Eating together encompasses more than food, something we are losing in our fast-food world but being reclaimed by the Slow Food movement. For desert people who lived with labor-intensive food gathering and preparation, the meal was the culmination and celebration of the efforts of many. When three strangers came to Abraham and Sarah's tent, staying for lunch was not about soup and a sandwich. Abraham first invited them to sit while a servant brought water to wash their feet. He offered them a "little bread", instructing Sarah to "make ready three measures of choice flour, knead it, and make it into cakes" (Gen. 18:6). Any bread-maker knows that making bread from scratch is no short process. In the meantime, Abraham ran to his field to get a calf for a servant to kill, quarter and prepare. Such rich desert hospitality paid off for Abraham and Sarah in the story—the strangers were from Yahweh, forecasting barren Sarah's immanent pregnancy.

"Company" comes from two Latin words, *com*, with or together, and *panis*, bread—sharing bread together. The full significance of this is lost where bread is only a portion of the food we enjoy, but in most parts of the world, bread is the staple that keeps people alive. A woman writing about food shortages in communist Europe explained that there were different shortages at different times, making the scarce item a luxury, whether fruit, milk or cheese. Each family had a small monthly allowance of meat, cheese and coffee, but never enough to feed a whole family. The basic food was bread. All other things could disappear for a time but when the shops said "No bread", it sent cold shivers through the community. In another cruel period of history, Primo Levi tells what happened when the Germans were defeated and simply deserted the concentration camps, leaving severely weakened prisoners to fend for themselves. Levi and two others went to the kitchens and hauled back a stove and leftover food so the prisoners in their hut could eat. Grateful, the others offered some of their bread to the three. Levi says:

> Only a day before a similar event would have been inconceivable. The law of the Lager [the camp] said: eat your own bread and if you can, that of your neighbors, and left no room for gratitude. It really meant that the Lager was dead. It was the first human gesture that occurred among us. I believe that that moment can be dated as the beginning of the change by which we who had not died slowly changed from *Häftlinge* [prisoners] to men again.[5]

Because of its central importance, bread is a metaphor for life itself and for making a living, since work provides our "bread" or food. This goes back to the Egyptians, called the "bread eaters", who perfected baking and established bread as their principal food and cultural and monetary measure—"number of breads" indicated someone's wealth, and wages were paid in bread.[6] For the Hebrews, Yahweh supplied "manna" in the wilderness (Ex. 16:1–36) that could be boiled in pots or ground to make cakes (Num. 11:8). There is still discussion as to what manna was but, like so many stories, its symbolism of Divine provision was more important than what was provided. Not surprisingly, Jesus was called "bread" because he brought spiritual "food" from GOD—"I am the bread of life. Whoever comes to me will never be hungry, and whoever believes in me will never be thirsty" (John 6:35).

The Jewish Passover (*Pesach*) was the Festival of Unleavened Bread, commemorating the exodus from Egypt (Ex. 12). Unleavened bread (*matzot*) signified that the fleeing Hebrews did not have time to allow their bread to rise. After the loss of the temple (70 CE), the Passover meal (*Seder*) became home-based with a ritual set down in the *Haggadah*. Traditions have varied through the centuries, but it still celebrates Jewish survival. The Exodus story is read. On the table are bitter herbs, reminders of Israel's slavery; a roasted lamb bone, a reminder of the Passover lamb; a roasted egg, a reminder of the *hagigah*, a festival sacrificial offering brought to the temple; a mixture of nuts, fruit and wine, reminders of the mortar the Hebrew slaves made; and a plate containing a vegetable to be dipped in salt water, a reminder of the pain of slaves who only ate basic food. Some Jewish women have reinterpreted their place and role at the *Seder*, given the patriarchal culture in which this ceremony originated. In a Minneapolis home, an orange symbolically appeared along with the traditional elements on the *Seder* plate. According to the story, Susannah Heschel, the Eli Black Professor of Jewish Studies at Dartmouth College, was lecturing in the "orange" state, Florida. An angry Orthodox Jewish man in the audience shouted, "A woman belongs in the *bime* (pulpit or raised platform in a synagogue) the way an orange belongs on a *Seder* plate."[7]

Jesus' last night with his friends was the Passover meal (except in John's Gospel). Anticipating his fate, he took the *matzah* (unleavened bread) provided and a cup of wine, asking his friends to remember him. This became the central Christian sacrament, developing into an elaborate ritual where Christ was symbolically re-sacrificed and the elements turned into flesh and blood. When the Reformation rejected this conversion of the elements, the laity could then receive the wine without fear of spilling Christ's blood, and the minister did not have to consume the consecrated leftovers. Whatever the theory, the ritual has moved a long way from early shared meals in homes, eaten out of a need of nourishment while remembering their last meal with Jesus. There is something powerful about sharing food with friends. Many times, when I have prepared dinner for guests and sat down with bread on my side-plate and wine in front of me, I have longed to take the bread and wine as symbols of friendship, no strings attached, no rules imposed, no magic chants, and say something to capture the moment and remember the Life that flows between us. Unfortunately these elements have been too long confiscated by rules about who can do this and in what setting, an *ad nauseum* church debate over which the first Christians would simply shake their heads in amazement. Has the Eucharist become an idol and the Divine imprisoned in wafers, wine and ordained hands until it is no more than a magic act? Has our obsession with Jesus' death concertina-ed that last evening together—the washing of feet, gathering of friends, sharing of a meal, premonitions of imminent disaster—into a blood-eating sacrifice? Have their hospitality, friendship and solidarity been reduced to a taste-and-sip, a wafer on the tongue, or a file-past dipping of a bread scrap into grape juice such that our focus is on not losing the soggy bread in the communal cup, rather than the meaning itself?

The French film *Babette's Feast* has become a "religious" film. Written by Karen Blixen (Isak Dinesen, 1885–1962) and made into an award-winning film, it tells of two spinster sisters, daughters of a deceased pastor who live a frugal, puritanical existence in an isolated village in Jutland, Norway, in the nineteenth century. Babette, a destitute widow fleeing Paris, becomes their servant and learned to cook their plain food. The pastor's flock begins to quarrel and remember old grievances as the sisters strive to keep the peace. When Babette wins the lottery, they assume she will leave, but Babette asks to prepare a French meal for the village as a celebration of the late pastor's birthday. She goes to Paris and returns, to the alarm of the sisters, with box-loads of strange and exotic food. The horrified sisters confess this sinful excess to the villagers, who decide to attend but not comment on the food, as if they had no sense of taste. At the beginning, they talk only of the weather and the good pastor, but things change as the sumptuous flavors and expensive wines thrill their taste-buds. Bitterness changes into sweet exchanges and peaceful contentment through this mystical transformation brought about by the sensual experience of taste. Babette tells the sisters she was a famous chef in Paris, that the dinner used up her new fortune and that the village would always be her home. They had all been "healed" through the sensation of food prepared with love.

Refusing the sense of taste has also been advocated as a way to the Divine. Such ascetic renunciation suggests that this natural sense is evil, a body–soul dualism that has beleaguered Christianity. "Would to God there were not these necessities [eat, sleep and drink], but only the spiritual refreshments of the soul, which, alas, we taste too seldom!" à Kempis wrote.[8] Yet if food is simply utilitarian fuel, why are there so many tastes and flavors—just to tempt us to sin? I am usually disappointed with octopus in restaurants, although I continue to try it, because I have an enduring memory of baby grilled octopus fresh from the sea in a beach-front restaurant in Plakia, southern Crete—none before or after have tasted like that. You will have your own examples. In a book about conditions in communist Europe, the author describes an old man eating his first banana after the Wall came down. He smelled it and felt it before putting it in his mouth, skin and all. "It tastes *so* good", he said. The skin must have been tough and stringy but, for him, just the act of biting represented the hope of a new future.

Both Judaism and Islam have a healthy question-mark against asceticism, precisely because they see it as a denial of GOD's good creation. The rabbis saw enforced privation as "sin"—we are to account for any enjoyments and pleasures we declined without sufficient cause.[9] However, Jews did have their food rules. According to Genesis, we are meant to be vegetarian—GOD gave humankind all the fruit and vegetables to eat, even the forbidden tree (1:29). It became more complicated with animals, however. Those with cloven feet who chew their cud—goats, sheep and oxen—are *kosher* (ritually fit for consumption), but ones without *both* attributes, such as pigs, are forbidden (Deut. 14:7–8). Animals must be slaughtered by a special slaughterer and hung so the blood drained out (*halal* or permitted meat for Muslims comes from animals slaughtered by severing the blood vessels, usually the jugular in the throat, while reciting Allah's name over the animal). Eggs from *kosher* birds can be eaten if free of blood spots, but only seafood with scales and fins, not shellfish. As for insects, a certain kind of locust is permitted, although I wonder why. I had a childhood horror of John the Baptist eating these in the desert. Locusts swarm on occasions where I live, a dark cloud sounding like cellophane being crumpled in front of a microphone, as all those legs rub together in flight. I can see why a plague of them stripping the crops might entice Pharaoh to release the Hebrews (Ex. 10:12–20)—no wonder John was a trifle grumpy at times.[10]

During Lent (the 40 days before Easter), some Christians limit their joy of taste in memory of Jesus' death. Originally, this fast was kept by eating only one meal, devoid of meat, fish, eggs and milky food—now Lent is more about reflection, prayer, study and generosity, with voluntary fasting as an aid. In Catholic England, Christians confessed ("shrove") on Shrove Tuesday to prepare for Lent. The village bell that rang to remind the faithful was called the "Pancake Bell", because foods being given up for Lent had to be finished off that day and the eggs, butter and fat were made into pancakes. The pancake race originated when a cook running late for church carried her pancake with her, still cooking in a pan. On the fourth Sunday of Lent (Mothering Sunday and also Refreshment Sunday), some loosening of food rules was permitted and relatives from afar returned home bringing gifts of food. That day's Gospel reading was the feeding of the 5,000 and people were sent home to feast until satisfied. Simnel cakes, from the Latin *simnellus* (special occasion wheat loaves) or the Anglo-Saxon *symel* (feast) were baked, covered with marzipan and stamped with the figure of Jesus, with twelve little marzipan balls representing the twelve apostles (or eleven if Judas had been dropped).[11]

Temporary abstinence and asceticism are different kettles of fish. The Buddha tried starving himself to gain enlightenment, but "all my limbs became like the joints of withered creepers," he said, "my gaunt ribs became like the crazy rafters of a tumble-down shed, my scalp became shriveled and shrunk and the skin of my belly clung to my backbone".[12] Instead, Buddhist monks eat in moderation, begging each morning for the meal they eat at lunchtime, with nothing until the next morning. Ramadan is a month of fasting for Muslims, but eating is permitted before dawn and after sunset. The Jewish Yon Kippur (Day of Atonement), is only a 24-hour fast. In Christianity, fasting and sexual abstinence appeared among some early Christians waiting for Christ's return, encouraged by the practices of the Greek philosophers. It lost general appeal, however, when Christianity became an imperial religion and serious fasting and punishment of the body, imitating Christ's suffering, moved to the monasteries. Bishop Athanasius (296–373 CE) wrote in his *Life of Saint Anthony*, a saint who had considerable influence on early monasticism:

> Anthony was a daily martyr to his conscience . . . and his discipline was much severer (than a martyr's), for he was always fasting, and he had a garment of hair on the inside, while the outside was skin, which he kept until his end. He neither bathed his body with water to free himself from filth not did he ever wash his feet, nor even endure so much as to put them into water, unless compelled by necessity.[13]

Food rituals concentrate our mind so we *think* about what we are doing. Saying a blessing over a meal reminds us that we are about to eat something that was once alive, even if we are vegetarians. Early tribal cultures living in reciprocity with nature thanked an animal for sacrificing itself and killed only the amount of meat needed. At the Parliament of the World's Religions (2009), Norma Kassi from the Wolf Clan of Old Crow, Yukon (Arctic Circle), described living in six to eight feet of snow, except for four months of the year beginning in March when her tribe travels on sleds over four mountains to the wetlands. Birds, salmon and caribou come there annually, providing their yearly food. Some 140 species of birds have been recorded, although tragically, possibly due to climate change, this has dramatically dwindled. The ravens announce the arrival of the caribou and one cup of blood from the first animal is drunk for spiritual strength. Men hunt only what they need, according to tribal rules, and take pride in caring for these wetlands where everything is sacred and each creature held in regard. The caribou numbers have also been shrinking but, in 2009, 20,000 came which they interpreted as a thank-you for caring for the habitat against an encroaching environmental disaster. Sensing dwindling salmon numbers, the tribe decided to take only 150 from the river last year—they only caught seven. These people living in such a delicate balance are thankful to what supplies them with food. Our global tribe also needs to develop thanksgiving rituals for what we need, not our greed, in order to preserve our delicately balanced planet.

The Japanese Tea Ceremony (*Chado*, the Way of Tea) speaks to *all* the senses with its simplicity, orderliness, harmony, companionship, equality and beauty. The goal is to realize tranquility of mind in communion with others. The student of tea arranges the objects artistically, understands timing and pauses, appreciates social graces and then applies all this beyond the tea room to daily Buddhist life. The principles of the Way of Tea are:

1   Harmony—between utensils, food, design and people, in tune with nature's rhythms.
2   Respect—a communal experience while respecting the dignity of each.
3   Purity—cleaning before and after for a harmonious ceremony, individual purification and release from attachments.
4   Tranquility—the aesthetic component of mood, quietness, oneness and freedom from worldly cares.

This "peace" created in the midst of a complex world is *wabi*, meaning "poverty", "simplicity" or "out of fashion" in the sense of breaking through artificiality to feel something of highest value.[14] Zen devotees have perfected this ritual in beautiful settings among manicured gardens, but any rituals with food or drink that intentionally make us pause and listen to our inner selves offer the chance of engaging that "highest value".

The sense of sight

"Everybody needs beauty as well as bread, places to play in and pray in, where nature may heal and give strength to body and soul alike."[15] North American Navajo wisdom describes their experience of the Sacred as:

Beauty behind me. Beauty before me.
Beauty above me. Beauty below me.
Beauty all around me.
(It starts) in beauty, and finishes in beauty.[16]

Their Creator Spirit Begochiddy called the creation "beautiful", meaning that all its parts were in harmony, and thus their central concern is the preservation of beauty at all levels of existence. The Hindu *Upanishads* describe "joyful play" as the Divine motivation for creating and re-creating the world in different cycles. This was no capricious act but acts of spontaneity and fun, illustrated in Hindu art as Lord Shiva dancing, Lord Krishna playing his flute and Divine Couples delighting in sexual love. According to Sufi Rumi, "God is like a beautiful woman in search of an undistorted mirror, so she can enjoy her beauty."[17] And consider the Divine satisfaction as each act of creation emerged "and God saw that it was good" (Gen. 1).

Is "good" a moral, aesthetic or physical description here? It is least likely to mean, in this context, *morally* good, yet early in Christian history, the creation story went sour with the taste of forbidden fruit and a theological overlay of sin and fallenness. Good became irrevocably paired with evil in a far-reaching obsession with morality and we lost the *aesthetic* goodness and beauty of human life and creation itself. Yet the "sight" of GOD is all about beauty, according to the religious writers. The psalmists waxed lyrical about the "strength and beauty" in GOD's sanctuary (Ps. 96:6) or their desire "to behold the beauty of the Lord" (Ps. 27:4). For Rumi, ". . . once you have perceived the beauty of God, the sciences lose their fascination"[18] and Thomas Aquinas, even while inheriting Christianity's moral negativity towards humanity, called the Divine the most beautiful thing in the universe. Alfred North Whitehead described God as "the poet of the world, with tender patience leading it by his vision of truth, beauty and goodness".[19] As for a contemporary voice, Australian Bishop E. J. Cuskelly (1924–99) said, "There is nothing more real than true poetry. There is nothing more poetic than the theology of God's Word working through all that is good and true and beautiful in our created world."[20]

For many of the world's religions, the visual has been more important than words in helping people "see" the Divine, even though they all realize that Divine Mystery is without form. Religious art has offered us windows for the imagination:

It is the creative process itself that momentarily transcends time, offering an awareness that something other than the ordinary can exist and, through that existence, reinvigorate the flawed aspirations of ordinary people.[21]

The Monstrance, the container which contains the Host (Eucharist wafers), was introduced in the thirteenth century so that people could *see* "the body of Christ" as well as ingest it. Monstrances became elaborately decorated in silver, gold and precious stones, and those taken on procession became so huge they needed a supporting carriage. Rather than the Bible stationary on a stand far off in the church chancel, it was processed down the aisle to accompanying music, liturgy and visual delight. The Bible itself was reproduced in stunning calligraphy and painted vignettes painstakingly done by monks so that, even for those who could not read, it was beautiful in itself, reflecting the glory of GOD. Its stories were also acted out in grand finery and action so people could enter into the drama themselves, rather than just hear it read.[22]

Paintings, murals and statues in churches highlighted the pain and agony of the crucifixion such that viewers reached out in devotion towards Jesus, the Word made visual, all the while subconsciously absorbing the theology of the day "read" from different symbols, attire and poses. In some paintings,

Jesus' divinity was emphasized, with haloes and heavenly habitations, while the Renaissance painted his perfect humanity. Words force readers to paint their own visual images, but art places the scene in front of us and invites us to come in and participate. Some art pieces are like videos with sequential events within one frame, while others are fixed on a particular moment. The "moving" pictures ask you to walk through the events, while the fixed pictures invite you to sit and meditate, your eyes doing the walking around the image. In San Marco in Florence, Fra Angelico's life-size scenes from the life of Jesus cover the walls of each monk's small cell, allowing them to "live" with Jesus and his disciples. As Jesus stretched out his hand to heal a beggar, that hand also reached out to engage the solitary monk.

Art critics forever tell us what is good and bad art and, no doubt, there are guidelines and fashions, or we would not have "Art Appreciation" courses, but art conveys meaning by speaking to the heart, a subjectivity that cannot be classified in generalities or imposed by another. There is a welling up in the heart and a reaching out to the Sacred in response to what the paintings suggest, given the experiences of the particular viewer. Take Holman Hunt's (1827–1910) painting, "The Shadow of Death", done in 1873. I had seen this painting in Sunday School lesson books and grew up with its brother, Hunt's painting of a handsome Christ, lamp in hand, knocking at the door of the heart, evoking emotions of longing and decision. I had never really *looked* at the "The Shadow of Death" until a student in my Religious Art course selected it as a painting that spoke to *her*. An overly-handsome teenage Jesus in his father's carpentry shop, bare-chested with nothing but a carefully draped loincloth, has paused for a moment, his arms stretched upwards to relax his body. His pose throws a shadow on the wall behind, a figure on a cross with its shadow hands touching the shop's wall-bracket of long nails. For those who might miss this not-so-subtle symbolism, a halo circles Jesus' head. Mary, kneeling on the floor beside Jesus, looks up and raises her hand in horror at the "shadow" of things to come. The painting worked for my student and others who heard her presentation—"This man died for me", it says and demands a response. Some months later, London's *Sunday Telegraph* featured this painting in an article headed "Seriously Soppy". Art critic Martin Gayford, admitting he is "positively allergic" to the Pre-Raphaelism style, wrote, "I find it hard to think, for example, of a more revolting painting than Holman Hunt's *The Shadow of Death* (1873) . . . everything about it is horrible—enormously talented and accomplished, true, but horrible." His litany of disapproval included the vulgarity of the idea, the texture "like glazed china" of everything in the carpenter's shop including the wood shavings, Jesus' "big cow eyes and an expression of camp idiocy" and the "shrieking colors" of turquoise and mauve,[23] yet for some of my students, who have the right to their own experiences, this was a window to the Sacred.

Since Christian art was a teaching tool employed by the Church to ensure that the illiterate learned the dogmas without ambiguity, paintings, for the most part, were realistic and contrived so that personalities could be recognized—Saint Peter holding his keys, Saint Catherine with a broken wheel and Mary Magdalene clothed in red. In a fifteenth-century Armenian illustrated manuscript of the early monastic Desert Fathers, the monks are doing nothing but standing and praying, but their clothes give us the necessary clues. Those in longer clothes lived in community, those with robes above the knees were more ascetic, while the true ascetes were naked (although the painter used long beards to hide significant parts).[24] Modern or abstract art, however, has taken up the challenge of the formless, unknowable Sacred, juxtapositioning symbols and objects to jolt us out of our myopic structured reality into the realm of metaphor, hints and suggestion. As Richard Holloway says, "In contrast to art that passionately notices things, such as a little patch of yellow on a wall, religion has a fatal weakness by trying to *explain* them."[25] For art to help us engage the Sacred today, it must first grab our attention, and then make us stop, look, think and respond, such as a painting of a black Mother GOD breastfeeding a white baby. We ask, what does this mean and how does this open a window to the Sacred for me?

The icons of Eastern Orthodoxy are exactly this—windows through which to glimpse heaven and be beckoned into the Divine presence. They are not holy pictures as in Roman Catholicism, but sacred things in themselves, charged with Divine energy and mediators between us and Mystery—the living Word in color. Judaism rejected any representations of the Divine (Ex. 20:4) and the Greeks thought gazing on the GODS invited insanity or blindness, but Roman portraits of the emperor were used to substitute for his presence—documents signed in front of such portraits were as binding as the emperor's actual signature. Once Constantine entered the Christian scene, artists were commissioned to paint holy pictures for imperial buildings, including portraits of Christ posed like those of the emperor. Emperor Justinian (527–65 CE) launched the golden age of Byzantine art in Constantinople and Ravenna and, just as Egyptians painted faces on mummies and the Holy Face miraculously appeared on objects, icons entered Christianity. They were revered until the eighth century when they were forbidden as idolatrous veneration of Christ's *humanity*, but were later accepted again as an expression of both Christ's divinity *and* humanity—the Divine was encountered through the humanity of Christ. While

Western art was absorbed with images of a twisted body on the cross as a bloody sacrifice, Eastern icons focused on Christ victorious over suffering and death, the serenely noble GOD-man.

Icon artists once included lay people, but the task was later assigned to monks in case lay painters were morally deficient. There were strict rules about icon design so that the faithful were not distracted by the "window", but looked beyond it to GOD. Icons varied with local flavor, however, as language dialects vary. Coptic icons (usually painted by lay people) reflected the early church simplicity against the extravagant Byzantine style. Ethiopian icons feature distinctly Ethiopian faces and history. In an icon museum in Addis Ababa, Ethiopia, I came across a battle scene with an inset of Saint George killing the dragon, a popular icon theme, where the "dragon" under the horse's feet was an Italian army officer, referring to Ethiopia's occupation by the Italians. While Western art went three-dimensional in the Renaissance, the Eastern church remained faithful to two-dimensional iconography which they saw as more appropriate for art as a "window" to Something beyond. Hand movements, clothing and colors are standardized and symbolically meaningful, even though no two icons are completely identical. Rules of proportion are not followed—important figures can be larger than they should be. Doors, windows and vegetation can be fanciful, indicating a spiritual rather than mundane world. The face dominates the icon, sometimes half-covered in drapes to add mystery. The body is subordinated to the head size, and enlarged eyes stare at eternity. Earth-colored faces indicate an historical person (*adama*—earth), wrinkled cheeks indicate ascetes, monks and bishops, and high, convex foreheads indicate wisdom and spiritual strength. Thin, elongated noses do not smell the world's scent but Christ's sweet odor, thin mouths reject sensuality and closed lips mean contemplative silence without need for earthly nourishment. Colors have significance—red is blood and sacrifice, purple is royalty, white is purity and Divine light, blue is for the Virgin and gold is divinity. Decorative metal over icon faces indicate a hesitancy to show the full beauty of the icon and thus invite idol worship. All icons are geared to exude the order and peace of a transfigured life, aiding meditation on the Mystery beyond by appealing to all our senses. Since an Orthodox church interior mirrors the cosmos, with the floor as earth and the ceiling heaven, icons represent the spiritual world present with us, and the iconostasis, the icon-covered partition that separates the sanctuary and altar from the body of the church, represents the boundary between the sensual and spiritual worlds, behind which dwells the Mystery not seen by the worshippers.

North American Indian sand paintings, while beautifully intricate and painstakingly done, are not art pieces in the sense of something permanent to capture and admire. They are action pieces, the tools of ceremonial medicine to restore harmony to individuals and the cosmos. In Navajo tradition, the sand painting is constructed on the floor and shows mythic figures connected with the cause of the particular illness. It must be replicated from memory—designs are never copied down. The sand painting becomes the mask, the tangible form in which the spiritual beings act. The person to be healed is brought into the sand painting and sand from the figures is placed on corresponding "sick" places of the person to affect healing. Once the ritual is performed, the painting is destroyed and the sand returned to nature.

> [The sand painting] is a cosmic map. It is a vehicle by which re-creation, health, and beauty in life and the world are achieved. The sufferer finds his or her way to health from within the sand painting and by becoming a part of it; in turn it disappears and becomes a part of him or her . . . The destruction of the picture corresponds to the dissolution of the tensions and imbalances that have given rise to the suffering.[26]

This is a totally foreign concept to cultures trained to honor the permanency of books and art. We talk about "non-literate" religions (Sam Gill prefers the term "exclusively oral") as if a written scripture is a superior stage and we become excited over ancient rock art, even as we recognize (as in Australian indigenous rock art) that the drawings were serially painted over each other as new situations arose, rather than considered permanent displays. "One of the greatest challenges facing the study of religion is to learn how to consider more fully the elements of performance, action and behavior", Sam Gill says. "It will amount to a radical rethinking of what we understand religion to be."[27]

While other Buddhist traditions also create elaborate, time-consuming mandalas (some from sand) on which to meditate, Zen Buddhists advocate spontaneous, sudden enlightenment without stages of meditation. "Buddhists see a way of living as the ideal," Masutani Fumio said, "religion is daily life—no more, no less."[28] Its art is therefore simple, spontaneous and uncluttered, preferring asymmetry to rigid form. Ink and brush strokes are laid down at speed, one stroke becoming a mountain, dabs becoming trees, and things not belonging to nature, like boats and fishing shacks, diminutive in the total landscape. Excessive white space suggested a dimension of reality *not* seen, like Zen nothingness or "no-action" suggests something deeper. Zen gardens are designed to be in harmony with the natural world—"The sounds of mountain streams are the voice of Buddha, and the shape of the mountains is the body of Buddha."²⁹ Simple and elegant flower arranging reflects the simplicity and harmony of unadorned nature. As Osaka Koryo says:

> In Japan we savor Zen through an extraordinary wide range of things. In this room flowers have been arranged, bringing nature in, and if we open the screens here a garden will lie before us; nature is constantly being brought in. Here we harmonize with something artistic and very great, and also very small. I think that in putting a vast world into something small there is the wondrous "flavor" of Zen. Even the ordinary person who knows nothing of Zen understands that much. Zen runs deeply in the transformation into beauty of everyday life. It is impossible to think of our life of taste apart from Zen.³⁰

The sense of hearing

Unless we are totally alienated from, or angered by religion, we can probably bring to mind a moment of worship (or many) in a religious tradition that held significance for us, whether a regular worship ritual, a funeral, a baptism, or a wedding. What was it about the worship that drew you in, that made you feel you were participating in something, not just repeating words? Many will nominate the *sounds* of worship, the appeal to our ears of music and chanting. Music draws us out of our mundane spaces into something more ethereal or more inward. This has happened to me a thousand times, but this one instance earned an entry in my ever-present notebook. At a religion conference, I was rushing between crowded hallways of academics loudly expounding on their version of the paper they had just heard, when it grabbed me and pulled me to a guilty halt in the midst of the chaos. Beethoven's *Ode to Joy*, wherever I hear it—church, symphony concert, commercial muzak—demands my soul, my life, my all. The melody could scarce struggle up above the chattering crowd from the foyer grand piano from which it came, yet even if it had been a whisper, it would have found me because my soul is attuned to that melody and always inescapably captured. Music is the language of the soul that transcends doctrines, debate, persuasion and argument—it is the Lord's song in a strange land.

According to Albert Schweitzer, the great organist and student of Bach's music, Bach rendered *visual* images in sound—a painter rather than a poet.

> If the text speaks of drifting mists, of boisterous winds, of roaring rivers, of waves that ebb and flow, of leaves falling from the tree, of bells that

ring for the dying, of the confident faith that walks with firm steps, or the weak faith that falters insecure, of the proud who will be abased, and the humbled who will be exalted, of Satan rising in rebellion, or angels poised on the clouds of heaven, then one sees and hears all this in [Bach's] music . . . Gothic architecture transformed into sound. What is greatest in this art so full of natural life . . . is the spirit that breathes from it.[31]

Many who walk away from church, because of outdated theology and grue-some medieval images in its hymns, still cannot resist the music, the old hymn tunes that *acted* on their hearts, even if the words now leave them cold. "[Music] has powers to alter and match moods, to sustain and evoke emotion, to induce trance or ecstasy states, to express worship, and to enter-tain", John Bowker says. "At the same time, it is supremely a corporate activity: it not only binds together performers and audience, it is an activity in which many people can be engaged at once . . . At moments of despair and of triumph, humans sing, and sing together."[32]

The sound of music includes chanting of the sacred sound "Om", the ritual chanting of Buddhism, Psalms sung in Judaism, Gregorian chants, recitation from the Mass or Prayer Book, liturgies, the Muslim call to prayer, the soaring *Hallelujah Chorus* or the contemporary choruses of Pentecostals. On my first visit to India, I awoke on Christmas Day in this Hindu country to the sound of church bells playing "O Come all ye Faithful". When we attended a church in Korea, the hymns we sang were all in Korean, but the good old Presbyterian hymn tunes had been transported intact and we sang lustily, using our own English words. When the minister later apologized in broken English that the sermon was all in Korean, my husband assured him that it was not the first sermon he had not understood! In the little town of Maletta on Mount Etna's slopes in Sicily, the shepherds still play bagpipes, the instrument of the Roman troops who introduced them into Scotland. For the nine days before Christmas, they descend to Catania on the coast and go from home to home, playing for three minutes around the family's crèche, having a brandy for the cold and then off to the next house, doing some 200 homes a day.[33] However you feel about bagpipes, they are following the instructions of the Psalmist, "Make a joyful noise to the Lord, all the earth; break forth into joyous songs and sing praises" (Ps. 98:4).

If we did a survey of human beings, asking them to identify the best moments of their lives, I am confident that the overwhelming majority would not be about something they read or learnt, but about something they expe-rienced through one or more of their senses. If we asked them to identify the moments they felt most in touch with the Sacred, however that is named, again the overwhelming majority would name an experience processed through their senses, rather than through a text. This is not very encouraging for us writers, but I also admit that it is true. Certainly it was for Bengali poet Rabindranath Tagore (1861–1941) who experienced the Divine with *all* his senses:

> Thou ever pourest for me the fresh draught of thy wine of various colors and fragrance, filling this earthen vessel to the brim. My world will light its hundred different lamps with thy flame and place them before the altar of thy temple. No, I will never shut the doors of my senses. The delights of sight and hearing and touch will bear thy delight.[34]

13

What is
Your Experience?

Be ye lamps unto yourselves,
be ye a refuge to yourselves.
Betake yourself no external refuge.
Hold fast to the truth as a lamp;
hold fast to the truth as a refuge.
Look not for a refuge in anyone besides yourselves.
                              —*The Buddha*[1]

o   o   o

Authentic experience makes a religion a true tradition.
Religious experience is, above all, human experience.
If religions are authentic, they contain the same elements of
stability, joy, peace, understanding, and love.
                              —*Thich Nhat Hanh*[2]

We have considered many aids to engaging the Divine and through which
we may feel the Divine engages us—people, places, things, rituals, communities and the senses—but for many, there is no need for intermediaries.
GOD has come to them in the quietness of a room, the glory of a sunset, the
still, small voice, the depth of the heart, and they have responded to this
epiphany using their own means of communication with the One. "God has
planted within you the desire to search for him", Rumi said. "Do not look
at your lack of strength and wisdom for the search. By planting within you
the desire to search, God is guaranteeing the strength and wisdom you need.
Also he is telling you that you are worthy of him."[3] On the other side of the
coin, this GOD-given desire to search has, for many, not been reciprocated.

They have strived, struggled and begged the Divine to come to them, or speak within them, in the quietness of a room, the glory of a sunset, the still, small voice, the depth of the heart, and they have felt nothing despite their longing to respond in their own way to the One. In a poem, I wrote:

> I burn a candle
> Spin a prayer wheel
> Count more beads
> Whirl dervish-like.
> Is Anyone there?
> I gaze deep within
> Repeat my mantra
> Meditate without food
> Abandon my all.
> Does Anything listen?[4]

Describing religious experience is more slippery than capturing a speck of eggshell in raw egg-white. Just when we think you have it cornered, it slips away again. We use the word "experience" all the time in religious talk, yet we mean different things by it. It can mean the sum of who I am, "In my experience, GOD is . . .", meaning that, if I look back over everything that has happened to me and everything I have read and thought, GOD seems more like this than that. Or, when I say "I have experienced GOD", I can mean that supernatural or out-of-the-ordinary surprises have happened to me and I see them as proof of GOD's attention. Or, I experience the Sacred through "doing" the sacraments, praying, walking a labyrinth or fasting. Or, it can mean that I have had visions, ecstatic feelings and Divine voice-mails where I have actually experienced GOD contacting me. To say that my considered reason and life-experience votes for Divine action rather than against it is hugely different from saying that GOD chats to me and acts as my personal Genie-in-the-lamp, yet the phrase "personal experience" is bandied around today without clarity as to what is being claimed.

Evangelical Christianity, at the time of my coming of age in the 1960s, was negotiating the widening chasm between fundamentalist creeds—"the plenary and verbal inspiration of scripture and its total inerrancy . . . the virgin birth of Christ, his deity, his bodily resurrection from the grave, and his pre-millennial return to reign on a purified earth"[5]—and biblical scholarship showing the Bible to be a human book with contradictions and cultural accretions, together with burgeoning scientific advances calling everything into question. A fortress mentality developed where, the more you "stood firm" to certain unquestionable "givens", despite evidence to the contrary, the stronger your faith. Personal GOD-experiences could be expected to bless this stance, assuring the believer of their eternal salvation. Interestingly, looking back, "assurance" was probably the most preached-about topic ("Blessed assurance, Jesus is mine") and, although it should come simply from Divine promises, the *real* proof of the pudding was a "personal experience" of a "personal Savior"—testimonies of how GOD personally communicated, wrought miracles, or appeared in ways beyond the mundane. I always thought this strange, because anyone could claim anything, and probably did. There was no way of proving whether a miracle happened, or whether one simply conjured up a warm, internal glow, or attributed an ordinary coincidence to the Divine. I never said this aloud—that would only reflect negatively on "Oh ye of little faith"—yet a lie-detector would have come in handy to allay the descending guilt of those who sat silently listening, with no epiphanies to report.

The surge of Pentecostal churches around the world is another expression of this "personal experience" religion. Although their emphasis on visible ecstatic experiences harks back to a splinter group in American Methodism in the early 1900s, the "new" Pentecostalism (Charismatic Movement) found its feet in the 1960s and became part of most mainline Christian denominations, as well as establishing many independent churches around the world. Here again, we are dealing with assurance, through an experience of GOD *beyond* traditional baptism, confirmation, or a "conversion" experience. The "Baptism of the Holy Spirit", accompanied by the ability to "speak in tongues", becomes the "proof" that the Divine Spirit has engaged and accepted you, giving you a "gift of the Spirit" as a membership badge. Intellectual reflection is subordinated to prophecy or direct messages from GOD; and dancing, clapping, raising arms to heaven and speaking in unintelligible "languages" (tongues) imitating diverse languages spoken at the Pentecost experience (Acts 2:7) are evidence of being "filled with the Spirit". Frank Schaeffer, who once worked alongside his conservative evangelical theologian-father, Francis Schaeffer (1912–84), has joined the Orthodox Church where life for him is no longer a constant search for personal supernatural experiences. He says:

Once you buy the evangelical born-again "Jesus saves" mantra, the idea that salvation is a journey goes out the window. You're living in the realm of the magic formula. It seems to me that the Orthodox idea of a slow journey to God, wherein no one is altogether instantly "saved" or "lost" and nothing is completely resolved in this life (and perhaps not in the next) mirrors the reality of how life works, at least as I've experienced it.[6]

So much has happened since the 1960s, when challenges to everything lay thicker on the ground than a Minnesotan snowfall. The Bible is seen by more and more scholars and church folk as a human story of ancient people in touch with GOD, rather than an inerrant Divine dictation or practical text-book for *every* event in twenty-first-century life. The Church and its tradi-tions have been found wanting, given their inability to move beyond ancient forms, language and concepts, and also the feet of clay displayed more prominently under clerical robes. "Truths" from medieval times and also the Enlightenment have had to be re-evaluated in contemporary contexts, current culture, science, technology and ecology. Teilhard de Chardin (1881– 1955), Christian visionary and scientist, full of awe about our evolving knowledge of the universe, said:

> If, as a result of some interior revolution, I were to lose in succession my faith in Christ, my faith in a personal God, and my faith in spirit, I feel that I should continue to believe invincibly in the world.[7]

All this must be taken into consideration when we do our theology for today. Theology is not just the responsibility of professionals, although they guide us in ways to think. *We* are also responsible, as individuals, for doing our *own* theology, our *own* talking about GOD, according to the way we have experienced our external and internal world. Every person has a theology, whether they call it that or not, but it must be a *working* theology, one that can function in our personal, professional and public lives. "The question is, how good, appropriate and functional it is," theologian Sallie McFague says, "we need a theology that 'begins in experience and ends with a conversion to a new way of being in the world.'"[8]

Experience has come into its own again as the basis for "knowing" (or not) the Sacred. This may seem a strange statement for those who think it never left, given the "evidence-based" personal experience of Evangelicalism and Pentecostalism I have just described. But personal "experience" based on hearing voices and cataloging miracles is not the experience I mean, although some may include this. It is life wisdom, lived action, personal history, collective stories, reason, feelings and emotions. It is about gathering up all that goes into the way we "know" things and applying it to questions about the Sacred. In a 1955 introduction to à Kempis' fifteenth-century *Imitation of Christ,* Brother Leo wrote:

> Knowingly or unknowingly, every normal human being has a philosophy of life. Some few persons, bereft of the power to grow, have a petrified

philosophy which knows no change or shadow of alteration; others, possessed of an undue admiration for what is ready-made, hold fast to some
cut-and dried philosophy; while the men and women who are blessed with
some realization of the mystery, the sublimity, and the sacredness of life,
make for themselves a philosophy which is incessantly being shaped and
modified by experience, by the passing of years, by travel, by friendship,
and by books.[9]

This is called contextual theology—considering our experiences in our
particular situations (context) and, from this reality, talking about GOD.
I said that this attention to life experience has come into its own again. Prior
to the 1960s, we dealt in "systematic" theology, meaning that any GOD-talk
or GOD-experience had to fit into an already existing cohesive system. For
example, since "the Divine plan for salvation" had been built around humanly
created categories of creation, fall and redemption, anything said had to fit
within that framework. If something did not fit, either from the Bible or
human experience, you simply ignored it, like a piece of puzzle from a different
puzzle box. This is why biblical scholar Marcus Borg called feminist theology
(a contextual theology) the single most important development in his lifetime,
because it challenged this fundamental way of doing theology.[10] Women began
to question their description as subordinate, sinful and suspect on account of
Eve's "sin", because this did not resonate with how they experienced themselves, life and GOD. If theology was "good news", it had to be good news
for women as well, and their questions challenged all three categories of
creation, fall and redemption. Using this contextual theology, the poor began
to question the master's reading of the Bible; blacks began to question white-
favoring theology; and indigenous people began to question colonial readings
of the text. As Anglican priest Steven Ogden says, "[R]eligion that does not
consider experience is bad religion."[11]

The courage for *me* to challenge inadequate religious "truths" came
through my experience. No matter how I tried to suppress doubts, they
grew more reasonable as the years went by. I finally reached the point, which
many theologians before me had reached, where I needed to address my
doubts face on, even at the risk of finding answers I did not want, or that
might lead me where I did not want to go. What I discovered was that
doubting what seems incompatible, incoherent or irrational is not ignorance,
weakness or inadequacy, but mature, honest, religious seeking. Authoritative
statements in religion must be treated the same way as authoritative statements in any discipline, open to question and challenge—any authority that
insists we believe certain things *against* our own experience must be tested.

In fact, I believe doubt is a gift, urging us to see through outdated "truths" and inadequate authorities.[12] Our life experience *matters* when we talk about GOD. We must not simply accept a religious package into which our lives must fit. According to Buddhist teacher Paramananda, we should wear our beliefs like a suit of clothes and not a suit of armor and be ready to shed them if our experience shows this to be necessary:

> What we have to be willing to do is place our trust in our experience rather than in our ideas about our experience. That means being able to experience on a level that is relatively free from prejudice and rigid ideas.[13]

If knowing comes from experience, how then do we "know"? Actually, the technical term is epistemology. I never needed that word until I began religious studies, by which time I was 40 and already had two degrees. What is amazing about theology is that you learn a whole new language so you can then say things you have always said. To say "I know" means that I am satisfied there is an authority by which I can know. Authorities come in different shapes. If you say "It's going to be a sunny day today" and I reply "I know", I mean (a) I heard the same weather report as you did—authoritative information; (b) the feel of my bones tells me it will not rain—personal experience; (c) I can tell by looking at the clouds—reasoning skills; (d) I'm omnipotent. We all know people who operate solely on the fourth type of authority, but for the rest of us, we use a mix of these at different times for different knowledge. By saying "I know" from experience, I am tempering each with the other and claiming my full humanity, rather than allowing others to ask, "By what authority are you doing these things and who gave you this authority?" (Matt. 21:23). There are times when we seek information from others about the Sacred (you *are* reading this book), there are times we reason things out for ourselves, there are times we intuitively feel things, and there are times when we feel "omnipotent"—connected with the Sacred. Sallie McFague says:

> There is no such thing as a complete theology; there are only piecemeal theologies, the best efforts of human beings to state what they have found to be undeniable through their experience of God and as members of the Christian community. It is as if a tiny bit of God is available to each creature, whatever aspect of God that creature needs and can absorb. Most of us cannot absorb very much of the infinite Divine Being . . . But a tiny bit is enough; that is, enough if it is deeply held, well understood, and carefully argued—and if it is open to the many other bits from other Christians as we all struggle to discern God's will for our world.[14]

We have to become our own theologians, deciding for ourselves whether Something engages us or whether we are simply listening to our echoes returning to us. *We* need to decide what is initiated beyond or deep within ourselves, or whether we have, in fact, invented GOD and belief in Divine communication. Faith is first-hand experience, whereas beliefs are second-hand, someone *else's* GOD-experiences cemented into doctrines by which we are told to live. "They knew the way and went to seek you [the Divine] along the narrow lane," Rabindranath Tagore wrote, "but I wandered abroad into the night for I was ignorant. I was not schooled enough to be afraid of you in the dark, therefore I came upon your doorstep unaware. The wise rebuked me and bade me be gone, for I had not come by the lane. I turned away in doubt, but you held me fast, and their scolding became louder every day."[15] A church friend became excited reading the progressive theology of Bishop John Shelby Spong and Professor Marcus Borg. Devouring all she could find, she shared her enthusiasm with her pastor who encouraged her, but became defensive when she asked why he did not preach this from the pulpit. When she volunteered to mentor Confirmation students, the pastor declined her offer and later told me that she was "too angry" for that—he preferred passive non-thinkers regurgitating the party line, or just being friendly, not those "angry" at clergy and church for keeping new ideas from them.

Many people who have turned to experience call themselves "spiritual" rather than "religious", but what does that mean? According to religion scholar Ursula King, spirituality is linked to "almost any longing of the human heart . . . for the permanent, eternal, everlasting—for wholeness, peace, joy and bliss".[16] These ideals have haunted human beings throughout history and fueled the desire to move beyond the limits of ordinary life to other levels of consciousness, inward experience and transformation. Australian theologian Tony Kelly uses similar words:

[Spirituality] stands for those neglected reaches of our humanity that cannot be quantified; an inwardness that superficiality often conceals or denies; a way of imagining a larger belonging to the community, to the world, to the ultimate reality. . . . It means to be a consistent protest against anything that would truncate our humanity, mutilate our sensitivities or stunt the creativity of imagination.[17]

An academic conference on religious experience in Warsaw (2010) described its focus in its call for papers thus, "Religion is also a deeply personal experience. Sometimes it is more or less possible to put the experience into words.

Sometimes it is just a feeling or an emotion difficult to verbalize, but nevertheless important for the meaningfulness of life and one's way of living." This recognition of hard-to-define personal experience at an *academic* level is in total contrast to the past. Twenty years ago, in the theological college in which I was involved, if a student offered his or her experience as an argument for a debated theological issue, the professors would not have been impressed. Although all the great church fathers and mothers throughout history wrote from their "embodied" experiences of life, this was never acknowledged as affecting their theological "mind", courtesy of that pervasive Greek dualism between body/matter and mind/spirit that devalued anything associated with bodiliness.

Spirituality is not an *escape* into the mind or its metaphysical playground, however—it is a lived *experience* involving and infiltrating all we are. When people call themselves "spiritual" today, they mean body *and* spirit, their whole being and existence in *this* world, enhanced through meditation, yoga, contemplative exercises or other ways of intentionally engaging the Sacred and recognizing the Spirit within. Spirituality is fully grounded in the earth, rather than a pie in the sky, and entails being fully human—"attending to the others here on planet Earth . . . finding out what makes others flourish . . . loving the neighbor . . . *knowing* the beloved others and feeling with them in their pain and joy".[18] While this is not meant to negate those who have left the world to live as hermits, monks and recluses, it does affirm those whose spirituality mixes with daily dishes, toddler demands and the stresses of the professional, corporate and social world. It calls into question the "flat, dead images of routine life" and challenges that "modern kind of corrosive pessimism that leads to paralysis rather than to the release of creative energies . . . [I]t is about where we radically stand, and where we move to from that point."[19] According to Ursula King, spirituality is "no longer a luxury of life, of mere interest to religious minorities or mystics . . . it now appears as an absolute imperative for human sanity and survival".[20] All this is a far cry from Thomas à Kempis' urging his fifteenth-century contemporaries to "keep thyself as a stranger and pilgrim upon the earth, who hath nothing to do with the affairs of this world".[21]

British journalist Malcolm Muggeridge (1903–90), who moved in a public and articulate way from atheism to Christian belief, was always cautious when questioned about what he believed and what church he had joined:

> Religion is . . . an experience, rather than a theory. It is something that people live, rather than something they can express as a theory of life. People who live the Christian faith seem to me to convey the reality of reli-

gion much better, more fruitfully, than any theoretical abstraction, any set dogma. One of the reasons that I don't in fact belong to any denomination is because I would resent very much being cross-examined about dogma.[22]

This is worrisome thinking for the powers that be if experience can be our guide and engaging the Divine is removed from places of worship and religious control. If the Divine is within us, or we can engage It in the world around us, we do not need temples, priests, sacraments or confession. It also asks serious questions about Christian doctrines that say Jesus Christ is the *only* incarnation of GOD and the Church is GOD's only ongoing "incarnation" on earth. Sallie McFague says:

[The incarnation] in its profound simplicity, means "God with us", God with the world and the world within God. The incarnation . . . is not merely or solely about Jesus. It is more radical than that, although for Christians Jesus is the paradigm of both God with us and the world within God. The incarnation reveals God as *always* with us and our being *defined* as within God . . . there is only one world, a world that God loves. Since God loves it, we not only *can* but *should*. In fact, loving the world (not God alone), or rather, loving God *through* the world, is the Christian way.[23]

Paying attention to our own experiences as knowledge of the Sacred can leave us vulnerable. If we *have* experienced Something engaging us, some epiphanies or visions vivid enough to keep us in faith for a lifetime, we are in good shape, but if we have *not* had such experiences, no matter how hard we seek them, does this mean, as John Calvin proposed, that we have simply been selected for eternal damnation or that there is no GOD to engage, as Marx and Freud suggested? What if descriptions of a Presence, Universal Energy and Ground of Being are simply hopeful interim descriptions before we take the inevitable plunge into non-belief? Or perhaps we do not *need* sense experiences of a Presence to have faith in Something More? Perhaps we can believe in Something simply because it makes more logical sense than nothing, or because we *need* Something in our sometimes frightening world—"God is not known, he is not understood; he is used," Professor Leuba said, "sometimes as a meat-purveyor, sometimes as moral support, sometimes as friend, sometimes as an object of love. If he proves himself useful, the religious consciousness asks for no more than that."[24] In this respect, our experience can mean a commitment to that which is needful.

Of late, I've been asking rather direct questions of people I meet, especially those stalwarts who have remained in the Christian fold as successive bottoms fall out of successive dogmas and we become less and less sure of who GOD really is, say nothing of the stories built up around the Divine. What is the basis for your persistence, I ask? Why do you stay wrestling with GOD when Bible and church have been relativized as authorities and the new atheists tell us it is all delusion? This word "experience" keeps popping up. After pages and pages of biblical and theological investigation, Albert Schweitzer finished his classic *The Quest of the Historical Jesus* with his personal experience of that quest:

> As one unknown and nameless He comes to us, just as on the shore of the lake. He approached those men who knew not who He was. His words are the same: "Follow thou Me!" and He puts us to the tasks which He has to carry out in our age. He commands. And to those who obey, be they wise or simple, He will reveal Himself through all that they are privileged to experience in His fellowship of peace and activity, of struggle and suffering, till they come to know, as an inexpressible secret, Who He is . . .[25]

This is not about acquiring faith, something not there before, but about faith evolving in a lived life. Television evangelists cajole us to "find faith", to make a decision, to believe a bunch of doctrines whether they make sense or not, but without confirmation from a lived experience, as time goes on such "faith" becomes a mind exercise rather than embodied truth. This "blind" or un-embodied faith despite personal experiences to the contrary is often sold as *great* faith, but a lived evolving faith, a confidence in Something, or in the search, or even just in *be*-ing, slowly matures if life experiences add more sense rather than less.

People struggle to describe this experience because it doesn't take theological sides, or wave banners, or expect others to sign up. It is simply part of who we are, just like our sense of humor or our aversion to injustice, not something to evaluate and analyze. It is the place where we currently stand, not "lights, camera, action" but a considered conclusion, given a cumulative lifetime of moments, thoughts, events and reflection. It is walking a path rather than bouncing from one signpost to the next. As a Zen writer explained, do not think about what you do, because the step ahead immediately becomes the step behind, so which is the step ahead and which the step behind? If we think about this, we will stop walking, because categories of forward, backward, first and last create a diversion. When we just walk, we are doing something—living.[26] Observing those in the concentration camp, psychologist and Holocaust survivor Victor Frankl (1908–97) noticed that a few men would walk through the hut comforting others and sharing their bread. This gave proof for him that a man can lose everything but the last of human freedoms, the power to choose one's attitude and way in a given set of circumstances—to choose to *be*.[27]

Can we differentiate between the experiences of GOD engaging us and us engaging GOD, or does one experience blend into the other? Those brave enough to speak for GOD describe a parallel search and desire. Julian of Norwich spoke of a Divine "quality of thirst and longing" without which "no soul comes to heaven . . . [a thirst] which will persist in him so long as we are in need, and will draw us into his bliss . . . we are his bliss, because he endlessly delights in us; and so with his grace shall we delight in him".[28] According to a revelation she received, "Any man or woman who voluntarily chooses God in his lifetime may be sure that he too is chosen."[29] Kashmiri saint-poetess Lal Ded (1320–92) wrote, "I was passionate, filled with longing, I searched far and wide, but the day that the truthful One found me, I was at home."[30] Saint Teresa of Avila (1515–82) described the soul of a just person as "nothing else but a paradise where the Lord says He finds His delight".[31] According to Thomas Merton, however, it is GOD who finds us. We can do everything possible in emptying our minds and trying to find our center, yet we will not find GOD:

No natural exercise can bring you into vital contact with Him. Unless He utters Himself to you, speaks His own name in the center of your soul, you will no more know Him than a stone knows the ground upon which it rests in its inertia.[32]

While these have suggested what the Divine thinks about *us*, I feel safer on the other foot—what human beings have felt about GOD. Leo Tolstoy experienced a "thirst for GOD" that he could not explain, coming from his heart rather than his head:

It was like a feeling of dread that made me seem like an orphan and isolated in the midst of all these things that were so foreign. And this feeling of dread was mitigated by the hope of finding the assistance of some one.[33]

Australian biblical scholar and Jesuit priest Antony Campbell moves beyond the traditional definitions and doctrines of GOD to reflect on the human search as he has experienced it:

When I seek to analyze my own faith in God . . . I find myself coming up against what I would call the whisper of spirit; alongside it, as companion, is the sense of wonder, the sense that the reality that is myself and the world and the universe around me is not sufficient to give an adequate account of its existence.[34]

At the other end of the scholarly quest, Sando, the veteran surfer in Australian Tim Winton's marvelous novel *Breath*, described the feeling of catching the deadliest wave:

When you make it, when you're still alive and standin' at the end, you get this tingly-electric rush. You feel *alive*, completely awake and in your body. Man, it's like you've felt the hand of God. The rest of it's just sport 'n recreation, mate. Give me the hand of God any day.[35]

If some of these experiences sound foreign to you, William James' classic book on religious experiences as "different strokes for different folks" sorts this out, the first psychological analysis of religious experience according to personality makeup. James said that some people see life optimistically and focus on the possible, while others focus on evil and its problems. Our different personalities determine what we seek in the Sacred and how we experience that search. Albert Schweitzer toured Europe giving organ concerts, wrote a book on Bach's music, produced the definitive book on the historical Jesus and went back to university to study medicine, all before the age of 30. Quite obviously, his personality type was different from a contemplative hermit or a Carmelite nun and thus his expectations of the Divine. As the Scottish academic Robert Leighton (1611–84) wrote:

Some travel on in a covert, cloudy day, and get home by it, having so much light as to know their way, and yet do not at all clearly see the bright and full sunshine of assurance; others have it breaking forth at times, and anon under a cloud; and some have it more constantly. But as all meet in the end, so all agree in this in the beginning, that is, in the reality of the thing.[36]

Wonder is a basic human emotion and experience, as Robert Fulghum reminds us in his little instruction book, *All I Really Need to Know I Learned in Kindergarten*. "Be aware of wonder. Remember the little seed in the Styrofoam cup: the roots go down and the plant goes up and nobody really knows how or why, but we are all like that."[37] This is the sacred experience for many—a Presence in the universe, a quiet assurance, a dimension of awe without need for proof or demonstration. It can be something ongoing, securely fastened to us, or an experience that comes and goes in special, or even "un-special" moments. Bede Griffith likened his experience of GOD to a child standing over an open trapdoor to a dark cellar, with the father standing below in the dark, telling him to jump.

Experiences can be comfortable like an old shoe, part of us. Australian Aboriginal Miriam Rose Ungunmerr speaks of *dadirri*, a contemplation she calls "an inner deep listening, and quiet, still awareness".[38] Theologian Bernard Lonergan (1904–84) was convinced that we are naturally programmed towards the Divine:

> There lies within [our] horizon a region for the divine, a shrine of ultimate holiness . . . The atheist may pronounce it empty. The agnostic may say that he has found his investigations inconclusive. The contemporary humanist will refuse to allow the question to arise. But these negations presuppose the spark in our clod, our native orientation to the divine.[39]

Saint Augustine's experiences with the Divine took him far beyond his everyday existence—"Sometimes you allow me to experience a feeling quite unlike my normal state, an inward sense of delight which, if it were to reach perfection in me would be something not encountered in this life . . ."[40] Or, our experiences can be surprising and unexplainable, like a jack-in-a-box in childhood. In a new book, *The Third Man Syndrome: Surviving the impossible*,[41] John Geiger catalogues stories of 100 climbers and adventurers across cultures, including highly secular people, who, in a moment of extreme danger, felt an unembodied Presence with them, encouraging them to make a final effort to survive. Ernest Shackleton (1874–1922) from the *Endurance* expedition to the South Pole felt a fourth man walking with his party when they were desperately hiking for help over a mountain on Georgia Island. American aviator Charles Lindbergh (1902–74), flying solo across the ocean without sleep, felt a series of presences helping in the cockpit. Many mountain climbers in dangerous circumstances have also recorded such experiences. Psychologists say it could be a coping mechanism or an "imaginary friend" as in childhood, while others speculate on a Presence—we can't know, but it *is* experienced, whatever the explanation. "God does not die on the day when we cease to believe in a personal deity," diplomat and mystic Dag Hammarskjöld (1905–61) wrote, "but we die on the day when our lives cease to be illumined by the steady radiance, renewed daily, of a wonder, the source of which is beyond all reason".[42]

When things happen that could simply be coincidental, they bring a smile of "connectedness" to our minds. A bishop quoted in a radio interview said, "When I pray, coincidences happen. When I don't pray they don't", which is like a Japanese *koan* on which you can't quite get a hold. I received a note from a friend whose father died in his prime. The family were having a hard time with this and my friend wrote of the comfort he found in learning, the day after the funeral, that his wife was pregnant—the passing of a life, the promise of a new one. Some might want to call this a miracle, but it is simply a reminder of the flow of life—not *what* happened and *why* but how events are interpreted to bring peace. In a similar story, I met a New Zealand man whose father was a promising economist and lay preacher. While preparing a sermon for the following Sunday on a flight home from a trip, his plane went into a mountain. The son hiked up the mountain and, sitting near the wreck thinking of his father, he saw a piece of charred paper caught on a twig. It was part of his father's sermon and the words were "We sorrow not as those who have no hope." His sermon was preached.

This does raise questions in a thinking person, however. While some may call a serendipitous coincidence an answer to prayer, others call it—a serendipitous coincidence. How do we know the difference between GOD-at-work and a lucky break? I seem to be a fairly lucky person, with things working out, for the most part, but how much of this is good planning, privileged circumstances, healthy genes, an intelligence to order things to advantage, 50–50 odds or GOD-ordained? And, when things *don't* work out, is that GOD—or not? Sometimes my husband will say something out of the blue that I was just thinking about. Is this telepathy, the consequence of living together for over 40 years so that certain topics spark shared memories—or is it Something More? Perhaps I have lived too long with people who claim every auspicious happening as "a miracle" or answer to prayer, even parking spots, yet make no comment when bad things happen, or they blame this on the Devil. When someone is healed because of prayer, why did the person get sick in the first place?

Personal experiences of GOD as visions, dreams, miraculous happenings, striking coincidences, Divine voice messages and supernatural occurrences are tracking points of spiritual progress for some Christians, while the wonders of the natural world or the "miracle" of love exhibited every day in families do not qualify for mention, because they are intoxicated with miracles rather than hard work and angels rather than ordinary people. By emphasizing the miraculous over the mundane, we constantly infer that Divine reality is *only* seen in supernatural events. As movies add more spectacular effects to create their visual worlds, television religion creates bigger and bigger miracles to sustain the "spiritual" world they sell to audiences—only out-of-control predicaments need apply and each miracle must be more sensational than the last. Jesus' life seems tame in comparison, especially when his death prompted no last-minute Divine rescue. "It is unfortunate but true", Sam Keen says, "that wonder is often experienced only on the frontier of the startling . . . A mature sense of wonder does not need the constant titillation of the sensational to keep it alive."[43]

For those who see GOD incarnate in everything in the world and the world in GOD, *everything* in life is a Divine encounter. This means that in every person and event, we "meet" the Divine. I remember sitting in a picnic area on top of a hill in central India with a Hindu colleague and his wife. I asked this serious thinker and gentle soul to talk to me about his ideas of the Sacred while I listened. As he ventured into many areas, not just theological but personal as well, this mountain-top experience became more than a conversation—it was the union of searching souls as I said "Yes" to all his GOD-talk, even though dressed in Hindu concepts, metaphors and expressions. I saw the Divine through the window of his life. In a similar way, we recently met a friend we had not seen since university days when both of us were in a very different theological place than we are today. I asked him and his wife to tell me how they experienced the Sacred now (you can see why some people may not want to have dinner with me). We took turns around the table, each answer triggering a memory in someone else—the Australian bush, the Grand Canyon, quiet and peaceful places, moments when serendipitous events become too dramatic to ignore as mundane. At this point, my friend raised his glass over the remains of our Thai food and said, "*This* is a sacred moment." After 40 years of traveling different roads in different countries with different careers and partners, we were together and finding, amazingly, that we had all traveled similar spiritual journeys and now could hardly catch our breath between saying "Yes, yes, yes" to the experiences of the other.

Experiencing or engaging the Divine is also the stuff of action—rituals, sacraments, prayer, and meditation—rather than messages or miracles. For such people, the absence of sensual experience is not seen as Divine absence—GOD has promised to be in the rituals and sacraments and "thus it is so". "I have never heard Him speak, but I know that he is within me," Thérèse of Lisieux said, "he guides and inspires me every moment of the day. Just when I need it, a new light shines on my problems. This happens not so much during my hours of prayer as when I'm busy with my daily work."[44] Mother Teresa, the woman most quoted in the last century as an example of sainthood, experienced dramatic visions and regular messages from GOD throughout the years she was pleading with superiors to allow her to leave the Loreto Order and begin her mission to India's poorest. After finally being granted her request and starting this work, she experienced many years of complete "darkness of soul", "agony of desolation" and complete emptiness. "Pray for me—for within me everything is icy cold", she wrote to her confessor. "It is only that blind faith that carries me through for in reality to me all is darkness. As long as our Lord has all the pleasure—I really do not count."[45] She was advised by her Archbishop to see this as a normal part of the mystical life and, perhaps, a wake-up call to investigate what might be amiss in her, despite her total sacrifice to the poor.

> God guides you, dear Mother; you are not so much in the dark as you think . . . You have exterior facts enough to see that God blesses your work. Therefore He is satisfied. Guided by faith by prayer and by reason with the right intention you have enough. Feelings are not required and often may be misleading.[46]

Though she could not feel Jesus' presence, Mother Teresa went to Mass every day, even a second Mass if possible, thinking "How beautiful to have received Jesus twice today." [47] She had faith in the teaching that the Real Presence of Christ was in the bread and wine and thus, by her actions, she was "experiencing" the reception of Jesus into her body, even while saying, "The place of God in my soul is blank. There is no God in me . . . He does not want me—He is not there."[48] Hers was a tremendous act of will against her feelings. Mother Teresa's seeing GOD work through her labors without experiencing any special moments would not suit everyone, but William James said:

> If religion be a function by which either God's cause or man's cause is to be really advanced, then he who lives the life of it, however narrowly, is a better servant than he who merely knows about it, however much. Knowledge about life is one thing; effective occupation of a place in life, with its dynamic currents passing through your being, is another.[49]

If this chapter seems like a collage of various human experiences, you have judged well, as this was its aim. We cannot collect experiences and sort them into boxes of genuine and not-so-genuine experiences, correct and incorrect claims, good and bad theology as we have tried to do in the past, just as we can't sort people into boxes as sane and unbalanced, naughty and nice, devout and shallow, although this has been tried as well. Our experiences are individually honed within the set of circumstances that attach to the word "mine". My twenty-month-old grandson Max's favorite word at present is "Max", said with a beaming smile as he pats his chest in the marvelous discovery that he is unique in himself and he has his own name. When he is at the dinner table in his high-chair, he works his pointing finger around the table, naming all those present and then, finally, the pat on his own chest—"Max!" Actress Ellen Burstyn, after making a retreat into Buddhism for a short while, wrote of her experience:

> I realized that although I loved the beauty of the temples, the tangkas [meditation paintings], the stories, and the teaching of the Buddha, I was a tourist here. This was not my path. That's when I understood deeply that with all my studies of other religions, basically I really am devoted to Jesus. I am not a church-going Christian, not a conventional one by most standards, but in my heart, Jesus is my guru.[50]

This is not a rejection of Buddhism but an acknowledgement that her identity has been shaped in a certain context and worldview, outside of which she feels not quite "at home". As the Dalai Lama tells people who wish to become Buddhists, stay in your own traditions and do what *all* religions tell us to do—practice compassion. "When we see someone overflowing with love and understanding, someone who is keenly aware of what is going on," Zen monk Thich Nhat Hanh says, "we know that they are very close to the Buddha and to Jesus Christ."[51]

Always there are those who recognize themselves in the words of Scottish psychiatrist R. D. Laing (1927–89) however—"It seems likely that far more people in our time neither experience the Presence of God, nor the Presence of His absence, but the absence of His Presence."[52] This gives us pause for thought as to where you or I fit in these categories at this very moment. Of Divine absence, Rumi said, "God hid himself so that people would have to strive hard to find him—and only then would they understand him for what he is"[53] but not everyone is as confident as Rumi that the Hide-and-Seek GOD will appear when the game ends and we call out "Come out, come out, wherever you are."

14

Engaging
through Prayer

> Everybody prays whether he thinks of it as praying or not. The odd silence
> you fall into when something very beautiful is happening or something very
> good or very bad . . . The stammer of pain at somebody else's pain. The
> stammer of joy at somebody else's joy. Whatever words or sounds you use for
> sighing over your own life. These are all prayers in their way.
>
> —*Frederick Buechner*[1]

It may seem a long way from the beginning to be talking about prayer, since
this is the most obvious means of engaging the Divine for some, yet it is
perhaps the most misrepresented and misunderstood path of all. Being an
addict for definitions leading into a discussion (my science background
oozing out), the word "prayer" comes from the Latin *precare*, to beg or
entreat, and is "the relating of the self or soul to God in trust, penitence,
praise, petition and purpose, either individually or corporately".[2] Meditation
(as distinct from contemplation) is a sub-species of prayer where the devotee
thinks about passages from scripture or some other writing for a deeper
understanding. Contemplation is a silent listening, the union of mind and
will with GOD through Divine grace. All assume direct access to GOD and
an expectation of a response, and all are the language of love—"they originate in love, sing of love, and invite us to dance in love—love, that is beauty
sublime. Love, that is God".[3] Although these are fluid categories, I will
concentrate on prayer in this chapter, leaving the following chapter to
explore meditation and contemplation. Once again, our attitudes to prayer
will depend on how we imagine the Divine and what we expect of GOD *and*
prayer. Australian educator Headley Beare says:

[W]e are engaging a living presence that (or whom) we cannot manipulate to our own ends, a power it is impossible to domesticate. In prayer we are not looking for ways to secure God's help for ourselves, but rather how we can make ourselves more fully available to God. It is about engagement with a here-and-now God, not a remote or a once-in-a-while encounter, but rather a daily intimacy that is profound, life-changing and absolutely real. We are dealing with a living presence to whose purposes we want to dedicate ourselves.[4]

A Buddhist is not striving to engage a living Presence but rather to free the mind from external burdens and entrapments so that one is fully awake and aware. The goal for the Hindu devotee is to move from the unreal to the real and find that the self (*atman*) is, in fact, GOD (*Brahman*). In prayer, Muslims acknowledge their creature nature before their Creator and bend their wills towards Allah in surrender (Islam means "surrender").

The definition of prayer as trust, penitence, praise, petition and purpose begins with a solid biblical word—"And those who know your name put their trust in you: for you, O Lord, have not forsaken those who seek you" (Ps. 9:10). Trustworthiness, reliability and refuge are also the Hebrew meaning of "truth", rather than the Greek idea of intellectual truth or ver-ifiable knowledge. Truth as trustworthiness is relational, something that stands up under testing from experience. Prayers of trust assume that, what-ever happens, things are in Divine hands and humanity is dependent on GOD. "[T]he privilege of speech with God is inestimable," wrote Sir Wilfred Grenfell (1865–1940), the British missionary doctor to Labrador and New-foundland. "When I can neither see, nor hear, nor speak, still I can pray so that God can hear. When I finally pass through the valley of the shadow of death, I expect to pass through it in conversation with him."[5]

Such reliability within the universe is encapsulated in the Hindu law of *karma,* where every action has consequences that come to fruition in a future time or a future life. In Islam, the phrase *insh'Allah* (if God wills) reminds us that nothing happens outside Divine will, even our salvation—"[H]e made some to believe in him and know him," Rumi said, "and he made others to remain ignorant of him."[6]

The doctrine of predestination held by some Christians also says that GOD foreknows and predetermines the outcome of all things and thus our only response is to trust GOD's grace and unmerited favor towards sinners. While this doctrine later became a source of fear, in case one was predestined for *hell,* its original intent was to offer assurance to those who trusted GOD.

Trust in the Lord and do good; so you will live in the land, and enjoy security. Take delight in the Lord, and he will give you the desires of your heart. Commit your way to the Lord: trust in him, and he will act. (Ps. 37:3–5)

There are many examples of trusting prayer where everything is simply put into GOD's hands, regardless of the outcome. While collecting material for this book, I received a letter from a couple working in an English-speaking international school in India. Although tucked away in the peaceful hills of the south, they were very concerned about the global unrest because their school hosted children from many war-torn, volatile nations who were unable to go home and were worried about loved ones. In the turmoil, the woman wrote, "How important it is for us to walk each day by faith, for our sight is limited, and our ability to control things is very small indeed. Our trust is that God does hold the whole world, and God's concern is for each individual." For Thérèse of Lisieux, rather than searching through books to find beautiful prayers to say with the Divine Office, she behaved like a child who could not read:

I tell God very simply what I want and He always understands. For me, prayer is an upward leap of the heart, an untroubled glance towards heaven, a cry of gratitude and love which I utter from the depths of sorrow as well as from the heights of joy.[7]

Such trusting prayer may give confidence when there is *visible* evidence one is truly in Divine hands, but many have felt their trust ignored or betrayed in the *absence* of assurance or Divine contact. Thérèse of Lisieux' namesake, Mother Teresa of Calcutta, spent many of her years in India in "such a deep loneliness in my heart that I cannot express it . . . How long will our Lord stay away?"[8] When assured that this feeling of Divine absence was par for the course, she told her confessor (my italics):

Please pray for me, that it may please God to lift this darkness from my soul for only a few days. For sometimes the agony of desolation is so great and at the same time the longing for the Absent One so deep, that the only prayer which I can still say is—Sacred Heart of Jesus *I trust in Thee.*[9]

The second type of prayer is penitence, where we seek forgiveness through confession and penitential prayers. For Hebrew people, penitence was prescribed on the Day of Atonement when Moses' brother Aaron had laid both hands on the head of a goat, the "scapegoat", and confessed the sins of the people before sending the goat into the wilderness to be freed—"The goat shall bear on itself all their iniquities to a barren region; and the goat shall be set free in the wilderness" (Lev. 16:22). This idea of scapegoat, something or someone taking the blame for others, has stayed with us in our secular language. In monastic Buddhism, confession and penitence are made to the *sangha* (community) in acknowledgement of failings, shortcomings and infringement of monastic rules so that the penitent can move on towards self-awareness. But penitence is more than listing sins and asking forgiveness—it is also the acknowledgement of how our human egos constantly get in the way and block out the Light. Rabindranath Tagore wrote:

I came out alone on my way to my tryst. But who is this that follows me in the silent dark? I move aside to avoid his presence, but I escape him not. He makes the dust rise from the earth with his swagger; he adds his loud voice to every word that I utter. He is my own little self, my lord, he knows no shame; but I am ashamed to come to thy door in his company.[10]

In Christianity, once original sin was named by Saint Augustine as an inevitable condition of human life, a penitential system developed where satisfaction or penance must be paid for each sin—it is not enough simply to be sorry. While this became more formalized in the Catholic tradition, confession of sins, whether privately or publicly, has been part of all Christian traditions. A mother told me how her little daughter came home from church school in tears one day. The children had been asked to write down how many sins they had committed that week. When the little girl wrote "none", she got into trouble both for lying and for being so unconscious of her sinful nature. In sharp contrast, a prayer from Aotearoa New Zealand assesses the human being thus: "I am a lovable person created by God. I give myself permission to enjoy being myself, to use my powers responsibly and to be a singer and dancer of God's new age."[11]

Mary Magdalene became the Christian icon of a penitent sinner, awarded this role by Pope Gregory I (520–604 CE) when he merged her with two other women, the "sinner" who anointed Jesus (Luke 7:37) and Mary of Bethany (John 12:3). Luke's Gospel identifies Mary "called Magdalene" as the one "from whom seven demons had gone out" (8:2), a tempting invitation for her later interpretation as "sinner" or prostitute, even though demon possession simply meant an illness and *seven* meant a severe illness. Mary became the *sexual* sinner whom Jesus redeemed and the model for all penitent women who lie somewhere between the extremes of wicked Eve and the unreachable Virgin. Mary Magdalene is portrayed in art, either in the exotic clothes of a prostitute or in ragged clothes half-covering her (or naked, covered by long hair) indicating her perpetual penitence. Thus she was successfully removed from church history by demotion and scandal as church leadership became all male. Only recently, she has been officially redeemed and restored as a leader of the apostles and significant enough to have the *Gospel of Mary* written about her.

Prayer as "praise" ties closely with worship. Even in Buddhism where worship is not addressed to GOD, there is plenty of praise offered to the Buddha, bodhisattvas and venerable leaders of monastic communities in gratitude for their teaching and wisdom. At the Parliament of the World's Religions (2009), the convention center foyer became the home-away-from-home for the monks and their master from Chinese Han Transmission Tantrayana Buddhism in Tasmania, Australia. From the monks' bowing to, and adoration of, their master, it was delightfully obvious that he was held in deep respect and worthy of their praise and honor. "God save our gracious Queen" and "God bless America" are also prayers of praise, both to the GOD that blesses and the object blessed. With an ineffable GOD beyond description and decoding, however, our public praise is always offered in limited language and using decidedly human (and male) visions of the Divine—the traditional daily prayer for a Jewish man praised God for not making him a Gentile, a slave or a woman.

Challenging more than gendering, Bishop John Shelby Spong questions the whole idea of liturgical prayers formed around a GOD in the heavens needing to be flattered to entice Divine favor and action, as with human authority figures. Kneeling, bending knees, kissing rings and bowing heads are derived from human systems that required the flattery of those in power. Spong says:

> What does it say about our understanding either of God or of ourselves that we think the proper behavior of the worshipper before the deity is the position of kneeling, the same position employed by beggars, slaves, serfs and others who judge themselves in the manipulative process to be inferior and inadequate?[12]

We are also encouraged liturgically to say dreadful things about ourselves in order to appear sufficiently worthless and thus to manipulate the Divine, Spong says—"miserable offenders", "no health in us" and not worthy to "gather up the crumbs" under the Divine table. While some readers might recoil in horror at Spong's analysis of liturgy embedded in our hearts and psyche, he raises important questions about our GOD-images and our understanding of human beings in a contemporary rather than medieval world. Spong also challenges the relevance of such language addressed to the Divine *within* us. Such communication is not about consciously wording something to an external Being, but rather the spontaneous, unspoken bursts from the heart at being alive in the wonders of nature and the belief that, in this world and within ourselves, the Sacred is present and revealed.

Praise as a response to and of love is integral to *bhakti,* the Hindu devotional tradition that crosses castes and is one of three yogic paths to salvation, along with ritual activity and spiritual knowledge. Here, *moksha* (liberation from rebirth) comes purely through devotion to the Divine, regardless of learning, wealth and class, and thus it appeals to the less powerful, especially devout women subordinated in a husband's family. *Bhakti* songs of praise and love were written in the vernacular, and each *bhakti* group worships one manifestation of the Divine—the *Shaivas* devoted to Lord Shiva, or the *Shaktas* devoted to Shakti (Divine Energy), the Great GODDESS and Shiva's consort. *Bhaktas* express devotion through images of passionate, erotic human love and, as a result, have composed some of the most beautiful poetry directed at the Divine. The famous *bhakti* poet Mirabai (*c.* 1498–1565), married to a crown prince but later a wandering mystic, referred to her Divine Lover Giridhara (a manifestation of Lord Krishna) as "the Dark One":

Something has reached out and taken in the beams of my eyes,
There is a longing, it is for his body, for every hair of that dark body.
All I was doing was being, and the Dancing Energy came by my house.[13]

The first Sikh guru, Nanak, incorporated Hindu *bhakti* hymns into the Sikh scriptures, along with Muslim Sufi hymns of praise where we "drink from his love, and become utterly intoxicated".[14]

For some, there is only one type of prayer. They may begin with a few words of introduction but soon gets to the real purpose—petition—where GOD is "reduced to the office of a village charity organization doling out small supplies to improvident applicants".[15] The sacred texts *do* invite prayers of petition—the psalmist says "Incline your ear, O Lord, and answer me, for I am poor and needy" (Ps. 86:1) and Matthew's Gospel says "Whatever you ask for in prayer with faith, you will receive" (21:22). In the Qur'an, Allah says, "I answer their prayers when they pray to Me" (Surah 2:186) and the Hadith (sayings of the Prophet) says that GOD "descends each night to the earth's sky when there remains the final third of the night, and He says:

Who is saying a prayer to Me that I may answer it?
Who is asking something of Me that I may give it him?
Who is asking forgiveness of Me that I may forgive him?"[16]

A prayer in the Sikh scriptures is very much to the point, although one wonders as to the *order* of things requested—"Hail, Hail, O Lord! You help your servants. I ask for pulse, flour and butter. I ask for decent clothes and shoes. I ask for a cow or a she-buffalo, I seek a fine Arab pony and a good wife."[17]

Irishman Paddy was working up a sweat because he had an important meeting and couldn't find a parking space. Looking up to heaven, he said, "Lord, pity me. If you find me a parking place I will go to Mass every Sunday for the rest of my life and give up my whisky." A parking space miraculously appeared. Paddy looked up again and said, "Never mind, I've found one." We laugh, but this represents how many people see prayer. Frank Schaeffer describes prayer in his family as a reminder to GOD not to let the Divine attention wander or forget what was expected. Since his mother had the stamina to literally "pray without ceasing", Schaeffer often wondered "if God ever tried to duck out of the room when he saw Mom coming":

> Praying out loud was also a way of advancing one's case, the advantage being that no one dared interrupt you or argue back. Moreover, prayer was a way to tell God to behave, to stick to being the God we said he was, and a way to remind God of his "many promises" so he wouldn't try to do anything odd or theologically inconsistent.[18]

People pray in the hopelessness of a situation, whether a missing child, a plane with engine trouble, or in the horrors of war. "I have been driven many times to my knees", President Abraham Lincoln (1809–65) said, "by the overwhelming conviction that I had nowhere else to go; my own wisdom and that of all around me seemed insufficient for the day."[19] The difficulty with claiming a direct cause-and-effect between prayer and an answer, however, is that it is almost impossible to isolate an event so completely that only the *prayer* could have been responsible. Many people attribute dramatic health cures simply to prayer, even though a physician accurately diagnosed the problem, a skilled surgeon operated, a well-trained chemotherapist balanced the right amount of drugs, and an efficient nursing team negotiated the known pitfalls to recovery.

The truth is, however, that prayers are not always answered as requested.

Is this the fault of our methods, the predetermined will of GOD, the complexity of the larger picture, or the impotence of GOD in the situation? People have dealt with "wrong" or no answers in many ways—GOD answered but said no, not yet, or not appropriate, or GOD saw a bigger picture unavailable on our local channel. Mystic Julian of Norwich decided that the trick was to become so like GOD that we only ask for what GOD wills:

> [God] teaches us to pray and to have firm trust that we shall have what we pray for, because everything which is done would be done, even though we had never prayed for it. But God's love is so great that he regards us as partners in his good work; and so he moves us to pray for what it pleases him to do. [20]

One of the most difficult theological questions around which we have to juggle our minds is Divine power. Can GOD do anything at all or is GOD limited by our choices (free will) and thus the consequences of human actions? Does GOD override situations in response to our prayers, like an omnipotent Teacher wiping the whiteboard clean of our childish felt-tip scratchings, or is Divine activity constrained by, or dependent on, what we do? For many, GOD is always in control, never limited or reduced by circumstances. Thomas à Kempis said:

> [God] giveth sometimes in the end that which in the beginning of thy prayer he deferred to grant. If grace were always promptly given and ever present at will, weak man could not well bear it.

However, à Kempis says, if this grace does not come or is removed, "it ought to be a matter of thankfulness; because He doeth always for our welfare whatever He permitteth to happen to us".[21] Yet is this the only way to interpret Divine intent and action? I hope not. Again, it depends on how we image the Divine. Sometimes Christianity is more about defending the straw GOD that humans have set up, explaining how this GOD thinks and acts, rather than allowing the "I am who I am" to *be*. So many people struggle with the shape in which prayer has long been molded and continues to be uttered in liturgy, as if we are still back in a medieval pew gazing up at the Big-Man-in-the-sky.

Praying is both an individual and a corporate act and, as such, they are different beasts and take different forms. The Lord's Prayer, the most commonly prayed public prayer in the Christian tradition, actually arose out of a discussion *against* praying in public. Adult Jewish men were expected to pray thrice daily in the direction of Jerusalem and before and after meals. Jesus encouraged them to do this in private. "Beware of practicing your piety before others in order to be seen by them", the chapter begins, and goes on to condemn those who give alms in a very public way and those who "love to stand and pray in the synagogues and at street corners, so that they may be seen by others" (Matt. 6:5). Jesus also criticized those who uttered long-winded prayers in public, "heaping up empty phrases" to be "heard because of their many words" (6:7), a charge not heeded by many who claim to take *all* of Jesus' words literally. Instead, when you pray, "go into your room and shut the door and pray to your Father who is in secret; and your Father who sees in secret will reward you" (6:6). What we now call the Lord's Prayer (which has parallels in the *Kaddish* and the Eighteen Benedictions used in synagogue worship in Jesus' time)[22] was then offered as an appropriate private prayer since "your Father knows what you need before you ask" (6:8).

This prayer also invites community use, however, with its "*Our* Father" and "Give us this day *our* daily bread." There is also precedence for public corporate prayer in both Hebrew and Christian traditions, as in most religious traditions. Corporate praying serves many purposes—maintaining the group's theology, binding a community with its past and encouraging solidarity through expressing the desires of the people, to name a few. In a sermon by an Australian Uniting Church minister, Revd Chris Udy, after the bushfires that ravished Victoria (2009), Udy commented on thousands of emails from around the world saying that people were praying for those threatened by the fires.

> They didn't expect their prayers to put the flames out; they didn't expect their prayers to change the wind; they didn't expect their prayers to save a particular life or to spare a specific building—they were praying to make a connection, to weave a kind of fabric of compassion—they were building a network of attention and concern, and shared sadness, and because they often came from people and places who'd also suffered heartbreak in the past—they also offered an affirmation that even this would pass, and there was hope, and there would be healing, and people would bring good things out of the bad—and if we're looking for God, that's where God was.[23]

Praying together assumes that those who gather are somehow connected to each other, whether in a Buddhist sangha, a silent Quaker meeting, or Friday prayers in the mosque. If we image the Divine within us and everything, this connection becomes greater than a shared tradition or common goal. The Indian greeting *namasti* means "The Divine in me greets the Divine in you." This connection is recognized when we pray together, but it becomes more difficult when public prayers are so encased in language specific to a particular tradition that others feel excluded. In the Rotary Club in Rochester, Minnesota where people come from all parts of the world for treatment at the Mayo Clinic, I sat one day with a couple of visitors. She was a Japanese Buddhist and he was a Muslim from the Middle East. The tradition in this large club was to have a different member offer a prayer at the beginning of each meeting, but strict instructions were given to pray *inclusively* such that anyone would feel welcome. On this particular day, a beautifully worded prayer was offered. The couple commented on how thrilled they were to pray with fellow Rotarians without feeling excluded or uncomfortable. We shared our "human-ness" as people making connections with each other and the Sacred, whether Christian or Hindu, American or African. Of course, some Christians in the group thought this was a cop-out, a missed opportunity to make covert appeals for conversion through a Rotary prayer.

In Roman Catholicism, prayers were said in Latin for centuries, even though lay people did not understand that language. The *Missal* dictated the words of the Mass while the Book of Common Prayer in the Church of England preserved formal prayers and daily offices that originated in the sixteenth century. Formal prayers in the Orthodox Church, the same over centuries, link worshippers with the "cloud of witnesses" from the past and also allow the supplicant to meet the Divine without the distraction of thinking of what to say. In some other Christian traditions, formal prayers are considered "soulless" and not as sincere as spontaneous words from the heart or through the nudge of the Holy Spirit. In charismatic churches, this also means "speaking in tongues". Others simply sit together in silence, *being* in the presence of GOD.

At the Parliament of the World's Religions (2009), one session focused on how various religions might pray together in public events, whether celebratory or tragic, such as 9/11. We are so bogged down in our words and imagery about the GOD *we* imagine that it takes great effort for some people to move into uncomfortable territory. The solution for some presenters was to avoid spoken prayers and draw people together with songs and sounds that were, in themselves, "language" to express shared feelings, whether an Australian didgeridoo, a Jewish shophar, a Buddhist chant, or the absence of sound—silent prayer and meditation. Yet words are our gift of communication, especially in the Abrahamic traditions, our ability to bridge gaps between each other. Thus we need also to struggle to *say* things that can be affirmed by us all, using images, such as the Sacred, that can encompass the breadth of religious traditions and talking about human transformation rather than salvation which has distinctly Christian meanings. An American Catholic priest in the audience at this session, however, who was in Manhattan in 9/11, thought that generic expressions mean that we leave our specific identities at the door. In a memorial service he attended 100 years after the San Francisco earthquake, diversity was celebrated by each religious tradition praying in their own way so that others *experienced* various religions at prayer, a pattern the Parliament adopted with worship services from various traditions beginning each day and open to all.

Prayers, public or private, are more than words—they are windows to the Sacred. Chants, mantras and liturgical prayers have been used down the centuries as tools to bring the supplicant into the Divine presence. Mantras (a sound, syllable, word, or group of words), originally from the Vedic texts of India, are about the sound vibrations and must be done properly to be effective. The sound is not just human, but superhuman—"to utter the mantra is to mimic the cosmic/divine in sound, and to perceive the mantra's sound vibrations is to make sensuous contact with that divine via the 'tactility' of the ears and mind".[24] Special mantras are passed down from guru to pupil (taking them from books does not work) and are used for mundane as well as religious acts, such as preparing meals, healing diseases, inviting business success and during childbirth. There are different types of mantras but all are about the freedom from language that allows us to transcend and commune with the Source, *the* Word.

> By meditating on various mantras, the devotee identifies him/herself with the corresponding levels of God, realizing progressively more subtle levels of consciousness, until ultimately reaching the direct experience of the divine presence.[25]

At a conference, a woman in her seventies told me her story. A devoted member of a Christian church all her life, she had raised her sons there, but both converted to Hinduism as adults through their own spiritual searches. The woman struggled with this but decided, rather than lose her sons, she would allow GOD to be greater than her GOD. Her sons meditate by chanting mantras as they walk and so she wrote her own mantras to the Divine and walks with them. Her sons love her for this but tease her a little as to whose chant better pleases the Divine.

Prayer is also action. Rules and rituals accompany the *manthas*, the sacred words of Zoroastrian prayer. Before praying (five times a day), both men and women wash all exposed parts of the body, untie the sacred cord around their waists, the symbol of their initiation, and face the light. Their prayers are from the *Avesta*, their sacred text, which has its own special alphabet so that they cease thinking in human or vernacular terms and enter a spiritual world. The words of the text become effective through recitation and enactment. Prayer beads (rosaries), for the repetition of prayers while counting the beads, are found in many religions—Christianity, Hinduism, Buddhism, Sikhism and Islam. In Sikh art, the founder Guru Nanak is often shown holding prayer beads and, in Islam, beads on the rosary represent the 99 beautiful names for GOD. The *komboschini* (prayer rope) counts prayers for Orthodox Christians. Fixed mantras with the counting action serve to transport a person into the Divine presence—I've often seen passengers bring out their beads as plane engines move from idling to a steady roar before takeoff. No doubt rosary beads gave inspiration to the "worry beads" of our high-tech world—strings of interestingly fashioned beads for CEOs to sift through fingers while pondering the next major move. For Tibetan Buddhists, the cylindrical prayer wheel, inscribed with a mantra on the outside with other mantras inside, has a similar purpose—turning the wheel "recites" the mantras, whether a small hand-held wheel or a huge wheel turned by water-power (or now, electric power).

Bodily postures are also important in prayer. Although less prevalent today, children of my vintage were taught to kneel beside their beds, eyes closed, hands pressed together in front of the nose, to recite a bedtime prayer. In my family, we said

Gentle Jesus meek and mild,
look upon a little child;
pity my simplicity,
suffer me to come to Thee.[26]

As I write it here, I wonder whether we knew what all the words really meant. American illustrator Norman Rockwell (1894–1978) cemented this childhood image in art, as he did with many themes of family life. His painting, *Bedtime Prayer*, casts a glow of remembrance across our faces—a blond girl kneels beside her bed, feet together and hands clasped in front of her, while her very large dog imitates her devout expression. In Frank Schaeffer's novel *Portofino*, ten-year-old Calvin Becker suffered massive embarrassment at his devout mother's propensity for long and vocal stream-of-thought prayers before meals in public restaurants in Italy, while he sat, eyes closed and head bowed, feeling the staring eyes and imagining the giggles of Catholic locals who, at most, briefly crossed themselves before eating.[27]

Raising arms towards heaven during prayer once symbolized reaching up along with our words to GOD in the heavens, as if our arms could somehow channel the prayers in the right direction. It is interesting that, even though science has shattered the medieval cosmology of heaven above and hell below, raising arms in prayer has become even more prevalent, especially in charismatic circles. For some Jewish men (now popular with some women as well), a prayer shawl made of wool and silk with fringes on each corner is worn at morning service and a similar undergarment worn throughout the day by strict Orthodox Jews. For Muslims who pray five times a day wherever they are, a special prayer mat (*sajj da*) is rolled out so that one end points towards Mecca. But such formalities are not for all. A working woman living in a high-rise tenement building said, "I throw my apron over my head when I want solitude; it is all that I can get."[28] All these aids to prayer, and many, many more not mentioned have one purpose—to help create "sacred space" in a mundane world.

Saint Augustine's words, "Our hearts find no peace until they rest in you", are both a threat and a promise, because many do *not* find peace or rest when they pray.[29] Religion scholar Karen Armstrong recounts the pain she suffered in the convent as a young nun when, despite everything she did and longed for, GOD was not there:

One of the most painful failures of my convent life had been my inability to pray. Our whole existence had God as its pivot. The silence of our days had been designed to enable us to listen to him. But he had never spoken to me . . . Every morning I resolved that this time I would crack it. This time there would be no distractions. I would kneel as intent upon God as my sisters, none of whom seemed to have any difficulties. I had never before had any problems of concentration. I had always been able to immerse myself in my studies for hours at a time. But to my intense distress, I found that I could not keep my mind on God for two minutes . . . Throughout my seven years, I hugged to myself the shameful secret that, unlike the other sisters, I could not pray. And, we were told, without prayer our religious lives were a complete sham. For several hours a day on every single day of the year, I had to confront and experience my abject failure. In other ways, my mind was capable and even gifted, but it seemed allergic to God. This disgrace festered corrosively at the very heart of my life and spilled over into everything, poisoning each activity. How could I possibly be a nun if, when it came right down to it, I seemed completely uninterested in God and God appeared quite indifferent to me?[30]

For French mystic Simone Weil (1909–43), "Attention, taken to its highest degree, is the same thing as prayer . . . Waiting patiently in expectation is the foundation of the spiritual life."[31] However, some wait patiently all their lives but only encounter a void.

In his book on prayer, Harry Emerson Fosdick recognized this "sense of futility—such as comes to one who finds that he has been speaking in the dark to nobody, when he supposed a friend was in the room". But Fosdick's solution, as it so often is, was to blame the supplicant—practicing the presence of GOD is not a casual thing "as though any one could saunter into God's presence at any time, in any mood, with any sort of life behind him, and at once perceive God there".[32] Instead, the supplicant must look for impediment within him or herself, "for sinister habits of thought, for cherished evils dimly recognized as wrong but unsurrendered, for lax carelessness in conduct, or deliberate infidelity to conscience . . . and above all for selfishness that hinders loving and so breaks the connections that bind us to God and one another".[33] How then does Fosdick explain away the unanswered prayers in the Bible to which he draws attention—Moses prays to enter the promised land but doesn't, Paul's thorn in the flesh remained and the cup of suffering was not removed from Jesus on the cross? Were all these through some fault of the supplicant?

Because of all the expectations and promises built up around prayer over centuries and because of our contemporary struggle with who GOD is and whether there is a GOD at all, prayer has become a problem for many. We need fresh ways and images to talk about prayer as engaging the Divine, just as we develop fresh and contemporary ways to imagine GOD. Revd Elizabeth Lerner from the Unitarian tradition says with honesty:

If nothing and no one is listening, then my prayer has a different function but the same form. It does me good, it keeps me humble, it keeps me honest, to express my yearnings and to address them to God even if that is my saddest and most foolish act because no one is listening. It does not hurt me; it helps me . . . If God does not hear me, or is not even there to hear me, it still does me good to get my yearning, my fear, my question, my grief, my anger *out,* to acknowledge it and express it and release it to the world . . . My prayers are honest, and they are mine.[34]

This may be sacrilege both for religious people who see belief in GOD as essential for prayer and also for atheists who would see such an attitude as proof of the delusion of religion, yet we need more honesty on the religious journey rather than tightly formulated answers that permit no doubt. Revd Felicia Urbanski, who used Lerner's quote in a sermon, moves us into the next chapter on meditation and contemplation:

> When it comes to prayer, whether we believe in God or not, does *not* really matter. I think this is the key. You do not need to "believe in" God in order to pray. We can *all* stand in awe before the grandeur and wonder of Life and the mystery of our existence. Just standing there looking at it all is a kind of prayer![35]

15

Meditation and Contemplation

There, in the silent depths [of the ground of our own being], there is no more distinction between the I and the Not-I. There is perfect peace because we are grounded in infinite creative and redemptive Love.

—*Thomas Merton*[1]

O   O   O

When the five senses and the mind are still,
and reason itself rests in silence,
then begins the Path supreme.

—*Katha Upanishad*[2]

Anyone who prays knows that this is not a one-dimensional affair. First, there is the language we speak (liturgy, mantras, conversational prayer) and the actions we do (clasped hands, bended knees, bowed heads)—what we usually call prayer. In the second dimension, we bring our minds to engage with our actions and words, pondering on a text or topic or deliberately fixing our thoughts on Divine things—meditation. The third dimension is where the heart takes over and "feels" what the mind is thinking, listening for GOD rather than speaking—contemplation. I realize we are dealing here with inadequate language to differentiate between different experiences when there is a patchwork quilt of experiences *within* each term and they inevitably merge with each other and annoyingly cross the boundaries we set for them. However, there does seem to be an evolution from prayer to meditation and contemplation, perhaps because we turn from speaking to listening, from asking to experiencing, from trying to engage the Divine to being engaged by It. Julian of Norwich said:

When our courteous Lord of his special grace shows himself to our soul, we have what we desire, and then for that time we do not see what more we should pray for, but all our intentions and all our powers are wholly directed to contemplating him.[3]

Most religions recognize this evolution in ways to engage the Divine. The Sikh tradition identifies six stages of prayer. The first stage is praying for *things*, which is where most people stay across religions and countries. The second is the realization that spiritual progress is better than transient worldly things, but the pull of the "world" competes with this new vision. As one saint said, "I am neither here nor there . . . Sometimes I do things that the meanest of mortals would not do, and other times there are flashes of saintly life. I am living a life of mental conflict."[4] The third stage has overcome worldly distractions and concentrates on devotion, feeling at one with GOD. Worldly things still cause strife but are now easily subdued. The fourth stage is a habitual state of peace and bliss where the mind has ceased to wander and revels in the Divine Presence, even feeling the ecstasy of a Divine Touch— "There is none but You and everything is in your play", Guru Arjan Dev (1563–1606), the fifth Guru, said. In the fifth stage, prayer can be abandoned because GOD is aware of all our needs—"You are present, wherever I look for You . . . You know every unsaid thought, O Lord." In the final stage, we are so in union with GOD that there is little for which to ask and what we do ask is in line with Divine Will—"Wherever His servant seeks, God is there and appears by his servant's side. What the servant desires of his master is granted." Prayer has become our life and any break in this is "tantamount to the agony of dwelling near the hole of a cobra", Guru Gobind Singh, the tenth Guru, said.

The term "meditation" is used more for a structured contemplation, a meditation *on* words from scripture or *on* a Zen *koan* (poem) in order to discipline the mind through concentration. "Contemplation" is about removing *all* thought to simply be silent and still in the Divine Presence— "freed from the disturbing influence of the passions and desires: it is a state of direct communication with God in which the mind transcends discursive activity and knows a presence or union".[5] Contemplation, according to Sam Keen, is a "receptive passivity", the difference between posing questions and relaxing in the presence of something, making ourselves available to it and allowing it to create its own categories in order to be understood:

Contemplation is the effort to evade the tyranny of the already known— a disciplined attempt on the part of the knower to allow the novel and the unique to create categories that will expand our knowledge.[6]

"What is the most beautiful sound in the whole world?" the audience was asked rhetorically by a Ch'an Buddhist master at the Parliament of the World's Religions (2009). "The sound of no sound", was his answer, meaning the exclusion of both wandering thoughts and the outside world. Silence and stillness, as opposed to sound, words and action, are the jewels of both meditation and contemplation. The Buddhist *Sutta-Nipata* says, "As in the ocean's midmost depth no wave is born, but all is still, so let the practitioners be still, be motionless, and nowhere should they swell."[7]

In our discussions across religions, however, meditation and contemplation do not stay put in these boxes to which we have assigned them, finding different expressions in every religious tradition, with the common belief that union with the Sacred is possible to achieve:

"[T]the sigh within the prayer is the same in the heart of the Christian, the Mohammedan, and the Jew." I have seen this unity with my eyes, heard it with my ears and felt it with all my being.[8]

Interfaith dialogue found an early home within the contemplative traditions as they shared meditation practices and experiences that transcended dogmas, institutional rules and truth claims. When you remove language and sound from the religious stage and encourage the inward journey, walls fall down. "Language is the finger pointing at the moon", Zen master Shunryu Suzuki (1904–71) said. "It is not the moon. When you understand what the moon is, the finger is not necessary any more. Different doctrines are just different fingers. There is one moon."[9] Thomas Merton, the Trappist monk who was involved in early Christian–Buddhist dialogue, said of religions, "[E]ven where there are irreconcilable differences in doctrine and in formulated belief, there may still be great similarities and analogies in the realm of religious experience . . . cultures and doctrinal differences must remain, but they do not invalidate a very real quality of existential likeness."[10]

When Henri le Saux (1910–73), a Franciscan monk from Brittany, went to India to "Christianize" India and its monastic institutions, he found instead that India had a gift to Christianity—the pearl of interiority. Benedictine monk Bede Griffith went to India to pursue le Saux' dream and ended up learning from the Eastern meditative traditions and marrying the monastic traditions of East and West—"It is not for nothing that in the Hindi language the only word that exists for teach is 'cause to learn'."[11] In the 1950s and 1960s, the Vatican sent monks to Asia and Latin America to help Catholic churches there develop their contemplative dimensions.

Instead, the monks found themselves converted to new monastic ways, learned from the indigenous traditions. Four years after Vatican II, monks from across countries and religions gathered together in Thailand to talk about what they shared in common, the deep desire for union with the Ultimate. At this meeting in 1968, Thomas Merton was accidentally and tragically electrocuted. On the morning of his death, he delivered a paper to the conference where he said:

> I believe that, by openness to Buddhism, to Hinduism, and to these great Asian traditions, we stand a wonderful chance of learning more about the potentiality of our own traditions, because they have gone, from the natural point of view, so much deeper into this than we have.[12]

Meditation in Buddhism seeks enlightenment. "Wakefulness is the way of life," the Buddha said, "the fool sleeps as if he were already dead, but the master is awake and he lives for ever . . . With great perseverance he meditates, seeking freedom and happiness."[13] Although the long-term goal is enlightenment, the immediate goal is tranquility, the calming or taming of the mind in the present (*samatha*) and using this calmness of mind to develop insight in order to see reality clearly (*vipassanā*). Meditation wakes us up, makes us aware of our feelings, our body and our perceptions and gives us the ability to understand and love. "To develop understanding, you have to practice looking at all living beings with the eyes of compassion", Thich Nhat Hanh says. "When you understand, you love. And when you love, you naturally act in a way that can relieve the suffering of people. Someone who is awake, who knows, who understands, is called a Buddha."[14]

Such awareness is called "mindfulness", which means being aware of what one is doing while doing it and of nothing else. If walking, rather than turning a jumble of thoughts over in the mind, a "mindful person" pays attention to the movement of his or her body, legs, breath and heartbeat. The most common exercise to establish mindfulness is paying attention to, and controlling, our breathing—"Breathing in, I calm my body. Breathing out, I smile. Dwelling in the present moment I know this is a wonderful moment."[15] This can be done at a meditation center or in the privacy of our room, but it can also be integrated into the everyday of life—breathing between phone calls, in quiet moments before the next class, or while walking between places. When we get angry, Thich Nhat Hanh suggests, we can enter our meditation "room", whether one with four walls or one within ourselves, and breathe to help us control and diffuse this anger. When a child is agitated, rather than a time-out, we can sit quietly with them and breathe to calm ourselves, for adults as much as the child—"This is the best education for peace."[16] We can also do slow walking meditation with our children for a few minutes at night before they go to bed, a special, shared moment between parent and child and a calming moment before sleep. All these methods are *aids* to meditation, and different people find different things effective. Buddhist teacher Paramananda tells the story of a farmhand who was given a sound to recite as a mantra by a passing guru. When the guru returned, he found the farmhand happy with his results but also discovered that the farmhand had mistaken the guru's mantra word for another, the Tibetan word meaning "cow". The guru corrected the farmhand, only to find on returning that the new word was not working. On a third visit, he allowed the farmhand to return to reciting "cow", and successful meditation returned to the farmhand.[17]

Meditation and being aware is not just about going inward, but about realizing our interconnectedness with the universe or, if that is a bit too all-encompassing for our little minds to grasp, our interconnectedness with what we can see around us. Paramananda wrote:

Sitting quietly in the midst of all this life, encourage an awareness of being part of this world, part of the manifestation of life. Feel that you are breathing in this world, in the middle of a breathing world. Be aware that you are made of the same basic elements that make up everything around you. See if you can encourage a sense of yourself as part of this remarkable phenomenon of life. Just sit quietly for a while, having a sense of your place in the world of things. [18]

Feeling our own sense of place also means feeling a sense of the rightful place of others, otherwise we are "imprisoned in our small selves, thinking only of the comfortable conditions for the small self, while we destroy our large self".[19] Various forms of Buddhism, because of their inwardness, have been challenged at different times as not having a "social conscience", but activist monk Thich Nhat Hanh preaches a Buddhism that is "engaged" with the world. When we eat meat, the grain fed to the animal would have fed thousands; when we eat bread, think of the poisons put on the crops; when we fly in a plane, think of the consequences of the fuel we use:

Meditation is to see deeply into things, to see how we can change, how we can transform our situation. To transform our situation is also to transform our minds. To transform our minds is also to transform our situation, because the situation is mind and mind is our situation.

Awakening is important . . . This is the real meaning of engaged Buddhism.[20]

Oneness with everything is the goal of the religions that came out of the Indian subcontinent—"the aim of life is to realize the great mind that includes everything and to practice accordingly".[21] It is to find everything in ourselves or ourselves in everything, the one in the many and the many in the one. This non-duality is foreign to the Greek philosophical roots of Christianity with its either/or dualities of GOD and humanity, mind and matter, men and women, good and evil, sinner and saved. Yet "many" and "one" are simply different ways to describe the whole. We call food cooked with Thai recipes Thai food and food cooked with Indian recipes Indian food, but both are food—*we* create the duality of Thai/Indian, good/bad, nice/not nice, right/wrong with our views, opinions and prejudices. *Zazen* in Zen Buddhism is a meditation free of analysing everything into its categories, "the unassuming attitude of just being present in each moment, accepting the non-dual reality of each moment with openness and clarity, being careful not to fall into partiality based on opinions and false views and being open to all possibilities".[22] If a bird sings during meditation, the practitioner does not consciously say "That is a bird", but simply becomes part of it and experiences it, disciplining the mind to allow it to be without being diverted by it. Instead of defining how life *should* be, we live with whatever happens, enjoying it and being completely involved—"Moment after moment we should live right here, without sacrificing this moment for the future . . . Everyone is a Buddha by simply practicing *zazen*, whether they have reached enlightenment or not."[23]

Meditation and contemplation found a friendly home in Christianity with the mystics, who seek the closest possible and direct union with GOD. Mystics have described their experiences in sexual imagery, in images of losing one's own self in the One, and as an "unknowing" of GOD as in darkness. Early mystics included the author of John's Gospel, Paul, the Desert Fathers, Saint Augustine and Dionysius the Areopagite, but mysticism blossomed in many directions in the Middle Ages with religious orders creating their distinct lifestyles, whether simplicity, silence, work, study or intense devotion to Jesus or Mary. In the Eastern Orthodox Church, hesychasm (from *hesychia* meaning stillness or quiet) developed out of the teachings of Saint Gregory Palamas (1296–1359), a monk from Mount Athos and later Archbishop of Thessalonica, who believed that, through meditation and self-discipline, one could attain a direct, experiential knowledge of GOD and the Divine energies here and now (deification). His opponents said this was not possible until the afterlife, but Palamas believed the saints had received this uncreated experience on earth, literally shining in their bodies as in a transfiguration. Their methods of prayer and meditation involved control of the breathing and posture, such that the monks were called *"omphalapsychoi"*—men with souls in their navels—because, to heighten the mystical experience, they focused their eyes on a place just below the chest, no doubt the origin of the expression "navel-gazing" today.

Meditation shapes the prayer life in most monastic orders in Western Christianity. "Blessed are they that enter far into inward things, and endeavour to prepare themselves more and more, by daily exercises, for the receiving of heavenly secrets", said Thomas à Kempis.[24] Although the Protestant reformers closed monasteries, the radical Reformation in Anabaptist, Quaker and Shaker forms encouraged the desire to be in direct communion and union with GOD by attending to the Divine Light within. With the contemporary turn to spirituality, meditation has come of age, even beyond the boundaries of religious groups. Borrowing the spiritual disciplines and experiences of monastic orders and Eastern meditation, small groups gather together, inside and outside churches, mosques and temples. The word "meditating" has become more popular than "praying" in places where the way we imagine the Sacred has turned inward. Because of its freedom from language, and thus from doctrinal speculation, meditation groups can work across religious traditions.

Sufism developed within Islam in order to ensure that the original devotional vision of the Prophet did not get lost in transition. Influenced at various times by Syriac Christian monasticism and Hindu asceticism, its followers sought to free themselves from human ego and weakness in order to live a life of love for GOD. They developed ways to produce ecstatic experiences of their relationship/union with GOD, initially raising alarm bells, given Islam's stress on the absolute transcendence and otherness of GOD. Sufis have similar language to other mystics—becoming true lovers of God and penetrating the mysteries of mysteries to understand the essence of God:

When a candle flickers in darkness, the moth flies into the flame and is consumed. The candle of God flickers in the darkness of the world, let us fly towards the flame, and be consumed by God's love.[25]

Rumi (1207–73), the author of these words, founded one branch of Sufism, the *Mevlevis* (Whirling Dervishes), whose *Sema* (whirling dance meditation) eliminates the distraction of the outside world. At the Parliament of the World's Religions (2009), a highlight of the Sacred Music and Dance evening was such a group in billowing white skirts and pillbox hats, circling in a personal spot as they also circled slowly around in the group circle, each deep in concentration on the hand held in front of them and never missing a step. Symbolically, the whirling recognizes that everything in the universe revolves, from electrons to the cycle of life and death, and so, by revolving, they are in harmony with everything. Whirling is not about losing consciousness or an ecstatic experience, but to unite the three parts of human nature—mind, heart and body—and deserting the ego or false self to reach Allah, the Real. The camel hair tall hat (*sikke*) symbolizes the tombstone of the ego and the wide white skirt the ego's shroud. When they remove their black coats at the beginning of the whirling meditation, this symbolizes being spiritually reborn. While whirling, the right arm is raised to the sky, receiving GOD's blessing, and the left hand, on which the devotee focuses, is turned to the earth. At the end of the *Sema*, they retire to their rooms for further meditation.[26]

In Hinduism, yoga brings disciples into union with the One where they discover that their "self" (*atman*) is actually *Brahman*.[27] This yoga (from "yoke", meaning to unite together and bring under discipline—as Jesus said "Take my yoke upon you and learn from me", Matt. 11:29), is not the commercial Western yoga in every community hall across the country, although this disciplining of the body, *hatha* yoga, was originally the precursor to the different forms of spiritual yoga. The yogic path you choose for your spiritual goal depends on your personality type—reflective, emotional, active, experimental or empirical. The common yogic goal is to control one's fluttering, fluctuating mind so that it can focus and move into higher states of consciousness and eventually to liberation—"Let the wise man vigilantly restrain his mind as he would a chariot yoked to bad horses."[28] For the philosophical type, *jnana* yoga offers a way through knowledge, with meditative exercises to reflect rationally and spiritually on the writings of the scriptures and sages. For the emotional soul, the *bhakti* yoga way of love (already discussed) directs our intense love towards GOD rather than reason. There are different Divine images in these two forms. Whereas *jnana* yoga imagines individual selves as tiny waves within the Infinite Sea (Brahman) or the all-pervading Brahman present in us and everything, *bhakti* yoga stresses Divine otherness:

> He who worships God must stand distinct from Him, so only shall he know the joyful love of God; for if he say that God and he are one, that joy, that love, shall vanish instantly away.[29]

To love and adore, one needs something to love, not something infinite and without personality, or simply a part of *us*. This *bhakti* love is expressed in repeating the Divine Name (*japam*) constantly, and this love relationship can be imagined in different relational metaphors, such as parent–child, friend–friend and lover–lover, and in different chosen Avatars (incarnations).

The third yogic way to union with the Divine is *karma* yoga—finding Brahman, not in monastic seclusion, but through work and in the bustle of daily affairs in the world. One meditates in a *jnana* or *bhakti* style while work is being accomplished. The fourth way is through psychological exercises, *raja* yoga, which seek to uncover, through mental exercises, various layers of the human being—body, conscious personality, the subconscious and finally Being itself. A person usually sticks to one yogic path and adapts his or her life around those practices. However, Hinduism also recognizes four *stages* of life—student, householder, retirement, and wandering ascetic—which are also taken into consideration when choosing a yogic path for any one period of life.

On the second level of the Melbourne Convention Center during the Parliament of the World's Religions (2009), Tibetan monks associated with the Dalai Lama set up an area for meditation. On one day, the monks created a huge mandala with colored powders. With amazing steadiness, patience and concentration, two artist monks tapped delicately on long silver cylinders (like elongated straws), controlling the flow of powder which "painted" a multi-colored pattern of circles, petals and the outlines of squares as the massive mandala took shape on a flat table. Even when two little children tried to climb onto the table for a better look, wrestling with each other for positions, the monks' demeanors did not change as they gently encouraged the children to play elsewhere. An older observer, wanting a photograph from above, climbed onto a fickle chair close to the table, which raised levels of stress in the observers but apparently not in the monks. After all this work, the mandala would be destroyed, representing the temporal nature of all things.

A mandala is a complex diagram used for meditation both in Hinduism and Buddhism. The word itself means a "circle" or "that which surrounds", since the circle symbolizes a universal natural form and cosmic wholeness. Within that circle, the complex design symbolically represents the cosmos, a geometric projection of the universe reduced to an essential plan, a cosmogram. The design follows a strict symbolic order such that the devotee can recognize what they are seeing and meditate through the layers from outside to the center to gain access to their highest levels of consciousness. In Hindu mandalas, Avatars are represented within the mandala—as circles or triangles pointed up and down to represent the male–female (Shiva–Shakti) principles. These Avatars aid the devotee to move towards the center—the *bindu* (navel) of the GODDESS, the symbol of love, the recognition of the Self and the visual equivalent of the sound "Om". Some mandalas are created large enough so that a person can actually step into that center, and a mantra is used when meditating on the mandala. The popular revival of the labyrinth is another form of mandala-style meditation and the symbolic striving for the center and the real self. Walking a labyrinth slowly and silently is a meditative, cleansing journey into the center and back again out in the world. We cannot lose ourselves in this process (as in a maze) since all paths lead to the center.

To aim at union with the Divine, the Divine has to be present, not somewhere off in the clouds, a Ground of Being rather than those forever-not-quite-touching fingers of GOD and man in Michelangelo's creation mural on the Vatican's Sistine Chapel ceiling. Interestingly in that painting, Eve is protectively nestled under GOD's other arm looking out, rather apprehensively I might add, before she is handed over to the earthly Adam. This part of the painting, GOD and Eve, is rarely featured, although it gives a better sense of Divine intimacy, albeit in anthropomorphic form, than the futile, eternally separated fingers of GOD and Adam. In Luke's Gospel, when asked by the Pharisees when the reign of GOD would come, Jesus said, "The kingdom of God is not coming with things that can be observed: nor will they say, 'Look, here it is!' or 'There it is!' . . . the Kingdom of God is among (within) you" (Luke 17:20–21). These words invite us to look both inwards and around us, rather than raising our eyes and hands to the heavens. This does not reduce GOD's location only to within the world as we know it, but acknowledges that what we know and experience of the Sacred must be experienced in our everyday world, or else it is just plain speculation. Speculation is a grand, ego-building exercise as we try to step into the mind of GOD, but it is always just that—speculation.

The Divine immanent in the world, however, means different things to different mystics. Some see it as being one with GOD (unitive) and some see it as being in the presence of GOD (numinous), where devotion is still directed to the Other. Philosopher Walter Stace (1886–1967) defined mysticism in a wordy but nuanced way as "the apprehension of an ultimate nonsensuous unity in all things, a oneness or a One to which neither the senses nor the reason can penetrate . . . [and] entirely transcends our sensory-intellectual consciousness".[30] In other words, this Mystery somehow abides within the cosmos, the world, nature and the individual's deepest self. "He who is in the sun, and in the fire and in the heart of man is one", says the *Maitri Upanishad*.

"He who knows this is one with the One."[31] This impacts the logistics of communing with the Divine. We are no longer addressing Something only up there in the heavens, with sign-in-and-out prayers that begin with "Dear God" and end "in Jesus' name". Rather, we are encountering That which is deepest within us and also in every sentient being, in the earth under our feet and in the air we breathe.

Words of address are no longer necessary if our soul (that strange little word that covers whatever we cannot otherwise explain) merges with the Soul of the universe, an internal, silent conversation between us and the Ground of Being. Here we are moving from meditating on something to contemplation or simply "be-ing" in the silent depth of ourselves, which some describe as union with the One. Jesuit priest and Zen teacher Robert E. Kennedy calls contemplative prayer "an empty and imageless prayer which is the naked intent of the will reaching out to God, not as I imagined him to be, or as he is in any of his works, but as he is in himself".[32] In the Qur'an, it is described thus: "Is He not closer than the vein of thy neck? Thou needest not raise thy voice, for He knoweth the secret whisper, and what is yet more hidden" (Surah 6:12). Christian mystic Meister Eckhart says, "God is nearer to me than I am to myself; he is just as near to wood and stone, but they do not know it."[33]

Prayer, meditation and contemplation, these three, but the greatest of these is . . . no, this is not about a hierarchy but about different ways to engage the Divine. Contemplation simply moves beyond the need for words or reflecting on a theme, to a simple gaze where reason is replaced by intuition and action by be-ing, paying attention to That of which we cannot speak. Thich Nhat Hanh says:

In Buddhism, our effort is to practice mindfulness in each moment—to know what is going on within and all around us. When the Buddha was asked, "Sir, what do you and your monks practice?" he replied, "We sit, we walk and we eat." The questioner continued, "But sir, everyone sits, walks and eats", and the Buddha told him, "When we sit, we *know* we are sitting. When we walk, we *know* we are walking. When we eat, we *know* we are eating." . . . When you have mindfulness, you have love and understanding, you see more deeply, and you can heal the wounds in your own mind.[34]

16

Engaging the Sacred in the World

> Leave this chanting and singing and telling of beads! Whom doest thou worship in this lonely dark corner of a temple with doors all shut? Open thine eyes and see thy God is not before thee! He is there where the tiller is tilling the hard ground and where the pathmaker is breaking stones. He is with them in sun and in shower, and his garment is covered with dust. Put off thy holy mantle and even like him come down on the dusty soil! . . . Meet him and stand by him in toil and in sweat of thy brow.
>
> —*Rabindranath Tagore*[1]

Although one of the great comforts of religions has been the vision of an afterlife, I am bold enough to say that this has also been one of the downfalls. Religions have invested so much mileage in promoting a future place of rewards where GOD lives, that humans have treated their existence in *this* world as trivial, temporary and, in many cases, a task and trial compared with what they hope to gain in the next. "Happy is he who always has the hour of death before his eyes, and daily prepareth himself to die," Thomas à Kempis said, "for to eat, and to drink, to sleep and to watch, to labor and to rest, and to be subject to other necessities of nature, is doubtless a great misery and affliction to a religious man who would gladly be released and free from all sin".[2] Thérèse of Lisieux called her childhood her "exile on earth", longing to be in heaven where she would know "unclouded joy"— granted she had lost her mother quite young and longed to be embraced by both her mother and Jesus. In the meantime, she went to church every day to sit beside the Blessed Sacrament:

> Sometimes I felt lonely, very lonely, but then peace and courage would come back to me if I repeated the line: "The world's thy ship and not thy home." [3]

"Salvation" was early narrowed down in Christianity to that which is necessary to gain entry to heaven, losing the original breadth of the word meaning "wholeness" and "liberation" in *this* life. GOD simply became the "police officer of little sins". Much of this theology emerged at times in history when the average life expectancy was no more than 40 and so belief in an afterlife was important. Also, for most of humanity, earthly life was a struggle and people were happy to leave it for something better. Today our lifespan is, on average, double that of medieval times and convictions about "streets of gold" are less firm, so we need to take a look around and live with what we have.

The deaths of young men in the war of the Maccabees (second century BCE) led Judaism to consider an afterlife, a concept they learned in exile amongst Zoroastrians and was still being debated in Jesus' day. Contemporary ideas in Judaism on an afterlife, however, are rather pragmatic. Jews do not see heaven and hell as places, but some imagine the soul reunited with the body "when the Messiah comes". This is why cremation is not accepted by some and organ transplants present a problem but, as a Jewish friend explained, this can be accommodated with the idea of a *mitzvah*, a good deed to save another's life. Jews are not preoccupied with sin because they don't see life as passing the big exam to gain heaven—the key factor is to live well here and now. Sin is not about depravity but about missing the mark, being less than fully human, certainly not a permanent stain on one's score sheet. The Jewish Paul said that, being "of the flesh" (human), "I do not understand my own actions. For I do not do what I want, but I do the very thing I hate" (Rom. 7:15). Although this was later interpreted as "proof" of original sin or "the devil made me do it", it was rather a description of a fallible human being who could use a little help from the indwelling Spirit to transform this tendency. Life was about making the best creative responses of which we are capable and, when we make wrong decisions, this is natural, not evil, because we are *not* GODS. This is the gist of the Adam and Eve story—they made a choice, as humans are supposed to do, qualifying them for independent human life *outside* the Garden. They disobeyed instructions, as humans do when they feel they are not the best solution and, when you think of it, *not* eating a fruit that gives knowledge of good and evil would seem a wrong choice. Like other ancient beginning stories, they were tested to see if they were worthy of, and ready for, not heaven but *humanity*! Judaism's buoyant attitude to life and nature also included a healthy attitude to sex as GOD's good gift, something Christianity would cover with shame, using this same story of Adam and Eve.

Hinduism's message is also a positive view of life in this world—you can have what you want but, in time, you realize what it *really* is that you want. Initially, human beings want pleasure and happiness in a world awash with beauty, but soon worldly success becomes more important. In time, this loses its appeal as people realize there is a deeper self beyond distractions and false ideas. They seek their true self (*atman*) and discover that it is no less than the Divine *Brahman*. This is not life-denying stuff but a move to become more intensely human, such that how we live as human beings in this life will influence the form we are given in reincarnated existences. Despite Buddhism's vision of enlightenment as the ultimate goal, either many lives away or through a sudden enlightenment that cannot be contrived, it also stresses the need to be "awake" and alive in every moment in *this* world. Thich Nhat Hanh says:

> We have to be in touch with ourselves and with other enlightened people and we have to be in the present time because only the present is real, only in the present moment can we be alive. We do not practice for the sake of the future, to be reborn in a paradise, but to be peace, to be compassion, to be joy right now.[4]

Nikos Kazantzakis and his friend were visiting Orthodox Christian monasteries on Mount Athos as part of their spiritual adventure. Full of life, wonder and enthusiasm, the young men asked a monk why the paintings over his monastery's cemetery entrance showed Christ crucified and not, as would be fitting, Christ risen. The monk became angry—"Our Christ is Christ crucified. In the Gospels did you ever see Christ laugh? He is always sighing, being scourged, and weeping—always being crucified."[5] This is also the feel in Thomas à Kempis' description of the life of saints who "imitated" the life of Jesus:

> [T]hey hated their lives in this world, that they might keep them until life eternal . . . They renounced all riches, dignities, honors, friends and kinsfolk; they desired to have nothing which appertained to the world; they scarce took the necessaries of life; they grudged even the necessary care of the body.[6]

But is this an accurate picture of Jesus of Nazareth? Do the Gospels portray Jesus' life as sheer misery, or did Jesus show us how to live abundantly in this world? Some people are so caught up with the idea that Jesus died for our sins (something Jesus did not spell out in the forms it takes in traditional Christianity) that they weigh Jesus' worth only in terms of his death. The theological question becomes, did Jesus, and those who followed him to death for a cause, live in order to die or did they die because they chose to live abundantly? When Jesus is valued only as a man born to die as a Divine pawn, we have totally missed the way he lived.

Sallie McFague calls for a whole new way of living in the world and engaging the Sacred *here and now*. It is not about longing for our "real" home in heaven as if we are somehow trapped in this earthly home, the Gnostic idea the early Church rejected. It is not about wallowing in our sinfulness and fretting about our personal salvation in order to keep our name on the heavenly list and ensure that as many others as possible get on that list, even while ignoring their sufferings in real life. "We have a place and a vocation: our place is planet earth, and our vocation is working with God toward the flourishing of all life in our home", McFague says. "If salvation is living appropriately on our planet, living as the one creature who can consciously help bring about God's beloved community, then sin is living in a way opposed to that goal . . . living a lie is living a selfish life; living the truth is living a deified life. The first assumes that life is found in the self; the second, that life is found in God."[7]

Such thinking presupposes that the Sacred is *within* the world, rather than located off somewhere else. It focuses on Divine Energy infilling and energizing everything as its Ground of Being. "There is not a single place in all the corners of the world", Shinto teaching says, "where God is absent."[8] According to Black Elk from the Sioux tradition, "The Great Spirit is everywhere, he hears whatever is in our minds and hearts, and it is not necessary to speak to him in a loud voice."[9] "Heaven"—where GOD's realm is—is here and now, the Divine is within us as John's Gospel says. Every crevice, every person and every event is filled with the Divine-at-work in what Thomas Merton described as "the joy of the cosmic dance which is always there. Indeed, we are in the midst of it and it is in the midst of us, for it beats in our very blood, whether we want it or not."[10] Religion scholar Ursula King prefers this metaphor of the "cosmic dance animated by the life-giving breath of the Spirit" to that of "journey", the more common description for the spiritual life. Dance is not solitary and it is also accompanied by music and rhythm, making it more dynamic:

While we dance, we also touch each other closely. We enjoy the sheer presence of another person, grow closer physically and emotionally, feel the sense of energy, delight and fun that accompany the exuberance of dancing. Thus it seems an appropriate metaphor to speak about the dance of life that involves body, mind and soul—our whole being. And life's dance is always interwoven with the dance of the Spirit.[11]

This move from the solitary journey to the intense, colorful involvement with others in the dance switches on lights in our minds and turns us from contemplating ourselves in our solitary corner to facing a world that demands our presence and invites us into the action:

> The largest setting for life's dance is the vast web of life, the continually ongoing process of universal becoming. We are part of the immense rhythm of being born and dying, integral to the evolutionary history of the cosmos itself.[12]

The answer to where and how we engage the Divine unfolds before us, free of sacred props, idols, saints and institutions. "The one who is more awesome than all the galaxies in the universe and nearer to us than our own breath" is inescapably part of this dance in which we all whirl and laugh.[13]

Being part of the cosmic dance where the Divine is present and participating is a wake-up call for religious people to come off their prayer mats, out of their churches and temples and engage the world and its crises. As Rumi said in his poetic imagery:

> If inner meanings were all that mattered, God would not have bothered to create the world. If loving God were purely a spiritual state requiring no outward expression, God would not have bothered to create the world. Just as lovers show their love through material tokens, God expresses his love through creation—and we must express our love for him by the way we use his creation.[14]

The 2009 Parliament of the World's Religions' theme was "Making a World of Difference: Hearing each other, healing the earth." Subthemes around which papers were presented were:

- Healing the earth with care and concern.
- Indigenous peoples.
- Overcoming poverty in an unequal world.
- Securing food and water for all people.
- Building peace in the pursuit of justice.
- Creating social cohesion in village and city.
- Sharing wisdom in the search for inner peace.

These were not random titles from a small committee trying to fill a program, but themes that emerged from previous parliaments and continue to present as urgent matters with which religious people must grapple if their visions of peace and justice are ever to become real. Six out of the seven subthemes are "worldly" themes addressing, not peoples' eternal salvation, future enlightenment or inward spirituality, but ways of living on *this* planet and taking responsibility for what we do.

Reflecting on these issues, I once wrote:

We litter with bricks and the steel of progress
placid farms, ancient springs, coastal dunes.
We drill the floors of teaming oceans
and scratch fatal scars across eternal hills.
With insatiable greed we rob
nesting places from birds
and existence from whole species.
When broken, outdated or drained dry,
we discard our toys in piles of metal,
our majestic hills of civilization.
Like wild children of permissive parents
we play with abandon and disdain
in this stunning planet God called good.
We fornicate, populate and consume
as if our exclusive right.
When will the bell toll
on our obscene madness?[15]

Many people see these issues simply as secular concerns and not part of their religious mission. To them, the earth has been provided by GOD for humans created in the Divine image, to plunder and destroy at will—were not humans assigned the task of "dominating" the earth and "subduing it?" And, they say, surely the Creator is also the Preserver? Can't an omnipotent, all-powerful GOD intervene to adjust the planet, if nothing happens apart from Divine will? And doesn't the Bible warn of end times, with earthquakes, wars and famines; and thus climate change, if it even exists, is part of the Divine plan for the end and Christ's return? As for the rights of indigenous peoples, wasn't it *GOD's* command to evangelize the world, bringing everyone out of darkness into the light of a westernized gospel? Didn't Jesus say, "I am the way, and the truth . . . *no one* comes to the Father except through me" (John 14:6)? As for poverty, doesn't GOD ordain who will be rich or poor, lord or serf, and anyway, isn't poverty also about laziness and irresponsible procreation? And justice—we've been doing that for years. Peace? We have to protect ourselves against the terrors (and terrorists) of this world and GOD fights on our side anyway, like the old Hebrew days. As for social cohesion in village and city and trying to integrate immigrants and foreigners, isn't that where all the trouble comes from, people of other religions challenging *our* lifestyle. Sharing wisdom in the search for inner peace? Now at *last* we're talking about something *religious*, so long as we don't have to talk with people from religions other than ours—*we* have the truth, the only truth, so help me GOD.

Propagators of the above arguments have GOD fairly and squarely tethered in the heavens outside our messy world, and that is where they want GOD to be. From that height, the Righteous One can send thunderbolts from the Divine fingers, and a heaven above where GOD dwells is an attractive option when we are freed from coping in *this* world. In traditional Christian portrayals of heaven, nothing much is said in detail, except that we will be "with GOD", yet *this* is the promise in the here-and-now world. I recently had a Christmas greeting from a friend whose GOD has to continually prove the Divine Self in ways that can be deemed miraculous. A family member was recently rushed to hospital and put in intensive care. With good medical staff and an efficient hospital, a series of crises was resolved, as is the day-by-day task of medical professionals. However, the story had to be recounted as a series of dramatic Divine interventions in order to "demonstrate GOD's hand" in everything that happened and prove a "faithful, loving Heavenly Father who can be trusted". The Divine working *within* events and people such that their creativity and skill achieved the desired goal is not as convincing as an external GOD intervening in the process to assure the supplicant of their great faith. I don't want to be cynical, but I have personally watched my spouse, during a very serious illness, test the best resources of the medical profession and I was deeply thankful and appreciative of their well-honed skills and investigative training, without having to celebrate *only* if I could detect something "supernatural" in the process.

Aleksei Leonov, the Russian cosmonaut who was the first person to walk in space, said as he gazed back at the earth, "The Earth was small, light blue, and so touchingly alone, our home that must be defended like a holy relic."[16] In a similar way, Clive James, a well-known Australian writer who would not call himself religious, said in a recent interview that he saw the world as "holy". According to theologian Matthew Fox, reverence is the only response to the universe, yet this "morality of reverence will also be a morality of responsibility—not a responsibility based on duty and fear of disobedience but a responsibility based on care for what we cherish and revere".[17] If the earth is holy, somehow infused with the Divine, this surely puts a different slant on paying attention to the cold, hard statistics of climate change and also our perspective on our greed and violation of the earth, the Divine womb. The Buddhist and Hindu concept of *karma*, that what we do results in consequences both in this life or a future life, is a brilliant model for ecology and sustainability. The Buddha said:

> As a mother watches over her child, willing to risk her own life to protect her only child, so with a boundless heart should one cherish all living things, suffusing the whole world with unobstructed loving-kindness.[18]

Yet how do we convince the world of this, especially the *religious* world that should be horrified about how the planet is treated? How can we rave about the beauty of GOD's creation and yet continue to abuse it and let most of the world's people suffer in poverty? "We do not need so much to accept Christ's sacrifice for our sins as we need to repent of a major sin", Sallie McFague says, "our silent complicity in the impoverishment of others and the degradation of the planet." If the world is GOD's "house", we inhabitants must keep the Divine house rules and "what God's house rules are . . . is one of the major tasks of Christian discernment".[19] While caring for the planet has not, for the most part, been led by religious bodies absorbed with the world beyond, the Dalai Lama states his responsibility to this earth, not as religious business but as *human* business and human survival, fostering compassion for the earth and all sentient beings as an inhabitant of this planet:

> [R]eligion is a kind of luxury. If you have religion, that is good. But it is clear that even without religion we can manage. However, without these basic human qualities, we cannot survive. It is a question of our own peace and mental stability.[20]

The image of the Divine *in* the world also raises questions about what the Divine *does* within the world. The Hindu *Upanishads* speak of GOD as the One "hidden in all things, all-pervading, the self within all beings, watching over all works, dwelling in all beings, the witness, the perceiver, the only one free of qualities".[21] While Intelligent Design proponents are hung up with the order and design of the universe as "proof" of a Creator, scientist John Haught suggests we take a closer look at what scientists actually *know* about the universe. As well as order and design, there is an ever fresh wellspring of novelty in the depths of the universe to which the theory of evolution points.[22] What if the Divine is not about order but about novelty, constantly working within an unfinished creation? What if God is not concerned with preserving some original Divine blueprint but with enabling the universe itself to participate in its own, ongoing creation? According to Swami Muktananda:

> God has appeared as the universe . . . it is a manifestation of the divine *Shakti* [Love] . . . You will see the divine *Shakti* darting with the speed of electricity through your whole body, through all its fluids, blood, prana [breath]. As you experience this *Shakti*, you will know what love is . . . First love yourself, then your neighbors, and then the whole world.[23]

Here, GOD is not the Being *doing* the loving but the *loving* or compassion itself. The Buddha told his followers, "Go forth into the world for the good of the many, for the happiness of the many, with compassion for the world, and for the benefit, the blessing, and the happiness of gods and humans."[24] When it all boils down, love and compassion are the centerfolds of religion, the dual themes of "love God [and] your neighbor as yourself" (Matt. 22:37, 39) and from the Hindu *Mahabharata*, "This is the sum of duty. Do nothing unto others which would cause you pain if done to you."[25]

In a recent interview with scientist Richard Dawkins, Australian interviewer Andrew Denton was determined not to allow the program to be monopolized by Dawkins' usual vitriolic recitation of everything evil and delusional about religion. Denton's carefully crafted questions left Dawkins either speechless or refusing to answer since they probed who Dawkins was as a person and what inspired or moved him beyond what he could attribute to science. When asked to name his moral guide, Dawkins hesitated, then said, "The Golden Rule—do to others what you wish to be done to you", a quote from Matthew's Gospel (7:12) but not an original idea, as Jesus acknowledged—"for this is the law and the prophets". *This* is the central message of all the religions that Dawkins calls "delusional". The Tibetan Buddhist Udana-Varga says, "Hurt not others in ways that you yourself would find hurtful"[26] and Confucius said:

> What one does not wish for oneself,
> one ought not to do to anyone else;
> What one recognizes as desirable for oneself,
> one ought to be willing to grant to others.[27]

If the gurus across the world's religions are right, engaging the Sacred in the world is to experience love and compassion, whether emerging from within us as we gaze at the beauties of nature, or seen in the eyes and actions of another, or motivating our energies towards justice and peace, or experiencing a loving Presence we choose to call GOD. Engaging this love is both to acknowledge its reality first in ourselves and to channel it into loving others and the whole world. "My God is found in the very power of shared human experience", Anglican priest Steven Ogden says. "In the midst of shared experience, we encounter presence, gracious presence as a sense of self-acceptance, warts and all, which enables us to live with a sense of courage and a willingness to respond creatively to the human predicament. Without a sense of self-acceptance, we are permanently and pathologically stuck in our own small world."[28]

Meeting the Sacred within the world as love and compassion and engaging this love will inevitably mean we have to get involved in anything that diminishes life for others and for the planet. Verses attributed to the founder of Taoism, Lao-Tzu (*c.* 600–300 BCE) read:

If there is to be peace in the world, there must be peace in the nations.
If there is to be peace in the nations, there must be peace in the cities.
If there is to be peace in the cities, there must be peace between neighbors.
If there is to be peace between neighbors, there must be peace in the home.
If there is to be peace in the home, there must be peace in the heart.[29]

In wondering why Lao-Tzu started with the big picture and worked back to the source of inspiration, spiritual teacher Anand Krishna suggests that humans are so engrossed in the world and their success and busyness that "the sweet but soft melody of [the] human heart can no longer be heard".[30] We can speak about world peace and raise money for world peace because people like big public ideas and, as with motherhood and apple pie, are in favor of them, but for Lao-Tzu, world peace was not possible until something changed within *ourselves*, something engaged *us* sufficiently to act. Engaging the Sacred within the world means becoming involved globally by acting locally in the particular confluence of circumstances into which we have personally been thrust. Canadian clergywoman Gretta Vosper says of this religion-in-the-world:

Rather than beseeching God's mercy, we find we are called to be god in the world to one another. Using the word *god* as a verb, we offer it to the world as we love and forgive and seek right relationships. We find in Jesus' ministry an incarnation of god simply because in much of his recorded work we see that drive to live out in his relationships all the goodness we associate with the divine: his challenges to the *status quo*, his recognition of brokenness, and his upholding of the oppressed . . . when we live out the values of love, mercy, compassion, and forgiveness, we, too, incarnate god. Or, in different terms, *when* we love, we experience and express our fullest humanity—our divinity.[31]

If we engage the Sacred here, what happens in the hereafter? Most religions have an answer for when we die. In Buddhism, there is no "self" to reincarnate, rather a causal influence as a result of karma that passes from candle to candle like a flame. Only when enlightenment ("blowing out") is reached does this process end. In Hinduism and its belief in reincarnation, there *is* an individual self, and the final discovery is not emptiness, but the realization that the self (*atman*) is *Brahman* (GOD). For Algonquin, Cherokee and Iroquois tribes of North America, there is a shadowy and vague afterlife, a "happy hunting-ground" reached after the soul is tested. In early Judaism, there was no concept of an existence after death until it became problematic to claim GOD's faithfulness in life and nothing in death. While Christianity would develop a full-blown account of heaven as the goal and crown of the faithful, there is surprisingly little talk of this, and little consistency about it, in the New Testament. While Christ's appearance to Paul on the Damascus road convinced him of a continuity of life "in Christ", Paul does not define either heaven or hell. John's Gospel uses the term "eternal life" for knowing and believing in Christ in the *present* life (John 6:47; 17:3).[32] As Bishop Spong says, "The fiery punishment that marks the traditional understanding of hell is mostly the gift of Matthew" with his translation of a continually burning rubbish dump in the Hinnom valley (Josh. 15:8, 18:16) into Gehenna, the fiery pits of hell, together with some heavy reinforcement from the "vision" of Revelation.[33]

On Norfolk Island in the Pacific, the old gravestones face east, the direction from which Christ will return. So there is no mistake on the last day, the ones facing west are people born out of wedlock and those who commit suicide. The Qur'an has vivid, literal pictures of *al-akhira*, the afterlife— those failing the Day of Judgement will burn in fire and those who pass will enjoy a garden of cool streams and beautiful women. With the exhumation of ancient Egyptian tombs, we have discovered their elaborate beliefs in a celestial afterlife for royalty, but during the 1900s BCE, the GOD Osiris promised ordinary people a continued existence tilling the "Field of Reeds" after the Day of Judgement if their hearts, weighed in a balance against the feather of truth, were declared justified—the unworthy were devoured by mythical creatures.[34] There are many more stories like this as we shine our flashlight across the world's religions, all representing human attempts to peer beyond the veil of death and find some comfort in a better and more permanent existence.

But who is eligible? Since Judaism did not teach an afterlife in its early days, the Adam and Eve story was simply a beginning story to explain why humans did not live with the GODs (the story is not even mentioned after Genesis 6). In Christianity, however, Adam and Eve would develop into a story of original sin, linked to Jesus through Paul's metaphor, the "second Adam", something Jesus never said of himself. Various theories arose to explain how Jesus' death redeemed humanity from its sin (atonement) and thus became their entry ticket into an afterlife—heaven. Whereas Jewish people saw human disobedience as a natural part of existence, John Bunyan (1628–88), the author of *Pilgrim's Progress*, described his feelings about his sinful self quite differently:

[M]y original and inward pollution, that was my plague and my affliction. By reason of that, I was more loathsome in my own eyes than was a toad; and I thought I was so in God's eyes too. Sin and corruption, I said, would as naturally bubble out of my heart as water would bubble out of a fountain.[35]

Salvation, rather than hope of heaven, was probably more about the fear of a hell so graphically painted in religious art and depicted with great relish in religious writings—"There shall the slothful be pricked forward with burning goads, and the gluttons be tormented with extreme hunger and thirst", à Kempis wrote. "There shall the luxurious and lovers of pleasure be plunged into burning pitch and stinking brimstone, and the envious, like rabid dogs, shall howl for grief. There is no sin but shall have its proper torture."[36] Such language has not disappeared. Only last month, my friend attended the funeral of a beautiful 80-year-old woman, a pillar of her church, who had died of cancer. The preacher began his eulogy, "She did not die because of her cancer. She died because of her sins", and went on to administer the full dose of fear to an audience who may be bound for hell. What we need saving from is this type of "salvation" that virtually makes a person a slave to weighing his or her actions and deeds every moment on a "Will I be saved or damned?" scale.

Copernicus and Galileo began the challenge to the medieval cosmology of heaven up there and earth below, and scientists and thinkers have kept the ball rolling down the centuries, such that today's understanding of the universe bears absolutely no resemblance to medieval times. Yet many people still mouth the old cosmological images cemented in our religious "truth packages". Where GOD is (heaven) has to be rethought with our ever-expanding knowledge of the universe, as do our Divine images. Just as serious scholars have refuted the story of Adam and Eve as the origin of sin and a cosmic fall, we have to renegotiate the whole idea of rewards and punishment—the word "sin" is so loaded today as to be next to useless. In our new image of an interconnected cosmos, "sin" is not about a moral list of "do's" and "don'ts", but about actions and attitudes that alienate us from this integrated whole, whether alienation within oneself, with one's neighbors, with all sentient beings or with the cosmos and its sacredness. We need to revisit the initial meaning of the word "sin" as "missing the mark", where an archer did not do something morally wrong but rather aimed off course and needed some realigning. Salvation (liberation) is the ongoing process of being realigned in this interconnected web with the Sacred, here and now, not for some afterlife in another realm. In Buddhist teaching, *dharma* is the way things really are, and failure to see them in this way means that one's world view is distorted or out of alignment, causing suffering. The Buddha taught his followers how to see things clearly, thus *dharma* also became the word for his teachings (handed down in Buddhist scriptures) that lead to enlightenment or liberation.

Some will no doubt launch the old cry, "Whatever happened to sin?", thinking I am going light on all the evil in the world, but this is simply perpetuating the old dualism—good and evil, male and female, black and white. Take black and white, for example. These colors are not complete opposites but shades along a continuum. When does black become grey? Is there only one color of grey? A grey sky certainly moves back and forth in color as the sun comes and goes and shadows fall, yet we still call it grey. Is grey a color or a process of reflection and refraction of light? Even grey paint changes, as some of us have realized to our horror, depending on the wall on which it is applied and its relation to the light. In the same way, what is good and what is evil? A mother bird feels immense satisfaction feeding a worm to her baby, but is this good news for the worm? No doubt worm bedtime stories paint birds as the ultimate evil. Hebrew thought inherited the idea of life as a dualistic cosmic battle between good and evil from the Zoroastrians, where Angra Mainyu is the hostile Spirit and Ahura Mazda the good Spirit. Both cosmic Beings existed from eternity and all evil must be eradicated for Ahura Mazda's final victory.

When this idea was incorporated into Christianity, Satan the obstructer in the Hebrew Bible, became Satan the evil one (Devil) in Christianity, locked in a cosmic battle with the good GOD. This set sin and evil up as human aberrations, something parasitic on our DNA to be removed, rather than recognizing, in a non-dualistic way, that good and evil are both natural possibilities on the human continuum and people are humanly capable of great love and great evil. When a person demonstrates immense altruism, we don't suggest that this is not a "natural" expression of being human (even if not common), yet when we observe human actions that we label evil, we want to attribute them to the Devil or to some unnatural, "sinful" nature. When Bertrand Russell was asked how he distinguished between good and evil without a belief in a GOD, he replied, "I don't have any justification any more than I have when I distinguish between blue and yellow. What is my justification for distinguishing between blue and yellow? I can see they are different."[37] The Buddha warned against this duality of good and evil:

People make a distinction between good and evil, but good and evil do not exist separately. Those who are following the path to Enlightenment recognize no such duality, and it leads them to neither praise the good and condemn the evil, nor despise the good and condone the evil . . . all the words that express relations of duality—such as existence and non-existence, worldly passions and true-knowledge, purity and impurity, good and evil—none of these terms of contrast in one's thinking are expressed or recognized in their true nature . . . Just as the pure and fragrant lotus flower grows out of the mud of a swamp . . . so from the muck of worldly passion springs pure Enlightenment of Buddhahood.[38]

In contemporary cosmology, where everything is engaged in the universe's interconnected dance of life, we can no longer name evil as the work of an extraneous Devil or something "acquired" by humans through some ancient fruit-eating story, and thus avoid taking full responsibility for it. We can no longer shrug off injustice here and now by saying there will be justice in heaven. We need to enter into the messiness of the world as co-workers with the Sacred for transformation, choosing, in each moment, wholeness for everything in the universe rather than alienation that leads to destruction and violence. If we believe in something we call the Sacred, contemporary cosmology tells us that It has to be part of this one indivisible, dynamic whole where there are no dancers, only the dance. As for what happens beyond death, this too must be described within this cosmic whole. The Hebrew creation story said that we came from dust and return to dust, something they observed in real life. The new cosmology tells us that we came, like everything else, from stardust. If that is where we return, we will remain part of the cosmic whole, whatever that might mean. As Albert Einstein said:

I feel myself so much a part of everything living that I am not the least concerned with the beginning or ending of the concrete existence of any one person in this eternal flow.[39]

To me, speculation about life beyond this world is unfruitful because we cannot know what is beyond death, just as we cannot imagine what "before birth" was like. This is not lack of faith—it is reality. It is not a denial of anything but openness to that which we cannot know. Rabindranath Tagore said of death:

I was not aware of the moment when I first crossed the threshold of this life . . . Even so, in death the same unknown will appear as ever known to me. And because I love this life, I know I shall love death as well.[40]

Those who long for death wish to be "with GOD", but that is already the reality for those who see the Sacred in this world. In his book on eternal life, Bishop Spong says:

I prepare for death by living. My commitment is to live as completely as I can and to drink in the sweetness which that particular day has to offer. While I am alive, I will plumb life's depths, scale life's heights, and share my life and my love with those who are fellow pilgrims with me in my time and space. When I die, I will rest my case in the "being" of which I am a part. That is where faith has taken me.[41]

17

Borrowing, Conquering and Adapting

What has been is what will be,
and what has been done is what will be done;
there is nothing new under the sun.
Is there a thing of which it is said
"See, this is new"?
It has already been,
in the ages before us.
—Ecclesiastes 1:9–10

In September 2005, the *Times of India* reported that over 1,500 *asanas* (yoga postures) from ancient Indian Vedic texts are being documented by the Indian Health Ministry and put into the ministry's Digital Traditional Knowledge Library, in order to challenge yoga instructors in the West who are trying to claim patents for these ancient positions. The health minister said, "The Library will protect India's traditional knowledge base." Another senior official told the reporter, "We are receiving reports of teachers trying to patent even our traditional yoga *asanas* . . . fooling people into believing that it helps certain diseases and then trying to name them themselves, by getting a patent. They have also tried to patent the syllable 'Om' . . . We will stop this."

Much of what religions claim as *their* revealed truth has actually been adapted from religions that went before. Our search for the Sacred develops a *déjà vu* when we start delving into other religious traditions. If we think we have a "new" truth, it probably means that we have a poor knowledge of the religious stories of others. Since we usually espouse a belief system lock, stock and barrel and do little investigation elsewhere, it is easy to believe that our religion is unique, but it stands to reason that most religions started in a previous tradition from which basic ideas were learned, even if the new religion has travelled far in another direction. Buddha grew up in what would later be called Hinduism, preserving many of its basic ideas—the law of *karma*, *moksha* (liberation) and the round of rebirth (*samsara*)—while adding a way of life that did not strive for extremes of knowledge or deprivation. Jainism emerged at the same time under its leader Mahāvīra (599–527 BCE), still talking of *karma* and *moksha* but following a more rigorous ascetic path. Hinduism took note of the Buddha's teachings, incorporating him into their stories as the eighth incarnation of Lord Vishnu; and not until the third century BCE, when Indian ruler Ashoka converted to Buddhism and promoted its teaching and ethics across India, did Buddhism become a separate religion and spread beyond India's borders.

Religious people take different stances about religions other than their own. Some reject all of them as wrong and want to obliterate them in the name of true faith. Some accept other religions as valid for others but inferior, still letting them exist side by side. Others accept some of the truths in other religions and appropriate parts that are attractive, while others see all religions as equally valid paths to the Divine and thus there is no need for conversion across religions. It is, therefore, not *inevitable* that different religions become enemies, but it has certainly happened this way in much of religious history. While new religions begin within a parent religion, usually as a corrective to it or fulfilment of it, the gulf widens in time between the new community and its mother tradition, either because the new group demands a pure form beyond the old or because the old tradition will not accommodate upstarts. The new group defines its differences as positives against the parent group's failures, and negative defining demands that people take sides, thus the battle begins.

The Hebrew people defined themselves against the religious ideas of Sumeria and Mesopotamia, even while sharing many common oral stories. According to religion scholar Jaroslav Pelikan, "The Babylonian poem known as *Enuma Elish,* which seems to have been recited once a year or even more often, contained enough parallels to the first two chapters of the Torah to have become known rather loosely as 'the Babylonian Genesis.'"[1] After his death, the Jewish Jesus was gradually described in Greek hero images and concepts. When Christians gained political power under Emperor Constantine, the persecuted became the persecutors, attacking Jews for not believing that Jesus was their Messiah. This began the long history of anti-Semitism in Christianity that would eventually permit the Holocaust. The Prophet Muhammad saw the Judaism of his day as attractive but ethnically exclusive and Christianity as distorting the message by claiming that Jesus was GOD, thus the Divine revelation he received moved beyond both of these traditions as a final revelation. Scholars still debate whether Martin Luther's brush with church authorities could have been resolved had the players been different, but it led to a 30-year religious war and spawned a series of new denominations, each naming their correct doctrines against an earlier reforming group. Joseph Smith pronounced Mormonism as a new revelation beyond traditional Christianity. In all these progressions, the way people engaged the Sacred or claimed to be engaged by It also migrated, taking new shapes, adapting old symbols and adding new meanings.

Many early religions practiced polytheism, where different functions were the responsibility of different GODS and GODDESSES. Without any sense of competition, people prayed to a specialist Deity for a particular need or, if hedging bets, to a few. In practical terms, this is not much different from praying to Jesus, Mary and the saints in a local village church and, for many villagers, the Catholic saints are not far removed from the Greek and Roman Deities that previously blessed their lives. Just as the ancient Romans wore a horn around their necks to protect them from the evil eye (the horn of plenty and a phallic symbol for good fortune), today's Romans wear the horn *and* the cross. In a hole-in-the-wall, but extremely fashionable, kitchenware shop in Sicily, an island oozing with Catholic tradition and ritual, the 30-something woman owner exuded secular sophistication and yet, in the back of her shop, not off in some corner but propped up on her fax machine, was a large photocopy of Jesus with light rays coming from his heart, a reminder of her spiritual connections, while in the pharmacy next door, a counter-top condom machine was carefully positioned to catch the eye of everyone checking out.

In the 1600s, the townspeople of Polizzi Generosa in Sicily pulled up a life-sized marble sculpture of the Egyptian GODDESS Isis, hidden in a well. She was moved into the cathedral where she held up the holy water font for years. In 1764, the statue was moved to the town square while church repairs were done, but when the people asked the bishop to place her back in the cathedral, he was appalled at a pagan GODDESS in the church and had the statue smashed to pieces. The horrified townspeople sent a protest letter to the bishop with a life sketch of Isis so she would be remembered, describing her beauty in detail:

She was of the whitest marble, her long hair hung loose over her shoulders and down her back. Three faces bloomed from her long neck. The one facing front was of a young woman. In the center of her forehead a flower bloomed inside a triangle, perhaps a symbol of the fertile Nile delta, which was her origin. Her left face was that of a bearded, wizened man, eyes wide open. The right face was of an androgynous child. The figure of Isis held two snakes in her right hand, their heads reaching up toward the sash girdling her tunic. In her left hand she held a semi-spherical object, which could have been a globe, or a loaf of bread.[2]

Isis had been the protectress of the grain crops that made Polizzi rich, her three faces the seasons of life—childhood, maturity and old age—and so "The people of Polizzi still mourned for her," Theresa Maggio said, "I saw her framed image in their bars, stores, and offices nearly as often as I saw crucifixes."[3]

In La Valle Dei Templi (Valley of the Temples) in Agrigento, Sicily, the Greek-built Temple of Zeus (fifth century BCE), one of the largest temples built in ancient times, was all but destroyed by the Carthaginians and then rebuilt, but then conquered by the Romans (210 BCE). In the fourth century CE, Christians destroyed it under Emperor Theodosius (347–395 CE). The site became known as the "Giant's Quarry" because so much of its stone was removed for other projects, most notably the Chiesa di San Nicola (Church of St Nicholas) further up the hill, built in the thirteenth century by Cistercian monks over the site of another ancient religious site. Likewise, the *duomo* (cathedral) at Siracusa sits on the site of a temple to Athena, Zeus' favourite child who emerged full grown and in full armour from his head. Built from the profits of the defeat of the Carthaginians in 480 BCE, it was incorporated into a Byzantine church in the seventh century CE. The massive, ridged temple columns still remain as part of the church, dividing the nave from the side chapels. The church became a mosque under the Arabs and returned to Christian use under the Normans. After the facade collapsed in the 1693 earthquake, it was rebuilt in baroque style, an architectural form that celebrated Catholicism's survival against Protestant reform. I was in Siracusa in April 2009 at the beginning of the G8 meetings on the environment and things had come full circle. For the occasion, a sculpture covered in silver paint had been brought from Washington DC and set up in the *duomo* square. Called "The Awakening", it was a giant, male figure with the classical bearded features of a Greek GOD emerging from the earth, revealing a face, two arms and knees and suggesting new life for the earth. A GODDESS figure would have been more appropriate coming from the earth however, given the idea of the earth as GODDESS and also Athena's history on this site.

Religious festivals and their dates are also about borrowings and adaptations. The Bible gives no date for the birth of Jesus and there is still debate as to how December 25 came to be chosen, but it was probably chosen because it was the feast of the "birthday of the unconquered Sun" (Romans revered the Sun as a GOD) or winter solstice, when the days following began to lengthen and the sun became stronger. Jesus would eventually be portrayed as the "new" Sun God. In a mausoleum under Saint Peter's basilica in Rome, there is a late third-century mosaic named *Christo Sole* (Christ the Sun) portraying Christ, with sun rays from his head, riding his chariot across the skies. Not only was the date borrowed but also the festivities to go with it. In the twelfth century, the Syriac Orthodox bishop Jacob Bar-Salibi wrote:

> It was a custom of the Pagans to celebrate on the same 25 December the birthday of the Sun, at which they kindled lights in token of festivity. In these solemnities and revelries the Christians also took part. Accordingly when the doctors of the Church perceived that the Christians had a leaning to this festival, they took counsel and resolved that the true Nativity should be solemnised on that day.[4]

History becomes interesting commentary when people today protest that Christmas has become a "pagan" celebration and urge us to "put Christ back into Christmas".

Similarly Easter, the feast of Christ's resurrection, has eclectic roots and branches. The death of Jesus, according to Gospel records, happened during Jewish Passover week. In the first few centuries of Christianity, a feast known as *Pasch* (Passover), an adaptation of the Jewish celebration, remembered Jesus' death and resurrection. It was later moved from the Jewish date to the following Sunday, with churches illuminated on the Saturday evening and new members baptized on Sunday morning. The Council of Nicaea (325 CE) settled Easter as the Sunday following the full moon after the vernal equinox, calculated with a table that synchronized lunar and solar months (Orthodox churches used the Julian date for the equinox and had a different Easter date from Western churches).[5] But there are other borrowings. According to the Venerable Bede (*c.* 672–735), who wrote a history of the English people, the word "Easter" comes from *Eostre* or *Eastre*, the Anglo-Saxon GODDESS of dawn or the spring GODDESS worshipped at this time of year—her name meant "to rise or be reborn" like the dawn. Despite church abhorrence of "pagan" ideas, many Easter customs have their roots in old Anglo-Saxon traditions. That cute Easter bunny appears because, at celebrations to GODDESS *Eostre*, a hare, the symbol of fertility, was sacrificed. In Hallaton,

Leicestershire, the famous Hare Pie Scramble takes place on Easter Monday, together with a "bottle kicking" game. The hare pie is blessed by the local church at the beginning of the day and then "scrambled" or fought over by local villagers. While some say the tradition had connections with the GODDESS *Eostre*, the locals claim the custom began when two women were saved from an angry bull by a startled hare and, in gratitude, gave money to the church for the vicar to provide a hare pie, bread and beer, over which the village poor fought (the pie is now made of beef and there is some debate as to whether it ever was hare). Eggs were given as gifts in Anglo-Saxon times, as a symbol of spring's reawakening or rebirth and thus they were adopted to symbolize Christian rebirth, both the resurrection and the rebirth of individuals through the Easter event. This ancient symbol has come down to us as painted and chocolate eggs. Celebrations belong to the people and are wound into their local lives such that the "show must go on", even if it has been "purchased" or conquered by another group with very different explanations.

Christians have always been good at packaging the Sacred, snatching it from others and claiming it as completely contained in their box alone. It is wrapped in special paper, tied with fancy ribbons and presented to others as if only ours to give away. The packaging serves to remove all traces of the Sacred in any other form or expression, as if the box was dropped already sealed, from heaven. But where was the Sacred *before* Christianity or *before* Judaism? Where was the Sacred in Africa *before* the missionaries came, a pertinent question when it is becoming more likely that the first humans *came* from Africa—where does that locate the Genesis creation story for literalists? Christians who refuse to study other religions because they have the only truth are ignorant of their own history of borrowing, conquest and adaptation. "Religion is a lot roomier than people think when they are looking at it from the outside," writer Ron Hansen said, "God has a long leash. You are allowed to roam."[6]

Mesopotamia at the time of Abraham had many city states, each with its own GOD. Battles between them were tribal rather than religious and, when a city was conquered, so was its GOD. When Babylon conquered a number of city states in the eighteenth century BCE to form Babylonia, its GOD Marduk became Babylonia's GOD, described in the Babylonian epic of *Enuma Elish*. Abraham's tribe left Ur about this time with *their* Deity Yahweh, one GOD among many—only later would Yahweh be equated with the one GOD of strict monotheism. Their chosenness did not make them missionaries—it was more about survival, where Yahweh would protect them if they obeyed and kept themselves pure. They were constantly overpowered by other nations but Yahweh rescued them. Christianity began with this Jewish story and, when eventually expelled from Judaism, created its own expanded story outside the synagogue.

More borrowing and adapting happened as Christianity established itself in the Mediterranean world and its story became more Greek than Jewish (Christians were 75 percent Gentile by the end of the first century). In Acts 17, Paul tells a universal story to the philosophers of Athens (Jesus and Judaism are not mentioned by name), drawing on what their own poets had said—"in [GOD] we live and move and have our being" (from sixth century BCE Epimenides of Knossos) and "for we too are [GOD's] offspring" (from third century BCE Aratus of Sicyon).[7] Their Stoic philosopher Epictetus (55–135 CE) had said, "When thou has shut thy door and darkened thy room, say not to thyself that thou art alone. God is in thy room"—which brings to mind Jesus' instruction to go into our rooms to pray (Matt. 6:5–6). Philosopher Socrates (469–399 BCE) said as he went to death, "We must obey not men but God", while the disciple Peter, facing persecution, said "We must obey God rather than men" (Acts 5:29).[8] Jesus, in this environment, was transformed from a human Jewish sage called a "son of God", as were many people in the Hebrew Bible (Hos. 11:1, Ps. 2:7; 2 Sam. 7:13–14), to a Greek "son of GOD", the title given to emperors. With the assistance of the virgin birth story (not in Paul's writings or the earliest Gospel, Mark), his birth became a Divine impregnation of a human woman like Greek GODS who spawned GOD-human offspring with human women.[9] This evolution of Jesus is perhaps the greatest borrowing and adapting story of all which, according to theologian Tom Harpur, also goes back to the stories of the hero figures of ancient Egypt.[10] The core of Christianity became a redemption story in terms of salvation, resurrection and heaven, yet the original idea of redemption in Israel meant restoration to kin and country, an idea that appeals to indigenous people, such as Australian Aboriginal people, who were ousted from their land:

> Postcolonial Christian theology needs to recover these older concepts of redemption in order to articulate fresh understandings of resurrection. In respect, Israelite and Jewish traditions could provide much needed conversation partners, both for Indigenous and non-Indigenous Christianity.[11]

Emperor Constantine's reign was a pivotal moment for Christianity, moving it from persecuted cult to imperial faith, with Constantine as head of the Christian Church. The faith declared by Constantine through the creeds became the only true faith. To show Christianity's triumph, churches were constructed on old "pagan" sites. In Rome, the Roman forum gave way to the new imperial religion, and a nearby temple to Zeus' twin sons Castor and Pollux became the basilica of Saint Cosmos and Damien, *Christian* twins. Since the cross had been superimposed on Constantine's sun emblem in a vision before his final battle for the imperial throne, it became the triumphal symbol of the emperor's new religion, although it had previously not been used by Christians as it was an object of offense. The Greek philosophers, not just the Jewish fathers, became recognized as forerunners of Christian thought, and Jews would later become demonized as Satan's people and their history erased from, or negated within, Christianity. Apart from accusations as Christ killers, they were said to perform ritual murders of Christian children, adding their blood to the Passover unleavened bread. These stories gave the excuse for Christian pogroms against Jews and, during the Middle Ages, Jews were expelled from almost every country in Christian Europe.

To celebrate Constantinople as a Christian city, Saint Sophia Cathedral was built and, by 380 CE, Emperor Theodosius made Christian belief mandatory in the East. As a sideline, what goes around comes around. Christian iconoclasts hacked at the wonderful mosaics on the walls of Saint Sophia before Muslim invaders captured the city and turned it into a mosque. Meanwhile in Rome where the Pope was head of the Western Church, hoards from the north invaded (410 CE), bringing Western Christian history to a halt (except in Ireland) until the ninth century with an alliance between Emperor Charlemagne and Pope Leo III. Europe owes the Irish for preserving Western Christianity—their beautifully illustrated manuscripts such as the Book of Kells (800 CE) would inspire artists in Charlemagne's court where Christian scholarship and an interest in ancient Greece and Rome were revived. The Middle Ages began the most powerful period of the Western Church when cathedral builders across Europe built their great "bibles" of brick and stone to tell the Christian story to the faithful.

Another strong claim to the one GOD of Abraham was gathering strength during this same period and the two were destined to meet. As religion scholar Reza Aslan says:

> One could argue that the clash of monotheisms is the inevitable result of monotheism itself . . . a religion of one god tends to be mono mythic; it not only rejects all other gods, it rejects all other explanations of God. If there is only one God, then there can be only one truth, and that can lead to bloody conflicts of irreconcilable absolutisms.[12]

Islam did not come out of nothing. The prophet Muhammad, not satisfied with either Judaism or Christianity, longed to revive the decaying society of Mecca. He received a Divine revelation that became the Qur'an, an Arab story encompassing Jewish and Christian stories as precursors to this final message. Islam spread quickly across the Arab world and, in 638 CE, Muslims captured Jerusalem, a holy place because, from the site of the ruined Jewish temple, Muhammad had been taken up into heaven in a dream. When Muslim armies arrived in Jerusalem, the temple site was derelict and local Jews helped Muslims clear the site to build their mosque, the Dome of the Rock (completed 691 CE). Everywhere, religions build on one another's sacred sites, either to claim superiority or to continue or expand the previous message. "New religions", writer Bamber Gascoyne says, "have moved, like hermit crabs, into the shells left by their predecessors."[13]

Islam flourished during its first four centuries, a leader in science, medicine and philosophy. The famous university mosque in Cairo was founded two centuries before Oxford University, and Muslim scholars were responsible for preserving the Greek philosophers, later rediscovered by the West. When Muslims entered Sicily in the seventh century CE, they changed the architectural and cultural landscape with irrigation, Eastern crops, mosques, madrasa schools and a flourishing culture from their Arab connections across the then known world. People could continue as Christians or Jews, but could not build new churches, ring church bells or read a Bible near a Muslim—but they were not persecuted.[14] In 1061, the Normans landed in Sicily and Christianity re-established itself, driving out Islamic culture and destroying its buildings and architecture. Noto, the last Arab stronghold in Sicily, yielded in 1091 when Roger I became the Pope's Sicilian representative. In the Church of Santa Chiara (Saint Clare) in Enna, a large tile mosaic in the center isle floor is called "The Triumph of Christianity over Islam", depicting a mosque with a minaret broken off and falling to the ground. The Cathedral in Mazara del Vallo, the first Sicilian city captured by Arab conquerors, has a facade scene of Roger I on horseback, killing a Moor lying underneath his horse. Scicli's Chiesa Madre (Church of the Madonna) houses a wooden statue of Madonna delle Milizie (the Madonna on horseback) because she is said to have fought at Roger I's side, making him victorious.

Given Sicily's eclectic religious history, architect monks included this mix in the churches they built—mosaics, Muslim horseshoe arches, arabesque and honeycomb designs. The stunning cathedral at Monreale (near Palermo) features arabic arches of varying styles and shapes, corinthian columns down the nave with acanthus leaves at their capitals entwined around the faces of the Greek GODDESSES Demeter and Persephone. The mosaics lining the cathedral walls, telling the Bible stories, are Byzantine and highlighted in gold. Mosaic floors imitate Moorish designs, while the Capella del Crocifisso (Chapel of the Crucifix) in the north apse is extravagant baroque dripping with marble draped curtains, cherubs, statues and angels, with the dove (Holy Spirit) in the ceiling surrounded by cherub faces peeping through the blue dome.

The Crusades were a dark moment in Christian history when Crusaders were promised heaven if they were killed in battle against "infidel" Muslims, fellow offspring of Abraham's GOD. When two groups fight for the honor of the same GOD, there are tragic results. The Crusades (eight in total), promoted as reconquering the Holy Land, conquered Jerusalem in 1099, the first Crusade. In 1182, Jerusalem fell to the Kurdish Muslim leader Salāh ud-Din (Saladin, 1138–93). The fourth Crusade got as far as sacking Constantinople in 1204 but, instead of returning it to the Eastern Church, the Western Church under the Pope took control. The Greek Church retook the city in 1261 and the Ottoman Turks took it in 1453. As each conquered the other, religious places of worship were razed in order to build the conqueror's variety. The exception is the beautiful mosque in Cordoba, Spain, where its Muslim-style verandas of striped arches lead into the center of the mosque which suddenly presents as a Gothic church sanctuary. Apparently, the invading Christians admired the beauty of the building and allowed it to remain, adapting it for their different religious purposes.

Goa, on the west coast of India, is another example of borrowing, conquering and adapting. Originally Hindu, Goa was taken over in the fifteenth century by the Muslim Moguls who destroyed Hindu temples and built mosques on those sites. In 1512, Portuguese Catholics landed on Goa beaches, defeating the Muslims. The Viceroy Arch between the beach and the town features a carving of this conquest with a triumphant Christian standing on a Muslim. Close by, the Church of Saint Cajetan is built over both the original Hindu well and a ruined Muslim mosque that used the carved stones from the Hindu temple in its construction. The massive Sé Cathedral in old Goa was built from money taken from local Hindus who would not convert and were executed on the lawn in front of the church. While Hindus in Goa were happy to add Jesus as one of their many Avatars, Goan Catholics thought otherwise. E. Stanley Jones (1884–1978), a missionary to India for many years, found Hindu scholars very open to the teachings of Jesus as his life resonated with their Indian experience—"[Jesus] could feel the darkness of the blind, the leprosy of the leper, the loneliness of the rich, the degradation of the poor, and the guilt of the sinner", one of them told

Stanley.[15] However, their openness to many paths to the Divine did not demand they forsake all others for Jesus, as many missionaries expected. On arriving in Calcutta and seeing the mighty Hugli River busy with many steamers and transport boats, Victorian travel writer John Stoddard said:

> I was informed that one of these ships had just brought from England 120 tons of gin and 40 tons of Bibles. If this proportion is maintained on all of them, we may discover why the advent here of Christian nations is not regarded by the natives as an unmixed blessing. It is, however, probable that the gin is chiefly for the Europeans, while the poor heathen have to take the Bibles.[16]

The Ajunta caves near Arungabad in Maharashtra state, India, are carved into the precipitous rock face in the gorge of the Waghore River. They were excavated around 200 BCE and abandoned in 650 CE in favor of the nearby Ellora caves. These 29 caves are covered with tempera murals of scenes from the life of the Buddha and Buddhist stories. Five of the caves were temples and 24 were monasteries, thought to have housed some 200 monks. The abandoned caves were forgotten until a British tiger-hunting party in 1819 saw what looked like arches in the overgrowth. In 1980, in the half-light of these caves, I met Mr Pimpare, an artist from Marathwada University, perched high on a ladder near one of the wall murals, diligently copying in watercolor the fading Buddhist themes. Since re-opening the caves, this marvelous artwork is under threat from the fumes and foibles of modern-day India. I purchased a watercolor as a reminder, which Mr Pimpare ceremoniously signed with the nearest pen, a thick blue felt marker. The more recent Ellora Caves, carved out of rock between 600 and 1000 CE, show a mix of religious traditions. Probably started by the Buddhist builders who abandoned the Ajunta caves, Ellora caves were further developed by pilgrims, both Hindu and Jain, traveling the caravan routes between northern Indian cities and coastal ports. Such is the accommodation between religions that branched from the same basic ideas and did not see the need to annihilate each other.

For the indigenous people of Australia, whose heritage goes back at least 40,000 years and perhaps much longer, everything around them, past and present, was infiltrated with the Sacred—linear time was not a factor as they followed the cycles of the seasons that constantly re-created the earth. The Sacred ancestors shaped the earth in the beginning times, sometimes called the Dreaming or the Law, an infinity that links the past with the present and thus determines the future. The ancestors still remain in those sacred sites, real and present today. There were many ancestral Spirits, each responsible for a different aspect of life, with the Rainbow Serpent the Creator-Spirit. After the white invasion in 1788, Aboriginal people were "missionized" by people who accepted only one true expression of the Sacred, the Christian GOD exclusively revealed in Jesus Christ. What was said by Native American people applied in Australia as well—"when [the missionaries] arrived, they had only the Book and we had the land. Now we have the Book and they have the land".[17] Some missionaries showed interest in indigenous beliefs and helped record them, but others forbade their continuation, considering both the ideas and their proponents "primitive". Early twentieth-century American preacher Harry Emerson Fosdick, although theologically progressive in his day, reflects this racial superiority in his analysis of the evolution of prayer:

> As power of thought confused and weak in an Australian aboriginal, becomes in a Newton capable of grasping laws that hold the stars together, so prayer may begin in a race or in the individual as an erratic and ineffective impulse, but may grow to be a dependable and saving power.[18]

In the 1970s, many Christian missions and government reserves, where indigenous Australians had been herded and deprived of traditional lands and connections, were returned to them. While most of these people were now "Christian", they are attempting to recover their original stories, lost either by force or buried under Christian overlays. In many cases, Aboriginal people did not completely surrender their past to the Christian story but incorporated the story of Jesus into their Dreaming and identified the Christian GOD with their Creator Spirit. They now understand themselves as people of two stories and two laws, the Hebrew and the Aboriginal beginning stories, which have many similarities. Australian Aboriginal theologian Graham Paulson wrote:

> If evangelization means the telling of the story of the gospel as it was acculturated in the western world, and translates into the subcultures of denominational religious institutions, then Aboriginal and Torres Strait Islander peoples have been very well evangelized. But if the process of evangelizing includes the telling of the biblical stories in ways which connect with our deepest spiritual expectations, evoking practices in tune with our own cultures, then we are not well evangelized at all.[19]

The story of conquest is similar wherever Western colonizing explorers went. While most of the adapting was on the part of the colonized, there was also reverse borrowing as aspects of indigenous cultures became exotic in the Western world. At the beginning of the nineteenth century, Native American lore was being taught at Boy Scout camps, even while non-indigenous Americans were insisting that "Indians" be converted from their uncivilized state. Americans have incorporated Native Americans into their Thanksgiving celebrations as part of GOD's blessing to the Pilgrims, dressing up like them and making doll replicas, while giving little thought as to whether indigenous peoples are equally thankful for their life and lot in today's America. Not until the era of nineteenth-century Romanticism did Americans start using indigenous names for places and streets, instead of transported names like New Hampshire and New England. By then, Native American culture had been lost or severely compromised and indigenous people were sadly decimated. Such naming accomplished two "white" desires—to separate themselves further from the England they fought against for independence and to appease the guilt at having destroyed the indigenous way of life. According to an Indian elder, when the white people arrived, they fell on their knees and prayed. Then they got up and fell on the Indians and preyed.[20]

At meetings of the American Academy of Religion, interest in interreligious dialogue with Native American scholars was initially greeted with hope and enthusiasm by these scholars, but disappointment followed when non-indigenous scholars simply recorded their stories to analyse and write about in papers, appropriating what fascinated them to "add" to *their* religious rituals, without also taking stands against injustices still perpetuated on indigenous people. Non-indigenous people have appropriated dream-catchers and corn woman images as their own, without trying to understand the thought and ritual associated with these symbols. Priests put peace pipes on church altars to identify with Native American people but some see this as claiming the power of the pipe along with all their other power. I was present at a meeting where Native American scholars were invited to dialogue with non-indigenous religious scholars and one woman refused— "Do you know how many times I have been asked to dialogue so that white people can understand our traditions and issues? Scores of times and nothing ever happens as a result. Things never change for us in terms of justice—all we do is help our dialogue partners feel good."

What does all this borrowing, conquering and adapting have to do with engaging the Divine, or the Divine engaging us? It tells us that there is something common about the human search for that which is beyond understanding and which we all struggle to name "correctly". New experiences, what some call revelations, often result in new religious groups who define themselves against each other with different words and truth claims. Those who wish to claim uniqueness need to examine the religious context in which their new ideas arose and on whose shoulders they stood for their better view of the Divine. As Ursula King says:

> There is incompleteness in each of the religious traditions; none is static or perfect. All are continually in the process of changing and being transformed—there is room and need for further growth in all of them.[21]

Thich Nhat Hanh also warns against claiming a unique, unchanging "truth". In Buddhism, clinging to what we know is an obstacle to learning new things, like a block of ice obstructing a stream. The Buddha told a story of a widower whose son was kidnapped when bandits destroyed his village. When the father came home and found a charred body, he cremated the body and carried his ashes with him. His son later escaped and knocked on his father's door, but the father would not open it or believe that it was his son. The child went away and they never saw each other again. Thich Nhat Hanh says:

> Guarding knowledge is not a good way to understand. Understanding means to throw away your knowledge. You have to be able to transcend your knowledge the way people climb a ladder. If you are on the thirty-fifth step of a ladder and think that you are very high, there is no hope for you to climb to the thirty-sixth. The technique is to release. The Buddhist way of understanding is always letting go of our views and knowledge in order to transcend. This is the most important teaching.[22]

18

Engaging the
Sacred Together

By me all this world is pervaded in my unmanifested aspect . . .
As the mighty air everywhere moving is rooted in the ether,
so all beings rest rooted in me.

—Bhagavad Gita[1]

○　○　○

The religions of the world are part of the human planetary inheritance, but
also so much more—a rich revelation of an inexhaustible divine ocean of
love, of compassion and mercy, and of the possibility of human dignity and
wholeness beyond all brokenness and wounds.

—Ursula King[2]

In a lecture for theological educators, Professor Dennis Edwards was describing the Sacred in the way I talk about the Divine, present in everything within the world and working within the laws of nature, rather than an interventionist Being acting on certain people in certain ways from outside the world, violating or bypassing its laws. While Jesus was the human face of Divine Love at one moment in history, the Divine was not absent from the world before or after that, but present in everything and always mediated through secondary causes within the universe. Because I knew that some present would find Edwards' words a challenge to their exclusive Christian claims, I was listening as *they* might be hearing these ideas and it struck me all over again that seeing GOD only through Jesus or through Christianity is not *possible* or *plausible* if we imagine the Divine as infusing everything in the universe. We cannot say GOD is ours only and that other experiences of the Sacred describe a different or false GOD. Huston Smith says:

235

It is possible to climb life's mountain from any side, but when the top is reached the pathways merge. As long as religions remain in the foothills of theology, ritual and church organization, they may be far apart.[3]

We can't argue that GOD only acts within those who "have faith", say the right religious words or do the correct rituals, if the Divine is in everything such that nothing in the universe is separated from It. We have talked about being "children of GOD" in our limited terms for so long but, if we see the Divine as the Life and Energy of the universe, we have to re-think what "children of the *one* GOD" might actually mean. Even as I write this, I feel embarrassed at spelling out something so obvious, but there are millions of people who still claim that GOD is theirs and has appeared exclusively and only to them.

GOD within everything in our ever-expanding cosmos displaces so many traditional Christian doctrines—the idea that sin entered the world through two human beings created in recent times in the billions of years of the universe's life; that GOD has only been encountered in the world through the life of one Jesus of Nazareth; and that salvation is obtained only through this one Divine revelation. Driving from O'Hare airport into downtown Chicago recently, I noticed, as we flashed by on the highway, a much larger than life statue of Jesus with flowing robes and outstretched hands in front of a stately old church, welcoming the masses into GOD's house. No doubt these arms once reached towards a grassy park in front of the church or even into a community square, but now the hands of Jesus scarcely miss touching the edge of the multi-lane freeway speeding towards O'Hare. Frozen in white plaster, Jesus looked helpless and impotent in what can now only be described as waving to the frantic commuter who cannot exit the highway at that point but, at most, can glance sideways for a fleeting drive-by blessing. This statue symbolized for me how the world has moved from church or temple as the center of community life, where few people travelled further than the next town, let alone to far-away countries from O'Hare airport. If we speak of GOD today, given our knowledge of the universe, GOD cannot be described only in the confines of our four church walls or the limits of our religious tradition, but encountered in everything and every part of the universe.

In the 1950s of my Australian childhood, the world most people experienced contained their town, perhaps their region, maybe their country, but rarely overseas. If people did travel overseas, everyone scrambled to view their slides on their return—now you have to *pay* people to look at your travel photos. Returning missionaries, who wanted financial support for their work, described other religions as "pagan" and the poor, unfortunate people living in the darkness and misery of these religions as going to hell. Traveler John Stoddard in late nineteenth-century India wrote that the Zoroastrian and Muslim religions, in comparison to Hinduism, were purity themselves because "they are free of all idolatry and worship one God alone". While admitting that Hindu sacred texts do appear to have some fundamental truths, Hinduism as practiced "becomes the most repulsive exhibition of idolatry, fanaticism and filth that one can well imagine; while the incessant demands for money made by the insatiable priests fill one with unspeakable pity for their deluded victims".[4] Fortunately, travel and global thinking have forced us to see that such statements about other religious traditions can be applied equally to aspects of our own and what we thought as superior and unique is found in many religions, often in forms more attractive and evocative than our own. We daily encounter people from other cultures and religions who shake our claims of exclusive truth. "All religions have caught visions of a transformed society," Ursula King says, "Hindus call it *dharmaraj*, the reign of righteousness: Christians the *basileia* or Kingdom of God; Muslims speak of *ummah* as the community of all believers and the Qur'an sees this community encompassing all humans. Spiritual needs are basic to humans. Everyone has such needs, even when not clearly articulated."[5]

Sri Jai Karunamayi, an Indian woman who spoke at the Parliament of the World's Religions (2009), described the world as many rooms in one house—Australia is a room, India is a room, Canada is a room. What we need, she said, is unity in the house. This metaphor becomes much more vivid in India where each son usually brings his wife home to a room in his parents' house, sharing the cooking facilities and main areas. Although the metaphor founders when we think of the traditional "hierarchies" within an Indian family, it reminds us that, since we don't (as yet) have the possibility of moving to another "house" or planet, we must share the one we have. This also means sharing the One we claim as Creator and Sustainer of our global house. Grace Cathedral (Episcopal) in San Francisco has as its mission statement:

We believe in one God, known to us in Jesus Christ, also known by different names in different traditions. We seek to transform the world, beginning with ourselves, celebrating the image of God in every person. We are a house of prayer, worship and service for everyone, welcoming all who seek an inclusive community of love.

In this book, I have tried to show how the human search to engage the Divine is something we share, even if we express our methods in different ways. I have suggested that the "great cloud of witnesses" that surrounds us is much wider than we might previously have imagined. I have described different religious responses to different experiences of the Sacred, allowing the differences to inform our own longings as human beings. We can read other religious ideas and simply think, "That's nice", "That's weird", or "That's simply wrong", but if we realize that we are all seeking the Sacred, known through human experience, we don't have to stay in our separate rooms in the world house. We can use the shared kitchen to compare stories over a meal, or relax in the shared living-room to ponder how the life story of another might resource the way we seek and engage the Divine. The aim is not to convert the other but to share life experiences, just as we share recipes, political opinions and our planet, and become more appreciative of both the similarities and the differences between us. We need more "world believers" according to Ursula King—people who, like world citizens who live in more than one country yet retain a strong sense of "home", can have deep roots in one faith but be able to relate to faiths other than their own.

> [T]he world needs more people who are spiritually multi-lingual and multi-focused. This is not arguing for relativism, but for true rationality between different faith perspectives and members of different faiths.[6]

King calls Diana L. Eck, Professor of Comparative Religion and Indian Studies at Harvard University, a "world believer". Eck, a United Methodist Church member who has worked for the World Council of Churches and is an expert on Hindu studies, says:

> Uniqueness, to me, does not mean that the "Jesus story" is the only story of God's dealings with humanity, nor the only true and complete story. The language of *only* is the language of faith, not of statistics.[7]

When pushed further as to how she combines her Methodist faith with her Hindu studies, she defines herself, not by boundaries of doctrines and labels, but by her roots—a seeker of the Divine. This is a far cry from the words of Matthew Gallatin who searched across Christianity to settle on the Orthodox tradition as the "true" faith:

> I believe that Jesus will soon mightily challenge the darkness and raise the standard of Orthodoxy high and brightly over this spiritually confused

world. Sometimes I dare to envision a Sunday morning where every church in the land is filled with the sounds of the Divine Liturgy; when every bell tower rings out the sound of unity—the hymn of the One, True Faith . . . It has been a thousand years since Jesus has seen such a day. I know He longs to see it come again.[8]

Can anyone claim that only one religion has the truth? Even if we studied the world's religions all our life, we could not enter completely into so many different religious traditions in order to make such a statement. And what does it mean to say a religion has the truth? Is it something that is measurable or demonstrable by a human scale and anyway, what would be the point? Yet this has been the stance of exclusivist faith traditions for centuries where such conviction is important enough to erect fences, conduct heresy trials, murder unbelievers and pronounce all other religions delusional. We are still picking up the pieces from centuries of colonial expansion based on this belief and on racist assumptions of superiority wound inseparably into it:

In the difference between a savage wanting nothing but nakedness, a straw hut, and raw food to content him, and one of us, demanding conveniences that lay tribute on the ends of the earth, our material progress can be measured. In the difference between an African dwarf, with no interest beyond his jungle's edge, and a modern scientist beating the wings of his inquiry against the uttermost bars of the universe, we can gauge our intellectual growth. In the difference between a pagan and his fetish, and Paul saying of his life in Christ, "I press on", our spiritual enlargement is measured. The greater a man is, the wider and deeper and finer are his desires.[9]

Not all encounters have been so tainted with Western superiority. Gideon Hawley (1727–1807), a missionary to the American Iroquois, wrote in his diary:

Asked Chief to let me have a path to his town and if he ever saw me coming over the mountains he would not, I hoped, shut the door against me. I told him . . . the smoke of our fires mist together in the same air— we drank of the same water and lived upon the same food and therefore be glad we might in every respects be one and spend a happy immortality together.[10]

People, for the most part, do not choose their religious tradition but are born into it. When asked in an interview why he became a Christian and not some other religion when he moved from atheism, British journalist Malcolm Muggeridge (1903–90) explained that, although he had worked among other religions, the *culture* in which he grew up was best expressed in Christianity:

> Perhaps had I been born in Burma, or China, I might have seen it differently. But I think it is true that the culture most people grow up in is related to the religion that appeals to them, and whereas everything in Christianity is related to the literature I love very much, the music I love, the buildings I know, the great Cathedrals, then that naturally predisposes one to find truth in that. Had I been born somewhere else, then I might have been different.[11]

Scientist and atheist Richard Dawkins criticizes those who talk about children as Muslim children, Jewish children and Christian children. They are just children, he says, born into various religious heritages. As we all know, put a group of toddlers together and they will relate, not according to their family's faith label, but on whether they *like* the other child, wish to *demolish* the other child, or think they can grab the other child's toy or cookie. Children differentiate on religious grounds *only* if taught this by adults, whether through segregation from those "not their type" or through derogatory caricatures of the "other" fed to them with breast-milk. Robert Fulghum's classic book title, *All I Really Need to Know I Learned in Kindergarten*, can be applied to religious intolerance as well.

With institutional religion's loosening hold, together with the multicultural mix in many countries today, there is a new freedom and interest in discussing with our school teachers, doctors, workmates and friends how they engage the Sacred in their particular religious traditions. Interfaith *and* intrafaith dialogue have become more important because of religion's overt or subtle role in political debate and global conflict. Whether we like it or not, our politicians make decisions about ethical and moral issues with considerable pressure from religious lobby groups, whether it be stem-cell research, abortion, funding for faith-based social services or legislation for same-sex couples and, while the tribal aggression rife in our globe today is often more about ethnicity, economics and ingrained hatreds than about religion, its *roots* are in religious ideologies and it is often played out with mandates snipped from various sacred texts. Just as political leaders are trying to understand nations with different religious perspectives because we now need them as allies, suppliers, or even places of refuge, ordinary people are talking across religious divides because we also need friends, sympathetic workmates and friendly professionals.

I find it difficult to separate intra-faith and inter-faith dialogue as I often have more in common with those under a different religious umbrella than with some Christians who claim absolute truth. Perhaps this is because I have honed my own ideas over years of struggle and find the efforts of another to return me to the correct "truth" of my heritage quite exasperating. Nancy Henderson-James writes about growing up in Angola and learning French from a Portuguese Catholic priest who was intimidated by teaching a young American *Protestant* girl. He had no idea that Protestants were also Christian—"You're excused from the Christmas lesson in the textbook", he told her.[12] *Inter*faith dialogue, on the other hand, allows me to enter the conversation as who I am in my faith tradition and meet another person who is at peace with who they are in theirs. Since neither is out to convert the other, we can converse with respect about our faith and each find fresh ways to be a better whatever-we-were-before. As Muslim scholar Reza Aslan says, the clash of monotheisms happens when faith, which is "mysterious and ineffable and which eschews all categorizations, becomes entangled in the gnarled branches of religion":

> Religion . . . is not faith. It is the *story* of faith. It is an institutionalized system of symbols and metaphors (read rituals and myths) that provides a common language with which a community of faith can share with each other their numinous encounter with the Divine Presence.[13]

When the theological concepts and language of any religion become ultimate and unchanging truth rather than culturally shaped, adaptable tools that allow us to describe our faith experiences to each other, we lose the possibility of dialogue, either within our tradition or beyond it.

Good dialogue about experiences of engaging the Sacred means listening, not for an opening to argue, teach or correct, but with a genuine hunger to learn from an equal. When we *do* talk, it is not to condemn, judge or manipulate the conversation, but to invite further revelations. My first question of a Buddhist would hardly be, "You don't believe in GOD, do you?" but rather, "How do you live out your convictions?" I once went to the Buddhist Information Center in a temple in Chang Mai, Thailand. An American Buddhist, not in monk's robes, asked if he could help and immediately said, "Do you know much about Buddhism?" That dialogue-stopper question required a "Yes–No" answer in order to categorize me, but it is not a "Yes–No" question. My answer would be "Yes", compared with the average lay person, but "No" compared with someone who has studied Buddhism over a lifetime. When I said I taught the world's religions, he fired off his standard question for those who ticked the "Know a bit" box—"So why do some people say Buddhism is not a religion?" I answered that some define religion as having a Supreme Being but, although this is correct, it was not the response he was geared to pursue. Ignoring *my* answer, he said, "Because it is not faith-based" and launched into his usual spiel, punctuated by more scripted questions of me to launch him into each new paragraph. His central interest was meditation and so, when he asked, "Do you meditate?" I suddenly remembered I had to leave because others were waiting for me. I knew that any answer I gave about my meditation habits would not be his correct one. Dialogue did not happen, even though I had visited the center with that hope in mind.

Wonderful interfaith dialogue spontaneously happens today around kitchen tables and cups of tea, between playgroup mums and dads as they watch their children and between office workers at lunch breaks. As we share experiences, hopes, frustrations and dreams about life, these inevitably will include our religious ideas and how they help or hinder our path. At one stage in my religious training, I read all the "must read" experts on interfaith dialogue, with their discussions about the "common ground" on which to begin so as not to privilege one side by giving value to something not equally rated in the other tradition (which is important), yet the basic issue for you and me usually boils down to "With whom will I dialogue?" or "How many of my friends and acquaintances are from faith traditions other than my own?" If the natural course of our lives does not move us into multicultural situations, we may have to reset our GPS if our paths are to cross with those who can share their different spiritual paths with us. A friend of mine belongs to an informal group of women from many faith traditions who meet each month for friendship, discussion and coffee. At one of their meetings around a large table, an enthusiastic Buddhist woman was explaining how Buddhists refrain from killing any sentient beings because of their belief in reincarnation. My friend was distracted by a blow-fly landing on the glasses and a jug of water in front of her. She knew how to catch flies—they take off vertically so if you clap your hands just above where a fly is sitting, it sees your hands move, takes off, and gets caught between them. In the middle of this discussion on not killing any creature, there was a loud clap and a dead fly fell to the table and bounced onto the floor. For a few seconds there was silence, then someone laughed and the whole room exploded. When they finally calmed down sufficiently to hear themselves speak, a Hindu woman assured my totally embarrassed friend that, since her intention not to allow diseases to spread was good, her action was permissible, but for the rest of the meeting, everyone remained a breath away from collapsing into laughter once again.

Our contemporary world recognizes how difficult it is to make universal truth claims—we even struggle to identify universal ethics. "Thou shalt not kill" means, for Jains, any life at all, even the smallest gnat breathed into the nose. At the Parliament of the World's Religions (2009), some Jain women who presented papers held a square of white fabric a few inches from their faces as they spoke. For some Christians, it means not killing a fetus, yet the same group of believers will happily consign a criminal to capital punishment. "Thou shalt not kill" was certainly not a *universal* instruction to the Hebrews. Since there is plenty of killing in the Bible with the Divine Warrior leading the army, it meant not killing kith and kin. Interestingly, Jesus went beyond the Big Ten to the many other Jewish commandments to select the greatest one, opting not for a religious rule but a way of living—love God and your neighbor (Matt. 22:37–39). I can never understand why some Christians in the United States think that hanging the Ten Commandments in school rooms and court houses will somehow purify the country. I would have thought that Jesus' commandment to love God and your neighbor might have more effect, especially since it came from their founder. This suggestion from Jesus that how we live is more important than what we believe is actually common to the founders of the world's religions and offers a good way forward for interfaith dialogue. The Qur'an says (my italics):

Lo! Those who believe (in that which is revealed unto thee, Muhammad), and those who are Jews, and Christians, and Sabeans—whoever believeth in Allah (GOD) and the Last Day *and doeth right*—surely their reward is with their Lord. (*Qur'an*, Surah 2:62)

At the Parliament of the World's Religions (2009), some 7,000 people from across many religions celebrated their need to listen to each other's engagements with the Divine. People squashed into the foyer of the plenary hall before the opening session, introducing themselves to each other and abuzz with anticipation. White Sikh turbans mingled with Buddhist saffron robes as Muslim women in hijab chatted with Hindu women draped in magnificent saris. Saami people from the Arctic, outfitted in strikingly designed garb, compared stories with sedately suited men with crosses hung around their necks. I introduced myself to Swami Parameshamanda next to me in the crowd, whose Calcutta-based order has ashrams across India, New York, London and Guyana. "How heavy is a polar bear?" he asked me after we had chatted for a while. He answered himself, "Heavy enough to break the ice. Thank you for breaking the ice and speaking with me." Once in the hall, a huge Buddhist bell on stage was sounded as an Australian

Aboriginal man, painted for ceremony, blew smoke as he danced to begin the celebration. An impressive combined choir and orchestra, complete with didgeridu (didgeridoo, a hollowed pipe instrument used by Australian Aboriginal people), performed "The Rise of Bunjil for Didgeridu, Choir and Orchestra" by Dmitri Golovko.[14]   Professor Joy Murphy Wandin (an Aboriginal elder known as Aunty Joy), carrying a large piece of bark with a branch from a eucalyptus tree, welcomed the crowd. "We celebrate your belief," she said, "we celebrate your right to be who you are"—generous words from someone whose people were decimated by others who did not celebrate *their* right to be who they were. The eucalyptus branch signified learning and its leaves indicated that the audience was welcome everywhere in this land. Part of Professor Wandin's blessing said:

> As you journey to our ancient land, travel gently on our Mother Earth, with respect and care. Hold the spirit of the sacred campfire always in your heart. May the spirits of our ancestors always watch over you.[15]

Other blessings were offered, one by one, from various religious traditions and accompanied by their dances, music and chanting—Zoroastrian, Hindu, Jain, Buddhist, Sikh, Jewish, Christian, Muslim, Baha'i, Aboriginal and Shinto. I couldn't help but think of the clouds of wisdom represented by these people, not just in themselves but in their ancient traditions, all seeking human transformation. The stage resonated with color, movement and sound, from a Hindu children's choir slapping their hands on their legs as they sang, to a young Jain dancer gloriously costumed in red and gold, to mature Buddhist women in black performing a sign language dance to a Buddhist sutra, to a multi-generational Sikh group chanting, swords held vertically in front of them, to an emotively sung Jewish invocation based on Deuteronomy 30:6, to a haunting chant in praise of Allah, accompanied by sitar, to an African man singing with every fiber of his body, "Blessed is the spot", words from the Baha'i prophet Baha'u'llah—and that was just the welcome plenary.

Seven days of meeting sessions with some 30 options in any one time bracket would take a book to describe in any adequate way (the program book itself was 300 pages), but perhaps some of the quotes and comments I scribbled down among the wealth of words and action might create at least a flavor. From the Chair of the Parliament's Council—"If we see the world as holy, as sacred ground, this means we need to do ecological, global care, justice and peace—every issue that engulfs our world has a spiritual shape."[16] From a Jewish rabbi who had listed today's global issues as war, environment, freedom, poverty and genetic engineering—"In a world where you can do everything, the moral question is whether you *should*."[17] From an elderly Afghani woman who has spent her life educating women and girls in Afghanistan—"Life is a struggle. Life is jihad. Jihad is struggle. People in Afghanistan have been struggling for 30 years . . . Religion is to give love and compassion, bring justice, help the neighbor and reach out to each other. We all know this", she added in a hopeful tone.[18] From a Sikh woman scholar—"Guru Nanak, our founder, said, 'How could women be inferior when they were the source of all creation, including men? . . . Women need education, employment and freedom of movement to go to both."[19] From a Benedictine sister—"Educate Western people about greed, not poverty—greed is something they know."[20] From a Hindu leader who identified depression ("like dressing a corpse") as a major issue for religions—"Faith-based organizations have a responsibility to make our world a happy society . . . When people say that everyone is going to hell in other religions, they create hell for everyone else."[21]

His Holiness Sri Sri Ravi Shanker grew up during Gandhi's non-violence movement where, if you became angry, there was something wrong with *you*, but now, he said, we glorify violence, whether from religious extremists or outspoken atheists—"Pride is being attached to violence", he said, which reminded me of Albert Schweitzer's letter from Africa to a friend during World War 2:

> We are all of us conscious that many of the natives are puzzling over the questions raised by the war. How can it be possible for the whites, who brought them the Gospel of Love, are now murdering each other, and throwing to the winds the commands of the Lord Jesus? When they put the question to us, we are helpless.[22]

Having watched the orchestra perform with such precision, in sync with the choir and soloists, Sri Sri Ravi Shanker offered a metaphor for the Parliament (which he called a "family reunion"). Each religion is playing its own instrument and we don't argue as to which is the best instrument. The key to harmony and not chaos is to "play our own instrument, don't fight, and all focus on the one conductor—GOD".[23]

When religious people talk together, it is not about conversion or the creation of some homogeneous religious community. It is about sharing the uniqueness we each bring from our personality, cultures, experiences and locations. Interfaith dialogue has been described as "passing over" from our own faith to another and then coming back and experiencing our own faith in a new light. It is another form of globalization where we are conscious, not only that we share an external world but that we also need an internal global consciousness, a sharing of spirituality and ethics so we can live together rather than forever be divided by religious exclusivity. In dialogue we discover how similar our struggles are as human beings and we can learn techniques from each other. It is about observing how we ask the same questions and how we interpret our answers. While operating on a broken leg-bone and on a minute blood vessel in the brain is very different and the procedure for one performed on the other might kill the patient, there are basic underlying techniques in common for surgery on the human body. Cancers act differently in different cell types and at different sites of the body, yet there are some common behavior patterns by which cancer cells multiply and invade that can provide answers for all oncologic specialties. If researchers only discussed the *differences* between cancer cells in leukemia and ovarian cancer, they would not learn anything from their *similarities*. Sri Ramakrishna (1836–86), the Bengali mystic who searched across many religions to experience the One, concluded:

> God has made different religions to suit different aspirants, times and countries. All doctrines are only so many paths; but a path is by no means God Himself. Indeed, one can reach God if one follows any of the paths with whole-hearted devotion . . . The devotee who has seen God in one aspect only, knows him in that particular aspect alone. But he who has seen him in manifold aspects is alone in a position to say, "All these forms are of one God and God is multiform." He is formless and with form, and many are his forms which no one knows.[24]

The last phrase grabs my attention—many are the Divine forms which no one knows. Whatever we think we have engaged as yet is never the Ultimate. Stepping out with the Sacred is always a journey, not a destination.

19

From Here
to Where?

A lifestyle is an art form. It brings life and wonder, joy and hope to persons
otherwise condemned to superficial living. Our times call for the creation of
lifestyles of spiritual substance.

—*Matthew Fox*[1]

○   ○   ○

The way not to drown
Is to swim far out
And dive deep down.
—*Anonymous*[2]

The last chapter of a book is always the most difficult to write. After the
luxury of wandering over many pages of words, the author has to call it quits
and gather her ramblings into some sort of closure. But "stepping out with
the Sacred" *has* no closure, just a point at which this book ends. I have
always found the Acts of the Apostles puzzling from this point of view. It
begins with a story of Jesus' ascension and the Spirit coming on Jesus' followers, a reasonable place to *start*, yet it ends with Paul living in Rome "two
whole years at his own expense" (Acts 28:30). "Two years" reveals that the
writer knew that something happened to Paul *after* two years. Scholars think
Paul was executed, so why didn't the author resolve his book thus? Besides,
where were all the other "acting" apostles? We'll never know—perhaps the
author had a deadline, even though actions of the same apostles the day *after*
the end of this book were as significant as the stories that made it into the
New Testament canon.

At the end of such a book, people expect to know what *I* think. I've tried

247

to include the voices of a great cloud of witnesses from the breadth of the human endeavor to engage the Divine. In a strange way, I don't really want to say what I think and thus funnel all that has been said by so many into one final position. As Robert Kennedy says of Zen Buddhism, the teacher tries to turn the student *away* from "answers" to life:

> The teacher is aware that the student is often looking for an answer, a safe harbor, a package he can wrap up and take home and put on a closet shelf. And so if the student's theme is saintliness, the teacher stresses the secular; if secular, he stresses the saintliness. Always the teacher nudges the student away from the shallows into the middle of life.[3]

People love boxed answers—"Tell me what to think and I'll blindly follow"—which is why we've had trouble in the past. Because I spent years of my life trying to believe what others said I *should* believe, I have a natural horror of other people simply adopting what *I* think. It may be sheer arrogance to assume this might happen, but we are very susceptible to people who do the work for us and then we rationalize our blind following with "humility"—others know better than us, especially if they have theological qualifications. Saint Augustine tramped through many philosophical and theological "schools" before settling on Christianity—"In your wonderful, secret way, my God," he said, "you had already taught me that a statement is not necessarily true because it is wrapped in fine language."[4] Like many of my theological contemporaries, I have moved beyond definitive definitions and doctrines of certainty as a way of life—"[A]ll these words and dogmatic statements are thoughts about God and emotions about God, they are not knowledge of God . . . organized religion domesticates and dwarfs God to a controllable and loveable size."[5]

We are currently in the postmodern era where we have realized there are many ways of seeing things and none are absolutely right for everyone and all time. Stephen Ogden calls it "a kind of organized chaos that questions the conventional wisdom of the past".[6] If we stand back and ask ourselves to name something of which we are certain (beyond the fact that $2 + 2 = 4$, if that is still in place), we will struggle, especially if asked to *prove* that certainty as well. We can say we are sure of our dog's love (if that is the case), but that is a faith statement and, like other things, open to change. I am comfortable if others wish to operate on claims of certainty but, for me, these only lead to disillusionment down the line if I am honest enough to allow my certainties to be tested. Thomas Merton said:

How many men fear to follow their consciences because they would rather conform to the opinion of other men than to the truth they know in their souls? How can I be sincere if I am constantly changing my mind to conform with the shadow of what I think others expect of me? Others have no right to demand that I be anything other than what I ought to be in the sight of God.[7]

Although it drives others to distraction, I believe that "uncertainty" is a *gift* to our age. I appreciate this gift, since I no longer have to squeeze myself into boxes in which I no longer comfortably fit nor settle on once-for-all decisions. It gives me freedom to approach every issue with the question, "What if the opposite is true?", and allow my thinking to go there. I have addressed questions that haunted me and been forced to challenge issues with which I was comfortable but should not have been. Examining the opposite invites all sorts of revelations since community "truths" have often been shaped to attract the vote of that community and may well be the preservation of the *status quo*, or surrender to consensus, rather than the truth we seek.

Writing this book has allowed me to trek across many landscapes and cultures, trying to understand their sacred experiences. I've visited people making outrageous claims about what GOD thinks and does and those who describe mystical experiences of sinking into the wonder of the universe and the Ineffable some call GOD. It has been a roller-coaster ride in a way, as I encountered again experiences and descriptions that had gone sour for me, encrusted in infallible doctrines of do's and don'ts. So many beautiful scriptural passages have been captured by dogmatic interpretations when they are better interpreted in more life-affirming and world-embracing ways. When my research took me back, for example, to that exclusive banner—Jesus is the only way, truth and life (John 14:6)—I stumbled instead on an anguished group of followers who had just realized their teacher would be arrested and killed (13:36–38). Their question, "How can we know where you are going?" was not seeking a theology of global salvation but some personal assurance in their particular place and time. Jesus told them not to be afraid because he had already shown them the way to GOD, just as the Buddha showed *his* followers the way he had found "enlightenment":

By your own efforts
Waken yourself, watch yourself,
And live joyfully.
Follow the truth of the way.

Reflect on it.
Make it your own.
Live it.
It will always sustain you.[8]

We live in a world of questions and answers, so naturally we expect that questions about the Sacred are answerable as well. For this, we look for authorities, but whom will we trust? I was recently talking with a religious educator preparing material for high-school students. The publishing house, trying to break the model that adults have the answers and youth the questions, prepared leaders' guides with the questions only, to encourage an egalitarian dialogue, but requests kept coming back from adult facilitators for the answers as well. I don't think this meant they did not know *how* to answer, but rather that lay people have been told what to think by religious experts for so long, without being offered the tools by which such "truths" are deduced, that they feel they must give *correct* answers. It's like the man on a galloping horse who was asked where he was going and called back, "I don't know. Ask the horse." Albert Schweitzer lectured and published in theology before he began studying medicine. He described the latter as a "spiritual experience":

> I had all along felt it to be psychically a danger that in the so-called humanities with which I had been so concerned hitherto, there is no truth which affirms itself as self-evident, but that a mere opinion can, by the way in which it deals with the subject matter, obtain recognition as true . . . How often does what is reckoned as progress consist in the skillfully argued opinion putting real insight out of action for a long time! To have to watch this drama going on and on, and deal in such different ways with men who had lost all feeling for reality I had found not a little depressing. Now I was suddenly in another country. I was concerned with truths which embodied realities, and found myself among men who took it as a matter of course that they had to justify with facts every statement they made. [9]

When my last book *Like Catching Water in a Net: Human attempts to describe the Divine* came out, among the many letters and emails I received was one from a woman who was struggling out of religious conservatism. She said how much she appreciated the book and how it had helped broaden the pathway of possibilities for her thinking about GOD, then went on:

Towards the end of your book I found myself thinking how you would end it. I needed your ending to retain the integrity that you had established along the way . . . yet I found an aspect of myself wanting a "comfort" stance, while knowing that such a stance would compromise all you had written. When I got to the end my sense was "Yes, this is how it is"—and it somehow then leaves the space for this remarkable journey—that has much to do with the inner voice/sense—to continue.[10]

I hope my readers feel the same about this book. There are so many ways people have engaged the Sacred, or experienced the Sacred engaging them, but these descriptions are merely tools for our own search, not rules or goals. Buddhist teacher Paramananda compares this difference to a map and the territory it describes—"Wisdom is not something that can just be taken on superficially; it has to be fully lived. It is a little like mistaking a map for the world itself. A map, however good, is just a map."[11] Unfortunately in religion, if the map doesn't conform to people's experiences, many think their experiences are wrong, not the map.

In 1995, I wrote a book called *In Defense of Doubt: An invitation to adventure.*[12] It came out of my own struggle with questions not permitted to surface in my particular religious tradition. This experience found its way into a poem:

One by one the deep roots
of my childhood faith
loosen and dislodge
of my own tugging –
and others'.
How many roots can break
with questions and doubts
before my soul dies?
Give me a new word of hope
to roll around my tongue
and test it for size and shape
against other sounds,
and throw it to the wind
to watch it create a world.
Don't let it return to me void.
Bring it back living and working,
resonating with promise and power
and carrying in its mouth
an olive branch.

In that book, I wondered why, since doubt leads to new ideas in most areas of knowledge, religious communities have regarded it with suspicion. Even when "naked" doctrines are paraded before us like the emperor's new clothes, we are told to believe, hoping the little boy will not cry out, "He's naked!", and expose us for the imitators we are. Hoards of people (if they have not already left) occupy church pews, living a dual existence by switching off to discrepancies in the stories so as not to surrender the camaraderie of the faithful—"You want to lead my reason blindfold like a hampered lion, check'd of his noble vigor—then, when baited down to obedient tameness, may it couch and show strange tricks which you call signs of faith."[13]

Yet doubt is not the opposite of faith and belief. The opposite of faith is to be without faith, and the opposite of belief is unbelief. Neither equate with doubt. Faith and belief are not synonymous. Faith is a response to experience, whether the love of a child or a conviction about soap powder brands. Beliefs are ideas, concepts and propositions formalized into "givens". Faith and belief are not even a package deal—you can doubt the beliefs yet still have faith about something. Doubt is rather the *discrepancy* when experiences (faith) do not line up with what we are told to believe. German theologian Dorothee Sölle, who had plenty of cause for doubt as she struggled to talk about GOD and faith after two World Wars, said:

> Faith without doubt is not stronger, but merely more ideological. The search into which living faith throws us cannot be content with cheap grace, naïve trust that all will go well, superficial charity which does not get to the root of things . . . It is not a sign of strong faith but of weak faith if our quest ends quickly and if faith shuns the light of reason.[14]

Science, medicine and education recognize that human explanations are always limited by language, concepts and knowledge, and that "truth" changes with new tools and circumstances, yet this has not been religion's stance. Doubts challenge authorities propagating "truth" and, in religion, the one challenged is claimed to be *GOD* (even though the Divine is always mediated through fallible, human agencies). As Bertrand Russell noted, "If there were a God, I think it very unlikely that he would have such an uneasy vanity as to be offended by those who doubt his existence."[15] The biblical heroes and heroines lurched from one crisis of doubt to the next. Sarah laughed when told of her impending pregnancy and the psalmists doubted Divine activity, or lack thereof. Martin Luther challenged the Church over salvation through works and, as I edit this chapter, Mary Daly (1928–2010) has died, the radical woman theologian who shocked her Catholic peers by suggesting GOD was not male. Doubts do not flag weaknesses—they test humanly constructed belief systems. The distinction is crucial. As successive bottoms fall out of doctrines that no longer fit our cultural and scientific worldviews, we don't "lose faith" by asking questions—we are seeking authentic answers.

Throughout this book, I have always allowed the option that there is nothing to engage. Many religious books simply nod their heads at this possibility and then assume a GOD anyway. In novels, many authors raise questions about Divine absence through their fictitious characters. In *The Shadow of the Wind*, Antoni Fortuny, a hat-maker, prays to be shown how to live at peace with his wife and child:

> He begged the Lord to send him a signal, a whisper, a crumb of His presence. God, in His infinite wisdom, and perhaps overwhelmed by the avalanche of requests from so many tormented souls, did not answer.[16]

A character in *The River Why* struggles, without success, to find GOD—"Whatever He did, however He did it, whoever and whatever He was or wasn't, if He wanted my attention, He'd have to leave off making Himself so scarce."[17] Devout people have always struggled with Divine absence and many have simply accepted the conclusion of no-God-at-all. GOD is always a faith statement since we cannot prove GOD either way. The standard question, "Do you believe in GOD?" is like a set of Russian dolls with smaller and smaller editions of themselves inside—"What do you mean by believe?", "What do you mean by GOD?", "Can I only answer yes or no?", "Why do you ask?" Some people ask for information, some ask to convert us and some ask to classify us within their narrow religious categories. Yet a "Yes" or "No" is not the point because our answer, if we think seriously about the subject, is evolving with our knowledge and experience. This book is about keeping the conversation going in a wider circle than simply our denomination or religious tradition. After reading my last book (which also went across religions), a Christian clergy friend said, "It sure made me realize that we've been promoting a fairly small cult, haven't we?" The global village in which we trade, seek education, travel and rub political shoulders requires that we also think together about religion.

There are those who have dismissed any notions of the Sacred *at all* and those who give up the search because they have not found an adequate idea of the Divine to inspire that search. Many atheists are more honest than those who stay in religion. However, I hear some raging against a straw GOD that most serious theologians have also long ago knocked down. Our images of the Divine must work in our twenty-first-century worldview and cosmology. That's a tall order, but it is the *only* order that makes sense. GOD needs to be believable in this amazing universe that continues to unwrap before us. The Divine within, Energy of the Universe and Presence allow us to speak without keeping our fingers crossed behind our backs and yet, take one step into most churches today and you are inundated with images of an old bearded GOD and hear praises sung to that same image.

There is a strong groundswell across religions under the umbrella name of "progressive" religious thought. This word "progressive" was attached to early expressions of the movement and stuck, although many are less than happy with the term. It is used in the sense of moving beyond traditional ideas and exploring the challenges of contemporary scholarship and scientific enterprise, of being open to all ideas rather than deciding there is only one answer—mine. However, the word also has the unfortunate connotation of suggesting something *superior* over those stagnant or regressing—we need a better term. Progressives, however, seek the Sacred *within* the universe, the only place humans can experience anything, Sacred or not, and they also have a considered hesitancy in describing this Sacred. A historian of religion who devoted 40 years to studying world religions came up with two things that religions have in common—"Belief in God—if there be a God" and "Life is worth living—sometimes."[18] Rather than this being apostasy or loss of faith, as some would say, it is a brave step out of traditional religious rules and assurances. Rather than the reliable old stepping-stones, the new stones are slippery and moss-covered, with chasms appearing between them. There may even be a missing half-mile of track or a fog so thick we can't see the next step. To continue on means a good few leaps in the dark and the hope that there *is* something on which to walk or else we will learn to fly. It may mean a cliff-face going down into nothingness, but we take these risks rather than remaining in something that has begun to decay all around us. Perhaps a better term is "constructive" religious thought with the double meaning of actually "constructing" something new with, around or over the rubble of inadequate doctrines, and "constructive" as leading to something positive and useful, rather than simply pulling down the old and giving it a good kick.

Mathematician Blaise Pascal (1623–62) experienced a mystical encounter that changed his life. He rejected the "proofs" for GOD put forward by church theologians, saying that reason is powerless before what humans cannot know, yet he also scolded those who called such believers "fools", because we can't rationally know either way. James Connor summarizes his argument, known as Pascal's Wager:

If God exists, and you believe in God, then throw the dice and you win an eternity of life, love and joy. If God doesn't exist, and you believe, and you throw the dice, then all you lose is the pile of meaningless pleasures you were sitting on. If God does exist and you don't believe, then you give up all hope of eternal life, and worse than that, you will one day find yourself in hell.[19]

Many still operate on this argument but the odds have shifted. Hell is no longer seen as a literal place by most, thus that threat is not in play, and heaven cannot be proven either way so that does not control people's decision as it did in the past. The "progressive" journey has therefore changed its beacons. Rather than moving towards some "light" in the future, it is about life here and now—finding the Sacred within everyday life. Rather than heavenly souls in transit or sinners being graded for the next life, we live deeply into *this* world and its joys, beauty, pain and suffering, as creatures of *this* earth in *this* moment. If religion is to survive in any authentic form, it will need to tap its essential oxygen from *this* world, rather than through some oxygen pipeline from another planet it calls heaven. Bishop Spong explains where he has arrived in his very public search for the Divine:

My search for "heaven" will cause me to turn to this life, to its very depths, for that is the only place where I now believe we can hear the echoes of eternity. In that search, I believe, we will discover that the word "heaven" points not to something external to us, but to something that is part of us . . . The time has come . . . for us to turn our spiritual telescopes around so that we no longer look outward for meaning or God, but begin to look inward. That is not to walk away from God . . . it is, I believe, to walk into God. The path is internal, not external, for it is identical with the walk into ourselves, and that is the journey that we must never refuse to take . . . I do not want to walk away from religion so much as I want to walk through religion and then beyond it. I want to walk into things that religion has never known. I do not want to abandon the wisdom of the past, but neither do I want to be bound by that wisdom, since wisdom is itself ever-changing.[20]

Buddhists have always known that to be truly alive is to be in the present moment, interconnected with everything and seeing all experiences as part of being human:

Do not pursue the past. Do not lose yourself in the future. The past no longer is. The future has not yet come. Looking deeply at life as it is in the very here and now, the practitioner dwells in stability and freedom.[21]

Our predecessors avoided living in the present by sublimating into their minds and souls, or by imagining the joys of heaven. We have our own effective avoidance methods, with reality television programmes like *Survivor* creating situations of intense danger, or intense social dysfunction like *Big Brother*, that play on our fantasies and remove us, for as long as we oblige, from real life. When real-life tragedies *are* beamed into our living-rooms through the same screen, we simply see them as reality television as well. As I write this chapter, horrific pictures of a massive earthquake in Haiti are flashing up on the television screen. I am actually looking at buildings under which people are still alive and I know, from Haiti's island location and lack of infrastructure, that some people will *die* even as I watch and even when global telecommunication has the capacity to bring their plight right into my living-room.

One hundred years ago, British mathematician Alfred North Whitehead (1861–1947) published three volumes of *Principia Mathematica* with pupil Bertrand Russell. Despite Whitehead's Church of England heritage, he was an agnostic, returning to religion but not a denomination later in life. With the collapse of Newtonian physics, Whitehead sought a philosophy that could incorporate all elements of knowledge into one language free of dualisms, including GOD and world. Science, at that time, was showing the universe to be one interconnected organism in constant flow and change, thus Whitehead's GOD must be part of this organism, not something separate from it. This was not the Abrahamic GOD but a space in his philosophical system that one could, if one chose, call GOD. Whitehead critiqued the dogmatism of the physical sciences of his day:

The reason for this blindness of physical science lies in the fact that such science only deals with half the evidence provided by human experience. It divides the seamless coat—or, to change the metaphor into a happier form, it examines the coat, which is superficial, and neglects the body which is fundamental.[22]

Whitehead's process philosophy influenced theology because it allowed us to talk about GOD within everything in the universe, rather than leaving a GOD-idea out of the discussion or setting GOD up in opposition to the world and science. Scientist and process thinker Charles Birch (1918–2009) describes this theology:

God does not affect directly the outward or objective aspect of things, that is the province of modern science ... God acts directly on the inner aspects of entities from quarks to humans by confronting them with possibilities and values ... Each one has its own degree of freedom to either respond or not. Presumably, the degree of freedom is greatest at the higher levels such as in the case of human beings. The nature of the entity at, say, the level of the electron is presumably much more fixed. The concept of God's involvement in the inner aspects of entities is akin to Tillich's concept of God as the "ground of being" ... When God influences the inner aspects of entities their outer aspects change. This perspective of divine activity is vastly different from the view that God directly changes the outer aspects of things, which posits that [God] can create new species in the twinkling of an eye. Instead God is never coercive, always persuasive. God is not a part-time operator. God's activity is continuous. God's action is not supernatural; it is natural.[23]

We hear so much today about the separation of science and religion that it does us good to be reminded of people who have thought in ways that do not demand compartmentalization or the destruction of one or the other. Even in the mid-nineteenth century, Leo Tolstoy questioned whether science answered everything:

[A] man's relationship to the world is determined not just by his intellect but by his feelings and by his whole aggregate of spiritual forces. However much one implies or explains to a person that all that truly exists is no more than an idea, or that everything is made up of atoms, or that the essence of life is substance or will, or that heat, light, movement and electricity are only manifestations of one and the same energy; however much you explain this to a man—a being who feels, suffers, rejoices, fears and hopes—it will not explain his place in the universe.[24]

In a similar tone, contemporary physicist Fritjof Capra sees science and mysticism as *complementary* aspects of the human mind, the rational and the intuitive areas—"Science does not need mysticism, and mysticism does not need science, but man needs both."[25]

Albert Einstein, Whitehead's contemporary (Whitehead also produced a theory of relativity), called himself an agnostic in that he did not believe in a personal GOD acting outside the laws of nature and dealing in moral issues. "I believe in Spinoza's God," he told Rabbi Herbert Goldstein in an interview, "who reveals himself in the orderly harmony of what exists, not in a God who concerns himself with fates and actions of human beings."[26]

I have never imputed to Nature a purpose or a goal, or anything that could be understood as anthropomorphic. What I see in Nature is a magnificent structure that we can comprehend only very imperfectly, and that must fill a thinking person with a feeling of humility. This is a genuinely religious feeling that has nothing to do with mysticism.[27]

In this way, Einstein said, "I am a deeply religious nonbeliever . . . This is a somewhat new kind of religion."[28] Einstein spelled out this "new religion":

The fairest thing we can experience is the mysterious. It is the fundamental emotion which stands at the cradle of true art and true science. He who knows it not and can no longer wonder, no longer feel amazement, is as good as dead, a snuffed-out candle. It was the experience of mystery—even if mixed with fear—that engendered religion. A knowledge of the existence of something we cannot penetrate, of the manifestation of the profoundest reason and the most radiant beauty, which are only accessible to our reason in their most elementary forms—it is this knowledge and this emotion that constitutes the truly religious attitude; in this sense, and in this alone, I am a deeply religious man. I cannot conceive of a God who rewards and punishes his creatures, or has a will of the type of which we are conscious in ourselves. An individual who should survive his physical death is also beyond my comprehension, nor do I wish it otherwise; such notions are for the fears or absurd egoism of feeble souls. Enough for me the mystery of the eternity of life, and the inkling of the marvellous structure of reality, together with the single-hearted endeavour to comprehend a portion, be it ever so tiny, of the reason that manifests itself in nature.[29]

To see ourselves as part of the magnificent whole of the ever-expanding and mysterious universe, with the Sacred as part of this cosmic dance, opens us up to "religious" wonder in the *full* sense of the word—from *religio* to "bind together", binding us to everything in the universe, including the Sacred. Such imagery does not ask that we define the Divine or separate out what is GOD and what is not, like trying to separate out the egg in a baked cake. When we are enveloped in a beautiful piece of music, we don't have to see the conductor to know she is central to the harmony, nor identify each instrument in order to enjoy the music properly—we participate in the total experience, whether hearers, conductor, trombonists or soloists. According to Bishop Spong:

We are now awakening to a sense of oneness with all that is; indeed, we are more connected than our minds can yet embrace. Self-consciousness begins to look like just one more stage in our development that will finally bring us to an awareness of our essential oneness with the universe, a oneness that binds together the material and immaterial things, and even our bodies and our minds, perhaps as a universal consciousness.[30]

Eastern religions have said this for eons. GOD is "pure consciousness", the *Svetasvatara Upanishad* said long before Jesus' birth.[31] According to the *Tao Te Ching*, "There is a thing inherent and natural, which existed before heaven and earth . . . It pervades everywhere and never becomes exhausted . . . I do not know its name. If I am forced to give it a name, I call it Tao, [the Way] and I name it as supreme."[32] "Days come and ages pass," Rabindranath Tagore said, "and it is ever he who moves my heart in many a name, in many a guise, in many a rapture of joy and of sorrow."[33]

How do we recover this sense of wonder at being within the whole, rather than hung up on separating the little drop that is us from the ocean? There are some very small people in my life who make everything else seem inconsequential. Some of my best experiences come packaged through their eyes as my grandchildren "see" something for the first time. It amazes me how well I remember certain of *my* childhood experiences, not day-to-day events but sense experiences—the feel of screw-top jars in my father's workshop, full of treasures of fuse wire, faucet washers, pen nibs and waxed string, and the smooth handle of his vice that held things securely, allowing my small hands to perform great creative tasks—yet I hardly remember details in last month's frenetic whirl. There is something in what Jesus said, "Unless you change and become like children, you will never enter the kingdom of heaven" (Matt. 18:3). It is not the quantity of experiences that matter in life but our ability to absorb these experiences so they transform us, whether the shiver of awe at a black and red beetle on the forest floor or the detailed perfection of a new baby's finger. Childhood is the time of first experiences that stay with us much longer than those in our satiated adult world where new experiences have to be continually created to keep our interest—new products, new movies, new partners, and new games. Some long nostalgically for the return of childhood naiveté, as if there are only a limited number of such experiences to be had. Yet we can make that "return" to wonder in the here and now if we look at the world around us as holy and sacred (with or without a GOD-concept), not in tired, outdated religious meanings locked in statues, doctrines and buildings, but as a living, interconnected, amazing whole of which we are a very tiny, but connected, part. We can be filled with awe through scientific exploration, walking in the wilderness, the eyes of a child and experiencing a Presence with us. These are not either/or categories, although we have long made them so. Sir Lloyd Geering describes a "new form of mysticism" he sees appearing with our contemporary concern for the planet:

> We may choose to use traditional God language of earlier mystics, or with some New Age mystics prefer the new Gaia language, or simply use the everyday human language of ecology—but in any case, we must now acknowledge, as did the ancients, that:
> • We came from the earth.
> • We remain creatures of the earth.
> • The hope of our species for a viable future depends on our mystical re-union with the earth.[34]

If we follow the momentum of this book's title of stepping out with the Sacred, faith is not about believing something but about living, about doing something, about being open to every moment in every way. It's not about having all the answers. Even if we could get them all catalogued, they would have changed before we filed the last one. My daughter emailed me the other day to describe her afternoon with her two toddlers. "We have spent the last hour on a picnic rug in the garden watching a sign-writer in the sky trying to write 'Jesus Lives', but every time he gets the 'L' finished, 'Jesus' has blown away and has to be redone." Sometimes our spiritual journeys are like that sign-writer, but we can't wait until we have crossed all the Ts. As the Buddha said:

> In the search for truth there are certain questions that are unimportant. Of what material is the universe constructed? . . . Are there limits or not to the universe? . . . What is the ideal form of organization for human society? If a man were to postpone his searching and practicing for Enlightenment until such questions were solved, he would die before he found the path.[35]

To be alive is to be constantly challenged with new information, doubting the old, throwing out some, retaining some and restructuring our collection before another challenge arrives. We don't "arrive" at faith, but live it. If we feel we have to define what we see as eternal truth, we will have to choose between certainty and agnosticism, rather than flow along the continuum between the two. Paul did not claim certainty—"For we know only in part, and we prophesy only in part . . ." (1 Cor. 13:9). Certainty cannot accept grey, believing that GOD has created the landscape in black or white. The land of certainty is like a child wandering through the woods, beckoned on all sides by gnomes, aliens and fairies, yet he has been told to follow only the red griffin without question. The beauty about grey is that it is the only area where movement and change *can* happen and, if you add a little light to grey, you get silver.

Joseph Bellamy, apprenticed to Calvinist theologian Jonathan Edwards (1703–58), was not afraid of grey—he read so widely and bought "so much work by heretics" that his library was hard to sell at auction after his death.[36] In the 1960s, Bishop John A. T. Robinson also accepted grey and wrote *Honest to God*, a book that rocked the Christian world. "All I can do is try to be honest—honest to God and about God," Robinson gave as his apology, "and to follow the argument wherever it leads."[37] It led a long way, opening up discussions that had waited for years to happen. People who follow the questions today, stepping out with the Sacred, continue to be the leaven in the bread, the salt in the soup and the light in the darkness when it comes to living with authenticity in our time and place. Such people are usually in the minority and in the margins of institutions, but they crystallize their thinking on the perimeter such that, when authorities are finally ready to embrace new thinking, the paperwork is done. Vatican II happened, not because these ideas emerged as the hierarchy chatted over coffee, but because a group of dynamic young priests and theologians worked diligently behind the scenes to prepare material for change. Gandhi lived out the teachings of his guru Jesus better than most Christians, and yet never signed on the Christian dotted line. He saw the glint in Jesus' eyes when he talked about justice and he absorbed Jesus' sense of outrage that accompanied his moral vision:

> A life guided by a compelling moral vision of what ought to be, animated by a sense of outrage at what is, articulated with respect for the common reason of humankind, and sustained by personal courage; that's what is needed.[38]

It's funny how we know what is needed, yet there is some great underground system of leg-irons that prevents us from even believing that it is possible.

And so to an ending, even though this does not end. Many people who talk honestly about engaging the Sacred do so with hesitancy. Some are simply thankful for rare moments of Presence. Steven Ogden talks about living mostly with Divine absence, except for fleeting moments when we experience Presence through a confluence of experiences and through people and community when we know something special has happened:

> . . . the experience of presence is always short-lived because presence, sweet presence is sheer presence sitting precariously on the edge of the abyss. Soon gone, we learn to live without it, wisely making do, half expecting another unexpected encounter with the presence of God in the world.[39]

Some encounter the Sacred in reflections *after* the event. Oxford academic C. S. Lewis (1898–1963) pondered what he might say to GOD after death:

> So it was you all along. Everyone I ever loved, it was you. Everyone who ever loved me, it was you. Everything decent or fine that ever happened to me, everything that made me reach out and try to be better, it was you all along. [40]

Others discover the Divine in nature. For writer David James Duncan, this was in sharp contrast to what he had experienced in a church:

> Intense spiritual feelings were frequent visitors during my boyhood, but they did not come from church-going or from bargaining with God in prayer. They came, unmediated, from Creation itself. In even the smallest suburban wilds I felt linked to powers and mysteries I could imagine calling "the Presence of God". In fifteen years of church-going I did not once feel this same sense of Presence. What I felt instead was a lot of heavily agenda-ed fear-based information being shoved at me by men on the church payroll.[41]

Others experience the Divine in union with themselves. Sufi Rabi'a (717–801) wrote of her need for the Divine Presence over all other rewards:

> O Allah, if I worship you for fear of hell, burn me in hell; if I worship you in hope of Paradise, exclude me from Paradise; but if I worship you for your own sake, do not deny me your everlasting beauty.[42]

Others do not *experience* GOD, but simply *live*. "How happy he is! For he sees that wakefulness is life", the Buddha said. "How happy he is, following the path of the awakened."[43] For others, there has been no engaging of the Sacred, no matter how much they have sought it. Bertrand Russell grew up without the comfort of someone with whom he could discuss his deepest questions. His doubts multiplied through teenage years and he later wrote, "Throughout the long period of religious doubt, I had been rendered very unhappy by the gradual loss of belief, but when the process was completed, I found to my surprise that I was quite glad to be done with the whole subject."[44]

Where, in all this, have you found helpful "tools"—or not—with which to continue *your* story of engaging the Sacred? This is the key as to whether this book has been of use. As for me, this is my story *for this moment*. I appreciate the words of writer Frank Schaeffer:

Honesty is the only thing that is satisfying about writing. And honesty is always filled with inconsistency. Since our opinions change, to be "sure" about anything—as if that opinion is fixed and will last for ever—is to lie. Anything we say is only a snapshot of a passing moment.[45]

Notes

Preface

1   Theodore M. Ludwig, *The Sacred Paths: Understanding the religions of the world* (New Jersey: Pearson, Prentice Hall, 2006), 3.
2   *Sydney Morning Herald*, February 11, 2009.
3   Sam Keen, *Apology for Wonder* (New York: Harper and Row, 1969), 22.
4   Keen, *Apology for Wonder*, 28.
5   Keen, *Apology for Wonder*, 27–34.
6   Richard F. Elliott, Jr, *Falling in Love with Mystery: We don't have to pretend anymore*. Electronic publication, 1.
7   Huston Smith, *The Religions of Man* (New York: Harper & Row, 1958, 1965), 10.
8   Huston Smith, *The Illustrated World Religions: A guide to our wisdom traditions* (New York: HarperSanFrancisco, 1994), 14.
9   Nikos Kazantzakis, *Report to Greco* (London: Faber and Faber, 1973), 479.
10 Kazantzakis, *Report to Greco*, 481–2.
11 Val Webb, *Like Catching Water in a Net: Human attempts to describe the Divine* (New York and London: Continuum, 2007).
12 Webb, *Like Catching Water in a Net*.

Chapter 1: Pinning Down the Sacred

1   *Adi Granth* (Sikh scriptures), quoted in Anand Krishna, *One Earth, One Sky, One Humankind: Celebration of unity in diversity* (Jakata: PT Gramedia Pustaka Utama, 2009), 7.
2   Noah Webster (ed.), *Webster's New Universal Unabridged Dictionary*, deluxe second edition (New York: Simon & Schuster, 1979) 1593, 538, 868.
3   Webb, *Like Catching Water in a Net*.
4   Julian of Norwich, *The Wisdom of Julian of Norwich*, Monica Furlong (ed.) (Oxford: Lion Publishing 1996), 48.
5   "Father" appears only fifteen times in the Hebrew Bible for GOD, denoting the head of a tribe rather than a hands-on parent. Of over 200 New Testament uses, almost half are crowded into John's Gospel with little emphasis elsewhere, because the author of this Gospel is painting a giant clan metaphor to show Jewish followers excluded from the synagogue that they are still part of the Father-GOD's clan.
6   Theresa Maggio, *The Stone Boudoir: In search of the hidden villages of Sicily* (London: Headline Books, 2003), 93.
7   Keen, *Apology for Wonder*, 69.
8   *Kena Upanishad*, quoted in Juan Mascaró (trans.), *The Upanishads* (Middlesex: Penguin Books, 1971), 52.
9   Quoted in John Bowker (ed.), *The Oxford Dictionary of World Religions* (Oxford: Oxford University Press, 1997), 220.

10 Quoted in Jane Hirschfield (ed.), *Women in Praise of the Sacred: 43 centuries of spiritual poetry by women* (New York: HarperPerennial, 1994), 94.

11 Lisa O. Engelhardt, *God is My Friend: A kid's guide to God* (St Meinrad, IN: Abbey Press, 2002), 2.

12 Quoted in Philip Yancey, *Reaching for the Invisible God* (Grand Rapids, MI: Zondervan, 2000), 37.

13 *Svetasvatara Upanishad*, quoted in Mascaró, *The Upanishads*, 87.

14 Thomas à Kempis, *The Imitation of Christ* (New York: The Macmillan Company, 1955), 171–3.

15 Rudolf Otto, *The Idea of the Holy* (London: Oxford University Press, 1923, 1980), xvi.

16 Otto, *The Idea of the Holy*, translator's preface, xvii.

17 Otto, *The Idea of the Holy*, translator's preface, xviii–xix.

18 Lawrence Krauss, *Does the Universe have a Purpose?* http://genesis1.asu.edu/~krauss/essay_Krauss.html.

19 Keen, *Apology for Wonder*, 15, 211.

20 Frederick Buechner, *Wishful Thinking* (London: Collins, 1973), 91.

Chapter 2: Location, Location, Location . . .

1 Guru Gobind Singh, quoted in Sikh Missionary Center, *Pearls of Sikhism: Peace, justice and equality* (Ann Arbor, MI: Sheridan Books, Inc., 2008), 54.

2 I am indebted in this analysis to Hans Schwarz in Donald W. Musser and Joseph L. Price (eds), *A New Handbook of Christian Theology* (Nashville: Abingdon, 1992).

3 Joshua R. Porter, "Ark", in Paul Achtemeier (gen. ed.), *Harper's Bible Dictionary* (New York: HarperSanFrancisco, 1985), 63.

4 The Ark disappeared at the time of the exile. Ethiopian tradition claims that it was taken to Ethiopia by the son of King Solomon and the Ethiopian Queen of Sheba and now resides in a church in Axum, inaccessible to anyone but the priest who guards it.

5 Mircea Eliade, *Patterns of Comparative Religion*, Rosemary Sheed (trans.) (Sheed and Ward, 1958; Lincoln, NE: University of Nebraska Press, 1996), 31.

6 John Shelby Spong, *Eternal Life: A new vision beyond religion, beyond theism, beyond heaven and hell* (New York: HarperOne, 2009),136.

7 Quoted in Musser and Price, *A New Handbook of Christian Theology*, 328.

8 Keen, *Apology for Wonder*, 88–90.

9 This is taken from the "Specifications for the Blessed Virgin Coronation" in the Musée de Villeneuve-les-Avignon.

10 à Kempis, *The Imitation of Christ*, 292–3.

11 à Kempis, *The Imitation of Christ*, 86.

12 According to several websites, this hymn was written by Philip Paul Bliss (1838–76) who heard a story told by preacher Dwight L. Moody of a captain trying to bring his boat into Cleveland harbor one dark, stormy night. The captain spotted the light from the lighthouse but could not see the lower lights, which had gone out. The captain asked his pilot, "Can you make the harbor?" The pilot replied, "We must, or perish, sir." They missed the channel and the boat hit the rocks and sank. Moody concluded, "Brethren, the Master will take care of the great light-house; let us keep the lower lights burning."

13 I can find no reference to the origins of this song, listed "anonymous" in *Pitcairn Hymns and Norfolk Favourites* (Norfolk Island, undated).

14 Julian of Norwich, *The Wisdom of Julian of Norwich*, 17.

15 John R. Hinnells (ed.), *Penguin Dictionary of Religions* (London: Penguin Books, 1995), 333.

16 Kazantzakis, *Report to Greco*, 227.

17 Kazantzakis, *Report to Greco*, 231–2.

18 Ursula King, *The Search for Spirituality: Our global quest for a spiritual life* (New York: BlueBridge, 2008), 156.

19 Katherine Bitney, "Ethics and the Goddess", in Dawne C. McCance (ed.), *Life Ethics in World Religions* (Atlanta, Georgia: Scholars Press, 1998), 10.

20 Bitney, "Ethics and the Goddess", 11.

Chapter 3: What Do Humans Want?
1 Smith, *The Religions of Man*, 12.
2 George Dennis O'Brien, *God and the New Haven Railway: And why neither one is doing well* (Boston: Beacon Press, 1986), 133.
3 William James, *The Varieties of Religious Experiences: A study in human nature* (New York: The Modern Library, 1902), 516.
4 Brennan R. Hill, Paul Knitter and William Madges, *Faith, Religion and Theology: A contemporary introduction* (Mystic, CT: Twenty-Third Publications, 1990), 162.
5 Hill, Knitter and Madges, *Faith, Religion and Theology*, 162–6.
6 Smith, *The Religions of Man*, 328.
7 Smith, *The Religions of Man*, 260.
8 Valerie Saiving, "The Human Situation: A feminine view", in Carol P. Christ and Judith Plaskow (eds), *Womanspirit Rising: A feminist reader in religion* (New York: Harper & Row, 1979), 26.
9 Saiving, "The Human Situation: A feminine view", 25.
10 Dorothee Sölle, *Thinking about God: An introduction to theology* (London: SCM Press, 1990), 14.
11 James, *The Varieties of Religious Experiences*, 28–9.
12 Goethe, quoted in James, *The Varieties of Religious Experiences*, 135.
13 Henry Alline, quoted in James, *The Varieties of Religious Experiences*, 156.
14 Florence Nightingale's complete writings are now available in a series of volumes: Lynn McDonald (ed), *The Collected Works of Florence Nightingale* (Waterloo, ON: Wilfred Laurier University Press, 2007–10).
15 Val Webb, *Florence Nightingale: The making of a radical theologian* (St Louis, MO: Chalice Press, 2002).
16 Florence Nightingale, 'Suggestions for Thought', quoted in Webb, *Florence Nightingale*, 231.
17 James, *The Varieties of Religious Experiences*, 477.
18 E. D. Starbuck, "Psychology of Religion", quoted in James, *The Varieties of Religious Experiences*, 82.
19 Thérèse of Lisieux, *The Story of a Soul*, John Beevers (trans.) (New York: Doubleday, 1987), 150.
20 Thérèse of Lisieux, *The Story of a Soul*, 154.
21 Smith, *The Religions of Man*, 314.
22 Elie Wiesel, *Memoirs: All rivers run to the sea* (New York: Schocken Books, 1995), 105.
23 Martin Luther, quoted in Howard Clark Kee and Irvin J. Borowsky, *Removing the Anti-Judaism from the New Testament* (Philadelphia: American Interfaith Institute/World Alliance, 1998), 167.
24 Kee and Borowsky, *Removing the Anti-Judaism from the New Testament*, 167.
25 Albert Schweitzer, *Out of My Life and Thought* (New York: Mentor Book, 1933, 1963), 117.
26 Schweitzer, *Out of My Life and Thought*, 119, 118.
27 Schweitzer, *Out of My Life and Thought*, 200.
28 Lloyd Geering, *Coming Back to Earth: From gods, to God, to Gaia* (Salem, OR: Polebridge Press, 2009), 151–2.

Chapter 4: Does the Sacred Engage Us or Do We Engage the Sacred?
1 Robert Van de Weyer (ed.), *Rumi* (London: Hodder & Stoughton, 1998), 27.
2 O'Brien, *God and the New Haven Railway*, 133–4.
3 Leo Tolstoy, *A Confession and Other Religious writings*, Jane Kentish (trans.) (Harmondsworth: Penguin, 1987), 33.
4 Karl Marx, *A Contribution to the Critique of Hegel's Philosophy of Right*, Introduction, 1843, first published in Deutsch-Französische Jahrbücher.
5 Marx, *A Contribution to the Critique of Hegel's Philosophy of Right*.
6 Keen, *Apology for Wonder*, 130.
7 Maggio, *The Stone Boudoir*, 101.

8 D. Hay, *Religious Experience Today: Studying the facts* (London: Mowbray, 1990).
9 Both surveys are quoted in Hinnells, *Penguin Dictionary of Religions*, 396.
10 *Newsweek*, August 29–September 5, 2005.
11 John Hick, *The New Frontier of Religion and Science: Religious experience, neuroscience and the transcendent* (Hampshire: Palgrave Macmillan, 2006), 206.
12 Julian of Norwich, *The Wisdom of Julian of Norwich*, 30.
13 Antony F. Campbell, *The Whisper of Spirit: A believable God today* (Grand Rapids, MI: William B. Eerdmans Publishing Co., 2008), 49.
14 Schweitzer, *Out of My Life and Thought*, 45.
15 Sallie McFague, *Life Abundant: Rethinking theology and economy for a planet in peril* (Minneapolis: Fortress Press, 2001), xiii.
16 Bede Griffiths, "The Golden String", quoted in Lucinda Vardey (ed.), *God in all Worlds: An anthology of contemporary spiritual writing* (London: Chatto & Windus, 1995), 88.
17 By the author.
18 Quoted in Hill, Knitter and Madges, *Faith, Religion and Theology*, 155.
19 Smith, *The Religions of Man*, 101.
20 Smith, *The Religions of Man*, 104.
21 Matthew Gallatin, *Thirsting for God in a Land of Shallow Wells* (Ben Lomond, CA: Conciliar Press, 2002).
22 Gallatin, *Thirsting for God*, 180.
23 Smith, *The Religions of Man*, 104–8.
24 Rupert Sheldrake, "The Rebirth of Nature", quoted in Vardey, *God in all Worlds*, 214.
25 Karen Armstrong, *The Spiral Staircase: A memoir* (London: HarperPerennial, 2005), 4–5.

Chapter 5: Earth as a Sacred Site

1 Keen, *Apology for Wonder*, 15, 211.
2 Billy Ireland, quoted in James Thurber, *The Thurber Album* (New York: Simon & Schuster 1952), 259.
3 Sallie McFague, *Super, Natural Christians: How we should love nature* (Minneapolis: Fortress Press, 1997), 67.
4 Steve Zeitlin, *The Four Corners of the Sky: Creation stories and cosmologies from around the world* (New York: Henry Holt and Company, 2000), 4–5.
5 Bronislaw Malinowski, quoted in Keen, *Apology for Wonder*, 70.
6 Roy Willis (gen. ed.), *World Mythology* (New York: Henry Holt and Co., 1993), 18–19.
7 Zeitlin, *The Four Corners of the Sky*, 30–1.
8 Keen, *Apology for Wonder*, 72.
9 Johann Gerhard, "The Image of God", in Herman A. Preus and Edmund Smits (eds), *The Doctrine of Man in Classical Lutheran Theology* (Minneapolis: Augsburg Publishing House, 1962), 29–30.
10 Spong, *Eternal Life*, 29.
11 Bertrand Russell, *Bertrand Russell's Best*, Robert E. Enger (ed.) (New York: Mentor Books, 1961), 34.
12 de Weyer, *Rumi*, 31.
13 Musser and Price, *A New Handbook of Christian Theology*, 328.
14 John Calvin, *Institutes of the Christian Religion*, John T. McNeill (ed.), (Philadelphia: The Westminster Press, 1960), I.III.1,43; I.V.1, 52; I.II.2, 48.
15 Calvin, *Institutes of the Christian Religion*, II:VI:4, 347-8.
16 Matthew Tindal, quoted in Karen Armstrong, *A History of God: The 4000 year quest of Judaism, Christianity and Islam* (New York: Alfred A. Knopf, 1993), 306.
17 William Wordsworth, "Lines . . . Above Tintern Abbey", in *The Poetical Works of Wordsworth*, Thomas Hutchinson (ed.) (London: Oxford University Press, 1904, 1959), 164.
18 Musser and Price, *A New Handbook of Christian Theology*, 331.
19 McFague, *Life Abundant*, 6.
20 By the author.

21 King, *The Search for Spirituality*, 172.
22 Thomas Berry, quoted in King, *The Search for Spirituality*, 172.
23 Quoted in Tony Kelly, *A New Imagining: Towards an Australian spirituality* (Melbourne: Collins Dove, 1990), 112.
24 Acharya Shrinath P. Dwiveda, President, Hindu Literary Society of Canada.
25 Marion Bowman, "A Tale of Two Celticities: Sacred springs, legendary landscape, and Celtic revival in Bath", *Australian Religious Studies Review* 20:1, 93–115 (2007), 113.
26 Lynne Hume, "Creation and Innovation in Australian Paganism", *Australian Religious Studies Review* 20:1, 45–58 (2007), 55–6.
27 Norman Habel, *An Inconvenient Text: Is a green reading of the Bible possible?* (Hindmarsh, SA: Australian Theological Press, 2009), 58.
28 Fyodor Dostoevsky, quoted in G. F. Maine (ed.), *A Book of Daily Readings: Passages in prose and verse for solace and meditation* (London: Collins, nd), 100–1.
29 Sir Peter Medawar, quoted in Alister McGrath and Joanna Collicut McGrath, *The Dawkins Delusion?: Atheist fundamentalism and the denial of the Divine* (London: SPCK, 2007), 18.
30 Norman Habel, private communication.
31 Paul Davis, quoted in Amantha Trenoweth, *The Future of God: Personal adventures in spirituality with thirteen of today's eminent thinkers* (Newtown, Australia: Millennium Books, 1995), 97.
32 Trenoweth, *The Future of God*, 103.
33 Trenoweth, *The Future of God*, 104.
34 Trenoweth, *The Future of God*, 107.
35 Campbell, *The Whisper of Spirit*, 30.
36 Campbell, *The Whisper of Spirit*, 34.
37 James, *The Varieties of Religious Experiences*, 484.
38 William MacNeile Dixon, "The Human Situation", quoted in Keen, *Apology for Wonder*, 13.

Chapter 6: Sacred Places
1 O'Brien, *God and the New Haven Railway*, 59.
2 Smith, *The Illustrated World's Religions*, 241.
3 ANZAC – Australian and New Zealand Army Corp.
4 The "Ode of Remembrance" is from Laurence Binyon's "For the Fallen", first published in *The Times*, London, in September 1914.
5 Jonathan Z. Smith (ed.), *The HarperCollins Dictionary of Religion* (New York: HarperSanFrancisco, 1995), 943.
6 Smith, *The HarperCollins Dictionary of Religion*, 944.
7 de Weyer, *Rumi*, 74.
8 Bowker, *The Oxford Dictionary of World Religions*, 367.
9 Rainbow Spirit Elders, *Rainbow Spirit Theology: Towards an Australian Aboriginal theology* (Blackburn, Victoria: HarperCollinsReligious, 1997), 38.
10 Rainbow Spirit Elders, *Rainbow Spirit Theology*, 35–6.
11 Rainbow Spirit Elders, *Rainbow Spirit Theology*, 45.
12 Hinnells, *Penguin Dictionary of Religions*, 77.
13 http://www.statemaster.com/encyclopedia/Plymouth-Rock.
14 This hymn "Jerusalem the Golden" was composed by Bernard of Morlaix (1146) and translated by John M. Neale in 1858.
15 Alan Philps, *The Telegraph*, London, July 31, 2002.
16 For this description of church art and architecture, I am indebted to an article by R. Kevin Seasoltz, "Transcendence and Immanence in Sacred Art and Architecture", *Worship*, 75:5 (September 2001), 403–31.
17 O'Brien, *God and the New Haven Railway*, 4.

Chapter 7: Sacred Things and Symbols
1 Robert A. Johnson, "Ecstasy", quoted in Vardey, *God in all Worlds*, 201.

2 Count Eugene Goblet d'Alviella, *Symbols: Their migration and universality* (Westminster: Constable and Co., 1894; New York: Dover Publications, 2000), 1.

3 Hans Biedermann, *Dictionary of Symbolism: Cultural icons and the meanings behind them*, James Hulbert (trans.) (New York: Meridian, 1992), ix.

4 d'Alviella, *Symbols*, 3.

5 Russell, *Bertrand Russell's Best*, 30.

6 John Stoddard, *John L. Stoddard's Lectures*, vol. 4 (Chicago and Boston: George L. Shuman & Co., 1912), 83.

7 d'Alviella, *Symbols*, xix–xx.

8 Rainbow Spirit Elders, *Rainbow Spirit Theology*, 13–14.

9 Stoddard, *John L. Stoddard's Lectures*, 21.

10 John Dominic Crossan, *God and Empire: Jesus against Rome, then and now* (New York: HarperSanFrancisco, 2007), 116–17.

11 Nancy Caldwell Sorel, *Ever Since Eve: Personal reflections on childbirth* (New York: Oxford University Press, 1984), 162.

12 Thérèse of Lisieux, *The Story of a Soul*, 105.

13 Stoddard, *John L. Stoddard's Lectures*, 38.

14 Michael Kelly, quoted in Eric Newby (ed.), *A Book of Travelers' Tales* (New York: Penguin, 1985), 140–1.

15 Thich Nhat Hanh, *Living Buddha, Living Christ* (New York: Riverhead Books, 1995), 6–7.

Chapter 8: Gurus and Go-betweens

1 de Weyer, *Rumi*, 78.

2 Kazantzakis, *Report to Greco*, 80–1.

3 Richard Rodriguez, *Hunger of Memory: The education of Richard Rodriguez* (New York: Bantam Books, 1982), 85.

4 Lytton Strachey, *Eminent Victorians* (New York: The Modern Library, 1918), 65.

5 Hinnells, *Penguin Dictionary of Religions*, 38–9.

6 Bishop John Shelby Spong online newsletter, Thursday August 13, 2009.

7 Hans Küng, Josef van Ce, Heinrich von Stietencron and Heinz Bechert, *Christianity and the World Religions: Paths of dialogue with Islam, Hinduism and Buddhism*, Peter Heinegg (trans.) (New York: Doubleday, 1986), 13.

8 de Weyer, *Rumi*, 75.

9 de Weyer, *Rumi*, 40.

10 Bowker, *The Oxford Dictionary of World Religions*, 1069.

11 Hinnells, *Penguin Dictionary of Religions*, 573.

12 His ideas were recorded in *The Book Which Tells the Truth* (1974), *Extraterrestrials Took Me to their Planet* (1975), and combined as *The Message Given to Me by Extraterrestrials: They took me to their Planet*.

13 Bukkyo Dendo Kyokai (Buddhist Promoting Foundation) (ed.), *The Teachings of Buddha* (Tokyo: Toppan Printing, 1987), 202.

14 Crossan, *God and Empire*, 28.

15 Sölle, *Thinking about God*, 19.

16 McFague, *Life Abundant*, 20.

17 Thomas Cahill, *Desire of the Everlasting Hills: The world before and after Jesus* (New York: Doubleday, 1999), 319.

18 http://www.catholic-pages.com/saints/process.asp.

19 Thérèse of Lisieux, *The Story of a Soul*, 53.

20 Thérèse of Lisieux, *The Story of a Soul*, 121.

21 Luigi Barzini, *The Italians* (Middlesex: Penguin, 1968), 63.

22 Barzini, *The Italians*, 163–4.

23 Thomas Merton, *Seeds of Contemplation* (Norfolk, CO: New Directions Book, 1949), 116.

24 Merton, *Seeds of Contemplation*, 26–7.

Chapter 9: Community, Clergy and Caretakers

1   Kazantzakis, *Report to Greco*, 184.
2   We note that the land GOD gave Jacob was the land taken from someone else who could no longer call it home!
3   Chandler W. Gilbert, *Seed Pods and Periscopes: Stories and reflections about living deeply and living well* (Jeffrey, NH: Charred Pencil Press, 2008), 73.
4   Bergen Evans (ed.), *Dictionary of Quotations* (New York: Avenel Books, 1968), 318.
5   Rodriguez, *Hunger of Memory*, 77.
6   Hick, *The New Frontier of Religion and Science*, 145.
7   Karen Armstrong, *The Case for God* (New York, Toronto: Alfred. A. Knopf, 2009), xiii.
8   Ludwig, *The Sacred Paths*, 17–18.
9   Warren Bird, Leadership Network's Director of Research, Hartford Seminary's Hartford Institute for Religion Research and Scott Thumma, Professor of Sociology of Religion at Hartford Seminary, *Not Who You Think They Are: The real story of people who attend America's megachurches*, www.leadnet.org/megachurch and http://hirr.hartsem.edu. 24,900 attendees of twelve mega churches across the country were polled between January and August 2008, the largest national representative study of mega church attendees to date.
10 Gerald White Johnson, quoted in John P. Bradley, Leo F. Daniels and Thomas C. Jones (eds), *The International Dictionary of Thoughts* (Chicago: J. G. Ferguson Publishing Co., 1969), 543.
11 Dava Sobel, *Galileo's Daughter* (New York: Walker & Co., 1999), 53.
12 Smith, *The Illustrated World's Religions*, 106.
13 Smith, *The Illustrated World's Religions*, 106.
14 Küng et al., *Christianity and the World Religions*, 46.
15 Hinnells, *Penguin Dictionary of Religions*, 35.
16 Lewis M. Hopfe, *Religions of the World*, ninth edition, revised by Mark R. Woodward (New Jersey: Pearson/Prentice Hall, 2005), 36, 38.
17 Quoted in Michael J. Cook, "Jews and 'Gospel Dynamics'", *The Fourth R*, 22: 2 (March–April 2009, 9–14), 14.
18 Hinnells, *Penguin Dictionary of Religions*, 282.
19 Hinnells, *Penguin Dictionary of Religions*, 392.
20 This material on Hebrew priests comes from Achtemeier, *Harper's Bible Dictionary*, 821–2.
21 Melanie Johnson-DeBaufre, "'That One' Takes a Village: the uniqueness of Jesus and the Beelzebul Controversy", *The Fourth R*, 22:5 (September–October 2009, 3–7), 3.
22 Musser and Price, *A New Handbook of Christian Theology*, 381.
23 See my doctoral dissertation for understandings of the ministerial role in denominations descended from John Calvin and John Wesley, *Ministry and Ordination in the Uniting Church of Australia: An historical, contextual and constructive theological study* (Ann Arbor, MI: UMI Dissertation Services, 1996).
24 Alfred Barrett, "Essay on the Pastoral Office, as a Divine Institution in the Church of Christ", quoted in John C. Bowmer, *Pastor and People: A study of church and ministry in Wesleyan Methodism from the death of John Wesley (17891) to the death of Jabez Bunting (1858)* (London: Epworth Press, 1975), 222–3.
25 Morag Zwartz, *Apostles of Fear: A church cult exposed* (South Australia: Parenesis Publishing, 2008).
26 Hinnells, *Penguin Dictionary of Religions*, 322–3.
27 Report from Jeffrey Fleishman in Cairo in the *Los Angeles Times*, March 2, 2008.
28 Val Webb, *Why We're Equal: Introducing feminist theology* (St Louis, MO: Chalice Press, 1999).
29 Tertullian, "On the Apparel of Women", quoted in John A. Phillips, *Eve, the History of an Idea* (San Francisco: Harper & Row, 1984), 76.
30 Huston Smith, *Why Religion Matters: The fate of the human spirit in an age of disbelief* (New York: HarperSanFransisco, 2001), 17.
31 David James Duncan, quoted in Gilbert, *Seed Pods and Periscopes*, 132.

Chapter 10: Sacred Texts and Holy Books

1   David James Duncan, *God Laughs and Plays*, quoted in Gilbert, *Seed Pods and Periscopes*, 143.
2   Armstrong, *The Case for God*, xi.
3   Armstrong, *The Case for God*, xi.
4   Richard Holloway, *Between the Monster and the Saint: Reflections on the human condition* (Melbourne, Australia: The Text Publishing Co., 2008), 52–3.
5   Unfortunately, Google as I may, I cannot find the author. It was a handout at an event with no credits given. Should anyone know the author, I would appreciate it – valmaurice@aol.com.
6   Mahatma Gandhi, quoted in A. R. Vidler (ed.), *Objections to Christian Belief* (New York: J. B. Lippincott Co., 1964), 59.
7   à Kempis, *The Imitation of Christ*, 324.
8   à Kempis, *The Imitation of Christ*, 103, 106.
9   Kazantzakis, *Report to Greco*, 55–6.
10 Smith, *The Religions of Man*, 229.
11 Sikh Missionary Center, *Sikh Religion* (Phoenix, AZ: Sikh Missionary Center, 1990), 255.
12 David L. Dungan, *Constantine's Bible: Politics and the making of the New Testament* (London: SCM Press, 2006), 52.
13 Dungan, *Constantine's Bible*, 61. Many writings disputed by Eusebius were eventually included in Jerome's fourth century Latin version after approval by church councils.
14 Dungan, *Constantine's Bible*, 9–10.
15 Roman Catholic Church ecclesiastical decree (1546), quoted in Jaroslav Pelikan, *Whose Bible is it: A history of the scriptures through the ages* (New York: Viking, 2005), 19.
16 Geoffrey Faber, *Jowett: A portrait with background* (Cambridge, MA: Harvard University Press, 1957), 143.
17 Bart D. Ehrman, *Misquoting Jesus: The story behind who changed the Bible and why* (New York: HarperSanFrancisco, 2005), 7.
18 From an American Academy of Religion lecture (2007) by Professor Bart Ehrman.
19 Peter Beresford Ellis, *The Druids* (Grand Rapids, MI: Eerdmans Publishing Co., 1994), 13.
20 Rodriguez, *Hunger of Memory*, 90.
21 This analysis is spelled out in Pelikan, *Whose Bible is it*.
22 Saint Augustine, *Confessions*, R. S. Pine-Coffin (trans) (Harmondsworth: Penguin Books, 1961), XI: 19, 268.
23 Buechner, *Wishful Thinking*, 12.
24 Hinnells, *Penguin Dictionary of Religions*, 35–7.
25 Hinnells, *Penguin Dictionary of Religions*, 572.
26 *Anguttara Nikaya*, quoted in Jack Kornfield (ed.), *Teachings of the Buddha* (New York: Barnes & Noble, 1998), 27.
27 Quoted in Smith, *The Religions of Man*, 42.

Chapter 11: Rituals as Religious Action

1   Armstrong, *The Case for God*, xii.
2   Joachim Wach, *The Comparative Study of Religions* (New York: Columbia University Press, 1958), 97.
3   *Arab News* report from Riyadh, October 2005.
4   "Liturgy", in *Webster's New Universal Unabridged Dictionary*, 1058.
5   Musser and Price, *A New Handbook of Christian Theology*, 415.
6   This varied with denominations. The Church in England retained many Catholic worship rituals, as did Lutherans, while at the other end of the spectrum, Quakers removed all ceremony including the Eucharist.
7   Faith Eidse and Nina Sichel (eds), *Unrooted Childhoods: Memoirs of growing up global* (Yarmouth, Maine: Intercultural Press, 2004), 93–4.
8   Gallatin, *Thirsting for God in a Land of Shallow Wells*, 80.
9   Smith, *The HarperCollins Dictionary of Religion*, 948.

10 Hinnells, *Penguin Dictionary of Religions*, 223–5.
11 Peter Fitzsimons, "The Fitz Files", *Sydney Morning Herald*, October 25, 2009.
12 Bowker, *The Oxford Dictionary of World Religions*, 122.
13 Henrietta Green, *Festive Foods of England* (London: Kyle Cathie Ltd, 1991), 44.
14 Hinnells, *Penguin Dictionary of Religions*, 376.
15 Murasaki Shikibu, *Diaries of Court Ladies of Old Japan*, quoted in Nancy Caldwell Sorel, *Ever Since Eve*, 153.
16 Hinnells, *Penguin Dictionary of Religions*, 288.
17 Paramananda, *Buddhist Reflections on Everyday Life* (New York: Barnes & Noble, 2001), 143.
18 Smith, *The Religions of Man*, 239.
19 Bowker, *The Oxford Dictionary of World Religions*, 192.
20 Monier Williams, quoted in Patton E. Burchett, "The 'Magical' Language of Mantra", *Journal of the American Academy of Religion* 76:4 (December 2008, 807–43), 833.
21 Hinnells, *Penguin Dictionary of Religions*, 361.
22 For the full story of Father Kennedy and this church, see Martin Flanagan (ed.), *Peter Kennedy: The man who threatened Rome* (Australia: One Day Hill Publishers, 2009).
23 Mark Twain, *Following the Equator* (1897), quoted in Wesley C. Camp, *Camp's Unfamiliar Quotations from 2000 B.C. to the Present* (New Jersey: Prentice Hall, 1990), 322.

Chapter 12: Sensing the Sacred

1 Saint Augustine, quoted in Harry Emerson Fosdick, *The Meaning of Prayer* (Nashville: Abingdon, 1949, 1962), 21.
2 Thich Nhat Hanh, *Being Peace*, Arnold Kotler (ed.) (Berkley, CA: Parallax Press, 1987), 4.
3 Sam Gill, *Native American Religious Action: A performance approach to religion* (Columbia: University of South Carolina Press, 1987), 4–5.
4 Diana L. Eck, *Encountering God: A spiritual journey from Bozeman to Benares* (Boston: Beacon Press, 1993), 100.
5 Primo Levi, *Survival in Auschwitz* (New York: Simon & Schuster, 1996), 160.
6 H. E. Jacobs, *Six Thousand Years of Bread: Its holy and unholy history* (New York: Lions Press, 1944, 1997), 31.
7 Susannah Heschel is the daughter of Jewish theologian, Rabbi Abraham Joshua Heschel.
8 à Kempis, *The Imitation of Christ*, 68.
9 Bowker, *The Oxford Dictionary of World Religions*, 97.
10 The Hebrew word for locust could also refer to the carob tree's edible bean-like pods, but locusts in swarming stage are still a protein source for desert people, so they were probably John's food. Achtemeier, *Harper's Bible Dictionary*, 572.
11 Green, *Festive Foods of England*, 12–13.
12 *Majjhima Nik ya*, quoted in Bowker, *The Oxford Dictionary of World Religions*, 97.
13 Athanasius, *Life of Saint Anthony*, quoted in Robert E. Van Voors (ed.), *Readings in Christianity* (Belmont, CA: Wadsworth Publishing Co., 1997), 85.
14 This description of the Tea Ceremony is from Sen Soshitsu, "Chado: the Way of Tea", *Japan Quarterly* 30, 1983.
15 John Muir, quoted in King, *The Search for Spirituality*, 166.
16 Quoted in Krishna, *One Earth, One Sky, One Humankind*, 16.
17 de Weyer, *Rumi*, 74–5.
18 de Weyer, *Rumi*, 79.
19 Alfred North Whitehead, *Process and Reality: An essay in cosmology* (New York: Free Press, 1978), 346.
20 Quoted in Kelly, *A New Imagining*, vii–viii.
21 Robert Withnow, *Creative Spirituality: The way of the artist* (California: University of California Press, 2001), 262.
22 Seasoltz, "Transcendence and Immanence in Sacred Art and Architecture", 403–31.
23 Martin Gayford, *Sunday Telegraph*, September 21, 2003.

24 Nira Stone, *The Kaffa Lives of the Desert Fathers: A study in Armenian manuscript illumination*, vol. 566 of *Corpus Scriptorum Christianorum Orientalium* (Belguim: Peeters Publishers, 1997).

25 Holloway, *Between the Monster and the Saint*, 143.

26 Gill, *Native American Religious Action*, 39.

27 Gill, *Native American Religious Action*, 9.

28 Masutani Fumio, "Religion as We See It", *Japan Quarterly*, 5 (1958), 30–1.

29 Mizuo Hiroshi, "Zen Art", *Japanese Quarterly*, 17 (1970), 161.

30 Haga Koshiro and Osaka Koryo, "Japanese Zen: A Symposium", *The Eastern Buddhist*, 10 (1977), 99–100.

31 Schweitzer, *Out of My Life and Thought*, 55–7.

32 Bowker, *The Oxford Dictionary of World Religions*, 667.

33 Maggio, *The Stone Boudoir*, 105.

34 Rabindranath Tagore, *Gitanjali: A collection of Indian songs* (New York: Macmillan, 1971), 89.

Chapter 13: What is *Your* Experience?

1   The Buddha, quoted in Kornfield, *Teachings of the Buddha*, 122.

2   Hanh, *Living Buddha*, 194–5.

3   de Weyer, *Rumi*, 82.

4   By the author.

5   Musser and Price, *A New Handbook of Christian Theology*, 169.

6   Frank Schaeffer, *Crazy for God: How I grew up as one of the elect, helped found the religious right, and lived to take all (or almost all) of it back* (Philadelphia: Da Capo Press, 2007), 390.

7   Teilhard de Chardin, quoted in Geering, *Coming Back to Earth*, 75.

8   McFague, *Life Abundant*, xiii.

9   Brother Leo, FSC, introduction to à Kempis, *The Imitation of Christ*, xxv–vi.

10 Marcus J. Borg, *The God we Never Knew: Beyond dogmatic religion to a more authentic contemporary faith* (New York: HarperSanFrancisco, 1997).

11 Steven Ogden, *I met God in Bermuda: Faith in the 21st century* (Winchester: O Books, 2009), 39.

12 For this discussion, see my book *In Defense of Doubt: An invitation to adventure* (St Louis, MO: Chalice Press, 1995).

13 Paramananda, *Buddhist Reflections on Everyday Life*, 93.

14 McFague, *Life Abundant*, 11–12.

15 Rabindranath Tagore, *Fruit-Gathering* (Madras: Macmillan India Ltd, 1943, 1985), 19.

16 King, *The Search for Spirituality*, 1, 28.

17 Kelly, *A New Imagining*, 16, 18.

18 McFague, *Life Abundant*, 22.

19 Kelly, *A New Imagining*, 6.

20 King, *The Search for Spirituality*, 56.

21 à Kempis, *The Imitation of Christ*, 57.

22 An interview with Malcolm Muggeridge in *Christianity Today*, April 21, 1978, 8–9.

23 McFague, *Life Abundant*, 13.

24 Quoted in James, *The Varieties of Religious Experiences*, 497.

25 Schweitzer, *Out of my Life and Thought*, 48–9.

26 Shunryu Suzuki, *Branching Streams Flow in the Darkness: Zen talks on the Sandokai* (Berkley: University of California Press, 1999), 79.

27 Victor Frankl, *Man's Search for Meaning*, quoted in Gilbert, *Seed Pods and Periscopes*.

28 Julian of Norwich, *The Wisdom of Julian of Norwich*, 29.

29 Julian of Norwich, *The Wisdom of Julian of Norwich*, 16.

30 Lal Ded, *Women in Praise of the Sacred*, 120.

31 Teresa of Avila, *The Interior Castle*, quoted in Robert E. Van Voorst (ed.), *Readings in Christianity* (Belmont, CA: Wadsworth Publishing Co., 1997), 201–2.

32 Merton, *Seeds of Contemplation*, 32.
33 Leo Tolstoy, written while contemplating suicide, quoted in James, *The Varieties of Religious Experiences*, 153.
34 Campbell, *The Whisper of Spirit*, 91.
35 Tim Winton, *Breath* (Victoria, Australia: Hamish Hamilton 2008), 76.
36 Robert Leighton, quoted in Vidler, *Objections To Christian Belief*, 77–8.
37 Robert Fulghum, *All I Really Need to Know I Learned in Kindergarten: Uncommon thoughts on common things* (New York: Ivy Books, 1986, 1988), 5.
38 Kelly, *A New Imagining*, 114.
39 Bernard Lonergan, *Method in Theology* (London: Darton, Longman & Todd Ltd, 1972), 103.
40 Saint Augustine, *Confessions*, R. S. Pine-Coffin (trans.) (Harmondsworth: Penguin Books Ltd, 1961), X:40:249.
41 John Geiger, *The Third Man Syndrome: Surviving the impossible* (New York: Weinstein Books, 2009).
42 Dag Hammarskjöld, *Markings* (New York: Alfred A. Knopf, 1964), 56.
43 Keen, *Apology for Wonder*, 23.
44 Thérèse of Lisieux, *The Story of a Soul*, 110.
45 Mother Teresa, *Come Be My Light: The private writings of the "Saint of Calcutta"*, Brian Kolodiejchuk (ed.) (New York and London: Doubleday, 2007), 163.
46 Mother Teresa, *Come Be My Light*, 150.
47 Mother Teresa, *Come Be My Light*, 213.
48 Mother Teresa, *Come Be My Light*, 210.
49 James, *The Varieties of Religious Experiences*, 479.
50 Ellen Burstyn, *Lessons in Becoming Myself*, quoted in Gilbert, *Seed Pods and Periscopes*, 139.
51 King, *The Search for Spirituality*, 70.
52 R. D. Laing, quoted in Vardey, *God in all Worlds*, 15.
53 de Weyer, *Rumi*, 42.

Chapter 14: Engaging through Prayer
1 Buechner, *Wishful Thinking*, quoted in Gilbert, *Seed Pods and Periscopes*, 63.
2 Bowker, *The Oxford Dictionary of World Religions*, 762.
3 Krishna, *One Earth, One Sky, One Humankind*, 16.
4 Headley Beare, *God-in-the-present-moment: Prayer in the twenty-first century* (Mulgrave, Victoria: John Garratt Publishing, 2008), 9.
5 Sir Wilfred Grenfell (1865–1940), quoted in Harry Emerson Fosdick, *The Meaning of Prayer* (Nashville: Abingdon, 1949, 1962), 38.
6 de Weyer, *Rumi*, 30.
7 Thérèse of Lisieux, *The Story of a Soul*, 136.
8 Mother Teresa, *Come Be My Light*, 158.
9 Mother Teresa, *Come Be My Light*, 165.
10 Rabindranath Tagore, quoted in Fosdick, *The Meaning of Prayer*, 129.
11 Bill Wallace, quoted in Maren C. Tirabassi and Kathy Wonson Eddy, *Gifts of Many Cultures: worship resources for the global community* (Cleveland, Ohio: United Church Press, 1995), 12.
12 Spong, *Eternal Life*, 101–2.
13 Mirabai, quoted in Hirschfield, *Women in Praise of the Sacred*, 134.
14 de Weyer, *Rumi*, 35.
15 Fosdick, *The Meaning of Prayer*, 117.
16 *Hadith Qudsi*, 35, published on http://www.usc.edu/schools/college/crcc/engagement/resources/texts/muslim/hadith/hadithqudsi.html.
17 Bhagat Dhanna, in *Sri Guru Granth Sahib Ji*, quoted in a handout on Sikh Dharma on "Stages of Spiritual Development" from Project Naad, www.ProjectNaad.com.
18 Schaeffer, *Crazy for God*, 150.
19 Quoted in Fosdick, *The Meaning of Prayer*, 6.
20 Julian of Norwich, *The Wisdom of Julian of Norwich*, 14.

21   à Kempis, *The Imitation of Christ*, 163, 98.
22   Achtemeier, *Harper's Bible Dictionary*, 575.
23   Revd Chris Udy, Killara Fiveways Uniting Church, Killara, Sydney, email communication.
24   Patton E. Burchett, "The 'Magical' Language of Mantra", *Journal of the American Academy of Religion* 76:4 (December, 2008, 807–43), 836 .
25   Burchett, "The 'Magical' Language of Mantra", 824–5.
26   Written by Charles Wesley, 1742.
27   Frank Schaeffer, *Portofino* (New York: Carroll & Graf Publishers, 1992, 2004).
28   Fosdick, *The Meaning of Prayer*, 158.
29   Saint Augustine, *Confessions*, I:1:21.
30   Armstrong, *The Spiral Staircase*, 58–61.
31   Simone Weil, quoted in King, *The Search for Spirituality*, 13.
32   Fosdick, *The Meaning of Prayer*, 75.
33   Fosdick, *The Meaning of Prayer*, 76.
34   Revd Elizabeth Lerner, quoted in Felicia Urbanski, "Prayer: Engaging the Sacred", Unitarian Fellowship in London, September 28, 2008, http://www.unitarianfellowshipoflondon.org/FUSept28,2008.pdf.
35   Felicia Urbanski, "Prayer: Engaging the Sacred", Unitarian Fellowship in London, September 28, 2008, http://www.unitarianfellowshipoflondon.org/FUSept28,2008.pdf.

Chapter 15: Meditation and Contemplation
1   Thomas Merton, *Thoughts in Solitude*, quoted in Vardey, *God in all Worlds*, 393.
2   *Katha Upanishad*, quoted in Mascaró, *The Upanishads*, 65.
3   Julian of Norwich, *The Wisdom of Julian of Norwich*, 45.
4   The following quotations from Sikh scripture come from an article on Sikh dharma, "Stages of Spiritual Development", handout from Project Naad, www.ProjectNaad.com.
5   Bowker, *The Oxford Dictionary of World Religions*, 236.
6   Keen, *Apology for Wonder*, 34.
7   *Sutta-Nipata*, Dines Anderson and Helmer Smith (trans.) quoted in Kornfield, *Teachings of the Buddha*, 79.
8   David James Duncan, *God Laughs and Plays*, quoted in Gilbert, *Seed Pods and Periscopes*, 135.
9   Suzuki, *Branching Streams Flow in the Darkness*, 104.
10   Thomas Merton, *The Asian Journal of Thomas Merton*, Naomi Burton, Brother Patrick Hart and James Laughlin (eds) (New York: New Directions Publishing, 1973, 1975), 312.
11   Murray Rogers, "Hindu Influence on Christian Spiritual Practice", in Harold Coward (ed.), *Hindu–Christian Dialogue: Perspectives and encounters* (Maryknoll, NY: Orbis Books, 1990), 199.
12   Merton, *The Asian Journal of Thomas Merton*, 343.
13   *Dhammapada*, quoted in Kornfield, *Teachings of the Buddha*, 1.
14   Hanh, *Being Peace*, 14–15.
15   Hanh, *Being Peace*, 5.
16   Hanh, *Being Peace*, 115.
17   Paramananda, *Buddhist Reflections on Everyday Life*, 53.
18   Paramananda, *Buddhist Reflections on Everyday Life*, 66.
19   Hanh, *Being Peace*, 68.
20   Hanh, *Being Peace*, 74.
21   Suzuki, *Branching Streams Flow in the Darkness*, 28.
22   Suzuki, *Branching Streams Flow in the Darkness*, 6.
23   Suzuki, *Branching Streams Flow in the Darkness*, 167, 174.
24   à Kempis, *The Imitation of Christ*, 174–5.
25   de Weyer, *Rumi*, 73.
26   http://www.whirlingdervishes.org/whirlingdervishes.htm.
27   For this discussion of yoga, I am indebted to Smith, *The Religions of Man*, 39–65.
28   *Śvetāśvatara Upanisad*, quoted in Bowker, *The Oxford Dictionary of World Religions*, 1058.

29 Smith, *The Religions of Man*, 40–1.
30 Walter T. Stace, *The Teachings of the Mystics*, quoted in Paul Alan Laughlin, "Pray without Seeking: Toward a truly mystical Lord's Prayer", *The Fourth R*, 22:6 (November–December 2009, 20–23), 20.
31 *Maitri Upanishad*, quoted in Mascaró, *The Upanishads*, 101.
32 Robert E. Kennedy, *Zen Spirit, Christian Spirit: The place of Zen in Christian life* (New York: Continuum, 1996), 33.
33 Quoted in Fosdick, *The Meaning of Prayer*, 82.
34 Hanh, *Living Buddha, Living Christ*, 14.

Chapter 16: Engaging the Sacred in the World
1 Tagore, *Gitanjali*, 11–12.
2 à Kempis, *The Imitation of Christ*, 54, 49.
3 Thérèse of Lisieux, *The Story of a Soul*, 58–9.
4 Hanh, *Being Peace*, 86.
5 Kazantzakis, *Report to Greco*, 208.
6 à Kempis, *The Imitation of Christ*, 34–5.
7 McFague, *Life Abundant*, 21.
8 Omoto Kyo, Michi-no-Shiori, quoted in Krishna, *One Earth, One Sky, One Humankind*, 6.
9 Black Elk, quoted in Krishna, *One Earth, One Sky, One Humankind*, 13.
10 Thomas Merton, quoted in King, *The Search for Spirituality*, 78.
11 King, *The Search for Spirituality*, 79.
12 King, *The Search for Spirituality*, 79.
13 McFague, *Life Abundant*, 23.
14 de Weyer, *Rumi*, 30.
15 By the author.
16 Aleksei Leonov, *The Home Planet*, quoted in Vardey, *God in all Worlds*, 538.
17 Matthew Fox, *The Coming of the Cosmic Christ* (New York: Harper & Row, 1988), 199.
18 Kornfield, *Teachings of the Buddha*, 5.
19 McFague, *Life Abundant*, 14.
20 Dalai Lama, *A Policy of Kindness*, quoted in Vardey, *God in all Worlds*, 432.
21 *Upanishads*, quoted in Robert O. Ballou, ed., *The Portable World Bible: A comprehensive selection from the eight great sacred scriptures of the world* (New York: Viking Press, 1944), 57.
22 John F. Haught, *God after Darwin: A theology of evolution* (Boulder, CO: Westview Press, 2000), 6–9.
23 Swami Muktananda, *Play of Consciousness*, quoted in Vardey, *God in all Worlds*, 406.
24 *Samyutta Nikatya*, Gil Fronsdal (trans.), quoted in Kornfield, *Teachings of the Buddha*, 124.
25 Mahabharata, quoted in Krishna, *One Earth, One Sky, One Humankind*, 57.
26 Udana-Varga, quoted in Krishna, *One Earth, One Sky, One Humankind*, 99.
27 Richard Wilhelm, *Confucius and Confucianism*, quoted in Krishna, *One Earth, One Sky, One Humankind*, 99.
28 Ogden, *I met God in Bermuda*, 75.
29 Lao-Tzu, quoted in Krishna, *One Earth, One Sky, One Humankind*, 99.
30 Krishna, *One Earth, One Sky, One Humankind*, 100.
31 Gretta Vosper, *With or without God: Why the way we live is more important than what we believe* (Toronto, Ontario: HarperCollins, 2008), 249.
32 Spong, *Eternal Life*, 9–10.
33 Spong, *Eternal Life*, 10.
34 Hinnells, *Penguin Dictionary of Religions*, 10.
35 Quoted in James, *The Varieties of Religious Experiences*, 155.
36 à Kempis, *The Imitation of Christ*, 59.
37 Quoted in John Hick, *The Existence of God* (New York: Macmillan, 1964), 183.
38 Kyokai, *The Teaching of Buddha*, 123–4.

39 Spong, *Eternal Life*, 29.
40 Tagore, *Gitanjali*, 107–8.
41 Spong, *Eternal Life*, 211.

Chapter 17: Borrowing, Conquering and Adapting
1 Pelikan, *Whose Bible Is It?*, 15.
2 Maggio, *The Stone Boudoir*, 73.
3 Maggio, *The Stone Boudoir*, 7.
4 Jacob Bar-Salibi, quoted in Ramsay MacMullen, *Christianity and Paganism in the Fourth to Eighth Centuries* (New Haven, CT: Yale University Press, 1997), 155.
5 Bowker, *The Oxford Dictionary of World Religions*, 301.
6 Ron Hansen, quoted in Gilbert, *Seed Pods and Periscopes*, 137.
7 Acts 17:28, Wayne A. Meeks, *The HarperCollins Study Bible* (San Fransisco: HarperSanFransisco, 1993), note 2093.
8 Socrates, quoted in Fosdick, *The Meaning of Prayer*, 2.
9 For a detailed account of this, see chapter 14, "Who Do You Say I Am?" in my book *Like Catching Water in a Net*.
10 Tom Harpur, *The Pagan Christ: Is blind faith killing Christianity?* (Crows Nest, NSW, Australia: Allen & Unwin, 2005).
11 Mark G. Brett, *Decolonizing God: The Bible in the tides of Empire* (Sheffield: Sheffield Phoenix Press, 2008), 199.
12 Reza Aslan, *No God but God: The origins, evolution, and future of Islam* (New York: Random House, 2006), xxiv.
13 Bamber Gascoyne, *The Christians* (New York: William Morrow & Co., 1977), 109.
14 Maggio, *The Stone Boudoir*, 222.
15 E. Stanley Jones, *The Christ of the Indian Road* (New York: Abingdon, 1925), 205–6.
16 Stoddard, *John L. Stoddard's Lectures*, vol. 4, 119.
17 Vine Deloria Jr, *Custer Died for Your Sins: An Indian Manifesto* (New York: Avon, 1969), 105.
18 Fosdick, *The Meaning of Prayer*, 8.
19 Graham Paulson, "Towards an Aboriginal Theology", quoted in Brett, *Decolonizing God*, 198.
20 Deloria, *Custer Died for Your Sins*, 105.
21 King, *The Search for Spirituality*, 53.
22 Hanh, *Being Peace*, 43.

Chapter 18: Engaging the Sacred Together
1 *Bhagavad Gita*, quoted in Ballou, *The Portable World Bible*, 65.
2 King, *The Search for Spirituality*, 65.
3 Smith, *The Religions of Man*, 6.
4 Stoddard, *John L. Stoddard's Lectures*, vol. 4, 84.
5 King, *The Search for Spirituality*, 41.
6 King, *The Search for Spirituality*, 62.
7 Eck, *Encountering God*, 89.
8 Gallatin, *Thirsting for God*, 183.
9 Fosdick, *The Meaning of Prayer*, 138.
10 Gideon Hawley, quoted in Elisabeth D. Dodds, *Marriage to a Difficult Man: The 'uncommon union' of Jonathan and Sarah Edwards* (Philadelphia: Westminster Press, 1971), 163–4.
11 Interview with Malcolm Muggeridge in *Christianity Today* (April 21, 1978), 8.
12 Eidse and Sichel (eds), *Unrooted Childhoods*, 165.
13 Aslan, *No God but God*, xxv–vi.
14 Royal Philharmonic Choir and Orchestra, Melbourne University Choral Society, Melbourne Percussion Ensemble, Andrew Wailes, Conductor, Alan Harris on didgeridu.
15 Professor Joy Murphy Wandin.
16 Revd Dr William Lesher, Chair of the Council for the Parliament of the World's Religions 2009.

17 Rabbi David Saperstein.
18 Dr Sakena Yacoobi, founder of Afghan Institute of Learning.
19 Dr Gurbux Kaur Kahlow.
20 Sr Joan Chichester OSB.
21 His Holiness Sri Sri Ravi Shanker.
22 Schweitzer, *Out of My Life and Thought*, 200.
23 His Holiness Sri Sri Ravi Shanker.
24 Sri Ramakrishna, quoted in Smith, *The Religions of Man*, 86–7.

Chapter 19: From Here to Where?
1 Fox, *The Coming of the Cosmic Christ*, 209.
2 Anonymous, quoted in Kennedy, *Zen Spirit, Christian Spirit*, 76.
3 Kennedy, *Zen Spirit, Christian Spirit*, 75.
4 Saint Augustine, *Confessions*, V: 6:97–8.
5 Kennedy, *Zen Spirit, Christian Spirit*, 38–9.
6 Ogden, *I met God in Bermuda*, 22.
7 Thomas Merton, *No Man is an Island* (Mariner Books, 2002), 191.
8 *Dhammapada*, Thomas Byrom (trans.), quoted in Kornfield, *Teachings of the Buddha*, 44.
9 Schweitzer, *Out of My Life and Thought*, 84–5.
10 Personal correspondence.
11 Paramananda, *Buddhist Reflections on Everyday Life*, 78.
12 Webb, *In Defense of Doubt*.
13 Seventeenth-century author, quoted in Fosdick, *The Meaning of Prayer*, 98.
14 Sölle, *Thinking about God:*, 4–5.
15 Russell, *Bertrand Russell's Best*, 30.
16 Carlos Ruiz Zafrón, *The Shadow of the Wind* (Melbourne, Australia: Text Publishing Co., 2001), 136.
17 David James Duncan, quoted in Gilbert, *Seed Pods and Periscopes*, 121.
18 Smith, *The Religions of Man*, 353.
19 James A. Connor, *Pascal's Wager: The man who played dice with God* (New York: Harper-SanFrancisco, 2006), 183–4.
20 Spong, *Eternal Life*, 143–4.
21 *Bhaddekaratta Sutta*, Thich Nhat Hanh, trans., quoted in Kornfield, *Teachings of the Buddha*, 11.
22 Alfred North Whitehead, *Modes of Thought* (New York: The Free Press, 1966), 154.
23 Charles Birch, *Science and Soul* (Sydney: University of New South Wales Press, 2007), 91.
24 Leo Tolstoy, *A Confession and Other Religious Writings*, 139.
25 Fritjof Capra, *The Tao of Physics*, quoted in Vardey, *God in all Worlds*, 811.
26 *New York Times*, April 25, 1929.
27 Albert Einstein, *The Human Side: New glimpses from his archives*, Helen Dukas & Banesh Hoffman, eds., (Princeton, New Jersey: Princeton University Press, 1981), 39.
28 Alice Calaprice (ed.), *The Expanded Quotable Einstein* (Princeton, New Jersey: Princeton University Press, 2000), 218.
29 Albert Einstein, *The World as I See It*, first published in *Forum and Century*, vol. 84, 193–4; (Minneapolis: Filiquarian Publishing LLC, 2006), 5.
30 Spong, *Eternal Life*, 152.
31 *Svetasvatara Upanishad*, in Mascaró, *The Upanishads*, 96.
32 Ballou, *The Portable World Bible*, 547.
33 Tagore, *Gitanjali*, 88.
34 Geering, *Coming Back to Earth*, 218.
35 Kyokai, *The Teachings of Buddha*, 296.
36 Dodds, *Marriage to a Difficult Man*, 60.
37 John A. T. Robinson, *Honest To God* (Philadelphia: Westminster Press, 1962), 28.
38 Boston Research Center for the 21st Century, *Newsletter* 10 (Winter 1998), 11.

39 Ogden, *I Met God in Bermuda*,122.
40 C. S. Lewis, quoted in Kennedy, *Zen Spirit, Christian Spirit*, 59.
41 David James Duncan, "What Fundamentalists Need for Their Salvation: in defense of truth, stewardship, and neighborly love", *Orion* (July/August 2005, http://www.orionmagazine.org/index.php/articles/article/156/).
42 Rabi'a, quoted in John Bowker, *God: A brief history* (London: DK Publishing, 2002), 336.
43 *Dhammapada*, quoted in Kornfield, *Teachings of the Buddha*, 1.
44 Bertrand Russell, *The Autobiography of Bertrand Russell* (Boston: Little, Brown & Co., 1967), 48.
45 Schaeffer, *Crazy for God*, 391.

Index

Gayford, Martin 156-7
Geering, Sir Lloyd 33, 260
Geiger, John 175
Gennaro, St 98
George, St 98, 158
Gerhard, Johann 49-50
Gill, Sam 146-7, 159
Giotto di Bondone 88
Gnosticism 209
Goa 230
Gobind Singh, Guru 10, 120, 196
Goblet d'Alviella, Eugene 75-6
GOD, images of 3-9, 14-15, 21
GODDESS tradition 21
Goethe, Johann Wolfgang von 28
Goldstein, Herbert 257
Grace Cathedral, San Francisco 105, 237
Granth Sahib, Guru 120; *see also* Adi
  Granth
Greek philosophy 49, 228-9
Greeley, Andrew 36
Gregory I, Pope 183
Grenfell, Sir Wilfred 181
Griffith, Bede 40, 175, 197

Habel, Norman 56
Hadrian, Emperor 66
Haiti 256
Halloween 140
Hammarskjöld, Dag 175
Hansen, Ron 226
Hardy, Sir Alister 36
Harpur, Tom 227
harvest festivals 138-9
Haught, John 20, 213
Hawley, Gideon 239
Hay, David 36
hearing, sense of 160-1
"Heaven's Gate" cult 91
Helena, Empress 66
Henderson-James, Nancy 241
Henry of Huntington 81
Heschel, Susannah 150
hesychasm 200
Hick, John 36-7, 102
Hinduism 6-9, 19, 25, 48-9, 63, 68, 71,
  75-8, 92-3, 112, 142, 148, 154, 181,
  202-3, 207-8, 216, 222, 237
Hitler, Adolf 80
Holloway, Richard 116-17, 157
Holocaust, the 31-2, 126, 222
holy books 115-28
"home", definition of 101-2

Hopi Indians 146-7
Howell, Vernon 91-2
human condition 24-7, 33
Hume, Lynne 56
Hunt, Holman 156

icons 158
imams 112-13
immanence 11
incarnations 92-5, 171
indigenous peoples 47-9, 54, 211, 231-3
initiation rites 140
Intelligent Design 213
interfaith dialogue 240-2, 245-6
Ireland, Billy 46
Islam 6, 88-9, 96, 107, 112, 120, 131,
  142-3, 151, 181, 201, 229, 237
Israel, State of 67

Jainism 222, 243
James, Clive 212
James, E. O. 35
James, William 24, 27-9, 59, 174, 178
Jensen, Archbishop 136
Jerusalem 65-8, 125, 229-30
Jesuits 70
Jesus Christ 37, 43, 49, 79, 90, 93-5,
  108-9, 135-7, 149-50, 188, 204,
  208-11, 222-7
Joan of Arc 38
John, St (and St John's Gospel) 10, 12, 78,
  123, 209, 216
John XXIII, Pope 67
John Paul II, Pope 67, 96, 98
Johnson, Robert A. 73
Johnson-DeBaufre, Melanie 109
Jones, Jim 91
Jowett, Benjamin 122-3
Judaism 9, 13, 31, 113, 125-7, 137-41,
  151, 157, 207, 216-17, 222-3
Julian of Norwich 2, 18, 37-8, 173, 187,
  195-6
Justinian, Emperor 157

Kandy 81-2
karma 181, 213, 216, 222
Karunamayi, Sri Jai 237
Kassi, Norma 153
Kazantzakis, Nikos xi, 19, 84-5, 100, 119,
  208
Keen, Sam viii-xix, 5, 8, 14, 35-6, 46, 49,
  177, 196
Kelly, Michael 82-3